Robert Home

A Précis of Modern Tactics

Comp. from the works of recent continental writers at the Topographical and

statistical department of the War office

Robert Home

A Précis of Modern Tactics
*Comp. from the works of recent continental writers at the Topographical and statistical
department of the War office*

ISBN/EAN: 9783337117351

Printed in Europe, USA, Canada, Australia, Japan

Cover: Foto ©Andreas Hilbeck / pixelio.de

More available books at **www.hansebooks.com**

A

PRÉCIS OF MODERN TACTICS.

COMPILED FROM THE WORKS OF RECENT CONTINENTAL WRITERS
AT THE TOPOGRAPHICAL AND STATISTICAL DEPARTMENT OF THE WAR OFFICE.

BY

ROBERT HOME,

MAJOR ROYAL ENGINEERS, COLONEL, ASSISTANT QUARTER-MASTER-GENERAL.

"If we take the best of the French system, and apply it to the best of our own, we shall infallibly beat the French whenever we meet them."—PRINCE FREDERICK CHARLES.

Printed *under the Superintendence of Her Majesty's Stationery Office,*
AND SOLD BY
W. CLOWES & SONS, Limited, 13, Charing Cross; HARRISON & SONS,
59, Pall Mall; W. H. ALLEN & CO., 13, Waterloo Place; W. MITCHELL.
Charing Cross; LONGMANS & CO., Paternoster Row; TRUBNER & CO., 57 and
59, Ludgate Hill; STANFORD, Charing Cross; and KEGAN PAUL, TRENCH,
& CO., 1, Paternoster Square;
Also by
GRIFFIN & CO., The Hard, PORTSEA;
A. & C. BLACK, EDINBURGH;
ALEX. THOM & CO., Abbey Street, and E. PONSONBY, Grafton Street, DUBLIN.
1882.

Price Eight Shillings and Sixpence.

NOTE.

The aim of the compiler of this book has been to collate the opinions of others, and to avoid as much as possible putting forward his own where original views have been expressed, he alone is responsible for them.

Instead of paraphrasing the sentences of writers of acknowledged worth, he has given their own words, and the marginal notes will assist the reader to refer to the original, or its translation, for the context, when fuller information is desired.

The compiler hopes this plan may be found convenient, as enabling the reader to gauge the value of the authorities, for on the subject of Tactics there is much diversity of opinion, and the works thereon vary considerably in merit, there being scarcely any theory, however preposterous, which may not be supported by a French or German quotation on the subject. Wherever continental writers are opposed, on points of importance, both sides of the question are given.

A list of the works which have been chiefly used in this compilation is appended.

R. HOME, *Major*,
Royal Engineers.

Topographical and Statistical Department,
War Office,
August 15th, 1873.

NOTE.

Some apology is due for the great delay that has arisen in preparing a second and improved edition of this book. At the same time I must thank many friends for their kind aid and assistance. Owing to press of work, a Second Edition has not been prepared, but at the request of Officers, the old Edition of 1873 is now reprinted.

R. HOME, *Major, R.E.,*
Colonel, A.Q.M.G.

Intelligence Branch, Horse Guards,
War Office,
August 15th, 1878.

LIST OF THE WRITERS WHOSE BOOKS HAVE BEEN MORE OR
LESS CONSULTED AND USED IN THE PREPARATION OF
THIS COMPILATION.

Jomini. "Traité des Grandes Opérations Militaires." Paris : Tanera, 1851.

Jomini. "The Art of War." Translated from the French by Captains Mendell and Craighill, United States Engineers. Philadelphia. Lippincott.

Jomini. " Histoire Critique et Militaire des Guerres de la Revolution." Bruxelles : Petit, 1840.

Charles de Savoye. " Reglement sur le Service des Armées en Campagne." Paris : Dumaine, 1873.

Vial, Capitaine, d'état Major. "Cours d'Art et d'Histoire Militaires." Paris, Dumaine, 1861.

Hamley, Colonel, C.B. "The Operations of War explained and illustrated." Blackwood and Sons, Edinburgh, 1869.

Wurtemberg, Duke of. "The System of Attack of the Prussian Infantry 1870–71." Translated by Captain Robinson, Rifle Brigade. Mitchel and Co., London, 1871.

Bugeaud, Maréchal de France. " Aperçu sur Quelques Détails de la Guerre." Paris, 1832.

" *The Prussian Campaign of 1866.*" A Tactical Retrospect (Captain May) : translated by Colonel Ouvry, C.B. Mitchel.

" *The Prussian Infantry.*" (Captain May.) Translated by Colonel Ouvry, C.B. Mitchel.

" *Tactical Deductions from the War of 1870–71,*" by A. v. Boguslawski. Translated by Colonel Graham. London : King & Co., 1872.

De Hardegg. "Science de l'état Major en General." Traduit par Dekervwer: Paris, 1856.

Dufour. "Cours de Tactique." Paris, 1840.

De Giustiniani. " Essai sur la Tactique de Trois Armes." Paris, 1844.

Napoléon. " Memoires pour Service à l'Histoire de France." Sous Napoléon : Paris, 1842.

Fallot et Legrange. "Colonels du Génie Belge ; Cours d'Art Militaire." Brussels, 1857.

De Clausewitz. "De la Guerre." Traduit par Neuens : Paris, 1849.*

Rocquancourt. "Capitaine d'état Major ; Cours Elémentaire d'Art et d'Histoire Militaires." Paris, 1834.

Wellington. "Selections from the General Orders." Gurwood. London : Parker, Furnival, & Co., Whitehall. 1867.

---

* An English translation of this valuable book has been published by Colonel Graham. Trübner & Co., 57, Ludgate Hill.

Vauchelle. " Cours d'Administration Militaire." Paris : Dumaine, 1854.

De Gerlache. "Sous Intendant Militaire Belge ; Administration des Armées en Campagne." Brussels, 1852.

" *Control Regulations.*" War Office. 1870.

Le Bourg, Chef d'Escadron. " Essai sur l'Organisation de l'Artillerie et son emploi dans la Guerre de Campagne."

Thiebault. " Manuel Général du Service des états Majors." Paris, 1813.

Frederick. " Secret Instructions for his Officers." Translated by Major Foster.

Frederick. " Secret Strategical Instructions of Frederick the Second to his Inspectors-General." Translated by Colonel Hamilton Smith. Coventry, 1811.

Napier. "History of the Peninsular War." London : Boone, 1832.

Thiers. "Histoire du Consulat et de l'Empire." Paris : Paulin, 1849.

Alison. "History of Europe from 1774 to 1852." London, 1849 and 1850.

Grivet. "Etudes sur la Tactique." Paris : Dumaine, 1865.

Stoffel. "Military Reports." Translated by Captain Home, R.E., Topographical and Statistical Department, War Office, London, 1872.

Wolseley. " The Soldier's Pocket Book for Field Service." Macmillan, 1871.

Kinglake. " Invasion of the Crimea." 1863.

Burgoyne. " Military Opinions." Field-Marshal Sir J. Burgoyne, G.C.B., edited by Colonel the Hon. G. Wrottesley, R.E. London, 1859.

" *The Army of the North German Confederation.*" Translated by Colonel Newdegate. King & Co., London.

Verdy du Vernois. " Studies in Leading Troops." Translated by Hildyard. King & Co.

" *La Fortification Improvisée.*" Par A. Brialmont, Colonel d'Etat Major. Paris : Dumaine, 1872.*

" *Franco-German War,* 1870–71 ; *official account.*" Translated by Captain Clarke, R.A., Topographical and Statistical Department, War Office.

Vinoy. "Campagne 1870–71 ; Siège de Paris ; Operations de 13° Corps." Paris : Plon, 1872.

Prince de Ligne. "Ouvres Military." Vienna, 1806.

Decker. " Tactique des Trois Armes." Traduit par Brack. Bruxelles, 1835.

Von Miller. "Leçons sur la Tactique des Trois Armes." Traduit de l'Allemand, by Huybrecht. Bruxelles, 1846.

" *The Frontal Attack of Infantry.*" Translated by Colonel Newdegate. London, 1873.†

" *The Elementary Tactics of the Prussian Infantry.*" Translated by Captain Baring, R.A., Topographical and Statistical Department, War Office, 1872.

" *The British Line in the Attack : Past and Future.*" Colonel Gawler. London, 1872.

Jackson. "Course of Military Surveying."

---

* Has been translated by Lieutenant Empson, R.A. King & Co.
† This little book is worthy of the closest study, and from its portability might well be in every officer's possession.

Chesney. "Recent Campaigns in Virginia and Maryland." Smith, Elder, and Co., London, 1873.

Borbstaed. "The Franco-German War." Translated by Major Dwyer.

"*Regulations for the Training of Troops for Service in the Field, and for the Conduct of Grand Manœuvres.*" Translated by Captain Baring, R.A., 1871.

De Brack. "Outposts of Light Cavalry." 4th Edition, 1869.

Von Moltke. "Observations on the Influence that Arms of Precision have on Modern Tactics." Translated by Lieutenant Crawford, R.A. Mitchell, 1871.

Todleben. "The Siege of Sebastopol."

Hohenlhoe. "On the Employment of Field Artillery." Translated by Captain Clarke, R.A., 1872.

Tellenbach. "The Art of Operating under the Fire of an Enemy." Translated by Captain Robinson, Rifle Brigade. Mitchel, 1872.

Bonie, Colonel.＊ "La Cavalerie, Française, 1870." Paris: Amyot, 1871.

"*Campaign of 1866 in Germany.*" Official Account. Translated by Hozier and Wright, Topographical and Statistical Department, War Office, 1872.

"*Conference Militaires Belges.*" Brussels, 1872. La Guerre des Bois.

De Looze. "Notions Sommaires de Tactique des Trois Armes."

Viollet le Duc. "Mémoire sur la Défense de Paris." Paris. Morel, 1871.

Frossard. "Rapports sur les Operations des 2nd Corps, de l'Armée du Rhin dans la Campagne, 1870." Dumaine, 1870. Paris.

Von Mirus. "Cavalry Field Duty." Translated by Russel. King and Co., 1872.

Scherff.† "A Study of New Infantry Tactics." Berlin, 1873.

De Cessac. "Guide Particulier de l'Officier en Campagne." Bruxelles, 1837.

De Folard. "Nouvelles decouvertes sur la Guerre."

Saxe. "Mes Rêveries."

De la Roche Aymon. "Introduction de l'Art de la Guerre." Paris. Dumaine, 1857.

Thiers. "La Défense de Belfort." Paris, 1871.

"*The Wellington Prize Essay.*" Lieutenant Maurice, R.A. Blackwood, 1872.

"*Essays written for the Wellington Prize.*" Crawford, Wolseley, Russel, Hildyard, Waller, King, 1872.

"*Three Months with the Army of Metz,*" by an Officer of Engineers, 1871.

Chesney. "Waterloo Lectures."

"*Experimental Tactics of Infantry.*" Colonel Newdegate, 1872.

"*Military Memorial of Prince Frederick Charles of Prussia.*" Translated by Charles Harcourt Graham, M.A.

"*The Minor Tactics of Field Artillery,*" by H. W. Hime, R.A.

Pelet. "Memoires sur la Guerre de 1809, en Allemagne." Paris, 1824-6.

Fisch. "Etudes sur la Tactique." Brussels. Muquault, 1872.

＊ Has been translated by Lieutenant C. F. Thomson, 7th Hussars.

† A translation of this very valuable and important book has been prepared by Colonel Graham, and is published by King & Co. It is perhaps a clearer exponent of modern Prussian views than any other work.

Lectures given by Colonel Hamley, C.B., when Professor of Military History at the Staff College.

Lectures given by Colonel Chesney, R.E., at various places.

Edinburgh Review.

Quarterly Review.

Articles in Magazines.

Journal of the United Service Institution.

Proceedings of the Royal Artillery Institute.

Professional Papers of the Corps of Royal Engineers.

Lectures given at the School of Military Engineering.

Articles in Military and other Newspapers.

Many valuable hints and much assistance from Major-General Walker, C., Military Attaché at Berlin ; and many other officers.

LIST OF PLATES.

		PAGE
	Sketch of Dessaix's advance at Marengo	*Frontispiece.*
I.	Formations introduced by Frederick the Great and Mesnil Durand	36
II.	Battle of Prague	38
III.	Battle of Leuthen	39
IIIₐ.	Skeleton map of the battle of Leuthen	39
IV.	Battle of Kolin	40
IVₐ.	Skeleton map of the battle of Kolin..	40
V.	Battle of Rossbach	42
Vₐ.	Skeleton map of the battle of Rossbach	42
VI.	Battles of Lonato and Castiglione	45
VII.	French formations	46
VIII.	Battle of Austerlitz	48
IX.	French formations	48
X.	Battle of Auerstadt	50
XI.	Battle of Busaco	58
XII.	Battle of the Alma	62
XIIₐ.	Details of battle of the Alma	62
XIII.	Illustration of a flank attack	70
XIV. XV. XVI. XVII. XVIII.	Illustrations of an infantry attack	96
XIX.	March of a German Division	166
XIXₐ.	March of an English Division	168
XX.	Defence of a wood	208
XXI.	Defence of a village	217
XXII.	Defence of Le Bourget	219
XXIII.	Post on the heights of Rainey	221
XXIV.	The heights of St. Cucufa and Colle St. Cloud	220
XXV.	Normal formation of an Italian Brigade	229
	Map of the environs of Metz, at the end.	

TABLE OF CONTENTS.

PREFACE.

	PAGE.
Necessity of general military information for officers	1
Theory not an absolute guide	2
Advantages of theory	2

CHAPTER I.

ORGANIZATION	3
Division of armies into companies, battalions, regiments, brigades, divisions, &c.—	
May, Vial	4
Companies—Boguslauski, May, Scherff	5
Battalions	6
Brigades—De Hardegg	7
Strength and composition of a German Division	8
„ „ French „	8
„ „ British „	9
Decker, De Préval, Giustineani, De Hardegg.	
Necessity for clear definitions—Jomini	10
Le Bourg, Decker, De Ternay, De la Pierre, De Préval, De la Roche-Aymon	10
Strength and composition of a German Army Corps	12
„ „ French „	13
„ „ British „	13
GENERALS, STAFF, AND DEPARTMENTS	14
Napoleon, Jomini, Folard, Rocquancourt	14-15
Plans should be known—Machiavelli, Bugeaud	15
STAFF, Duties of	16
Wellington, Vauchelle, Grimoard, Hardegg, Jomini, "Army of North German Confederation"	17-18
Verdy du Vernois, Napoleon	19-20
Staff should not interfere	20
Correspondence to go through staff—Jomini	21
CONTROL DEPARTMENT, Duties	21
Extract from Control Regulations, Vauchelle, Grimoard, De Gerlache, De Lavarenne, De Cessac, Saxe	21-26
ARTILLERY, Duties—Jomini	27
Von Miller, Napoleon, Le Bourg	27
"Army of North German Confederation," May	28
ENGINEERS, Duties	28
Thiebault, May, "Army of North German Confederation," Napoleon, "Organisation of Peninsular Army"	28-33

CHAPTER II.

	PAGE.
BRIEF SKETCH OF THE HISTORY OF TACTICS ..	33
Tactics have developed, not changed	33
Gustavus Adolphus, Chemnitz	34-35
Frederick—Formations	35
Prague—Jomini	37
Leuthen—Jomini, Napoleon	38-40
Kolin—Jomini, Napoleon ..	40-42
Rossbach—Jomini, Napoleon	42-43
Peculiarity of Fredrick's Tactics ..	43
Mesnil Durand's proposals ..	44
Revolutionary Armies	45
Italian Campaign, 1796 ..	45
Lonato, Castiglione, Rivoli ..	45
Tagliamento, Marengo	45-46
Austerlitz	47
Jena ..	49
Auerstadt	49
Eylau, Hardships, Army exposed to—Napoleon ..	53
Essling	53
Wagram	53
Regimental Artillery	54
Formation of Macdonald's Corps ..	55
Alterations in French Tactics	56
Invasion of Russia ..	57
Alteration of Prussian Tactics, " King of Prussia's Order, 1813 "	57
Busaco—Napier	58
Albuera ..	59
Waterloo—Jomini's conversation with Wellington	59-60
Origin of Prussian Company	61
The Alma ..	61
„ Moltke's remarks on	62

CHAPTER III.

INFANTRY TACTICS	64
Motives which sway men—Napier	64
Discipline—Napier ..	64-65
Panics..	65
Education—Stoffel ..	65
Training and Discipline—Napoleon	65
Good arms—Stoffel ..	66
Manœuvring under fire impossible	67
Kinglake	67
Action of small bodies	68
Breaking up of battles into detached fights—Scherff	68
Flank attacks—Boguslauski, Clausewitz ..	69-70
Problem to be solved at present day	70
Relatively speaking, attack has gained more than defence—Scherff, Boguslauski	71
Breech-loaders enable a greater fire to be given now than formerly ..	74
Danger of the indiscriminate use of the word " loose " ..	74-75
Attack on St. Privat—Duke of Wurtemberg	75
Moral causes at work—General Walker	76
" King of Prussia's Order, 21st August, 1870 " ..	77
Attack, individual, not loose—Scherff	77
Necessity of large areas to train troops	78
Necessity for supports	78
Kinglake	79
Skirmishers must not be sent by driblets ..	79

PAGE.

Sir John Burgoyne 79
Scherff, Gawler 80-82
Lines of battle 82
May 83
Fighting line to carry its own reserve 83
Chesney, Kinglake, Napier 83-84
Area of action greater now than formerly 84
General ideas as to formation 84
Zones of fire—Tellenbach 86
Advancing under fire 86-87
"Cabinet order of Emperor of Germany".. 88
Skirmishing by sections 88-89
Circumstances under which an attack is now possible 89
Frontal attack of infantry—Scherff 90
Shock or bayonet now requisite as well as fire 91
Last stage of attack—Scherff, Gawler 92-93
Reason why small columns are preferable 93
Duty of supports—Scherff 94
State of matters when the "general advance" is ordered.. 95
Skirmishers not to be left behind—Scherff.. 95
Frontal attack of infantry 95
Effect of development of tactics on British troops 96
Napier, Bugeaud 96
Disadvantages ; small numbers 98
Small companies preferable to large.. 98
Frontal attack of infantry 99
Loss of officers.. 99
Paramount necessity of complete training of troops 100
Necessity for tactical information 101
Proposal to extend the main body 102
Small columns suffer less from fire than lines 102
Desirable to advance with main body in small columns, to give moral
   support to skirmishers ; frontal attack of infantry 103

THE DEFENCE (II.) 103
   Pure defence useless—Von Moltke.. 103
   Moral superiority of attack 104
   Sir John Burgoyne 104
   Advantages of defence 105
   Convergent and divergent fire 106
   Occupation of positions 107
   Vollies impossible—Boguslauski 107
   Defence, taking the offensive 107
   Defence should be offensive in character 108
   Offensive use the defensive carefully 108

CAVALRY (III.) 109
   Cavalry in the field at the present day 110
   Duties of cavalry 110
   Action of cavalry by no means a thing of the past 110
   Von Moltke, May 110
   Bredow's charge at Mars-la-Tour 111
   Boguslauski, Borbstaedt 111-112
   Reserves indispensable—Wellington 113
   Second line—Prussian instructions 114
   Effect of rifled guns 115
   Opportunities afforded to small bodies of cavalry.. 115
   Proposals for attack—Boguslauski 116
   Austrian regulations 116
   Reconnaissance of ground requisite.. 117
   Bonie : "Official account of war of 1866"—Napier 118
   Flank attacks 119
   Action of French cavalry at Gravelotte—Bonie 119

PAGE.

Cavalry covering an army—Von Mirus 120
De Brack 120
Necessity of spreading cavalry out, whether advancing or retreating .. 121
Bonie; "Three months with the army of the Rhine" 123
Comparison of French and German cavalry 124

ARTILLERY (IV.) 125
Difference between rifled artillery and smooth-bore guns.. 125
Use of artillery in the field 126
Necessity of unity of action; campaign of 1866; Wochenblatt.. .. 127
Corps artillery and divisional artillery—Becker 128
Duties of divisional artillery—Todleben 129
Independence of artillery 129
Direction of corps artillery 130
Artillery escorts, not now required as a rule 131
Artillery to move seldom and rapidly 131
Position of Artillery—Hime; "Campaign of 1866" 131
Necessity of artillery being in front—May.. 132
Masses of artillery—Boguslauski, Hohenlohe 133
What artillery should fire at—May, Waldersee 133-134
Mitrailleuse 135

ENGINEERS (V.) 135
Peculiarities of Napoleon's campaigns 135
Field fortification most backward of branches of art of war—Napoleon 136
Use of field fortification—May, Duke of Wurtemberg, Viollet le Duc 136-137
Fieldworks important, as partially solving the question of flank attacks
   —Chesney 137
Duties of Engineers in the field twofold 138
Mounted sappers—Brialmount, Frederick 139
Tactical relation of fieldworks to the troops—Brialmont.. 140
Evil effects of separation of direction: Königgrätz 141
Use in modern war 142
Village of Vionville—Frossard; Battle of Gravelotte 142-143
Tools 143
Necessity of tactical instruction for engineers 144

CHAPTER IV.

COMBINED TACTICS 141
Arms of the service must not be interchangeable 144
Necessity of Generals having full control of auxiliary arms—Vinoy 145-146
Proportions of the arms of the service 147
Napoleon; Prussian army 147
Infantry the chief arm; Losses in action 148
Way in which battles begin 149
Mars-la-Tour 150
Action of artillery and engineers 151
Tendency of armies to extend 152
Concentration may be weakness 153
Decisive points to be held; parallel with permanent fortifications .. 154
Concentric attacks—"Campaign of 1866" 154-155
Reserves: many, and not one great one 156
Campaign of 1866 156
Langensalza 156
Numbers of troops to the yard 156
Artillery should never be kept in reserve 157
Action of small bodies of cavalry 158
Penetration of the enemy's position and lodgment 159

CHAPTER V.

	PAGE.
MARCHES ..	161
Importance of marching	162
Armies cannot march in line of battle	162
Guibert, Clausewitz..	162
As a rule must adhere to the roads	162
Campaign of 1866; De Ternay, Napoleon	162-163
Rates of marching—Colley ..	163
Length of columns ..	164
Opening out—Clausewitz, Fallot, Lagrange, Thiebault..	165
Order of March—De la Pierre, Von Waldersee ..	166
Verdy du Vernois, Colley ..	167-168
German march across the Lauter ..	169
Army orders..	170
Corps orders ..	171
Advanced guard orders	172
Position of auxiliary arms ..	173
Verdy du Vernois, Clausewitz, Le Bourg..	173-174
Keeping up the touch	174
Advanced guards ..	174
Rear-guard—Verdy du Vernois, Fallot, Lagrange	175
Bugeaud, Napier	176
Bazaine's retreat	177
Tendency to turn troops out too early	177-178
SUPPLY OF TROOPS	178
Rations must be carried by the men	179
Men must be watched to see they don't eat all their food at once	179
Rations carried by Prussians	179-180
Distribution—De Gerlache, Grimoard	181
Requisitions requisite—Clausewitz	182
Fallot and Lagrange..	182-183
Necessity of care ..	183
Lecture of General V. Kirchback ..	183
THE ORGANIZATION OF THE COMMUNICATIONS OF AN ARMY, INCLUDING RAILWAYS	185
Meaning of "Organization of Line of Communications"	185
Three ways by which armies can be fed ..	186
Division of supply into two great branches	189
Division of transport into three portions ..	190
Wellington's organization of his line of communications	191
Organization of German line of communications..	192
Changes in war caused by use of railways..	196
Imaginary example of organization of railway communications in England ..	199

CHAPTER VI.

ATTACK AND DEFENCE OF WOODS AND VILLAGES ..	203
Peculiarities of wood fighting: Prussians and French ..	203
Training of soldiers now more requisite than ever	204
Outskirts of wood to be held	205
Examination of a wood ..	207
Putting a wood in a state of defence	207
Attack of a wood ..	210
VILLAGES ..	212
Great part they have played in war	212
Must not now be held as formerly..	213
Examination of a village ..	214

	PAGE.
How a village should be defended..	215
Ideal case	217
Attack of villages—Frederick, Duke of Wurtemberg	219
Positions round Paris	220
Bougival	220
Rainey	221
Le Bourget	222

APPENDICES.

	PAGE
Italian Committee on Infantry Tactics recommends section skirmishing; German opinion opposed	224-23 t
Order for marches—General Crawford	235
War strength of Infantry	258
„ „ Cavalry..	259
„ „ Artillery	260
„ „ Engineers	262
Losses in Battles ..	263

PREFACE.

In the following pages an attempt is made to compile a book, that may be useful to students of the military art who are not near good libraries, and who do not possess the large number of volumes that are written on military subjects. This book has been chiefly prepared to aid officers in the examinations which they must pass for promotion, and to give them the views of a large number of eminent soldiers. It is hoped that it may direct the attention of officers to the military writers referred to, and induce a study of their writings, as opportunity may offer.

The form of this book is based on that of the well-known work by Charles de Savoye, "Règlement sur le service des armées en campagne annoté d'après les meilleur auteurs qui ont écrit sur l'art Militaire."

An attempt has been made to avoid all technicalities used in either artillery or engineer science, except such as should be well known to officers of every branch of the army, for the duties of each arm of the Service overlap and blend into one another, and the higher the grade an officer attains, the more requisite it is that he should be acquainted generally with the duties of those arms of the Service to which he himself does not belong; by this means alone can we hope to obtain that intelligent co-operation, that harmonious working of all branches of the Service together, which makes a perfect machine out of the various elements composing an army, and at the same time gives the surest guarantee of success. In armies, as elsewhere, there is a tendency for everyone to think his own branch, that which he has studied most and knows best, the most important; such feelings are very natural, and in the lower grades often do much good; but as men rise in the Service it is desirable that they should know something of the duties of other branches, and the difficulties others have to contend with : such knowledge tends to produce cordiality and forbearance. Cavalry officers falling into command of mixed forces will not then expect their infantry to gallop, infantry officers will not seek to bind the cavalry to the pace of their infantry. A knowledge of the capabilities of other arms will enable officers to use those arms to the best advantage as occasion offers.

B

It should, however, be borne in mind, that it is impossible to lay down fixed rules of action. Nearly every military regulation should be followed by the words " according to the ground and according to circumstances." Rules are but guides, which must be intelligently, not blindly, followed.

Jomini.

Suppose a committee of the greatest generals,—Napoleon, the Archduke Charles, and Wellington, &c.,—assembled, aided by the ablest artillery and engineer officers, they could lay down no fixed and immutable laws on the art of war, especially on Tactics.

Practice and experience alone can decide many points; practice and experience alone can give the power of applying rules; but theory, by which is really meant the experience obtained by others, is not the less important and valuable.

Bugeaud.

When attempts are made to lay down principles in war, a large number of officers at once solve the problems by saying *everything* depends on circumstances. As the wind blows, so must the sails be set. But if the proper sail, and the proper amount of sail suitable to each wind, is not known beforehand, how can sail be made at all ?

Clausewitz.

A man who spends a portion of his life in seeking to throw light on the various portions of a difficult subject will, in all probability, do more and go further than he who seeks to understand it in a hurry. The object of theory is to spare each fresh student the trouble of classifying and subdividing the subject he studies, in order that he may carefully examine it in all its bearings. Theory brings the subject before him classified and arranged : it forms the mind of the future commander, or, rather, it points out how he may form it for himself. But theory must be left behind on the battle-field. A wise teacher limits himself to the development of the intellectual capacity of his pupil, he does not seek to keep him in leading strings all his life.

Vial.

War is not, as some say, a game of violence and chance. It is, says Napoleon, a game, but a very serious game, where reputations, armies, and empires are the stakes. It is the triumph of force, of force skilfully prepared and organized, guided by intelligence and genius, acting in accordance with certain principles of art ; force subservient to the highest social virtues, courage, self-denial, and devotion. As for chance, doubtless it plays its part in war, but true art consists in rendering this part as small as possible, and the object of principles is to subdue chance by prudence, wisdom, and calculation.

And it must be remembered that in war the instrument used is not an inert, but a living mass, changeable, and susceptible of great enthusiasm or the reverse.

Principles are but guides, which must be revised, examined and verified after each war, after each discovery that may be brought to bear on the military art. The great successes of Gustavus Adolphus, Frederick, Marlborough, Napoleon, Wellington, Von Moltke, are but due to careful consideration and appreciation of the effects of various discoveries on the art of war. There is no finality in the art of war.

CHAPTER I.

ORGANIZATION.

The difference between an army and a mob, is discipline, and discipline alone confers on bodies of men the power of manoeuvring.

Hamley. Manœuvres are the quick, orderly change of highly-trained and flexible masses from one kind of formation to another, or their transference from point to point of a battle-field, for purposes which become suddenly feasible in the changing course of the action.

Drill is a means to discipline, but drill is not discipline, which may be defined as obedience to superiors.

It is perfectly clear that to establish and maintain discipline there must be personal contact between the superior and the inferior, and as one man can influence only a limited number of his fellow men, it follows that the size of the first "body," "unity," or "division" into which a mass of men is divided, must bear some relation to the number of inferiors of average attainments, that can be influenced by one superior, also of average attainments. Upon this basis must ultimately rest the division of armed bodies of men into companies, battalions, regiments, brigades, Divisions, army-corps, armies.

There is also another set of ideas that must be taken into consideration, when the organization of men into separate bodies is considered; not only must soldiers be disciplined, but they must also be paid, fed, armed and clothed. Hence the division of men into organized bodies should be such as will facilitate administration. There are therefore two distinct sets of ideas that have to be taken into account; these may be termed administrative ideas, and tactical ideas.

It has already been observed that discipline can be best maintained by personal contact of a superior with inferiors, and as the provision of food, arms, and clothing for men, keeps the superior in contact with the inferior, and induces the latter to lean on, be governed and guided by the former, it follows that, if possible, the first tactical division should correspond with the first administrative division, or, in other words, that the smallest independent tactical command (the company) should also be the smallest administrative division.

B 2

Prussian
Infantry.
Captain May.
(Translated
by Ouvry.)

The Captain commanding a company is the only officer between whom. and the soldier a personal relation subsists in peace time. He knows every individual soldier in the most intimate manner, and the soldier on his part is aware that his Captain so knows him. It is upon this relation that the uncommon influence rests which he, above all other officers, has over the individual soldier, as well as over the whole company.

The soldier sees his nearest home in his company, and he has under all circumstances a decided feeling for his Captain, even though it be one of hatred. In most cases, however, it is a feeling of love, confidence and respect. The intimate and continual intercourse between them allows no room on either side for acting ; each must appear as he really is, and thus, together with the bad qualities, the good ones also which they both possess must come to light. They become accustomed to one another, have their fits of ill-temper at times on both sides, but when at length the hour comes that they are finally to part, there is an earnest feeling of sorrow which cannot be suppressed. With regard to the higher grades of officers, such as officers commanding battalions or regiments, the soldier on the contrary has no personal relations with them, neither have the officers with him ; he has a respect for them according to regulation, otherwise he is for the most part indifferent. At the very most he knows whether his General keeps him long at drill and annoys him or not, and particularly whether he has any ridiculous habits. It requires very especial qualities in the higher ranks in order to make a real impression on the soldier, and he who does not possess these qualities can at most try, by acting and coquetry, to make himself take with the men, but which in the long run tends to an opposite effect. However proud of his position a Colonel may be at the head of his regiment, the soldier looks on his Captain as by far the most important personage, and should the Colonel take to bullying the Captain on parade, to show the soldier what a great man he is, the result usually is that the soldier respects the Captain the less, but certainly the Colonel not the more. The beautiful relation between the soldier and his Captain is a corner stone of our army, and not one of the least firm ones. The highest reward which the soldier can obtain during his service springs from his Captain, viz., the confidence of his company leader, and he on his part will find the attachment of his subordinate the most precious reward which will fall to him in his lifetime.

Vial.

The art of war enables a mass of men to be so organized and disciplined that their efforts may be directed towards the same object. It transforms a confused multitude of men into a trained and obedient body of troops. Lastly, it allows an entire army to be moved on the field of battle in accordance with one will, one idea, that of the General officer commanding. If only 100 men have to be moved, certain subdivisions are requisite to give them a cadre and commanders. There must be some definite instruction for both men and officers, there must be, in a word, principles, rules, and theories. What is true for a company is even still more the case for an army. To organize an army is to establish subdivisions and give chiefs to each, in order that they may be instructed and moved in accordance with the will of one man. A single man cannot command directly 100,000 men. Intermediate commanders who command bodies of greater or less extent, and who deal directly with a smaller number of subordinates, are requisite. Thus a General-in-Chief commanding 100,000 men deals directly with only the Generals of five or six Army-Corps. Each General of an Army-Corps deals only with four or five Generals of Division, each General of Division with only two or three Generals of Brigade, each General of Brigade with two or three Colonels, and so on to the Corporal of a squad who commands only eight to twelve men. There is thus a chain of responsibility from the General to the last man.

In all armies in the world the company has been invariably considered as the first, or smallest independent command; the Captain of a company being the executive, and commanding, drilling, paying, and looking after the men composing his company. And with the view of keeping up a company feeling, arrangements are generally made in regiments for working as much as possible by companies. The size of the company and the position occupied by the Captain, however, vary much in different armies.

In the English Army a company on a war footing has varied from 80 to 120 men—the Captain being on foot, and the battalion usually consisting of eight to ten companies. This system was pretty generally adopted in most armies except the Prussian, where the companies are about 250 strong and the Captain is mounted. In no army is so much dependence placed on the Captain, or company leader, as in the Prussian; but it is requisite that Prussian examples be not slavishly followed. Many customs that suit the German temperament would be bad, and positively dangerous, if introduced blindly amongst other nations.

Some German writers have proposed to do away with all links between Commanders of companies and Generals, making the company the tactical unit. This is however opposed by others, with perhaps more reason, as will be seen by the following extracts:—

One of the chief props of this edifice, built up of obedience and confidence, is the Company Chief. On him falls the chief labour of training and instructing the soldier. In constant communication with one another, the men come to know him thoroughly, and he learns to know them. The name by which the Company Chief is commonly known to the Prussian soldier, that of "company father," explains his position. In battle, the Company Chief leads the principal tactical unit and is first and most before the soldier's eyes. — Boguslawski. (Translated by Lumley Graham.)

In action the mounted officers are obliged to dismount, which makes that supervision and direction impossible which is so very easy in peace manœuvres. Frequently the dismounted field officer, somewhat unaccustomed to rapid movements over stalk and stone, is scarcely able to keep up with his battalion ; the breaking up into columns of companies is for him a solution of his difficulty. — Captain May's Tactical Retrospect. (Translated by Ourry.)

He thinks that certainly the four officers commanding the companies will know what to do, so he attaches himself to a company. The original officers commanding lines are in the same predicament, their lines are broken up and scattered in all parts of the battle, thus they have to give up all ideas of commanding them, and attach themselves to the first company of infantry that offers, and, in order to do something, command that. It thus happens that some companies, favoured by chance, have, besides their own Captain, a Major, a Colonel, and a General as well.

The officer in command of a battalion should not take the direction of part of the companies on himself, but should rather lead all the four equally. Should foreign armies think of imitating our company column fights they must take into consideration how it stands with them with regard to fundamental principles, that is, the relation between their officers and men. They will otherwise adopt the disadvantages without gaining the benefit. — Prussian Infantry. Captain May (Translated by Ourry.)

Despite all the dissertations upon the definition of a tactical unit, the most fanatical partisan of the company column must allow that the company [a German company 250 men] is too weak to suffice for the three phases of the attack if an affair of any importance is to be undertaken. 12 company columns, each acting for itself, cannot fulfil what is required for the preparation — Scherff.

and execution of an attack, and à fortiori they must fail in the last period. But three battalions can undoubtedly accomplish what is requisite.

What is thus generally true for companies applies also, though in a less degree, to single battalions. Three battalions, acting each for itself, may succeed pretty well in preparing and executing an attack, but will find it very difficult to accomplish the last stage. We will return more in detail to this subject, we merely point out here that in breaking up the object of the attack into several distinct portions, that we consider it absolutely requisite not to deal with any force smaller than a battalion.

The question as to whether a company on the German model is, or is not, a tactical unit, is really a very unimportant one, and must depend to a great extent upon the meaning attached to the words. If by 'tactical unit' is meant a body that can fight independently, it would appear that a division is the real tactical unit, as it includes all arms of the service. A battery of artillery is continually termed a tactical unit, but it does not fight separately. The fact is that the words tactical unit vary entirely according to the point of view. To a General Commanding an army the army-corps are tactical units; to a General Commanding a division, brigades are tactical units; to a General Commanding a brigade, battalions are tactical units; to an Officer Commanding a battalion, companies are tactical units. So far then as the company is the basis of military subdivision it is a tactical unit, but no further.

The question as to how many companies should compose a battalion may be well answered by referring to Napoleon's words,—"No man can command more than five distinct bodies on the same theatre of war." Taking also into consideration that the size of the company is limited by the number of men that can be influenced by one man, it appears that the Prussian system of four companies is a correct one.

But it by no means follows that this is the only solution to the problem, or even the best. The more personal intelligence there is distributed through a body of men, the larger the number of officers there are in that body trained and competent to lead it, the more efficient will that body be when placed in the difficult positions of actual combat: taking this, and the fact that the Prussian proportion of officers leaves no margin for sickness or loss, and that the front of a Prussian company is, from the fact of its being three deep, smaller than that of those nations that habitually form their troops two deep, also that the use of troops in extended order has been greatly increased of recent years, it would appear desirable to reduce the size of the companies considerably below the Prussian standard. While at the same time every effort should be made to increase and draw tighter the bonds between the Captain and his company, giving the Captain greater interest in, and control over, the company. Taking all the bearings of the question into consideration, it appears that the formation which best suits the requirements of the present day, is one of the battalion into wings, each wing into four companies of 100 to 125 men each. The wing will thus be a small four-company battalion, and the number of men—100 to 125 in each company —will be such that it can be handled and led by one officer with ease. A half-battalion—a wing—will then be nearly the strength of a battalion in peace time.

With regard to half-battalions, they cannot be considered as altogether strange to our peace customs, as a peace battalion is just equal to a half-battalion in war, and these half-battalion formations were proved to be good in three glorious battles.   *Schellendorf. (Translated by Ourry.)*

Two or more battalions united together compose a brigade, which is commanded by a General Officer of the lowest grade, termed a Brigadier; a Brigadier has also a Staff Officer, termed a Brigade-Major.

A brigade means generally a tactical body composed of two or three regiments of the same arm, either infantry or cavalry. The term 'brigade' is also applied to from four to eight batteries working together. In the Engineers, the term 'brigade' is also applied to detachments destined to perform one and the same duty, and whose force is variable (2 to 20 men).   *De Hardegg.*

A Division is the first body that is composed of all branches of the Service, hence it comes more nearly to the definition of a tactical unit of an army that any other body; the Division being composed of all arms, is thus at the base of all army formations. An army composed in peace time of Divisions, and the organization of which goes no further, can in war time be easily formed into army-corps. Doubtless it is desirable to have army-corps, or even armies, formed ready to take the field, but such formations entail much cost, and the advantages they confer are so far problematical as hardly to warrant the expenditure they entail. If then the Division be carefully formed, its various component portions correctly adjusted, and it be furnished with a proper staff, it would seem that the higher formations of army-corps and army may be left to be completed when absolutely requisite on the outbreak of war; provided the principles on which they should be formed, and their composition, have been carefully elaborated, and clearly laid down.

A Division is composed of two or more brigades of infantry, two or more batteries of artillery, one or more companies of engineers, one or more cavalry regiments.

In Prussia, military matters have received much attention, perhaps more than in any other country in Europe, and it may not be uninteresting to give the composition of a German Division :—

8

TABULAR STATEMENT of the Composition and Strength
of a German Division.

WAR ESTABLISHMENT.

	Officers.	Non-Commissioned Officers and Men.	Buglers, &c.	Paymasters and Administrative Officers.	Surgeons.	Farriers.	Hospital Orderlies, &c.	Train Soldiers.	Workmen.	Total.	Riding.	Draught and Pack.	Carriages.	Field Guns.
											Horses.			
Staff of Division	4	14	...	...	...	...	...	13	...	31	26	2	1	...
1st Brigade { Staff	2	3	...	...	.	...	...	7	...	12	12	2	1	...
{ 2 Regiments Infantry	138	5,912	122	6	12	...	24	130	6	6,350	116	124	32	...
2nd Brigade	140	5,915	122	6	12	...	24	137	6	6,362	128	126	33	...
1 Regiment Cavalry ...	...	23	589	13	1	3| 5	4	37	2	677	691	16	7 |...
1 Division Field Artillery ...	...	18	561	8	...	5| 4	4	30	4	634	140	370	41 |24
Total Division ...	...	325	12,994	265	13	32| 9	56	354	18	14,066	1,213	640	115 |24

This force is a very handy complete Division, but it will be observed that it does not embrace engineers, which, in the Prussian Army, form a body attached to the corps, not to the Division.

In France, there has been no definite rule laid down as to what a Division should consist of, but in the army that took the field in 1870 a Division was usually composed as follows:—

TABULAR STATEMENT of the Composition and Strength of a French Division in 1870.*

	Officers.	N.-C. Officers and Men.	Horses.	Guns.
Staff of Division	10	..	..	.
1st Brigade { Staff	2	..	..	..
{ Battalion of Rifles ..	23	773	13	..
{ 2 Regiments of Infantry of the Line .. }	126	4,291	59	..
2nd Brigade { Staff	2	..	..	..
{ 2 Regiments of Infantry of the Line .. }	128	4,327	54	..
Artillery (Divisional)	11	417	343	18
Engineers (Divisional)	4	77	16	..
Total	306	9,885	485	18

* The 1st Division of the 4th Corps.

NOTE.—The want of Cavalry in this Division is apparent. Cavalry in the French army was attached to the Corps; and separate Cavalry Divisions were formed for the army. This system left the Divisions without even a couple of squadrons as orderlies, escort, or messengers.

In the British Army, a Division will, on actual service, be formed as follows:—

A DIVISION OF INFANTRY.

(Approved by His Royal Highness the Commander-in-Chief, 18. 7. 71.)

	Officers.	N.-C. Officers and Men.	All Ranks.	Horses.	Guns.
Staff	13	6	19	36	—
*2 Brigades of Infantry (6 Bns.)..	194	6,398	6,604	82	—
1 Battalion of Rifles ..	31	1,066	1,099	10	—
1 Regiment of Cavalry	27	607	634	559	—
3 Batteries Field Artillery ..	21	547	568	436	18†
1 Company Royal Engineers ..	5	186	191	44	—
1 Troop Military Police	2	73	75	65	—
1 Infantry and Artillery Reserve Ammunition Column .. .. }	6	206	212	253	—
Total..	299	9,104	9,403	1,862	18

* Details of the actual War Strength of a Battalion of Infantry, a Cavalry Regiment, a Battery of Artillery, and a Company of Engineers, are given in the Appendix.
† One 9-pr. Battery; two 16-pr. Batteries.

It is not known who first proposed the Division and army-corps. It is reasonable to suppose that it was gradually arrived at. | Decker.

The system of forming armies in Divisions was first thought of and tried by the Marshal Broglie in the war of 1760, but it was then very imperfect, as all useful things must be which have to contend at first against routine and prejudice. | De Préval.

Turenne was the first in France who divided armies into Divisions, but after his time this happy idea was for a long time forgotten. During the Seven Years' War the French Army, and that of Duke Ferdinand, were formed into units somewhat similar to Divisions, but no rule seemed to govern this formation, which was more apparent than real. In 1795, the Division formation was adopted by the French Republican armies. The Divisions were then composed of all arms of the Service. They had a special staff and administrative bodies, each was composed of four demi-brigades of infantry, or twelve battalions, four to eight squadrons of cavalry, one to two companies of artillery, with eight to twelve guns, the effective being 10,000 to 15,000 men, according to the strength of the battalions and squadrons. Austria adopted this formation in 1805, Prussia in 1806, Russia in 1807. | Giustineani.

Prior to this period armies were formed into advanced guards, first and second lines and reserve, also into wings, there being distinct commanders for these bodies, also distinct commanders for the infantry, cavalry and artillery. Traces of this formation remain in some armies even now. The commanders were often detailed for the day, and there was no bond of union between the commander and those he commanded, as there is between a Divisional General and his Division.

A division is either mixed, in which case it is termed an army Division; or it is composed of one arm of the Service, in which case it is termed a cavalry or infantry Division. Such a Division is composed of two or three brigades. | De Hardegg.

This word 'division' is also used in Austria, Prussia, and Bavaria, to denote a body composed of two squadrons. In the infantry of a certain class, as in rifles, it is used to denote a body composed of two companies. These cavalry divisions have generally a field officer in permanent command. In the infantry, such divisions are commanded by the senior Captain. In Russia, divisions of artillery are formed by the junction of four or five batteries.

Jomini. The preceding, says Jomini, shows how much improvement is requisite in military nomenclature. It is absurd to call a body composed of twelve battalions a Division at the same time that two companies are termed a Division. I do not pretend to say if it was a confusion between these two words that caused the formation of the heavy masses at Waterloo. However that may be, it is requisite in all armies that perfectly distinct terms should be used to denote a Division of twelve battalions and a Division of two companies, or one-fourth of a battalion.

The same confusion exists in English as to the words,—fort, battery, brigade, staff, &c. No term should convey two distinct meanings, nor should a *general* term be adopted to express a separate, special, or definite meaning without an explanatory word, otherwise inconvenience and confusion of ideas are produced. Terms cannot be too clear and distinct.

Le Bourg. It is, besides, desirable to have some Divisions of greater strength than others, because a General may wish to give the command of certain Divisions to such trustworthy officer as he may wish to detach for important operations requiring the aid of a large body of men. Many Generals wish that Divisions should be composed of three brigades, because when a Division fights singly it will then have two brigades in line, one in reserve, whilst the organization in two brigades, by which only a portion can be in reserve, is vicious.

Decker. Divisions should, as much as possible, be of the same strength and organization, in order that if possible they may be employed in the same way, and with equal confidence. It is important to form Divisions in peace corresponding to the territorial divisions ; if this be not done, when war breaks out the General-in-Chief finds himself entirely absorbed in a long and difficult operation.

It may be easily understood that a Division newly formed cannot be of the same value as one that has been in regular working order for some time. The custom of fighting and working together causes to arise between the corps a confidence and friendly feeling which tends greatly to produce success. Generals thus know completely the men, and are known and appreciated by them.

De Ternay. If the military institutions of a country are so bad as to separate the troops of the same Division in peace time, they should be brigaded and put in Divisions as soon as possible. The manner in which the military machine is put together at the opening of a campaign exercises much influence over the manner in which it performs its duties.

De la Pierre. Mixed Divisions and brigades appear to be more generally used now than formerly. In addition to the requisite artillery, a company of engineers to execute various works, a detachment of police to maintain discipline, and a sufficient number of men of the administrative services to transport stores, hospitals, and provisions, are attached. In short, a Division is organized so as to provide entirely for its own wants.

De Préval. Napoleon recognized the truth of these facts, too late, when he saw the inconvenience of having no Divisions or brigades of cavalry attached to the corps and Divisions of infantry.

De la Roche-Aymon. In approving of the distribution of cavalry amongst the Divisions and brigades, light cavalry only is referred to ; Cuirassiers or heavy cavalry should never be thus scattered. They form masses of reserve cavalry, and should be used only in great actions and battles. General Hoche, when he took command of the Army of the Sambre and Meuse, desiring to remove what he considered to be an inconvenience, united all his cavalry into separate Divisions. But in avoiding one error he fell into another not less dangerous, by destroying the mutual support of the various arms—depriving them of their reciprocal support. He would have derived greater advantages from his cavalry, says Jomini, had he left the Hussars, the Chasseurs, and even the Dragoons with the Divisions, forming his reserve only of heavy cavalry.

The advantage of mixed Divisions and brigades has been so fully recognized in the Prussian Army as a principle of organization, that each Division is composed of cavalry, artillery, and infantry; this combination allows them to manoeuvre on all kinds of ground, and enables them to advance without danger and inconvenience. This arrangement further forms General officers and accustoms them to the command of mixed bodies, and enables them by practice to determine the strength and weakness of the various arms of the Service.

Army-corps are formed by the junction of two or more Divisions together.

The following is a detail of an army-corps of the German Empire :—

TABULAR STATEMENT of the Composition and Strength of a German Army-Corps.

WAR ESTABLISHMENT.

Field Troops.	Officers.	Non-Commissioned Officers and Men.	Buglers, &c.	Paymasters and Administrative Officers.	Surgeons.	Farriers.	Hospital Orderlies, &c.	Train Soldiers.	Workmen.	Total.	Riding.	Draught and Pack.	Carriages.	Field Guns.
General Commanding and Staff	14	93	...	1	...	1	...	41	...	150	121	10	4	...
1st Division—														
Staff of Division	4	14	...	...	...	...	...	1	...	31	26	2	1	...
1st Brigade { Staff	2	3	...	...	...	...	...	...	...	12	12	2	1	...
{ 2 Regiments Infantry	138	5,912	122	6	12	...	24	130	6	6,350	116	124	32	...
2nd Brigade	140	5,915	122	6	12	...	24	137	6	6,362	128	126	33	...
1 Regiment Cavalry	23	5-9	13	1	3	5	4	37	2	677	691	16	7	...
1 Division Field Artillery	18	561	8	...	5	4	4	30	4	634	140	370	41	24
Total 1st Division	325	12,994	265	13	32	9	56	354	18	14,066	1,213	640	115	24
Total 2nd Division	325	12,994	265	13	32	9	56	354	18	14,066	1,213	640	115	24
*1 Battalion Rifles	22	985	17	1	2	...	4	24	1	1,056	16	24	10	..
Total of 2 Divisions	672	26,273	547	27	66	18	116	732	37	29,188	2,442	1,304	240	48
†Cavalry Division—														
Staff	4	14	...	...	...	...	...	13	...	31	26	2	1	...
1st Brigade { Staff	2	3	...	...	...	...	...	7	...	12	12	2	1	...
{ 2 Regiments	46	1,178	26	2	6	10	8	74	4	1,354	1,382	32	14	...
2nd Brigade	48	1,181	26	2	6	10	8	61	4	1,360	1,394	34	15	...
1 Battery Horse Artillery	4	141	2	...	1	1	1	5	2	157	117	92	16	6
Total Cavalry Division	104	2,517	54	4	13	21	17	180	10	2,920	2,931	162	41	6
Artillery Reserve—														
Regimental Staff	2	2	1	...	...	1	...	6	...	12	10	2	1	...
1 Field Division (4 Batteries)	18	561	8	...	5	4	4	30	4	634	140	370	41	24
1 Horse Division (2 Batteries)	10	283	4	...	3	2	2	20	4	328	244	186	21	12
Ammunition Train	20	767	18	...	10	9	9	784	10	1,627	239	1,358	230	...
Total Artillery Reserve	50	1,613	31	...	18	16	15	840	18	2,601	63	1,916	293	36
Pioneers	30	879	15	6	5	2	4	313	...	1,254	82	430	83	...
Military Train Battalion	35	495	...	16	29	12	507	935	148	2,177	646	1,689	598	...
Administrative Services	1	43	...	127	76	...	328	381	18	974	232	328	92	...
Field Post	..	...	...	53	...	...	...	24	...	77	...	56	12	...
Grand Total of Field Troops	906	32,613	647	234	207	70	987	3,446	131	39,341	6,787	6,895	1,363	90

* The Battalion of Rifles is attached to either of the two Divisions at the discretion of the Officer Commanding the Army-Corps.
† The Cavalry Divisions in the field are not attached to the Army-Corps, but to the armies; they vary, being sometimes composed of two, sometimes three brigades, of two or three regiments each.

The following is a detail of a French army-corps, as formed at the beginning of the war of 1870; but, as has been already stated, the French have no absolute form for an army-corps:—

Tabular Statement of a French army-corps in 1870.[*]

	Officers.	N.-C. Officers and men.	Horses.	Guns.
General Staff	16	..	62	..
Artillery Staff	7	..	..	..
Engineer Staff	8	..	..	..
Military Staff	35	..	62	..
Civil Staff	6	..	..	..
Total Corps Staff	41	..	62	..
1st Division	306	9,885	485	18
2nd Division	312	9,995	506	18
3rd Division	315	9,931	475	18
Cavalry Division	190	2,279	1,569	..
Reserve Artillery	24	925	778	36
Artillery Train, Small and Great Gun Ammunition	8	503	563	..
Pontoniers	5	133	6	..
Artificers..	1	75	2	..
Reserve Engineers	4	140	67	..
Military Train	12	570	601	..
Administrative Corps	19	236	2	..
Hospital Department	42	236	67†	..
Police	5	87	62	..
Total	1,283	34,995	5,245	90

* The 4th Army Corps. † 22 Ambulances, 8 Wagons, 396 Cacolets.

Note.—None of the French Corps were completely horsed during the recent war. The Pontoon Train, for example, requires 240 horses, it had but 6. The Battalions were all under horsed, as were the other services.

The following is the establishment of a British army-corps formed for active service :—

An Army-Corps.

(As approved by His Royal Highness the Commander-in-Chief, 18. 7. 71.)

	Officers.	N.-C. Officers and Men.	All Ranks.	Horses.	Guns.
Head-Quarter Staff	21	12	33	64	—
3 Divisions of Infantry	897	27,312	28,269	5,586	54
1 Brigade of Cavalry	92	2,039	2,131	2,001	6
Corps Artillery :—					
Regimental Staff	4	2	6	11	—
3 Batteries Horse Artillery ..	21	516	537	537	18
2 Field Batteries	14	382	396	308	12
Army-Corps Reserve Ammunition Column in 3 sections.	18	516	534	549	—
Engineers :—					
Regimental Staff	2	1	3	5	—
1 Company Royal Engineers ..	5	186	191	4	—
1 Pontoon Train	4	247	251	154	—
1 Telegraph Troop	4	245	249	120	—
Total	1,082	31,458	32,540	9,376	90

The union of two or more army-corps forms an army. To which is usually assigned in addition one or more Divisions of cavalry, and sometimes a reserve of artillery, as was done by the Austrians in the war of 1866, and by the French in 1870.

Having thus given generally an account of the various sections into which bodies of armed men must be divided, in order that they may work together for one end, and be submitted to one authority, it appears desirable to give some account of the nature of the duties devolving on the General who commands, the Staff who aid him in carrying out his duty, and the various branches of the service.

In most armies the various functions are divided between three great departments. The control, or intendance, the artillery, and the engineers.*

The demarcation between the duties performed by these various bodies differs in various armies, but the difference between the three bodies is sufficiently marked to constitute a well-defined distinction, although the exact line of division between the duties of each, may not be the same in all armies.

In the British Service, an army is commanded by either a Field-Marshal or a General; an army-corps by either a General or Lieutenant-General; a Division by either a Lieutenant-General or Major-General, and a brigade by either a Major-General or a Colonel with the rank of Brigadier-General. The following remarks upon the duties of a General Officer are interesting, as showing how much depends on him, and how requisite it is, that at all times he should receive the cordial support of his subordinates.

Napoleon.

Nothing is more important in war than the command. When war is made against a single power, there should be but one army acting upon one line of operations, and directed by one General.

Jomini.

The most essential qualities for a General will always be greatness of character or moral courage, which produces resolution; next, coolness or physical courage, which masters danger; knowledge comes only in the third line, but it is a powerful auxiliary, it would be blindness to despise it. But, as I have already said, I do not mean great erudition, a *little* well understood is better, but, above all, a General should have a mind thoroughly imbued with guiding principles.

In addition to these qualities there is personal character. A brave, just, upright man, knowing how to value merit in others, but not jealous of it, one who can use it for his own ends, such a person will always be a good General, and may even be a great man. Unfortunately an anxiety to be just to merit, is by no means a common quality. Mediocrities are always jealous and inclined to make bad selections, fearing lest the world should say that they are led, and forgetting that he who is placed at the head of an army has

---

* A Department of the Army is a body that serves the Army generally, producing or supplying something that is of general utility, and for the supply of which the Department is responsible. The Artillery and Engineers are thus Departments of the Army. They are, however, different from the Control Department, inasmuch as they have a tactical relation with other troops, which it has not.

They are thus *Arms of the Service* as well as *Departments of the Army*; and this double function is the peculiarity of these two bodies.

almost the entire glory of success, however small may be his share in obtaining it. I think then that the best way of obtaining a General, when there is no great leader who has given proofs of ability, will be

1st. To select as General, a brave man, bold in action and unconquerable in danger.

2nd. To give him, as his Chief of the Staff, a man of great capacity, of a frank-honourable nature, with whom the General may live in good fellowship. The glory is sufficiently great to yield a portion to a friend who has helped to prepare success.

The first quality in a General is to be cool-headed, to estimate things at their just value ; he must not be moved by good or bad news. The sensations that he daily receives must be so classed in his mind that each may occupy its appropriate place. Reason and judgment are only the result of the comparison of well-weighed ideas. There are men who from some physical or moral peculiarity of character, make of each thing a picture. No matter what knowledge, intellect, courage, or good qualities they may have, these men are unfit to command. Generals-in-Chief must be guided by experience or by their own genius. Tactics, manœuvres, the science of the engineer or the artilleryman may be learned from books ; but the knowledge of great tactics can only be acquired by experience and by the study of the history of campaigns of great Generals. *[margin: Napoleon.]*

Gustavus Adolphus, Turenne, Frederick, Alexander, Hannibal, and Cæsar have all acted on the same principles,—holding their own force united, being vulnerable nowhere, seizing rapidly, important points,—such are the principles which lead to victory.

A General-in-Chief should ask himself several times every day—If the enemy appear in my front, on my right or on my left, what would I do ? If he cannot at once give a satisfactory answer, he is in a bad position, he is not acting wisely, he must alter his dispositions.

It is a general idea that coup d'œil does not depend on the individual, that in short it is born. We do not concur in this idea. We all have coup d'œil in proportion to the intellect and good sense that Providence has endowed us with, but it may be improved and trained. To this end our imagination must think always of war, when we hunt, travel, walk, or ride. *[margin: Foland.]*

Napoleon did not leave the front until the first attack took place. He then retired to some place where he might watch events. He generally selected one near the main attack, but out of fire. Had he occasion to quit this place he left an officer to say where he had gone, and left others as he went along to point out where he could be found. *[margin: Rocquancourt]*

It is needless to say that a certain amount of reticence is requisite on the part of a General, but this reticence may be carried too far. Men will always work better when the reason of the exertion demanded from them is made apparent to them, and will carry out orders with greater precision when treated as intellectual beings, and not as machines. The contrast between the two following extracts shows the progress modern war has made in this respect. The more improved the arms in use become the higher does the intellectual power of the soldier rise in value as compared with brute force.

You cannot injure your enemy more than by concealing your intentions. It is for this reason that Metellus, who commanded the army in Spain, being asked what he intended to do next day, replied : If my shirt knew that, I would put it into the fire. *[margin: Machiavelli.]*

Marshal Bugeaud is of a different opinion. He says the plan, at the moment of execution, should be known to as many as possible of those who have to carry it out. Far too often these things are wrapped in mysterious silence. *[margin: Bugeaud.]*

At the moment of action, if possible, even the soldiers should know the plan, each then, even the private, helps intelligently.

The duties of a General in command, even of a small army, are so great, necessitating such constant thought and care, and requiring him to be present at so many places at one time, that it is impossible for any one man to perform these duties. Hence in all armies a General is aided and assisted by officers termed " Staff Officers."

STAFF.

There are few words in the military vocabulary which are used to denote a wider range of meaning than the word 'staff.' Jomini has referred in strong terms to the errors that the indiscriminate use of the word ' division' may produce, and it is therefore desirable to arrive at a clear definition of the word ' staff.' Staff is used in a twofold sense,—first, to denote all officers not in actual personal command of troops; for example, the Paymaster, Adjutant, and Quartermaster of a regiment, are termed the Regimental Staff, that is to say, they are officers who deal with all the companies, and are not like the Captain, Subaltern, or Major, who actually command, or belong to certain defined portions of the regiment, as the companies or wings.

In this sense, Surgeons not attached to regiments are termed Staff-Surgeons. Similarly officers on the General Service List of the Indian Army, are termed officers of the Indian Staff Corps; similarly, the commanding officers of Artillery and Engineers, officers of the latter arm not attached to companies, and officers of the Control Department and subordinate branches are termed officers of the Staff. They are for general duty with the army, and are not attached to troops; but although all these officers belong to the Staff, they are not Staff Officers in the proper acceptation of the word.

The Staff Officer is an officer who acts as the eye and ear of the General, or other officer to whom he is attached, who conveys his orders, collects information for him, and represents him when he is not present. If the General of an army be compared to the head, the Staff, as Hardegg says, may be justly compared to the nerves which convey the volition from the head to the different members.

The position of a Staff Officer should be clearly understood, in order that the duties falling on him may be properly appreciated. He knows the General's plans, and from constant personal intercourse with him, is fully aware of all his intentions, and is consequently able to say what he would order under certain circumstances. Having no real authority of his own he can only act and give such orders as the General may direct. He has no authority as the commanding officers of Artillery and Engineers have over their own corps and the Controller has over his own department, he is simply a portion of the General commanding. The duties of a Staff Officer require great tact, readiness, and knowledge of all branches of the army.

In foreign armies, as the Austrian, Prussian, Russian, and French, there is one Staff; that is to say, the staff duties are undivided, and are performed by a body of officers who are selected in various ways, but who all perform staff functions. There is an officer with the head-quarters of each army, army-corps, or division, termed Chief of the Staff, who is the senior Staff Officer and takes the orders of the General commanding the army, army-corps, or Division, on all matters; he is aided by as many Staff Officers as may be requisite. All correspondence to and from the General with the commanding officers of army-corps, Divisions, or brigades, and with the commanding officers of Artillery and Engineers, and the Intendants or Controllers, passes through his hands, he registers the General's decisions and orders, and conveys them to all concerned. It is his special function to consider and bring to the General's notice, the effect that any regulation proposed by the head of any department, may have on the other departments, and to obtain and submit to the General Officer the opinions of the departments so affected. Belonging to no department or arm of the service, the Staff Officer should know the ideas, feelings, and peculiarities of all, and consequently be able to arrange impartially between them; this is a matter of no little importance, for if any department has the power of settling questions relating to itself, or the responsibility of bringing to the General's notice complaints against its own action or negligence, suspicion is invariably produced as to the impartiality of its action.

Further, each head of a department naturally looks on his own department as the most important object, and hence views everything from a lower stand-point than the Staff Officer who sees the working of all departments.

Every Staff Officer must be considered as acting under the direct orders and superintendence of the superior officer, for whose assistance he is employed, and who must be considered as responsible for his acts. To consider the relative situation of General Officers and Staff in any other light would tend to alter the nature of the Service, and in fact to give the command of the troops to the subaltern Staff Officer instead of the General Officer. *Wellington.*

The Chief of the Staff has no personal or immediate authority, except over the Staff Officers of the army; but he exercises, in the name of the General commanding, all such functions belonging to the latter as he may choose to delegate. Consequently he opens and signs all the daily orders, issuing and signing, " by order" of the General, all orders that the General does not sign himself. The Chief of the Staff is responsible for the whole detail of the army. He collects and submits to the General accurate reports on the state of every branch of the Service, and he directs all measures requisite to put these services in order to be taken, if the officers commanding and the Intendant-in-Chief have not of themselves done so. *Vauchelle.*

The *raison d'être* of the Chief of the Staff is to give the General, who is

C

both the will and intelligence of the army, time and leisure for the thought requisite to worthily accomplish his great mission.

The relations of the Chief of the Staff with the Generals commanding, and with the Intendant-in-Chief, are the same as those of the General, whose mouth-piece he is.

There is this difference between the Chief of the Staff on one side, and the General Officers commanding troops, the Artillery, the Engineers, and the Intendant-in-Chief on the other, that the latter exercise under the direction and in accordance with the orders of the General commanding-in-chief a secondary but personal authority, which they derive both from their grades in the Service and their letters of service, while the Chief of the Staff, whose duties are more extended and more variable, exercises only a delegated and variable authority. Thus his functions differ as he is employed under a Turenne, or a Villeroi, a Pichegru, or a Rossignol.

Grimoard. The Staff of an army consists of a number of selected officers whose chief or chiefs, if there are several, take the orders of the General with reference to all details concerning the feeding, the movement, or quartering of troops.

Hardegg. The object of the Staff in the existing state of warlike administration, is to be the organ by which the commandant of an army or a fraction of an army watches over the detail of the administration of the troops under his command under every circumstance.

Jomini. A good Staff, says General Jomini, is indispensable for the well-being of an army ; it should be considered as the nursery from which a General selects the instruments to serve him, as a collection of officers whose knowledge helps his own. There is thus harmony between the genius which commands and the talents of those who apply his designs.

Grimoard. The details that a Staff officer has specially to look after, are the subsistence, the movement, and the quartering of troops, and as these three are the most indispensable things in war, it is requisite to unite them in the same hand as much as possible, at the same time relieving the General of all details, and leaving him all his faculties for the combination and execution of his military plans. This is the reason that has led to the introduction of staffs in an army. Their special duties are to maintain and watch over due order, in all branches of the army, but having no particular authority over the troops, their duties only embracing the weaving together of details.

Army of North German Confederation. (Translated by Colonel Newdegate.) Non-military men often hold wrong ideas of the *rôle* of the Chief of the Staff of a large Division of the army, especially of the nature of his relations with the Commander-in-Chief in war. They think that his first duty is to act as an adviser to his chief, and even that he officiates as the proper strategical agent at head-quarters. This is not the case. The Commander-in-Chief is the deciding principal ; he alone bears the responsibility. His Chief of the Staff is nothing more than his first assistant, the principal organ for communicating his individual will to the troops ; and if the Chief of the Staff sketches a plan of operations or the dispositions of a battle, he did not give his own ideas but those of his Commander. The position of a Chief of the Staff is no doubt a most important one. He has even to represent his chief under certain circumstances, but he then only acts according to the intentions and upon the principles imposed by the latter.

These relations do not prevent the General commanding from sometimes desiring to learn the opinions and views of his Chief of the Staff, and even of adopting them ; but it is then a voluntary act of confidence in the intelligence of his subordinate. The history of wars no doubt shows that certain Generals, otherwise very capable, do not unite all the qualities required for so high a mission, and that a Chief of the Staff has been placed beside them who was capable of supplying precisely the qualities in which they were deficient. One can recall the combinations Blücher-Gneisnau, Radetzky-Hess. But these are exceptions to the normal rule.

The officer of the General Staff is at hand to assist the Divisional General. This officer has to exempt his General from the detail of communicating orders, and in action he is specially destined to assist him in a knowledge of the situation and of the ground, in order that the latter may be able to make his dispositions judiciously. This can only be attained by absenting himself temporarily from his commander, who cannot be everywhere at once, and should change his place as seldom as possible, but he must not go away oftener, nor remain absent longer, than appears absolutely necessary; moreover, he should never absent himself on his own responsibility. The Staff Officer's place is at the side of his General, whom he should only leave on obtaining his order or permission to do so. Occasions for this come often enough; even when the engaged line of a division is not immoderately extended, its commander, from his station in rear, can, as a rule, only observe the general features of the course of the action. He can see when the action is at a standstill, when it advances or retires, but he frequently does not know the reason why in one place no progress is made, while in another the troops are even beginning to give way, yet if he wishes to go everywhere personally he must give up at once his superintendence over the whole; or the ground in front of his position hides the movements of a portion of his troops, and of the enemy, the reports arriving do not suffice to give a clear idea of them, yet the General must not leave his place, as he must keep the greater portion of his troops in view. Further, even for the reconnoitring of ground, especially when on the offensive, there is not time enough for one individual to take a view of the proportionally great extent of ground necessary for a Division; moreover, the troops arriving must be provided with orders, and still they cannot be judiciously disposed, without, at least, an idea of the ground.

In all these cases the leader of great bodies of troops requires an officer upon whose judgment he can rely, who can go to the different places instead of himself and then observe for him, and for this purpose the officer of the General Staff is principally destined. The latter can only fulfil his task if he has been specially trained for the duties of it. Moreover, apart from this, it is also his business to look to everything by which he may be able to lighten his commander's duties and assist him in their performance. The Staff Officer must understand, therefore, in action, not only how to take in the situation of the bodies of troops to which he is attached, with regard to the general state of the engagement, but he must be able to judge rightly its several periods as well as the features of the ground, and this requires very thorough training. The greatest difficulty he incurs with a Division is that a correct judgment can only be formed by his maintaining a constant view of the whole state of affairs, whereas his duty often takes him from the spot from which alone he is able to obtain it. This officer, therefore, on returning to his commander, after having been despatched anywhere, must always immediately endeavour to obtain information of anything that has occurred during his absence. He cannot possibly trouble the Divisional General at such an important time with questions, and inquiries in the Staff would only furnish him with incomplete information. If, therefore, his General does not of his own accord impart to him his knowledge on the subject, the Staff Officer easily loses the complete information which is so necessary for him.

Arrangements for providing wagons for the eventual transport of the wounded, the direction of the train and of the prisoners, the delivery of reports to superior authorities, and the providing of a guide who knows the ground belong to necessary details. The latter may appear superfluous, but is far from being so.

In the first place, even if in possession of the most detailed map, the whole of its sections cannot be carried in the sabretache, and an unexpected course of events may necessitate the use of sections whose employment was only reckoned upon for the following day, and which are consequently not at hand in the moment of need. Thus it happened that in the Staff of an officer holding a high command, which was richly provided with materials for maps, not a single section relating to that portion of the ground could be found upon entering the battle-field of Königgrätz.

And even when they are on the spot errors cannot be avoided. During a rapid ride, in which the direction is often changing, and the attention is distracted by passing events, the run of a map may be lost even when actually in the hand. Lastly, with the best maps mistakes are easily made about points some way off, church towers behind woods and such like.

The old saying, that a messenger tied to a string is better than the finest map, has still its full force, and it is well in every large staff to commission one officer with the sole duties of reconnoitring the ground.*

We may take this opportunity of remarking that the training in reading maps is not always undertaken in a sufficiently practical manner. The value of survey maps in war requires no further proof; but in order to practice oneself in plans for use in action the looking over and general understanding of them does not suffice. It is much more necessary to be able to observe, as it were, a landscape in one's mind, as has been often attempted in these sketches. Let it be supposed that one arrives at any spot and asks which portion on the map corresponds with the landscape from this position. In this way previous practice will be so much the more useful at a future time in making judicious dispositions of ground.

Napoleon.

To be able to read a map, to understand a reconnaissance, to be able to issue orders, to be able to give a clear statement of the most intricate movements of an army,—such are the requirements of a Staff officer.

The functions of a Staff Officer are thus of a very extensive nature, and to discharge them well, he must have not only considerable knowledge but also a great amount of tact and good humour. A fussy Staff Officer does much harm, he is always interfering with the heads of departments, pointing out *how* they should do their duty. It being his proper place to take obstacles out of their way, to smooth their relations with others, and to bring to the General's notice any neglect on their part. The moment a Staff Officer, using his position on the Staff of a General, prescribes *how* any definite action is to be performed, he removes the responsibility for the due execution from the shoulders of the executive officer whose duty it is, on to his own. Confusion and friction must ensue from such a course of action. It is impossible to over-rate the importance of a Staff Officer's duties, or the knowledge he requires to fulfil those duties adequately, but a Staff Officer must never forget that more harm than good may be done by interference with details. The way in which an executive officer carries out his duty often depends on his peculiar temperament, no two men placed in similar positions will act exactly in the same way. Within wide limits their conduct must be judged by results; to attempt to bind all to one standard, would be to destroy all individuality: consequently details should be invariably left to those whose duty it is to

---

* The following extract is remarkable, more especially when it is remembered that the ground was that fought over by the great Frederick, and close to the Prussian frontiers. "The wood of Maslowed was not distinctly marked on the maps, so that its extent and depth were unknown. From east to west it is about 2,000, from north to south about 1,200, paces long." [Prussian official account, campaign 1866. Translated by Hozier and Wright.]

execute orders. Through the Staff all correspondence of all kinds should pass, and in the Staff office, that is to say, the General's office, all decisions should be carefully registered for future reference. If this be not done there will be much confusion.

The commanding officer of Artillery, the commanding officer of Engineers, and the Intendant, claim to deal with the General-in-Chief, and not with his Chief of the Staff. Nothing should prevent the closest intercourse between these functionaries and the General, but he should see them only in presence of the Chief of the Staff, and send him all their correspondence, otherwise confusion is inevitable. *Jomini.*

CONTROL DEPARTMENT.

The Control Department is charged with the supply of all stores of every kind, both *munitions de guerre* and *de bouche.* The head of the Control Department in the British service under existing regulations does not deal with the Staff but with the General commanding; all correspondence for the Controller is taken by that officer to the General commanding, who settles it, the Controller being the means of communication on all questions connected with barracks, fuel, light, powder, shot, arms, engineer appliances, boots and clothes, as well as for food, forage, and money.

The Control Department in the English Army is unlike the Intendance of any foreign army, performing many duties which in foreign armies are not performed by that body, and, on the other hand, having nothing to do with duties that in foreign armies are performed by the Intendance.

The Controller is bound to be well acquainted with all the armament of works within the command, and the stores required for the same.

He is bound to repair all military stores of every kind, and he is bound to have all reserve stores kept up to the proper quantities and to concentrate them in reserve depôts.

A Controller will consult with the officer commanding as to the place of supply depôts, and as to what things are to be got on the spot.

The Controller will conduct his duties under the direct orders of the officer commanding, to whom he may be attached. He will be the adviser and agent of the officer commanding in all matters connected with the raising or issue of money, the supply of provisions, stores, clothing and transport. He will relieve him as far as possible of all details connected therewith. *Extracted from the Control Regulations.*

The Controller will hold towards the officer commanding, and towards the heads of other departments within the command, with reference to Control services, a position analogous to that held by the officer of the General Staff, with reference to military services; excepting that while the Controller is under the immediate command of the officer commanding, he is at the same time responsible to the Secretary of State for War that the duties of his department are conducted in strict accordance with the instructions laid down in the regulations, and with any special instruction that may be given to his predecessors, or that may from time to time be conveyed to him.

The Controller will not be warranted in departing on any occasion from his instructions upon his own authority. Should circumstances at any time render a deviation therefrom in his opinion necessary or expedient, before reference can be made to the War Office, he will submit the case to the officer commanding, and obtain a written sanction for the deviation, reporting the full particulars to the Secretary of State for War. The Controller will be held responsible for any measure that may be adopted on his recommendation.

Should the Controller receive orders from the officer commanding inconsistent with War Office Instructions or Regulations, and which may not have proceeded from his (the Controller's) suggestion, it will be his duty respectfully to point out this inconsistency to the officer commanding, and to solicit a special authority in writing for the deviation, which, being granted, must be implicitly obeyed. A report of the circumstance, countersigned by the officer commanding, together with a copy of the correspondence, will be transmitted by the Controller to the Secretary of State for War, who will hold the officer commanding responsible for the measures ordered by him.

Should the officer commanding and the Controller, or either of them, consider that they have not sufficient power, or should they be in any doubt how to act, reference will be made to the Secretary of State for War. When it is necessary to promulgate in "orders," a decision of the General officer commanding, or an instruction referring to Control services, the Controller will submit in writing, for the approval of the officer commanding, a draught or memorandum of the terms in which the communication is to be made, and having obtained the initials or signature of the officer commanding to the document, will then transmit it to the Adjutant-General or proper military Staff officer to be put in orders. In cases in which the decision of the officer commanding does not require promulgation by an order, the intervention of a military Staff officer will not be required. The Controller will communicate the decision to the persons concerned direct, and in writing with his signature affixed, adding the words, " by decision of the General officer commanding."

When the troops are brigaded, the Controller will be in direct communication with the Brigadier on all subjects appertaining to Control duties, and will submit any question which may require decision or consideration to the officer commanding the division or garrison.

The Controller is charged with the appropriation of barracks, and their custody when vacant and not dismantled.

In order to obtain information as to the best mode of supplying the troops, the Controller will use every endeavour in all situations in which he may be placed to ascertain the resources of the country in cattle, grain, forage, fuel, &c., and the means of transport by land or water, the established rates and prices of the country, the state of the roads, the communication by land and by inland navigation, together with all other information of a local nature that may be useful.

The Controller will be responsible for the proper organization and for the economical and efficient working of the transport service, whether furnished by the Army Service Corps or provided locally.

The Controller will make himself acquainted with the quantity and nature of the various articles for which land transport would be necessary should the army take the field, and he will ascertain the resources of his district in respect of auxiliary transport.

The Controller will have in readiness plans for the movement of the force or of parts of it, with specifications of the equipment, animals, and stores necessary. These plans will be kept corrected in accordance with the progress of events.

The Controller will be the medium of communication with the War Office on subjects relating to Control services, but he will submit all letters and communications for the perusal and observation of the officer commanding, except those relating to matters of ordinary routine, which the officer commanding may not require to be submitted to him.

It will be the duty of the Controller to prepare for the officer commanding all correspondence on Control subjects, whether local or with the Secretary of State for War. He will preserve in his office all letters and other records relating to those duties, including the correspondence addressed to the officer commanding. He will be prepared at all times to lay those records before the officer commanding when required to do so, and to furnish him with full information on all points connected with Control duties.

The Controller is responsible that the officers of the Army Service Corps preserve discipline and efficiency in the establishment under their orders.

In France the organization and execution of the various administrative services, the supervision and continual control of the interior economy of corps and detachments, forms a portion of the duty of the Intendance, as well as the authorization of all expenses, the verification and audit of accounts of issues and consumption of all kinds, either of money or articles obtained in the country or of prizes made by the enemy—in short all the details of the administration, except what is connected with the matériel of the Artillery and the Engineers, form a portion of the duties of the Intendance. The Intendants and Sous-Intendants have no duty transaction but with the commanding officers or Chief of the Staff of the army, army-corps, division, or brigade to which they are attached. *Vauchelle.*

The Intendant, or Chief Commissary of an army, has under his direction the agents who supply the following provisions :—Forage, hospital requisites, clothing and camp equipment transport, the supply of articles used by the troops in barracks or on the line of march. The provision of the subsistence of the army is the first duty of the Intendant, all else is subordinate to that. *Grimoard.*

Armies have frequently to be fed by forced requisitions ; these requisitions are ordered by the General commanding, the custody and distribution of what is obtained by requisitions falls to the Intendant.

The following remarks on the subject of requisitions are interesting :—

However careful and foreseeing the administration of an army may be, it will often be compelled to seek assistance from the inhabitants of the country occupied by the army : compulsory demands for assistance are then made. These demands are termed "requisitions" when they are in kind, "contributions" when in money. *De Gerlache.*

Requisitions are therefore demands on the enemy's country ; they are made without any pretence of justice, only by the right of the strongest ; that necessity commands them ; they are in short a kind of fine to help the cost of the war.

The same right of war, which authorizes requisitions of provisions in an enemy's country, also permits requisitions of money.

The adoption of such measures, and the amounts demanded, the mildness or harshness with which they are enforced, are entirely political questions.

The power of calling for contributions in money in an enemy's country when occupied, belongs exclusively to the General commanding-in-chief. The amounts so obtained are paid into the military chest to the credit of the treasury, and are included in the general resources, to meet the wants of the army.

When a General-in-Chief determines to call for a contribution in money, the Intendant-in-Chief will furnish him with a report on the state and resources of the country, upon the taxes already charged on it, and upon the chances of the sum demanded being realized.

Grimoard. M. Paris du Vernei, the most able Intendant the French army had, lays it down as a principle, that so far as possible requisitions in kind, especially in grain, are to be avoided. He says with great truth that when the inhabitants get frightened about their own food they hide their corn, and famine often thus succeeds rapidly to abundance. He considers it better at all times, even for the country itself, to demand money and buy corn with it.

If bread is demanded, the size and shape of loaf used in the country should be accepted ; it will be easier to distribute it, than to insist on the bakers providing loaves similar to those used by the army.

De Gerlache. Requisitions should if possible be moderate in amount and frequently renewed, this will divide the pressure of their charges more equally ; they are at all times most vexatious to the people. If contributions in money can be obtained they are always the safest, easiest, and most politic, it being far more economical to provision an army by purchase than in any other way. But it always happens that although the amount of a contribution is stated in coin, yet practically in war a portion must be taken in coin, a portion in paper, a portion in provision, a portions in labour. This latter portion is termed "a requisition."

One advantage of contributions in money is that they avoid waste, and produce a certain amount of trade in the country, which may slightly alleviate the burdens of the people.

A system of requisitions is essentially a bad one, and a wise administration will use it as little as possible, and with great circumspection, and then only for the first and pressing wants of the army, or if the people wish it to enable them to pay the contributions more easily ; nevertheless, at certain times and places requisitions have to be resorted to, and it is then advisable to place them under strict rules.

It is most imprudent to give too much power to the local authorities, much time will be lost and very little done. An official of the army must be present at the division of the amount, and must assure himself of the means of executing the requisition ; otherwise the envy, small hatreds, and passions of little towns influence the division, and when arbitrary acts are either done or authorized in war, such feelings should not be excited.

When an urgent requisition is demanded, the chief inhabitants are immediately ordered to supply a certain portion, according to their estimated ability ; and the representatives of the Government are the first so called on. Shopkeepers should only pay their *pro rata* share, whatever may be the state of their stores.

When the leading men of a town are thus dealt with, it is unlikely that they will spare any one, and they will be just to their fellow citizens ; if this be not done there will be neither justice in dividing the requisition nor punctuality in bringing it.

It is most essential to watch the agents entrusted with the duty of obtaining the requisition for furnishing a requisition may be made the pretext, and furnish the occasion, for the most vexatious interference with the people.

However, if the orders are very explicit, and if civilians acting as commissaries assist the military commissaries, a great many abuses and vexations may be avoided. But if the quantity or quality of the provisions has been unsuitably fixed, and if the country be handed over to the agents of the Intendance and these happen to be dishonest, avarice will find a thousand ways of inflicting misery on the inhabitants ; and as Olennius, of whom Tacitus speaks, demanded skins of a uniform pattern, the agents will be most difficult to satisfy. The quality will never be good enough, the measure will not be of the proper weight, or the weight of the proper measure, the corn will not be clean enough, the bullocks will be too small, too thin, and everything will be too little, or bad. These disputes will be finally settled, but the country and the army will suffer.

Notwithstanding the most careful consideration and foresight, requisitions must be made in every country where there is war. The *army must live*, and no consideration should stop the staff when this imperious law has to be obeyed. A town or a village always contains food and supplies of different kinds for an army which is at hand ;—to find the means of extracting them, that is the problem.

Under such circumstances, and in accordance with orders to be issued by only the Commander-in-Chief or the Commandants of Corps, the Chief of the Staff will select the places on which a contribution is to be levied, its amount and nature. De Lavarenne.

An officer or a Sub-Intendant (or better still, a treasury *employé* if money has to be received) is entrusted with overseeing the contribution in a certain district, and when the duty is completed the Military Intendance divide the proceeds as may be directed. This officer or Sous-Intendant will be accompanied by a detachment composed of a force of cavalry and infantry, commanded by an officer whose duty it is to respond to all demands made on him, either to furnish sentries over persons' houses, to aid the local authorities, by main force, or even to make house to house visits.

For such an operation (as for foraging) a party is told off proportionate to the value of the contribution, the neighbourhood of the enemy, or the dispositions of the inhabitants. The commanding officer is responsible that all requisite measures are taken to ensure the execution of the order.

This is one of the most delicate and unpleasant duties with which an officer can be charged. The officer entrusted with this duty, prior to leaving his garrison, camp, or post, should receive an exact list of the villages which are to contribute, the nature and the amount of contribution each is to furnish. He should know the places that the provisions, forage, &c., should be sent to. He should be informed of the roads leading from the place he is in to the various villages, and from the villages to the magazines. He should be informed if the enemy is in the neighbourhood of the country called on to contribute, and what is the force assembled. He should also know the feelings and character of the inhabitants. He should ask information on all these points in the greatest detail, and he should ask for and get a covering order to protect him against any odium that may arise from having to resort to extreme measures. He should also keep a journal noting down all marches or operations of any kind, and he should call on the chief inhabitants to sign as to the state of the contributions levied. De Cessac.

Prior to moving off he should inspect his men, and give the clearest instructions as to pillage. As in reconnaissances, detachments to levy contributions should not be too large—too large a detachment frightens the people, who hide their cattle, their corn, and forage, leave their houses, and go to seek and warn the enemy.

Large detachments fatigue an army—they can be followed and easily attacked.

Small detachments on the contrary go everywhere, arrive at unexpected moments, return with ease, and, consuming little food, can easily hide in small woods and ravines. For these reasons an officer sent to levy contributions should take only a small detachment. A detachment sent for such a purpose should be composed one-half of infantry, one-half of cavalry ; it should be accompanied by guides and interpreters ; fresh guides should be procured each day, for peasants rarely know any but the roads close to their own houses.

The Commandant of the detachment will arrange so as to arrive about the middle of night near the village on which the contribution is to be levied. He will place his men in an advantageous position, and will send an interpreter, accompanied by two infantry officers, to find out if the enemy is in the village ; they will go quietly through the streets, and will listen attentively, and examine everything. If an enemy is in the village they will answer his challenge, and return as quickly as possible. If nothing indicates the presence of an enemy they will return and report to the Commandant if the enemy is in possession ; so soon as the scouts return the party will retreat : if there is no enemy, two mounted non-commissioned officers and an interpreter will be sent into the village. They will go to the chief man in the place, who represents the Government : it will be very advantageous if the guide or interpreter knows the man. He will be at once told that a strong body of the enemy is close at hand, and that guides are requisite, and that he must come and speak to the commanding officer. This will generally induce him to open his door ; he will be then taken without noise to the Commandant.

While this is going on the Commandant will surround the village with small parties of seven or eight men to prevent any one leaving it or going to warn the enemy who may be near at hand.

As soon as the chief man shall have been brought to the Commandant, he will be told of the orders given to require a sum of money, a quantity of provisions, forage, carts, or labourers. He will be directed to place in the hands of the Commandant five or six hostages chosen among the chief people of the place, also the children of the principal inhabitants. When these hostages have been given, the magistrate will be allowed to go, and a very short time will be allowed to get the contribution ready and on the road for the army. If the contribution cannot be at once supplied, the hostages will be taken away, and the people will be informed that if the contribution does not reach the army on a certain day the village will be burned.

The following is an example of a requisition :-

"Notice.

"*Nancy*, 23rd *January*, 1871, 4 p.m.

"The Prefect of the Meurthe sends the Maire of Nancy the following order:—

"If to-morrow, the 24th January, at 12 noon, 500 workmen from the workshops of the town are not at the railway station, the foremen first, and a certain number of the workmen next, will be seized and shot."

If the magistrates refuse to furnish the contribution, the Commandant will threaten to burn their houses and farms, and will prepare to carry out his threats if they are not submissive.

To compel villages to pay their contingent, the magistrates should be written to and informed that if, at a certain hour on a certain day, they have not furnished the proper quantity of money, provisions, forage, carts, or labourers, a party will be sent to burn the farms and houses. On the day appointed the detachments sent for this purpose will go to the village, burn one house and threaten to burn all the rest if the contribution be not at once forthcoming. As the weight of contribution becomes excessive, if it is not equally divided, and as the magistrates of a country occupied by an enemy invariably divide contribution in an unjust way, the officer charged with this operation will point out the means for raising this tax, and he will watch that the contributions demanded are fairly divided.

So soon as the inhabitants have furnished the contributions levied on them, the detachment will escort it close to head-quarters, leave a small party to take it in, and proceed to the other villages.

When the whole of the contributions have been obtained, the detachment will return to camp, the Officer Commanding will halt it a short distance from the camp, and will examine the men's haversacks. If any stolen property be found the culprits will be at once punished.

Saxe.

Before returning into quarters all the men should be marched to a certain place, and if any stolen property be found the thieves must be hung without mercy.

De Lavarenne.

It is prudent not to take the same road when returning, as the inhabitants may obtain a small force of the enemy to attack the convoy, or even do so themselves.

Great firmness is requisite to prevent deception on the part of the inhabitants, and in such a delicate operation the return of the party is likely to be the most difficult. It will be prudent, therefore, to use pack horses to carry money on in place of carriages. These animals can cross fields, bye-roads, or bad ground more easily than wagons.

ARTILLERY.

The Artillery of an army is commanded by a General Officer, who is styled the Commanding Officer of Artillery. He has to assist him, a staff which is composed of two branches, one being charged with the duty of Adjutant-General, or personnel, the other being charged with the matériel; the head of the matériel branch is termed the Director of Park; both these subordinates are if requisite helped by other officers of Artillery.

The Artillery of an army-corps is commanded by a Major-General, or Brigadier-General, assisted by a similar staff.

The Artillery of a Division is commanded by a field officer who has a staff officer charged with both the personnel and matériel of the Division.

The Commanding Officer of Artillery with an army is charged not only with the command of all the Artillery, but also with the supply of the 1st and 2nd reserves of small and great gun ammunition, as well as with the important duties which devolve on that corps at sieges.

The most suitable means of obtaining the greatest advantage from the artillery is by giving the chief command of that arm to an Artillery General who is not only an artillerist but a good tactician and strategist. This General disposes not only of the general Artillery Reserve, but also of one-half of the guns attached to the division and army-corps. He can thus, in concert with the General Commanding-in-Chief, determine the moment and place where large masses of artillery can best contribute to victory. But such a massing of artillery must never be made, except by order of the General Commanding-in-Chief. The Commandants of Artillery and Engineers have always made a portion of the Staff of the army. *Jomini.*

The Commandant of Artillery should be endowed with great coolness and intelligence. He should be close to the commanding officer of the Division so long as his presence with his batteries is not absolutely requisite, in order that he may follow the course of the action and subordinate the artillery to its movements. *Von Miller.*

It is a duty of the Commandant of Artillery to know the whole of the operations of the army, since it is his duty to supply arms and ammunition to the different divisions composing it. His connection with the Commanding Officers of Artillery at the advanced posts should keep him aware of all the movements of the army, and the direction of the great parc is subordinate to these movements. *Napoleon.*

The General commanding the Artillery has authority over all the troops of the arm. He may, with the approval of the General commanding, make all such changes in the personnel and matériel as he thinks advisable. He issues orders to the Generals commanding the Artillery of army-corps, and receives their reports, the Central Reserve and Grand Park receive orders only from him, he fixes the depôts as well as the marches; finally, he sees to the supply of the army from the parks and convoys. *Le Bourg.*

He lives close to head-quarters, and when marching to attack an enemy he accompanies the General in all his reconnaissances, in order to select the places most suitable for his guns. In action he remains close to the General to receive his orders, if he does not himself direct the movements of the reserve at decisive moments.

The Chief of the Artillery Staff receives from the Staffs of corps and divisions reports and states of their situation, both as regards personnel and matériel. He sends them all orders issued by the commanding officer of Artillery, and the General Staff of the Army. The Director of Park is charged with the supply of ammunition and all articles required for repairs, or exchanges if these cannot be supplied by the Corps and Divisional Parks. He keeps the commanding officer of Artillery aware of all expenditure of ammunition. The commanding officers of the Divisional Artillery receive orders from the Generals commanding the divisions to which they are attached as regards their marches and the military position they should occupy; but, as regards interior economy and matériel they receive orders from the commanding officer of Artillery, whom they keep acquainted with changes from day to day, the state of their supplies, and their wants.

The Army of the North German Confederation.
Newdegate.

Although the cannon is the arm of all Artillery, yet the diversity of object and manner of employment, as well as the different kinds of guns dependent thereon, and the various modes of serving them, have necessitated a different instruction for the men, and a division of all into two categories—siege artillery and field artillery, which last is divided into field and horse, the latter provided with mounted gunners. This division, however, concerns the men of the corps, not the officers. The artillery officer is not destined for one only of the categories mentioned above, but rather for employment in either, and is educated accordingly. He is, as it were, a universal artilleryman.

Captain May.
Tactical retrospect.
Ouvry.

The leader of the Artillery of an army should be a General of the first class.

ENGINEERS.

The Engineers of an army are commanded by a General, who is styled the Commanding Engineer. He has to help him a staff, composed of an officer discharging the functions of Adjutant-General, and a Director of Park.

The duties of the Engineers are the conduct of engineering operations at sieges, the construction and maintenance of field telegraphs, mining, bridging, surveying, or such other military engineering duties as the General Officer Commanding may direct.

Thiebault.
(Hand Book of Staff Duties.)

The works that the engineers are charged with make them as important in peace as in war. During peace they make or repair everything connected with their Service, everything that war may have destroyed. They perfect and complete systems of defence. They fortify frontiers and the coast, taking advantage of the ground—as water, marshes, woods, or mountains.

During war they are employed on reconnaissance, which they make either themselves, or in which they accompany General and superior officers. They open and make roads for the different arms of the Service; they are employed to choose positions, sketch ground, and on the itinerary of routes, on the trace and construction of field fortifications, the intrenchment of camps, the attack and defence of fortresses.

In battles the Commanding Engineer and his Staff remain close to the General to give him all the information he requires as to the ground, the positions he wishes to take or the movements he may desire to make, and to execute immediately, with the companies of sappers held ready at hand and provided with tools, any work the General may wish, either on the line, on the flank, or rear. In addition to these duties which, as Engineers, they are charged with, these officers may in some cases be employed as Staff officers.

An engineer who employs all his time in fortifications, exchanges voluntarily the position of a soldier for that of an artizan. An engineer who is a good soldier and an indifferent architect, will always be serviceable ; even though his constructions may, in a measure, fail in an artistic point of view, an indifferent construction at the right place, is better than an artistic production at the wrong one. *Captain May. Tactical retrospect. Ouvry.*

The great importance of the Commanding Engineer in an army can only be appreciated when he is seen at the side of the General Commanding-in-Chief, superintending the whole strategic and tactical position, and seizing the opportunity when his own branch of the Service can advantageously co-operate in the battle.

The Pioneers, the officers of which are taken from the Engineer corps, are not properly a tactical body, but a technical one ; that is, a body of soldiers appointed for the execution of such building and numerous other technical works as become indispensably necessary in war. Although they are not organized for combat, yet their *rôle* in war is none the less important, and is one also of no less danger than that of other troops. They are very frequently obliged to execute their works exposed to the efficacious fire of the enemy, and with passive endurance. They are also charged with mining operations, the most terrible warfare of its kind. In a technical point of view the men of each pioneer battalion are divided into pontoniers, sappers, and miners. *Army of the NorthGerman Confederation. Newdegate.*

They are charged with the construction of field works, placing villages in a state of defence, erecting barricades, piercing loopholes in the walls of houses and gardens, &c., they also render essential assistance to the infantry under opposite circumstances at the capture of such localities, by the removal of barricades and the destruction of walls : all under the enemy's fire. A brilliant example of this took place at the storming of Le Bourget (30th October, 1870).

Their duties also include the formation of obstacles to impede the enemy's march, such as abattis, the destruction of bridges and roads, and, in antagonistic circumstances, the removal of the same obstacles in favour of their own troops. Finally, they furnish the men required for the technical service of the field telegraph and field railway. The *rôle* of the Pioneers is therefore very comprehensive. At sieges the other arms, especially the Artillery, naturally had their full share in the brilliant result (siege of Strasburg). But the chief merit belongs to the Engineer, who has to determine, in such a war problem, the basis of the whole attack, namely the choice of the attacking fronts and the laying out of the parallels and works generally.

The Permanent Committee of Engineers, composed of the chief and superior officers of the corps, which meets daily at Berlin under the orders of the Inspector-General of Engineers, is of great importance. It decides the necessity of new works of fortification, orders their construction, and examines and publishes new technical inventions and improvements.

The great requisite for the Commanding Engineer of an Army, who must design and direct all the works of his arm of the service, is sound common sense. *Napoleon.*

The foregoing is a brief sketch of the duties performed by the various departments of the Army, and the places they fill in the military machine.

It is difficult, if not impossible, to lay down hard and fast lines dividing these duties one from the other.

In many cases they blend together, and there must always be certain duties which are common to both. Consequently it is most desirable that officers should see a little beyond the limits of their own special branch of the army. To the effective working of all departments heartily, with good will, and without jealousy, the great result, success, is due.

As the British Army is not permanently formed in corps and Divisions, and as a large force has made no field campaign (Sebastopol was a siege) in continental Europe since 1815, it may not be uninteresting to give a brief account of how these duties were performed under the Duke of Wellington. The following is taken from the preface to his General Orders, published with his authority and approval by Colonel Gurwood.

Gurwood. The Staff of the army at head-quarters was composed as follows :—

Personal Staff of the Commander-in-Chief.

The Military Secretary.
The Commandant at Head-Quarters. (An Assistant Adjutant-General).
The Aides-de-Camp to the Commander-in-Chief.

The Adjutant-General's Department.

The Adjutant-General.
The Deputy Adjutant-General.
Assistant Adjutant-Generals.
Deputy-Assistant Adjutant-Generals.

The officers of this department were charged with all the detail of duties, returns, correspondence, discipline, &c. Although the organs of head-quarters, and of the General Officers Commanding Corps and Divisions to which they were attached, for all orders and communications, the responsibility of the duties they performed rested with the General Officer under whose orders they served, and for whose assistance they were employed.

The Quartermaster-General's Department.

The Quartermaster-General.
The Deputy Quartermaster-General.
Assistant Quartermaster-Generals.
Deputy-Assistant Quartermaster-Generals.

The officers of this department were charged with embarkation, disembarkation, equipment, quartering, halting, encamping, route marching, and the occupation of positions of the different divisions and of the troops, at the stations to which they were respectively attached, under the authority and responsibility of the General, or other superior officer in command.

Staff attached to Head-Quarters.

An Assistant Quartermaster-General to superintend the billeting, the quartering and baggage of the head-quarters.

A Staff Surgeon.
A Chaplain.
An Assistant Commissary-General.
An Assistant Provost-Marshal.
An Assistant Baggage-Master.

Corps attached to the Head-Quarters.

The commanding officer of Royal Artillery, with the Staff of his corps, having a general superintendence of the artillery and ammunition attached to the corps and divisions, also the battering train and the reserve artillery and ammunition. The Commanding Royal Engineer, with the Staff and other officer belonging to his corps having a general superintendence over the officers of Engineers, the corps of Sappers and Miners, pontoons, and the engineer park, consisting of the siege material and the entrenching tools, &c., belonging to the army.

The officer commanding the corps of Guides (an Assistant Quartermaster-General), in charge of the post-office and the communications of the army.

The officer commanding the Staff Corps of Cavalry in charge of the police of the army, and other confidential duties.

The Provost-Marshal and his assistants, having charge of prisoners of war, deserters from the enemy, and all prisoners tried, or to be tried, by general court-martial, and having authority to inflict summary punishment for all offences committed under their observation.

Civil Departments attached to Head-Quarters.

The Medical Department, consisting of Inspector-General of Hospitals, Deputy Inspector, Physicians, Staff Surgeons, Apothecaries, Dispensers, Assistant Staff Surgeons, Hospital Assistants, &c.

The Purveyor's Department, consisting of a Purveyor to the Forces, with deputies and assistants in charge of the hospitals, hospital material, arms and accoutrements, clothing and necessaries of men in hospital, also of the funeral expenses of men who died in hospital.

The Paymaster-General's Department, consisting of Paymaster-General, assistants, &c.

The Commissariat Department, consisting of Commissary-General, Deputy Commissary-Generals, Assistant and Deputy-Assistants, Commissariat Clerks, &c. This department was divided into two branches—Stores and Accounts.

The Storekeeper-General's Department, consisting of the Storekeeper-General and his assistants, having charge of the field equipment, tents, &c., and the heavy baggage of the army.

The Comptroller of Army Accounts, with inspectors, &c., to whom all accountants, except Commissariat accountants, render their accounts.

Divisions.

The army in the field was divided into divisions, each commanded by a Lieutenant-General or Major-General, having local rank as Lieutenant-General, with the following staff :—

Two Aides-de-Camp.
One Assistant Adjutant-General.
One Deputy-Assistant Adjutant-General.
One Assistant Quartermaster-General.
One Deputy-Assistant Quartermaster-General.
One or two officers of the Royal Engineers.
One Staff Surgeon.
One Chaplain.
One Assistant Commissary-General, with a deputy, clerks, &c.
One Assistant Provost-Marshal.
One Baggage Master, with assistants from the Staff Corps of Cavalry.
One Storekeeper of Ordnance in charge of reserve ammunition, under the officer commanding the Royal Artillery attached to the division.

Each division was composed of two or more brigades, each consisting of two, three, or four battalions, the light companies of which were formed when in presence of the enemy into a battalion under the command of a field officer or senior Captain of the light companies of each brigade.

The brigades were commanded by a Major-General, or a Brigadier-General, or Colonel on the Staff, with the following staff :—

One Aide-de-Camp.
One Major of Brigade.
One Deputy-Assistant Commissary-General, with clerks.

To each division of infantry a brigade of Artillery was attached, the officer commanding which was under the immediate orders of the General commanding the division, although under the general superintendence of the commanding officer of the Royal Artillery at the head-quarters of the army.

When two or more divisions were placed under the second in command, or other officer of high rank, to act as a corps, a similar Staff was attached to the corps to assist him in the command of it.

One or more brigades of Artillery were in general attached to the corps, in addition to the divisional Artillery. Also a force of Cavalry in proportion to the duties of the corps.

The Cavalry was also composed of divisions, each division consisting of two or more brigades, and each brigade of two or more regiments of Heavy or Light Cavalry.

To each brigade of Hussars or Light Cavalry a troop of Horse Artillery was usually attached when in the advance of the army or before the enemy, under the immediate orders of the General commanding the brigade. The General Officer commanding the Cavalry had a Staff attached to him similar to that of a General Officer commanding a corps.

In addition to the foregoing, what is called the matériel was attached to the army, independent of the army in divisions, viz.,—

> The Battering Train, under the orders of the officer commanding the Royal Artillery.
> The Pontoon Train, under the orders of the Commanding Royal Engineer.
> The Engineer Park and siege matériel.
> The Wagon Train, under the orders of the Quartermaster-General, attached to the hospitals, to the commissariat, &c., or to divisions, as circumstances might require.
> The Ordnance Store Train.
> The Commissariat Wagon Train, and the other transport of the army.

In the principal towns through which the army passed a hospital station was usually formed, to which, besides the necessary medical and hospital staff, there was a depôt staff consisting of

> A Captain Commandant.
> A Subaltern Adjutant.
> An Assistant Commissary-General.
> An Assistant Provost-Marshal.

Particularly if the station should be a town of consideration, with a magazine on the line of supply.

These stations, of course, changed as the army changed its lines of operation.

The port of embarkation, or disembarkation, formed the chief depôt of the army, and was under the command of a superior officer, with officers of the Adjutant and Quartermaster-General's departments attached to him, exclusive of the usual garrison staff.

Officers of the Quartermaster-General's department, officers of the Royal Engineers, and Royal Staff Corps,* were employed on topographical surveys, reports of roads, bridges, and resources of the country.

---

* The Royal Staff Corps was formed in 1800, and termed originally the "Quartermaster-General's Corps." It had the same establishment as a battalion of infantry, both of officers and men. The officers were not allowed to serve on the General Staff (General Order, 14th April, 1815). This corps was organized and armed as a body of infantry, but trained to the duties of field engineering. The officers were mounted and expected to perform the services of the Quartermaster-General's department. The Field Officers ranking as assistants, and the Captains and Subalterns as deputy-assistants, receiving when in the field forage and other allowances according to their Staff rank. The qualification for an officer was a military education, and four-fifths of the soldiers were mechanics. This corps was not broken up until many years after the termination of the late war, its services having been made available in the colonies.—JACKSON.

In addition to these, regimental officers were employed by the Generals commanding divisions as officers in observation beyond the outposts of their respective divisions, to obtain information with respect to the movements of the enemy in front, and for the purpose of reporting upon the resources, roads, rivers, bridges, and other military features of the country unoccupied between the outposts of the two armies.

CHAPTER II.

BRIEF SKETCH OF THE HISTORY OF TACTICS.

It is repeatedly said that tactics have been altered, that the use of rifles and breech-loaders, supported by rifled artillery, have completely changed the system of fighting, and that a new leaf must be turned over. In one sense this is true; in another it is an error, and a mischievous error.

It is quite true that the introduction of improved arms has produced very considerable modifications in the method of fighting; but those modifications are not so much changes, as the growth and development of principles that have been known for hundreds of years. And it is a most dangerous thing to ignore all experience obtained prior to the introduction of improved arms, for it is only by a careful study of the development of tactics, that the true direction in which improvement is possible can be determined.

There has been no period when it could be justly said, "Those are old, these are new tactics." The improvements have followed gradually and naturally on each succeeding improvement in firearms. The flint-lock, percussion-cap, rifle, and breech-loader have each necessitated changes. And as the breech-loading rifle is but a development of the flint-lock musket, so tactics, as existing now, are but a development of what they were 100 years ago. It is quite true that there are certain periods when great changes seem to take place, but these are really periods coincident with great wars, when the minds of people in general are turned to military subjects, and many startling discoveries appear then to be made, which were well known, discussed, and practised years beforehand, but which have escaped notice until peculiar events have forced them into prominence. It is desirable therefore, before giving an account of the development of tactics produced by the introduction of breech-loading rifles, and tested in the actual school of war in 1866 and 1870, to give a brief sketch of the gradual growth of the art, compiling the sketch from the many authors* that have written on the subject.

Going back to the history of Greece and Rome, we find that the same causes that produce alterations in tactics now, were at

---

* Perhaps the most useful of these books is that of Grivet, "Études sur la Tactique," which has been freely used.

D

work then. We find the undisciplined armies of Persia, composed of nations and tribes of warriors, chiefly mounted, overcome by the steady discipline and firmness of the Greek phalanx. The same phalanx was overcome by the Roman legion, which was more mobile, employed a greater number of missile weapons, and could work over rough ground with far greater ease than the phalanx, which very quickly got disorganised on uneven ground.

B.C. 216.

The order of battle of the Romans did not apparently include a regular reserve until after the Carthaginian wars had taught the lesson that victory often fell to the General who could bring up a reserve at the last moment. Subsequently the Romans invariably employed strong reserves of both horse and foot.

After the fall of the Roman Empire, cavalry became almost the only force used; this arose chiefly from the political and social state of Europe at that time, armies being to a great extent formed of the retainers and followers of great feudal chiefs, and the infantry being composed of the poorest people, of little account and badly armed.

The English at this period were remarkable for gaining several great victories. Cressy, Poitiers, and Agincourt—all gained by tactical arrangements in consonance with the arms used. The long-bow, the weapon the English infantry used, being superior both in range, accuracy, and rapidity of fire to the cross-bow, the usual weapon of foreign archers. The tactics of the English were simple, and consisted in taking up a position where the enemy had to attack them, discharging great flights of arrows on him as he charged with heavy masses of cavalry, and charging him when in disorder, on the flank, with cavalry posted on the wings for that purpose.

Subsequently the Swiss infantry, by its victories at Morgarten, Sempach, and Noefels, raised the estimation in which infantry was held in Europe, and all armies soon had companies of Swiss infantry, usually employed as the Guard of the Sovereign.

The general introduction of firearms showed that armies, to be successful, must be composed of large bodies of men so armed, and that they must be mobile. From this resulted a gradual preponderance of infantry and the reduction of the defensive armour men carried.

Gustavus Adolphus was the first General who grasped these facts, and who also saw that mobility must be dependent on discipline.

The changes introduced by Gustavus Adolphus were very similar in their tendency to those consequent on the use of breech-loaders. They were increased mobility and development of fire.

The usual formation of the Swedish troops was in six ranks, but in action they deployed so as to form three ranks. Each brigade consisted of two regiments, each regiment of 1,800 men, divided into eight companies, each of which had 72 muskets

(margin notes:) 1346. 1415.

Gustavus Adolphus, 1611.

and 54 pike men, the latter being in the front rank and using the pikes to cover and protect the musket men while they fired. The cavalry was formed three deep, and although furnished with firearms, its instructions were to charge, and not to trust to fire.

The tactics adopted by Gustavus Adolphus conduced greatly to his many victories, his opponents, adhering to the heavy deep columns at that time in use, were compelled to guard against being outflanked by the formation of their opponents, to place all their troops in one line, while the Swedes were enabled to form the troops in several lines. Consequently, when the line of the imperialists was forced at any part they could never bring up fresh troops to support the decisive point.

Many improvements in soldiers' equipment were introduced by Gustavus Adolphus, such as lightening the musket, dispensing with the rest, introducing the wheel-lock in place of slowmatch,* and also cartridges, thus enabling the soldier not only to fire but also to load more rapidly. He also made artillery more mobile, and added regimental guns which fired case shot, to the battalions of infantry.

The tactics of the great Swedish King were largely dependent on his improvements in arms. And it was to the clear conception he had of the effect of firearms on the movement of troops, that much of his success was due. Few leaders have ever equalled or surpassed him, in handling troops.

No one ever equalled Gustavus Adolphus in leading his army against an *Chemnitz.* enemy or conducting a retreat so as to prevent loss, nor in encamping his troops, or strengthening his camp with field works. No one knew fortification, attack, and defence, so well as he did. No one could divine the intention of his enemy or take advantage of the chances of war more ably than he did. He took in at a glance the whole position, and drew up his troops so as to profit by every opportunity. The three points that he exceeded all others in were tactics, organization, and arms.

After the death of Gustavus Adolphus, the art of tactics remained stationary for many years, although numerous improvements, both in arms and organization, were made by Turenne and Saxe. But no General appears to have taken up the question of tactics, organization, and arms, as a whole, until Frederick *Frederick.* the Great, following in the footsteps of Gustavus Adolphus, *1749.* showed that victory would fall to the General who distinctly understood the bearing of these subjects on one another, and again we find improvements taking the same direction—development of fire and mobility. It is said that the fire of the Prussian infantry was so rapid that each man had a piece of leather to protect his left hand from the heat of the barrel.† The troops were formed in three ranks, the battalion being composed of ten

---

* Fire was produced by means of a piece of pyrites, or flint, fixed in the cock being brought rapidly against a revolving hammer.

† Evidently due to the large charge of powder then used. It is not a little remarkable that rapidity of fire has twice placed Prussia at the head of the military nations of Europe, in 1749 and 1866.

companies, and the greatest care being taken to preserve correct distances and alignments, so as to enable every man to fire. The movements were always in open column, which wheeled into line to the pivot flank and advanced on the enemy. There were no skirmishers of any kind.

The cavalry was formed two deep, and trusted entirely to the effect of its charge, and not to firearms.

The Prussian order of battle was at that time invariably in two lines, cavalry on the wings and infantry in the centre.

The battalions of the first line were deployed, with six paces interval between them. The battalions of the second line were also deployed but as the first line was usually stronger than the second, the intervals between the battalions of the second line varied and were greater than those of the first line. The cavalry was also formed into two lines on the flanks, a few Hussars being detached beyond the flank of the general line to cover it. The artillery was usually placed in heavy batteries on the front. Frederick's battles may be divided into two distinct phases,—

1st. The movement, termed his oblique order of battle, by which he sought to place himself obliquely on the flank of his opponent.

2nd. The action of the troops after they became engaged.

The very short range of weapons at the period to which we refer enable troops to get personally engaged after passing over short spaces. Frederick's tactics consisted, once the troops were engaged, in rapid firing and repeated bayonet charges.

The method that Frederick adopted in forming his troops on the line of march, and in order of battle are best given in his own words :—

At eight o'clock the advanced guard composed of six battalions of Grenadiers, a regiment of infantry, ten squadrons of Dragoons, and two regiments of Hussars, will march. It will proceed fourteen miles, halt, and form the camp. (*Vide* Fig. 1, Plate I.)

The following day the army will follow, the infantry of the two lines of the right wing forming the second column, the infantry of the two lines of the left wing the third column. The cavalry of the two lines of the right wing the first column, the cavalry of the two lines of the left wing the fourth column, the baggage in rear, the heads of the column will be in line, preceded by a small advanced guard. (*Vide* Fig. 2, Plate I.)

One or two days before leaving, the baggage will be sent to the rear under a strong escort : if the country is open the rear-guard will be formed of cavalry ; if defiles have to be passed they must be occupied the day before by infantry.

When the army marched to the front in four columns, right in front, it formed line of battle as follows : The battalions marched in open column of companies, the cavalry in open column of troops or squadrons ; while the advanced guard engaged the enemy and the King examined the ground, the columns wheeled to the right if right in front, to the left if left in front, and marched in two long parallel columns, seeking to place themselves obliquely on one of the enemy's wings ; when the signal was given, the two columns halted, and wheeled right or left into line. (*Vide* Fig. 3, Plate I.)

When the army retreated the operation is precisely similar, only the battalions or squadrons of the second line move off the first.

When near the enemy the army invariably marched in two columns, all

Fig. 1.

Advanced Guard.

Fig. 2.

Army marching to the front in four columns.

Cavalry left wing

Second line   First line

Infantry left wing

Second line   First line

Infantry right wing

Second line   First line

Cavalry right wing

Second line   First line

Fig. 3.

Army marching in four columns forming line to the front by changing direction to the right.

Cavalry   left wing

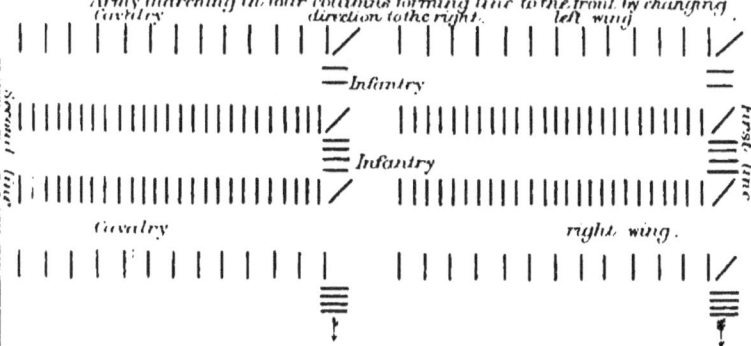

Infantry

Infantry

Cavalry   right wing.

Fig. 4.

Battalion.

8   0   6   2   1   3   5   7

Light Company   Grenadier Company

Fig. 5.

Regiment

Flank Companies

Fig. 6.
Battalion in Column

L.C. ═══════ G.C.

2 ═══════ 1

4 ═══════ 3

6 ═══════ 5

8 ═══════ 7

Fig. 7.
Regiment in column

Fig. 8.

Deployment of 6 Battalions.

the first line being in one column, all the second line in the second column. The army thus moved in open column of companies along the front of the position occupied by the enemy.

It is quite evident that troops to move in this manner must have been most carefully drilled, as otherwise the distances would be lost and great confusion ensue.

Such formations and movements could never take place in presence of an enemy who could manœuvre, neither could they have taken place in the presence of long-range weapons, as the wheel into line must have been made at a considerable distance from the enemy, and a long advance in line under fire would have been necessitated.

Frederick the Great himself showed better than anyone else how such a method of attack should be defeated. To the better understanding of the tactics of the Prussian King, which have had a great influence over English tactics, the following short *1757.* descriptions of the battles of Prague, Kollin, Leuthen, and Rossbach are added. The battles of Prague and Kollin succeeded one another, but Prague and Leuthen, which are successful instances of a flank attack, are given first.

Frederick had invaded Bohemia with two columns, one, under Battle of his personal command, advanced from Saxony; the other, under Prague. 12th the command of Marshal Schwerin, advanced from Silesia by May, 1757. Buntzlau and Brandeis. These two columns converged on Prague (*vide* Plate II.).

The Austrian leader, Prince Charles of Lorraine, took up a position close to Prague, with his left resting on the Cziskaberg heights close to the Moldau, his right resting at Kyge, being covered by a series of marshy ponds, extending from Nieder Micholup to Kyge, where the stream that joined these ponds turned to the left and ran along the front of the position, discharging itself into the Moldau at Lieben. Another Austrian army, under Daun, was advancing from Vienna, and was close at hand, the road by which this force was advancing on Prague, ran behind the Austrian position. The Austrians formed their line of battle, as was usual at that period, in two lines, with the cavalry on the flanks. Prince Charles desired to keep the Prussians in check until the arrival of Daun; hearing of Schwerin's near approach, he threw back his right from Kyge so as to form a *crochet* on the high ground extending from above Sterboholy towards Hortlorzes.

A crochet can only be considered a good means of defence when the *Jomini.* enemy, already moving to attack, has been compelled to divide his force to reach the flank he threatens. In all other cases a crochet, or as it is better known, the order "*en potence*," if used to protect a flank against an army that can manœuvre, is a remedy worse than the disease it is used to cure. It is manifest that the flank or extremity of the crochet must be as well protected as the line itself; if it is not, it is useless. It, in addition, has this great fault, that the troops near the salient angle cannot retire without getting mutually jammed, and without falling into disorder and confusion.

If the troops have to advance, a great gap is left at the salient, which must be filled by closing to the right or left, which may cause great disorder, and have the most fatal consequences at the moment of attack. Further, a skilful general will soon find means for opening a cross-fire on the salient angle, which will take the battalions at the salient both in flank and front.

Frederick, desirous of supporting Schwerin, and crushing Prince Charles before Daun could arrive, crossed the Moldau at Podhaba, and effected a junction with Schwerin, the united armies occupying a position extending from Streziskow on the right towards Sattalitz on the left. Frederick's army was thus parallel, or nearly so, to the Austrians.

He could not attack them on their left, which was supported by the Maldan and Prague, their front was also too difficult to be attacked, he therefore resolved to attack their right. To effect this he wheeled his army into open columns of companies left in front, and circled round the Austrian right, penetrating between the ponds which extended from Micholup to Kyge. The Prussians formed their line and attacked the high ground above Sterboholy, which was undoubtedly the key of the Austrian position; at the same time they attacked the villages of Kyge and Illoupetin. The Austrians vainly attempted to resist, and were rolled up and forced to retire into Prague.

It will be seen that the Austrian leader made no attempt to attack the Prussians on their line of march, or to prevent the junction of the two armies. The very strength of the Austrian position in front prevented their leaving it to attack the Prussians, who were thus to a great extent protected during the flank march. The best roads by which the Austrians could advance to attack Frederick during his flank movement were closed by his attacks on the villages of Kyge and Illoupetin.

Battle of Leuthen, 5th December, 1757.

Frederick, although personally he had gained great successes in the west at Rossbach,[*] had suffered much in Silesia, his armies had been defeated, his towns and his generals captured, and when he took command he found himself with only some 30,000 dispirited men to face 80,000 Austrians flushed with success.

Jomini.

A series of fortunate events may dull the greatest minds, deprive them of their natural vigour, and level them with common beings. But adversity is a tonic capable of bringing back energy and elasticity to those who have lost it. Frederick was in this state; he assembled his generals and staff officers, and informed them of all his losses, told them he counted on their zeal, constancy, and that courage and love of country which had always animated them, and that they must snatch from the enemy the advantages he had obtained.

He directed them to point out these things to the officers, and even the soldiers of the army, to prepare them for the great events that must take place. That they must attack the Austrians wherever they could find them, regardless of their numbers.

The army moved at break of day from Parchewitz, and

---

[*] As this book does not pretend to deal with military history, or with strategy, but merely with tactical questions, it is not requisite to observe the chronological order of Frederick's battles, or to do more than treat of each as a separate unconnected event.

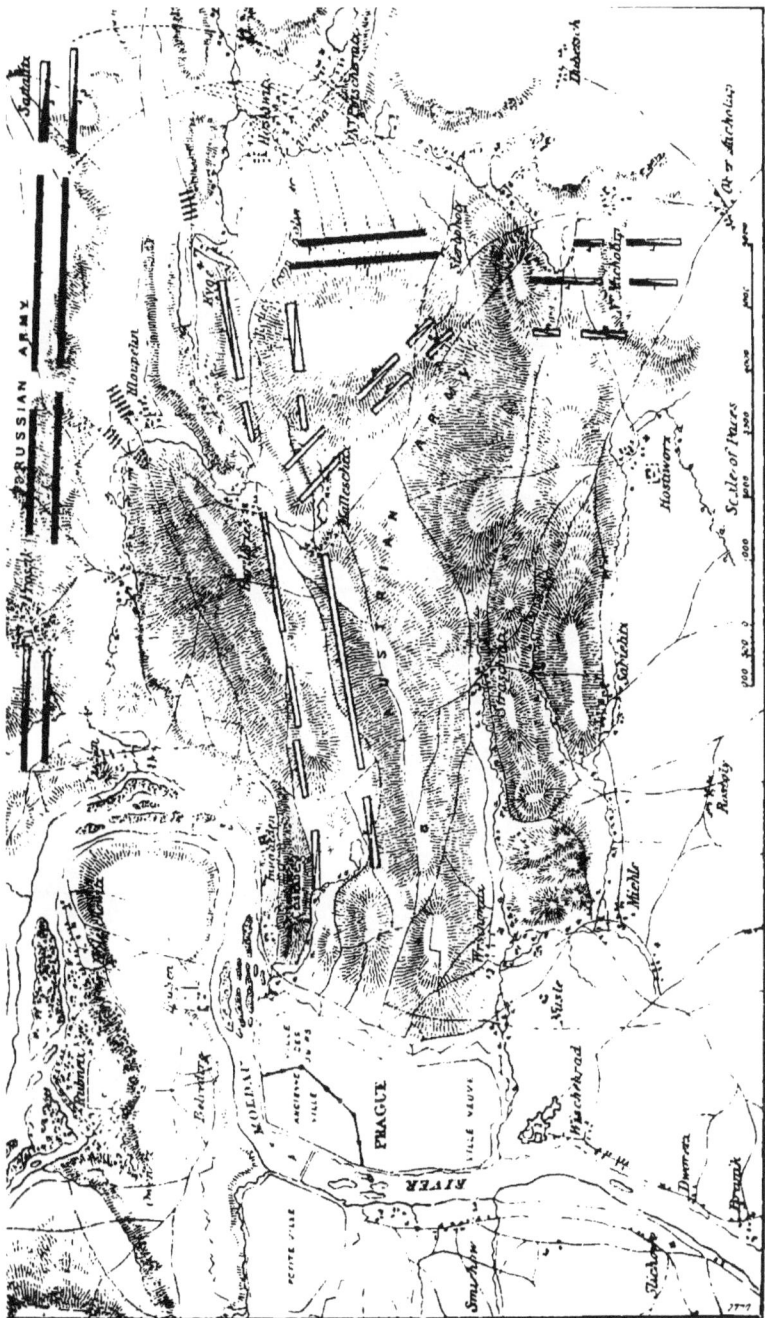

BATTLE of PRAGUE.

DANGERFIELD, LITH. 22. BEDFORD ST COVENT GARDEN

PLATE III.

BATTLE
OF
LEUTHEN.

A. B. *Change of front attempted by*
the Austrians
C. D. *Prussian Attack*

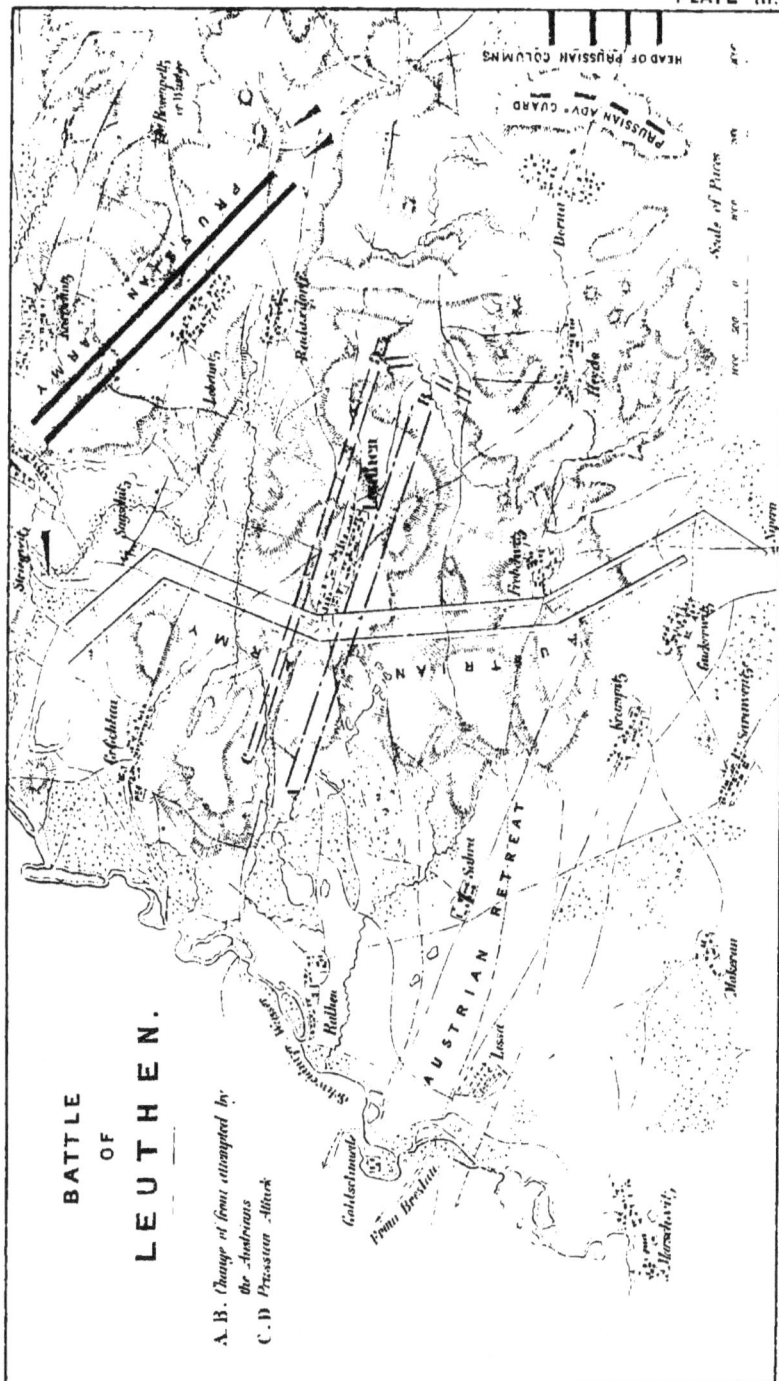

HEAD OF PRUSSIAN COLUMNS

PRUSSIAN ADV: GUARD

PRUSSIAN

AUSTRIAN

AUSTRIAN RETREAT

Scale of Paces

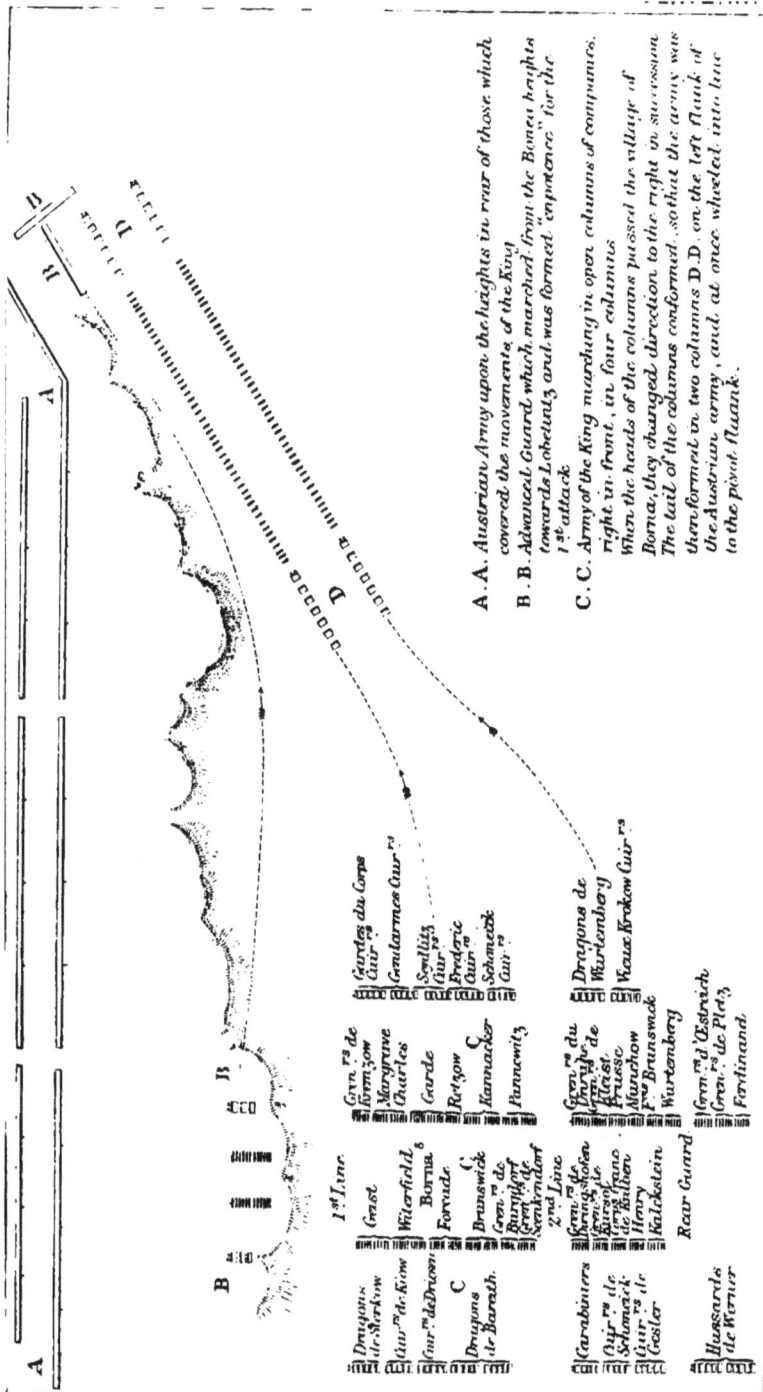

SKELETON MAP OF THE BATTLE OF LEUTHEN.

A

B

B

D

D

A

B

B

C

D

D

A. A. Austrian Army upon the heights in rear of those which covered the movements of the King.

B. B. Advanced Guard which marched from the Borne heights towards Lobetintz and was formed to prepare for the 1st attack.

C. C. Army of the King marching in open columns of companies, right in front, in four columns. When the heads of the columns passed the village of Borne, they changed direction to the right in succession. The tail of the columns conformed, so that the army was then formed in two columns D.D. on the left flank of the Austrian army, and at once wheeled into line to the point flank.

Dragons de Morlow
Aus.Ptc.Kiow
(inr.de)Driese
Dragons de Barath

1st Line
Gessl
Witerfield8
Borna
Forade

2nd Line
Brunswick
Com.rd de Burghoff
Gront Neukirchent

Carabiniers
Cuir.rd de Schmerach
Cuir.rd de Coslar

Grn.rd de Brunshohen
Graw.la
Kirsey
Henry
Kalkstein

Rear Guard

Hussards de Warur

Grn.rs de Forrizow
Marqrwe Charles
Garde
Retzow
Kannacker
Panncvitz

Grn.rs du Prusse
Munchow
Fre Brunswick
Wurtemberg

Grnm.rd d'Estrich
Gnm.rd de Pla.3
Ferdinand

Gardes du Corps Cuir.rs
Gendarmes Cuir.rs
Senlitz Cuir.rs
Fredgric Cuir.rs
Schmacki cuir.rs

Dragons de Wurtemberg
Vaux Krokow Cuir.rs

DANGERFIELD LITH. 22 BEDFORD ST COVENT GARDEN

marched in the following order to Neumarck. The advance guard was composed of 800 volunteers and 10 battalions, 34 squadrons of hussars, 15 squadrons of dragoons, and 10 guns.

The army followed in four columns (Plates III and IIIA), it marched by wings right in front, the first was composed of the two lines of cavalry of the right wing, the second of the two lines of infantry of the right wing, the third of the left wing of the infantry, the fourth of the left wing of the cavalry; the artillery followed the two infantry columns.

The Prussian advance guard met and drove in a force of the enemy near the village of Borna, and obtained information as to the exact position of the enemy. The Austrian right rested on Nipern, protected by a large wood and some ponds, their centre rested on Leuthen, their left on Sagestchutz. A "crochet" was thrown back to protect this flank, which extended from Sagest-chutz to the pond of Gohlau, the Austrian retreat being by Goldschmiede.

The sharp attack made by the Prussian advanced guard on the Austrians at Borna, joined to their not being able to discover what the Prussians were about, induced Daun, their leader, to move his reserve to the right wing. Frederick, who knew the ground, determined to attack the Austrian left, and refuse his own. So soon as the heads of his column had passed through Borna he changed direction, to the right, and, filed into two lines. The ground in front of the Austrian position favoured the manœuvre ; and the weather was cloudy. So soon as Frederick's advanced guard passed the villages of Kartchutz and Striegwitz on their right, they were ordered to wheel into line and attack. This was done, and they captured the village of Sagestchutz. Under fire of its 10 guns the main body wheeled into line and advanced against the Austrians, whose reserve having been moved to the right were unable to withstand the Prussians. They formed a "crochet" with Leuthen at the salient, thus showing front in two directions, but the right of the "crochet" being unsupported was charged and destroyed by the cavalry of Frederick's left wing, and the Austrians fled in great confusion.

This battle is an epoch in the annals of the military art, and contained not only the theory but also the practice of the system of which Frederick is the author. It will be seen that his army formed an oblique angle with that of his enemies. This oblique order, in the opinion of the ablest military men, decided the victory ; hitherto people had an imperfect idea of its application, and no general had been able to seize its advantages. Since then the German generals have for a long time made it the basis of all their orders of battle.

The nature of this order shows that the attack must be made on a wing, and that the part of the line to attack must be strengthened, in order to crush and take in flank and reverse the wing. However, as the enemy has also means of sending reinforcements to the threatened point, he must be deceived, so as to keep him in doubt as to the actual point of attack, until everything is ready, then he must be attacked with vigour, to surprise and deprive him of the power of making a combined defence.

Speaking of the conduct of the Austrian leader in deploying his whole force, Jomini says:—

Jomini.

It is a great error when an army that is superior in numbers waits to be attacked, and particularly when it deploys the whole of its force. It is far better to show only a force capable of containing the enemy, and to hold the remainder in hand in three or four heavy columns ready to strike divers places, and manœuvre on the flanks of the enemy to gain various points. In fact, a large army deployed is not so mobile as if it were in columns. To immobilise troops not engaged is to forget the first principles of tactics. A portion only of the reserve should be deployed, if it be desired to awe the enemy by a great display of force. In my opinion the conduct of the King at Leuthen contains the principles on which all warlike action is based, namely, to put in action at the most important point of a line of operations, or of an attack, a larger force than the enemy has there. This may be done either by marching, or strategic movements, or by manœuvres, or by a selection of the form of attack.

Napoleon.

The battle of Leuthen is a masterpiece of movements, manœuvres, and resolution. Alone it is sufficient to immortalise Frederick, and place him in the rank of the greatest generals. He attacked a stronger army than his own, in position and victorious, with an army composed partly of troops which had been just defeated, yet he won a victory without paying too dearly for it.

All his manœuvres at this battle are in conformity with the principles of war. He made no flank march in sight of his enemy, for the armies were not in sight. The Austrians expected him, after the combat at Borna, to take position on the heights in front of them, and while they thus waited for him, covered by rising grounds and fogs, and masked by his advanced guard, he continued his march and attacked the extreme left.

Neither did he violate another principle not less sound, of not abandoning his line of operations. Daun did everything that could be done under similar circumstances, but the Prussian cavalry and their masses continually came up before his troops had time to form.

These battles show generally what is termed Frederick's oblique order of attack, successful. The following is an instance of its failure, or rather an instance of how, if the troops moving to a flank are attacked on the march, it is exceedingly probable it will always fail.

Battle of Kolin, 14th June, 1757.

The Austrian army sent to relieve Prince Frederick Charles, blockaded in Prague, advanced along the Olmütz-Brünn-Prague road as far as Kolin ; Frederick, leaving a force before Prague, moved to meet Daun. The King moved in his usual formation, covered by an advanced guard consisting of 55 squadrons of hussars and dragoons, and seven battalions of infantry. On debouching from the village of Planian, the Austrian army was found posted on the southern side of the road on a semi-circular range of heights, extending from Krzeczor on the right to Brzesan on the left (Plate IV). The first line was posted half way up the slope, the second on the crest, the front was covered by villages and difficult ground, and bristled with batteries which swept all the approaches.

The King resolved to attack the Austrian right flank, or that nearest their line of retreat. He directed his advanced guard to advance along the main road until nearly opposite Krzeczor, and then leaving the road to move towards Radosvesnitz, intending to support the advanced guard by the whole army and take up

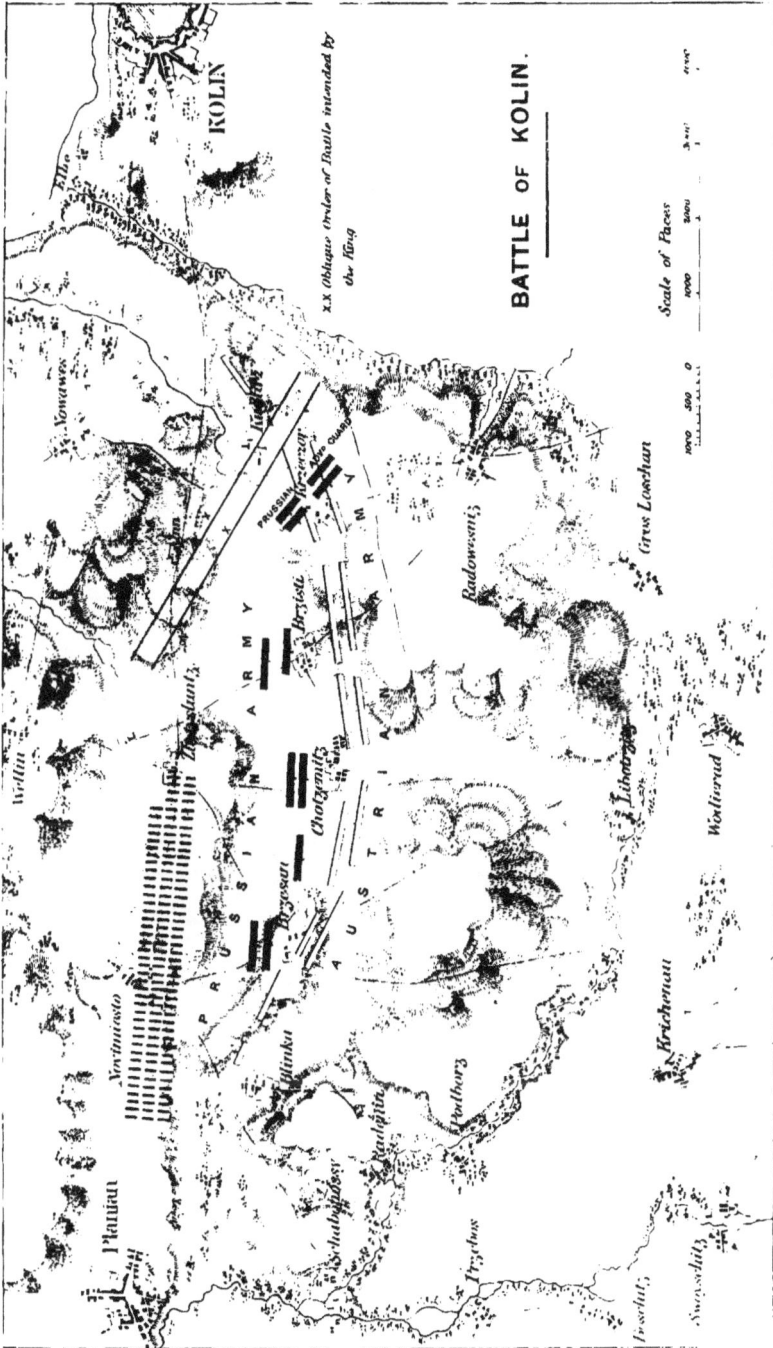

PLATE IV

BATTLE OF KOLIN.

Scale of Paces

X.X *Oblique order of Battle intended by the King*

Fig. 2

The Prussian army was encamped in three lines in rear of Planian, the Infantry in the first two lines, the Cavalry in the third. The army moved off in open columns of companies, left in front, each ten forming a column. The head of the columns on reaching the line at B, was to change direction to the right and march on Kaurzim, C, in order that the columns might be placed in line of battle, by simply wheeling to the right without any deployment.

Fig. 2. Shows an army marching by lines (doubling its columns at D, & requisite when the reach E, the 1ˢᵗ and 2ⁿᵈ columns forming the left wing allows the right wing (c) proceed and file in rear of it, thus again forming only two columns

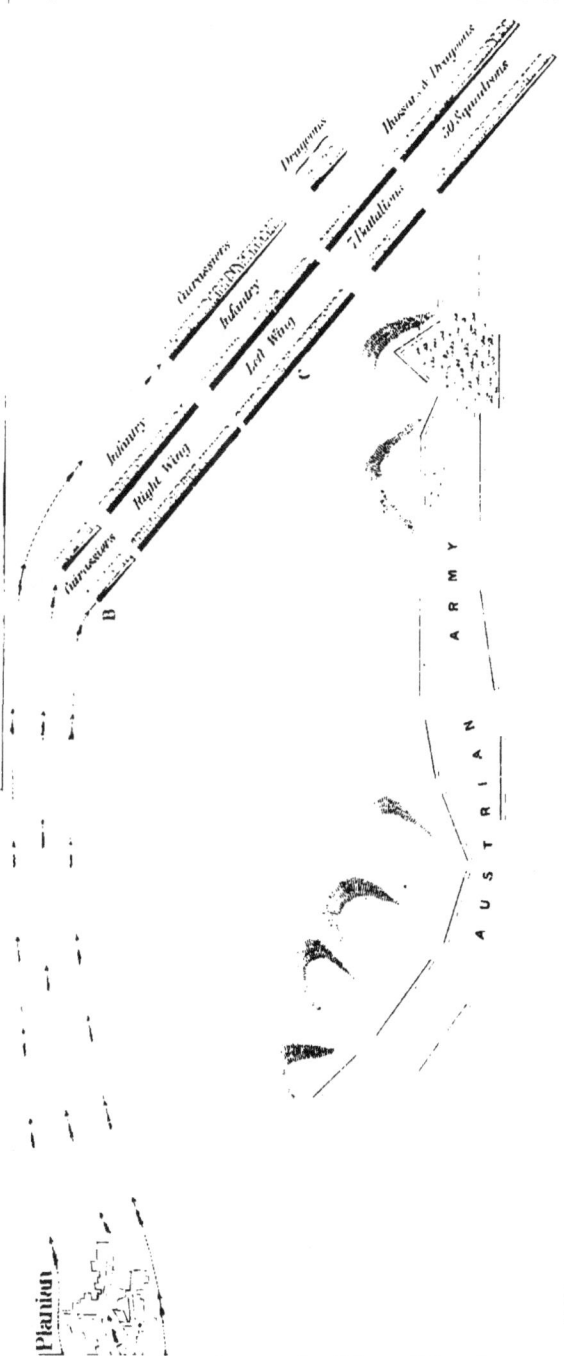

Planian

Curassiers

B

Right Wing

Infantry

Left Wing

Cuirassiers

Infantry

Dragoons

Hussars & Dragoons

7 Battalions

30 Squadrons

AUSTRIAN ARMY

E

D

SKELETON MAP OF THE BATTLE OF KOLIN.

DANCERFIELD LITH 22, BEDFORD Sᵀ COVENT GARDEN

the position XX, from which he could advance and roll up the
Austrian line. This projected movement is shown on Plate IVᴀ
more distinctly. The advanced guard had reached Zlatysluntz,
and the head of the main body Novimesto, when it became
requisite to halt to correct the distances as much distance had
been lost by defiling through the town of Planian, and regular
distances was one of the things essential to Frederick's tactics.

The advanced guard moved as directed, wheeled into line,
and carried the village of Krzeczor.

But while this was being done, the army in its march along
the front of the Austrian position was much disquieted by the
Austrian light troops, who continually attacked their right flank ;
a battalion leader being much pressed, ordered his battalion to
wheel to its right, as this was the order to form line, it was
taken up by the whole army in rear, who wheeled into line also
and attacked the Austrians near Chotzemitz while the leading
portion continued its march ; a large gap was thus left in the
long columns, and the general commanding the first portion,
hearing the firing, looked back, saw the remainder of the army
in action, and wheeled to his right and attacked also ; thus,
instead of forming the line XX, the Prussian army made four
disconnected attacks along the front. The Prussians fought
well, and renewed their attack five or six times, but were
unable to carry any of the Austrian positions, and were compelled to retreat with heavy loss.

The Prussians in their march formed an arc, of which their enemy were Jomini.
the chord ; they could then in less time place a greater force in action at the
principal point ; this, even with two armies of equal force, is always decisive.

If it be acknowledged that the most advantageous attacks are those made
by a concentrated effort on the extremity of an enemy's line, it becomes absolutely requisite to take measures to gain this extremity by masking the movement.

If this precaution be neglected, the enemy can follow the march of the
columns which wish to outflank him, can offer them always his front, or take
them in flank, as was done by the King at Rossbach.

The march may be concealed by darkness, by the ground, or by a fierce
attack on the enemy's front, which may draw his attention to that side. The
last means are the best, as night movements are less sure and less regular
than those made in the day.

I think that to threaten a considerable front it is better to use small detachments than a regular advanced guard. The size of the detachments should
be regulated by circumstances, and they should be supported by cavalry and
horse artillery.

This battle shows clearly the danger of flank movements in
the presence of an enemy, even when they happen to be as bad
tacticians as the Austrians then were; why the King should
have undertaken a march along the front of the Austrians, to
attack their right flank when he might have attacked their left, it
is difficult to say. Success, had it been achieved, would doubtless
have been more complete by an attack on the right than the left.
But the latter was feasible, the former was not. The wheel to
the right made by the battalion commander, which upset the

King's arrangements, was not the cause of the attack failing, so much as it was the consequence of an attempt to move troops under a close fire to a flank. If the troops front as they did in this case, the movement miscarries, and the best troops will be found to get demoralised if they suffer from an enemy close at hand, who they are directed to disregard and make no attempt to resist. The Austrian light troops (Croats), who annoyed the Prussians so much, appear to have been unopposed, Frederick never using skirmishers. The only prospect of success his movement could have, was by covering it with a powerful body of skirmishers to attack and drive back the Croats, while the main body moved to the flank.

Napoleon.

At the battle of Kolin it is difficult ts justify the attempt to turn Daun's right by the flank march made from 600 to 1,000 yards from the heights occupied by the enemy. This operation was rash, and opposed to the principle of war. Never make a flank march before an enemy in position, especially when he occupies the heights at the foot of which you must march.

The King might have attacked the Austrian left, he was admirably placed for doing so ; but to try and march under a fire of musketry and artillery from an entire army, occupying a commanding position, is to imagine that that army has neither guns nor small-arms. To say that the King's manœuvre failed because a battalion leader, wearied with the fire of the Austrian skirmishers, wheeled into line and attacked to his front is an error. The movement the Prussian army made was one demanded by the greatest necessity,—viz., its own safety, and that instinct which forbids men to allow themselves to be killed without defending themselves.

A comparison between the battles of Prague, Leuthen and Kolin will show why the flank movement succeeded in the one case and not in the other.

Battle of Rossbach, 5th Nov., 1757.

The battle of Rossbach is especially valuable as showing how, when an incompetent general tried to ape Frederick's tactics and attack him on his flank, he managed to change his front and deliver a crushing defeat. The King crossed the Saale at Weissenfels, and advancing beyond Schortau, found the Franco-German army occupying a position in three lines extending from Gulgen Hugel on the left, to beyond Branderoda on the right ; finding this position too strong to attack, Frederick retired and took up a position extending from Bedra to Rossbach ; he occupied this position in three lines, the infantry being, in the first two lines and the cavalry in the third line (*vide* Plates V and VA). Soubise, who commanded the allied army, finding the Prussian right and centre well protected by a small stream, resolved to attack their left at Rossbach, this flank being slightly *en l'air*, he moved off in three columns, cavalry in front and rear at first, but subsequently with all the cavalry in front. The moment the movement was discovered, the King directed Seidlytz to move with all the cavalry under cover of some slight hills to circle round the Jams Hugel height, and meet the head of the enemy's columns, by taking up a position between Lundstaedt and Reichertswerben, the infantry followed in the same direction.

Soubise, seeing the Prussians, as he thought, retreating,

PLATE V

BATTLE
OF
ROSBACH.

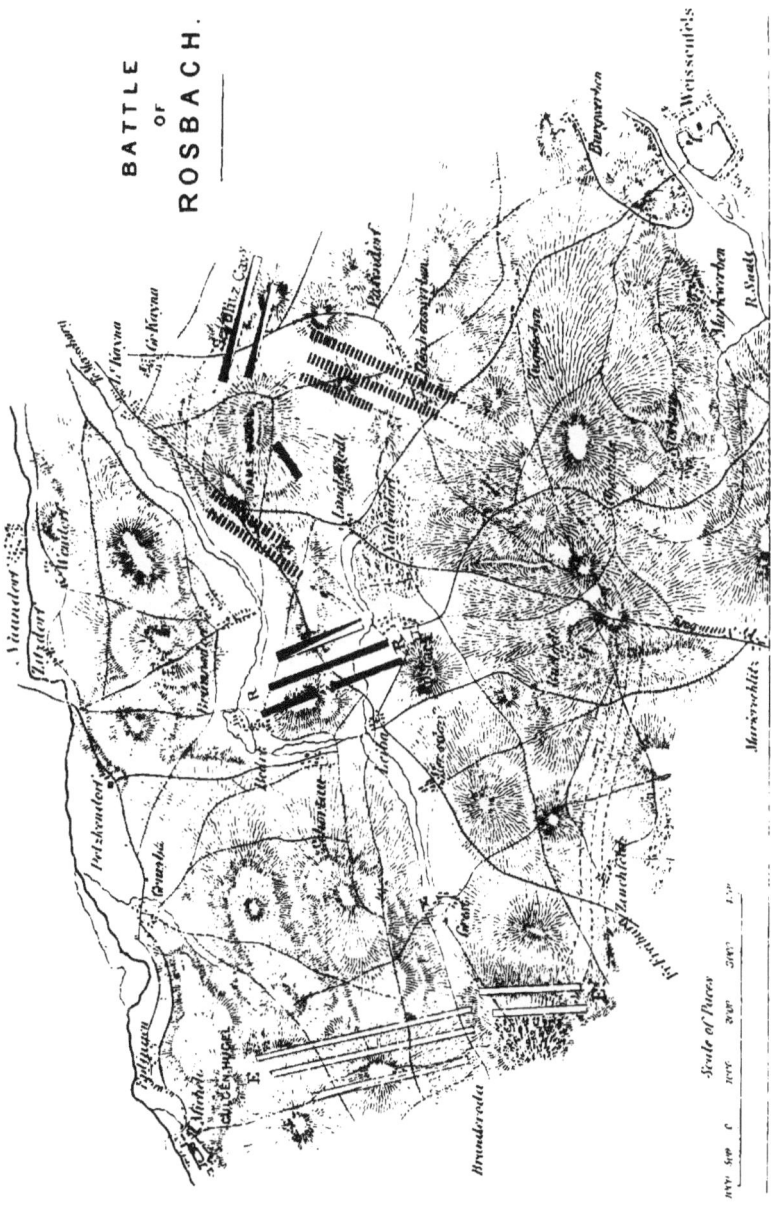

Scale of Paces

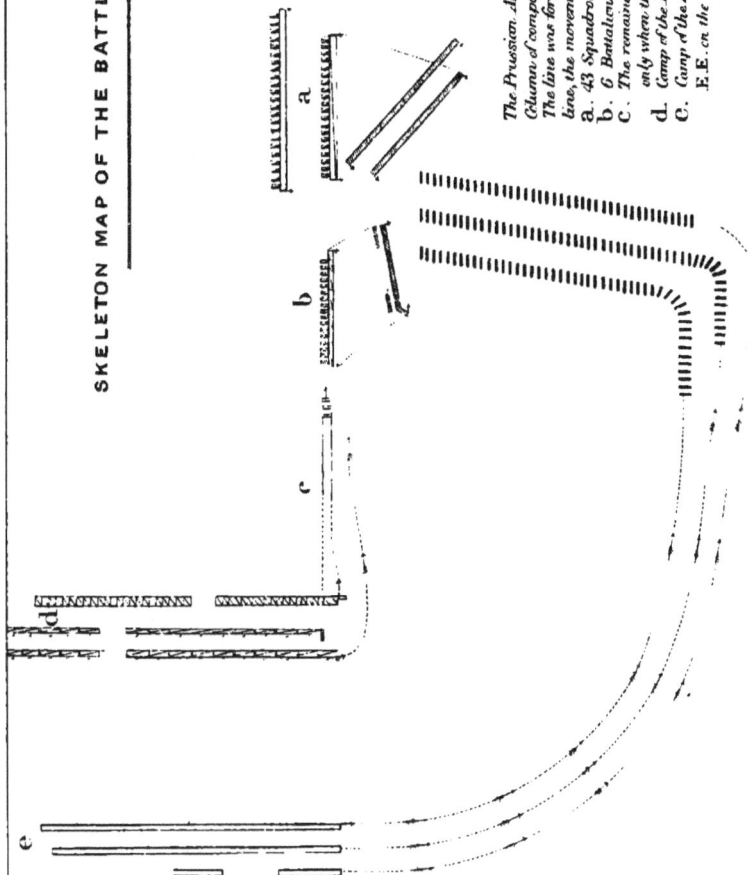

SKELETON MAP OF THE BATTLE OF ROSBACH.

The Prussian Army marched left in front, the Infantry in open Column of companies; the Cavalry in open column of Troops. The line was formed by a simple wheel on the rovt Flank into line, the movement being concealed by the heights.

a. 43 Squadrons
b. 6 Battalions
C. The remainder of the Infantry marching in lines which arrivd only when the Battle was completed
d. Camp of the King marked R.R. on the plan of the Battle.
e. Camp of the Allied Army during the 3rd and 4th October marked E.E. on the plan.

hurried on to intercept them. As he debouched past Reichertswerben he saw Seidlytz, who had marched left in front, appearing past the Jams Hugel, and thought this was only a rear-
guard. Seidlytz wheeled his squadrons into two lines, placed
his artillery on the Jams Hugel, and immediately charged the
Franco-Austrians. They were driven back in confusion. Soubise
attempted to deploy, but failed. The Prussian infantry coming
up to the support of the cavalry took the allied columns in
flank. The Prince de Soubise was consequently unable to
deploy his army, and the whole fled in the greatest confusion.

Such was the battle of Rossbach, where 22,000 men, led with prudence and   Jomini.
vigour, lost only 300 killed and wounded, while they defeated more than 50,000,
with a loss of 800 killed, 6,000 prisoners, and 72 guns.

Frederick had watched his enemy's movements without being disconcerted.
He guessed their intentions, and so soon as he knew what they were going
to do he calmly took his measures. His march behind the Reichertswerben
plateau gave him a great advantage. This apparent flight excited the vanity
of the enemy, who neglected all precautions, and hurried on so fast that they
confused their ranks; the heads of their columns got suddenly under the
Prussian fire, and could not deploy. The King seized the favourable moment,
ordered his cavalry to charge, and the small infantry force that was up attacked
without orders. An inch of ground, a moment lost, would have given the
allies the space and time requisite to deploy. But the manœuvres of the King
were so exact that victory was compelled to crown them.

A General who commands an army that can manœuvre should, as much
as possible, attack his enemy when on the line of march, even if he be superior
in number.

It will be observed that the Franco-Austrian army moved
without any advanced guard, and were consequently utterly
ignorant of Seidlytz's movements or of what the King was
doing.

After remarking on the quality of the Franco-Austrian army,
Napoleon says:—

Such troops, commanded by such officers, cannot undertake a flank move-   Napoleon.
ment against a well constituted army.

The manœuvre of the King of Prussia was natural, and he merits less praise
than his adversaries do blame; for their march, made without being protected
by a corps in observation, or covered by flankers, or an advanced guard to
secure them against surprise in a hilly country, and in a foggy season of the
year, was so imprudent that it dictated to the King what he should do.
Frederick, at Kolin, lost only his army; Soubise, at Rossbach, lost both his
army and his honour.

Plate VA shows the movements of the two armies clearly, and
the striking similarity there is between Soubise's movement and
that of Marmont at Salamanca; a study of the latter battle in
Napier's Peninsular War is strongly recommended as affording
an illustration not only of the evils of extending too much to a
flank, but also of how a flank attack can be met.

It will be seen that the system followed by Frederick had
many disadvantages. Amongst these were the slight depth of
his line of battle, the want of reserves, the want of skirmishers,
the impossibility of properly commanding the troops when

spread out in such long lines and columns. General officers in command had their troops scattered over a long front, which they could neither overlook nor direct; but the admirable drill, steadiness, and manœuvring powers of the Prussian Army gave it, when opposed to troops who were not possessed of those qualities, such a pre-eminence, that Frederick's successes were due to these qualities rather than his tactics.

The Prussian Army formed for many years the model of other armies, and the tactics of Frederick are the basis of what are termed "Linear tactics."

1774. In 1774, Mesnil Durand proposed a system which exercised great influence over the tactics of the wars of the Republic and Empire.

He proposed to form battalions in close columns of grand divisions or double companies, and that all deployments should be on the leading double company; he recommended battalions in ten companies, two of which were invariably to skirmish.

When the battalion was deployed these companies were on the flanks slightly in rear, so that between battalions deployed in line there was the front of two companies, regiments being composed of four battalions (Fig. 4, Plate I).

When several battalions worked together they were to be formed in line of double company column at deploying intervals, covered by the whole of the flank companies as skirmishers.

Columns,* said Mesnil Durand, mass the greatest amount of force in the smallest space, and alone can, on account of the narrowness of the front and the greatness of the intervals between them, give free movement to cavalry or artillery, but these columns must be linked together by thick chains of skirmishers. Infantry has two weapons to fight with, and it should have two distinct formations: line is the best for firing, column for manœuvres and attack. In every case, without exception, that formation should be used which is the most suitable at the moment.

The primitive formation of all troops should be in line of battalions at deploying intervals. So formed any requisite manœuvre may be easily carried out. The shallow formation has a natural tendency to make men halt and fire, the order in column has a tendency to make men advance.

When troops are deployed in two lines with cavalry on the flanks, they are weak everywhere, are incapable of the least manœuvre, and the cavalry, artillery, and infantry do not support one another.

When, on the contrary, each battalion is in column, the flank companies being in the battalion intervals, the cavalry placed in rear can easily and unexpectedly charge to the front: this order is strong everywhere. It threatens the enemy with the fire of the skirmishers, the weight of its columns, and the charge

* The following is a *précis* of Mesnil Durand's views.

PLATE VI

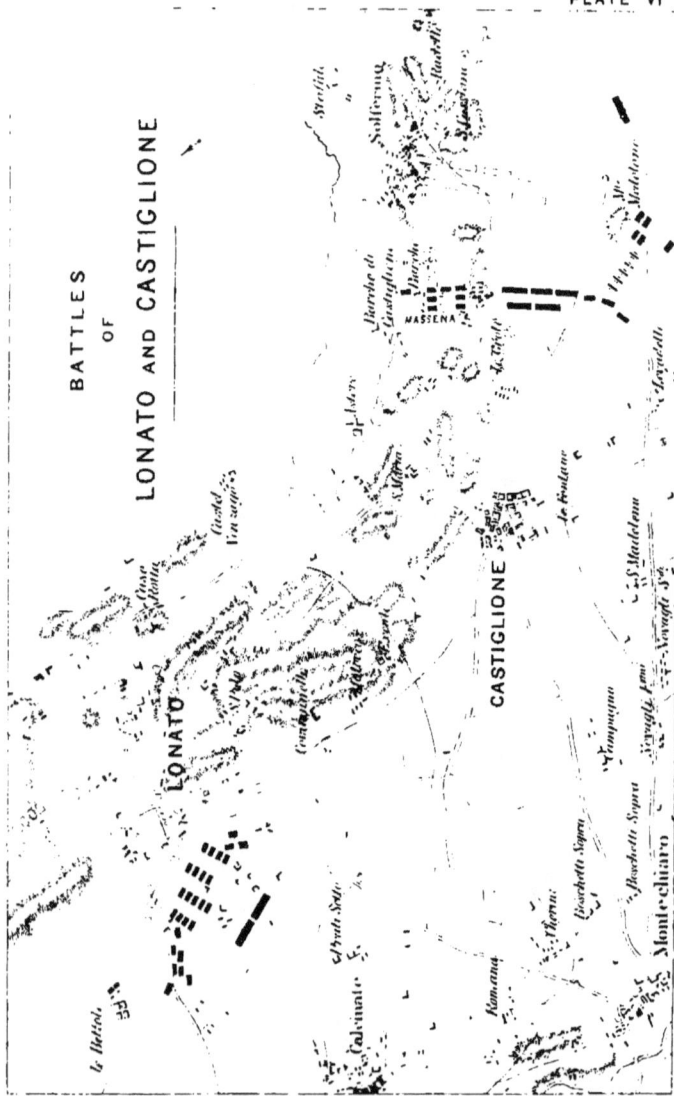

BATTLES
OF
LONATO AND CASTIGLIONE

LONATO

CASTIGLIONE

MASSENA

DANGERFIELD. LITH 22, BEDFORD ST. COVENT GARDEN

of its cavalry. An army so formed can march and manœuvre with the greatest case and rapidity.

The views here given (which are a synopsis of Mesnil Durand's proposals) were those in vogue at the French military schools,* when Napoleon was a student. They fell in with the peculiar character of the French revolutionary armies. Small battalion columns, covered by clouds of skirmishers, was the basis of these tactics; the long and difficult drill necessary to acquire the exactness of movement required by the linear tactics was needless, more depended on the courage and skill of individuals than accurate drill. Hence the proposals of Mesnil Durand were adopted by the French Army, and formed the basis of the regulations of 1776 and 1791.†

These tactics were those which were more or less the basis of the movements of the French Army in Italy in 1796. They were by no means reduced to a system; much was left to the individual enthusiasm of the soldier, and to the effect produced by the large number of educated men the revolution, and consequent universal service, had placed in the ranks, which of course greatly increased the moral power of the Republican Armies. *Napoleon's Italian Campaign.*

At Lonato and Castiglione the French worked in battalion columns at deploying intervals, the columns being columns of double companies covered in front by skirmishers. At the latter battle the division of Massena was formed with the centre battalion of each demi-brigade, equivalent to a three-battalion regiment, deployed, the flank battalions being in double column of companies, or column of divisions,‡ as termed by the French (*vide* Plate VI). *3rd and 5th August, 1796.*

At the battle of Rivoli, the French worked entirely by battalion columns, covered with skirmishers, and when on the defensive, as during the course of that celebrated battle they often were, these battalion columns were deployed into line three deep. The average strength of the French battalions was on this occasion only 470 men: hence the units that actually fought the battle were small columns, covered with skirmishers. Deducting the skirmishers and men not in the ranks, the actual strength of the columns handled could not have been much more than 300 rank and file, which, formed in double column of companies, would not be very different from the Prussian company column of the present day. *14th January, 1797.*

When Napoleon forced the passage of the Tagliamento, *16th March, 1797.*

* Particularly Brienne.
† The same writer advocated the formation of company columns, for exactly the same reason as he advocated battalion columns,—viz., that the formation could be changed more readily from line to column when requisite ; these company columns have since become celebrated. The formation of the battalion in grand divisions or double company column is shown on Fig. 6, Plate I. The regimental column of four battalions is shown on Fig. 7, Plate I, and the proposed method of deploying a six-battalion column from the centre is shown at Fig. 8. It will be observed that this deployment is very similar to that of the British army at the Alma (*vide* Plate XII).
‡ Until 1870 termed "Grand Divisions" in the British service.

his formation was still that of demi-brigades,* the centre battalion deployed, the flank battalions in double company columns covered by skirmishers (*vide* Plate VII. Fig. 1). And the reason assigned for this formation was that the demi-brigade, consisting of 24 companies, a fire of 12 companies, or one-half, was obtained, and the flanks of the lines were protected by the columns ready to form square, if charged by the superior Austrian cavalry. But the composition of the French armies at this date was peculiar: they had large numbers of intelligent, well-educated men in the ranks and inferior grades of officers, who sought the profession of arms, not only on account of the law of universal service, but of the fact that the revolution and consequent paralysis of trade and commerce had destroyed almost all other openings for young men.

The formation of Dessaix's column at Marengo was peculiar as showing the same ideas at work.

Dessaix advanced in direct echelon from the left. The leading demi-brigade, the 9th Light Infantry, having its flank battalions in column of double companies, its centre battalion deployed into line three deep. The next demi-brigade, the 30th of the Line, was deployed, and the last, the 69th of the Line, being formed as the 9th. This formation gave a very considerable amount of fire, pushed in like a wedge, and kept the flank well protected from the Austrian cavalry, which were threatening the French advance (*vide* Fig. 2, Plate VII. also Frontispiece).

The formations which have been described as marking the French tactics up to the year 1800, may be summed up as follows:—A large use of skirmishers, taken not from selected regiments but from companies of the battalions immediately in rear, united with the independent action of small battalions. The French battalions on paper did not exceed 700 men; a paper battalion of that strength can rarely put 600 men on parade, which, when skirmishers and staff were deducted, would give some 400 to 500 men for the force composing the independent command. Thus great latitude was given to individual commanders.

Up to this time there were really no regiments in the French Revolutionary Army; what were termed demi-brigades took their place, and consisted of three battalions. The whole of the arrangements were of that irregular character that must characterise armies hastily put together.

After the assumption of the Imperial title, Napoleon prepared for the invasion of England, and in the large standing camps formed at Boulogne and elsewhere on the coast of the English Channel, many improvements and alterations were made both in organization and tactics; conscription with substitution was introduced in lieu of universal service, and the more settled state of the country and Government, causing many openings

---

* Three battalions formed a demi-brigade.

PLATE VII.

Formation for attack of a Demi Brigade at the

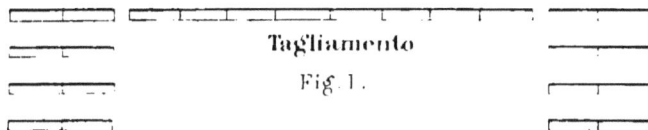

Tagliamento

Fig. 1.

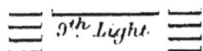

9ᵗʰ Light

Formation of Desaix's
Column at Marengo
Fig. 2.

30ᵗʰ Line

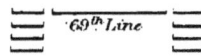

69ᵗʰ Line

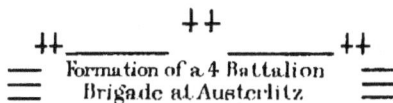

Formation of a 4 Battalion
Brigade at Austerlitz
Fig. 3.

Fig 4.

Formation of a 10 Battalion Division at Austerlitz

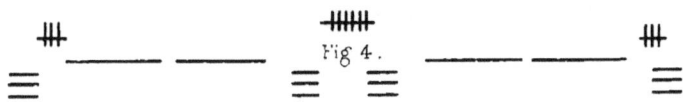

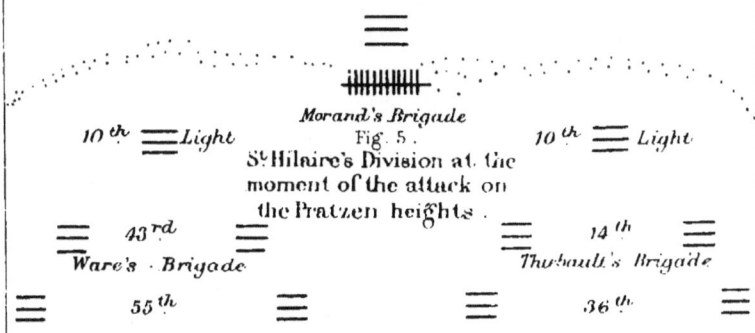

Morand's Brigade
Fig. 5.

St Hilaire's Division at the
moment of the attack on
the Pratzen heights.

10ᵗʰ Light

10ᵗʰ Light

43ʳᵈ

14ᵗʰ

Ware's Brigade

Thibault's Brigade

55ᵗʰ

36ᵗʰ

in civil life, drew off much of the intelligence that had been previously forced into the army for want of a vent elsewhere. The army formed at Boulogne still, however, possessed many of the old elements that gave the early Republican armies such great moral power; it possessed also that firmness and steadiness, which it takes many months to give troops.

Formed for a most difficult enterprise (the invasion of England), trained with the greatest care and skill, it undoubtedly was the finest army the Emperor Napoleon ever commanded. One of the changes, perhaps not an improvement, was the alteration of the old three-battalion demi-brigade into a regiment of two battalions. It was this army that fought the battle of Austerlitz. The tactics of the French during this battle are worthy of notice. Austerlitz, Dec. 2, 1805.

The allies, Austrians and Russians, resolved to quit their position at Olmutz and turn the right of the French Army; they marched in five columns, one being entirely composed of the reserve cavalry; the army was covered by an advanced guard of three columns under Bagarthion. On the 2nd December the French troops were drawn up in the following order: on the plain between Girscikowitz and Santon, Caffarelli's division, composed of the 13th Light, the 17th, 51st, 30th, 61st, all two-battalion regiments, or ten battalions. The division was drawn up in three lines of battalion double-company columns at deploying distances.

Suchet's division, composed of four regiments, or eight battalions, was similarly drawn up in two lines.

The corps of Bernadotte in the centre was drawn up as follows: Drouet's division, composed of three three-battalion regiments; and Rivaud division, of three three-battalion regiments, was drawn up in battalion double-company columns at deploying distances. On the right, St. Hilaire's division in the same formation in front of Puntowitz, Levassus' brigade of Legrand's division was in front of Kobelnitz. Beyond Girschikowitz was Vandamme's division. On the extreme right, upon a rising ground and in the ditches in front of Tellnitz, General Legrand's division, the 26th regiment being at Sokolnitz. The batteries attached to each division of infantry were in the brigade intervals. The reserve cavalry under Murat was behind Lannes' corps, the guard upon the plateau behind Girschikowitz, drawn up in two lines of battalion close columns at deploying distances, 40 guns being placed in the intervals. The cavalry of the guard was in close column of squadrons.

Some days before the battle the Emperor had ordered a new formation for the Infantry. Each brigade was to have its first regiment deployed, the second formed in close column of double companies on the flanks, the 1st Battalion of the 2nd Regiment beyond and in rear of the right of the deployed regiment, the 2nd Battalion on its left (*vide* Figs. 3 and 4, Plate VII). If the division had five regiments, the fifth regiment was to be placed 100 yards in rear of the centre. The artillery in the intervals between the brigades and on the flanks.

The Emperor Napoleon, writing to Soult and Bernadotte on the 26th December, 1805, says: "You will, by observing this "formation, be able to oppose a line of fire to the enemy, and "yet have close columns ready to attack him if requisite."

These dispositions are a further instance of the fundamental rule in infantry fights, that the second line must not be independent of the first line, of which it is the support and immediate stay. The order of linked brigades was thus conformable to what history shows as having occurred in every battle. The ground on a battle-field is generally so cut up by obstacles, and so formed, that each brigade has usually a distinct object to attain. The second line can rarely, if ever support the first line without forcing it again into action, for the passage of lines, as laid down in books, can rarely, if ever, be carried out. These formations are also a condemnation of the system of deploying an entire division in front line, and an entire division in second line.

At Austerlitz, when the heights of Pratzen were attacked, the battalions previously deployed were formed in double company columns on the centre. St. Hilaire's division, upon which some of the hardest fighting fell, was formed at the moment of actual contact, as shown in Fig. 5, Plate VII.

Upon the Pratzen heights the infantry composing the 4th Austro-Russian column marched in open column of companies left in front to follow the 3rd column marching towards Sokolnitz, when it suddenly saw Soult and Levasseurs' infantry climbing quickly up the heights; the tail of the 3rd column and the whole of the 4th column wheeled to the right into line exactly according to Frederick's tactics. Kutusoff, who saw that the Pratzen heights were the key of the position, sent to seek assistance from the Prince of Lichtenstein who sent him four cavalry regiments.

The French columns did not reply to the fire of the Austro-Russian infantry, but advanced with shouldered arms.

The 10th Light Infantry, paying no regard to the village of Pratzen, where the two leading battalions of the 4th column were posted, pushed straight up the heights.

It was supported by Thiébault's brigade, whilst Waré turned the village, took the battalions posted there in flank, and crowned the heights. Vandamme's division came into line with Waré and attacked the Russian column, which was now formed in several lines, its right thrown back on the high ground towards Kzernowitz, where a considerable force of artillery was placed. When 100 paces off, the French deployed, and opened a heavy fire from two ranks. But the Austro-Russians, owing to their numerical superiority, held the French in check until the latter advanced with the bayonets and forced the first line back on the second. Six battalions, concealed by a rising ground, attacked the left of the division, but were driven back by the 4th and 24th Regiments; these regiments did not fire a shot, but merely used the bayonet. Soult's divisions were formed as shown on Fig. 4, Plate VII.

PLATE VIII

BATTLE
OF
AUSTERLITZ.

Scale of Metres

PLATE IX.

Fig.1
Formation of Suchet's Division at Jena

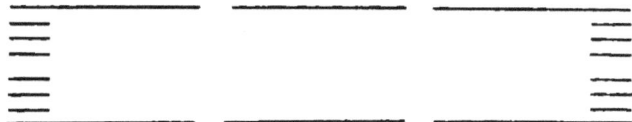

Fig.2
Flank March of Massena at Wagram.

Fig.3.
Formation of Macdonald's Corps at Wagram.

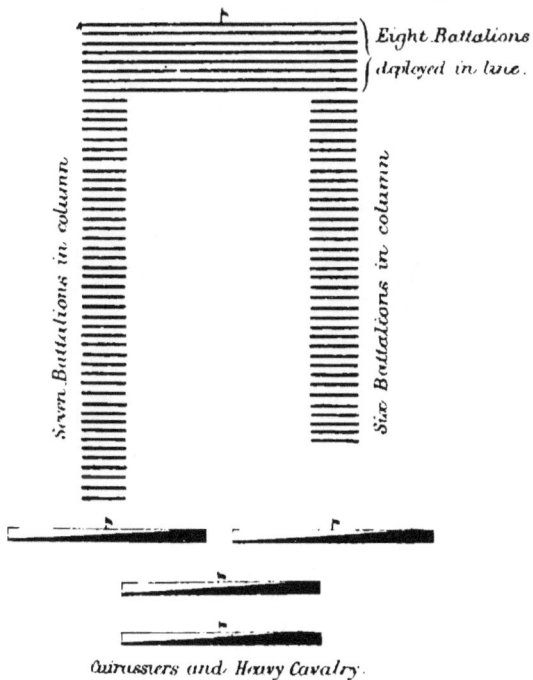

Eight Battalions
deployed in line.

Seven Battalions in column

Six Battalions in column

Cuirassiers and Heavy Cavalry.

DANGERFIELD. LITH. 22. BEDFORD ST. COVENT GARDEN

Meantime the tail of the 3rd column had formed line. The Russian regiments, Fanagorisky and Rhynsky, of the 2nd column, and the Austrian brigades, Guzczeck and Rottermund, or 20 battalions, occupying a long line, advanced to surround a battalion of the 10th Light Infantry; they were, however, charged by that battalion, supported by the 14th, 36th, and 43rd, and driven back. The other battalion of the 10th was driven back until supported by Levasseur's brigade. The French then remained masters of the heights, and the allies fell back.

In the centre, Bernadotte and the guard got on the heights without firing a shot.

Almost the last act of this battle was the destruction by the Russian cavalry of the 1st Battalion of the 4th Regiment, which got into disorder when pressing the Russians. It is a common fault of the French infantry to get into confusion during an attack, and not to preserve their ranks: from this cause many disasters have happened, for the enemy's cavalry coming up unexpectedly always takes troops so dispersed at a great advantage.

At this period the French Army was at its highest point, the old soldiers of the revolution were still in the ranks in considerable numbers, the officers were well taught and trained in the best of all schools, that of successful war.

On the breaking out of war with Prussia in 1806, the Emperor Napoleon formed the flank companies of the various battalions into permanent battalions of grenadiers and voltigeurs; the battalions of the line were thus reduced to six companies, each of which had a normal strength of 100 men, but which actually in the field could not have had many more than 80 men.

At Jena the tactics of Frederick the Great came into actual contact with those of Napoleon, and although that battle was decided by circumstances other than the actual fighting, yet the formation of the French troops presents some points of interest. The French troops were usually drawn up in line of battalion double company columns at deploying distance, and attacked in that order, covered by skirmishers. *Jena, 14th October, 1806.*

Fig. 1, Plate IX., shows the formation and mode of attack of Suchet's division, but the tactics at that time used by the French Army are perhaps best shown by a study of the battle of Auerstadt, where Marshal Davoust, with his corps alone, defeated the main body of the Prussian Army, about 66,000 men, which, however, attacked him piecemeal, and not all at once. This battle possesses much that is worthy of study; it was on the part of the French, who were greatly out-numbered, for a long time a defensive battle, and offers a good illustration of French formations. *Auerstadt, 14th October, 1806.*

Believing that the French Army was moving towards Leipzig and Dresden, the main body of the Prussian Army, about 66,000 men, moved from Weimar towards Naumburg, with the view of getting behind the Elbe, and obtaining support from

E

the fortress of Magdeburg. One wing of the army, under the Prince Hohenlohe, was left to cover the movement. The force under the Prince Hohenlohe fought the battle of Jena, with the main body of the French Army under the Emperor Napoleon. Davoust's corps, which should have been supported by Bernadotte, but, for reasons which it is superfluous to mention, was not, had to sustain the attack of the Prussian Army.

The main road from Weimar to Naumburg led through the village of Hasenhausen, crossing the Saal at Kösen (*vide* Plate X).

Davoust had three infantry divisions, those of Gudin, Friant, and Morand. Early on the morning of the 14th October, 1806, he crossed the Saal at Kösen, and leaving a battalion to defend the bridge, advanced towards Hasenhausen, Gudin's division leading, covered by cavalry; after a slight cavalry action, Davoust formed Gudin's division, which consisted of the 25th, 85th, 12th, 21st Regiments of the line, or eight battalions, with six squadrons of cavalry, on the north of the Weimar-Naumburg road, which here runs nearly due east and west (*vide* Fig. 1, Plate X).

The 85th Regiment was placed in the village, with a strong body of skirmishers in some woods in front, the 25th was deployed into line on its right, the 21st also deployed, being in second line and the whole of the 12th Regiment, that is to say, two battalions, was formed in close column of double companies, on the extreme right and slightly in rear, so as to cover and protect the flank of the deployed line.

In this formation the division was attacked by the Prussian infantry (General Schmettau's division), who were unable to make any impression on it; they were then charged by large bodies of cavalry under Blucher. The French met this attack by forming the 12th Regiment into regimental square, the right battalion of the 21st into battalion square on its right company, the right battalion of the 25th into battalion square on its left company, the left battalions of these regiments, partly covered by the wood, still remained in line. The Prussian cavalry were beaten back with great loss, and were charged as they retired by the six squadrons of Gudin's division which, up to this period, had been sheltered behind the infantry (Fig. 2).

Meantime Friant's division came up, and was pushed to the right of Gudin's division, which, being thus supported on the right, moved the 12th Regiment from that flank along the rear to the south of Hasenhausen, when it deployed one battalion with its right flank on the village, the left flank being covered by the other battalion in double company column ready to form square slightly in rear (*vide* Figs. 3 and 4).

The Prussians still attempted to force the French out of Hasenhausen, and tried to turn their left flank, where the only troops as yet in position consisted of the two battalions of the 12th Regiment formed as above described.

Wartensblen's division pushed well to the south of Hasen-

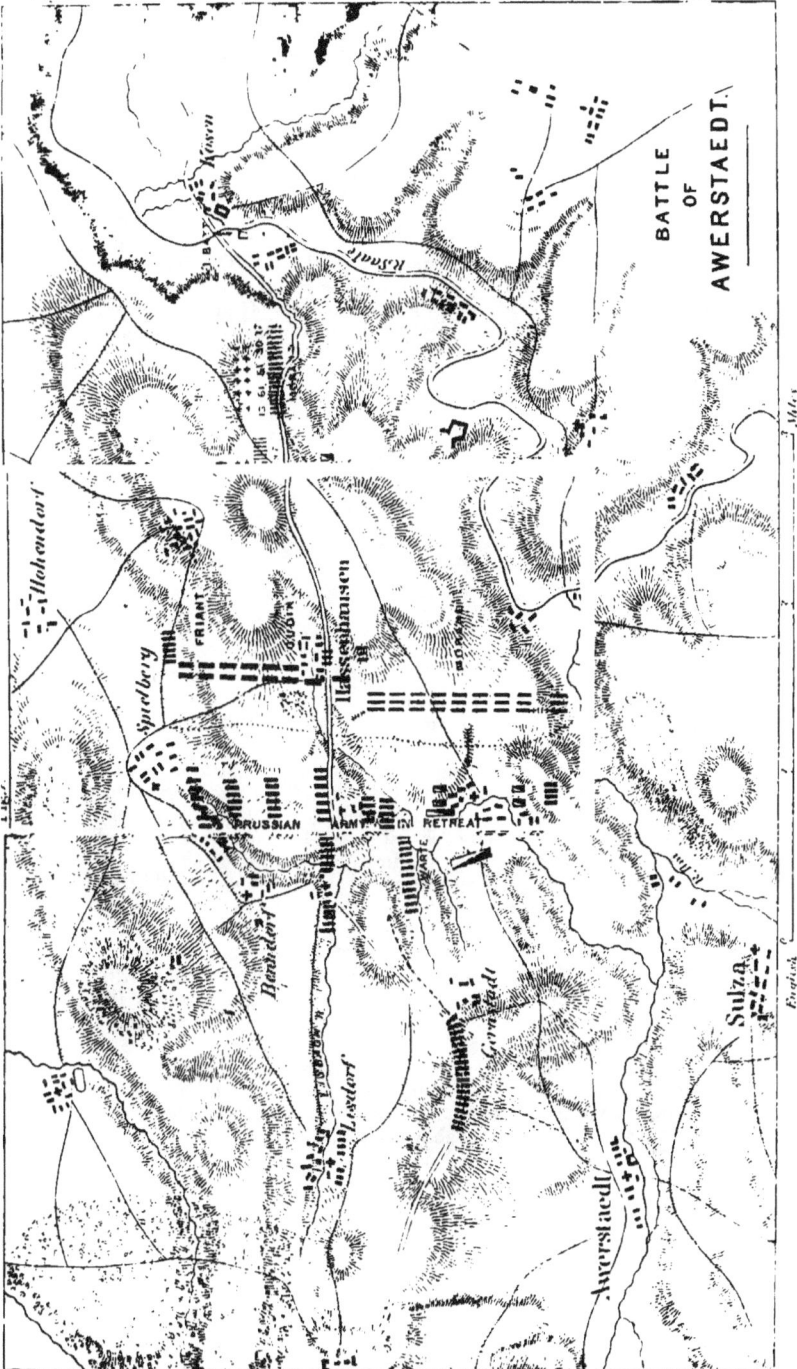

PLATE X.

BATTLE
OF
AWERSTAEDT.

the fortress of Magdeburg. One wing of the army, under the
Prince Hohenlohe, was left to cover the movement. The force
under the Prince Hohenlohe fought the battle of Jena, with the
main body of the French Army under the Emperor Napoleon.
Davoust's corps, which should have been supported by Bernadotte, but, for reasons which it is superfluous to mention, was
not, had to sustain the attack of the Prussian Army.

The main road from Weimar to Naumburg led through the
village of Hasenhausen, crossing the Saal at Kösen (*vide* Plate X).

Davoust had three infantry divisions, those of Gudin, Friant,
and Morand. Early on the morning of the 14th October, 1806,
he crossed the Saal at Kösen, and leaving a battalion to defend
the brid   towards Hasenhausen, Gudin's division
leading,   slight cavalry action,
Davoust   95th.
85th, 1
six squ
burg re
1, Plat
    Th
body
ploye
secon
two
on t
prote
    I
infa:
make any impression
bodies of cavalry under Blucher.
by forming the 12th Regiment into regimental squares,
right battalion of the 21st into battalion square on its right
company, the right battalion of the 25th into battalion square
on its left company, the left battalions of these regiments,
partly covered by the wood, still remained in line. The Prussian cavalry were beaten back with great loss, and were charged
as they retired by the six squadrons of Gudin's division which,
up to this period, had been sheltered behind the infantry (Fig. 2).

Meantime Friant's division came up, and was pushed to the
right of Gudin's division, which, being thus supported on the
right, moved the 12th Regiment from that flank along the rear to
the south of Hasenhausen, when it deployed one battalion with
its right flank on the village, the left flank being covered by the
other battalion in double company column ready to form square
slightly in rear (*vide* Figs. 3 and 4).

The Prussians still attempted to force the French out of
Hasenhausen, and tried to turn their left flank, where the only
troops as yet in position consisted of the two battalions of the
12th Regiment formed as above described.

Wartensblen's division pushed well to the south of Hasen-

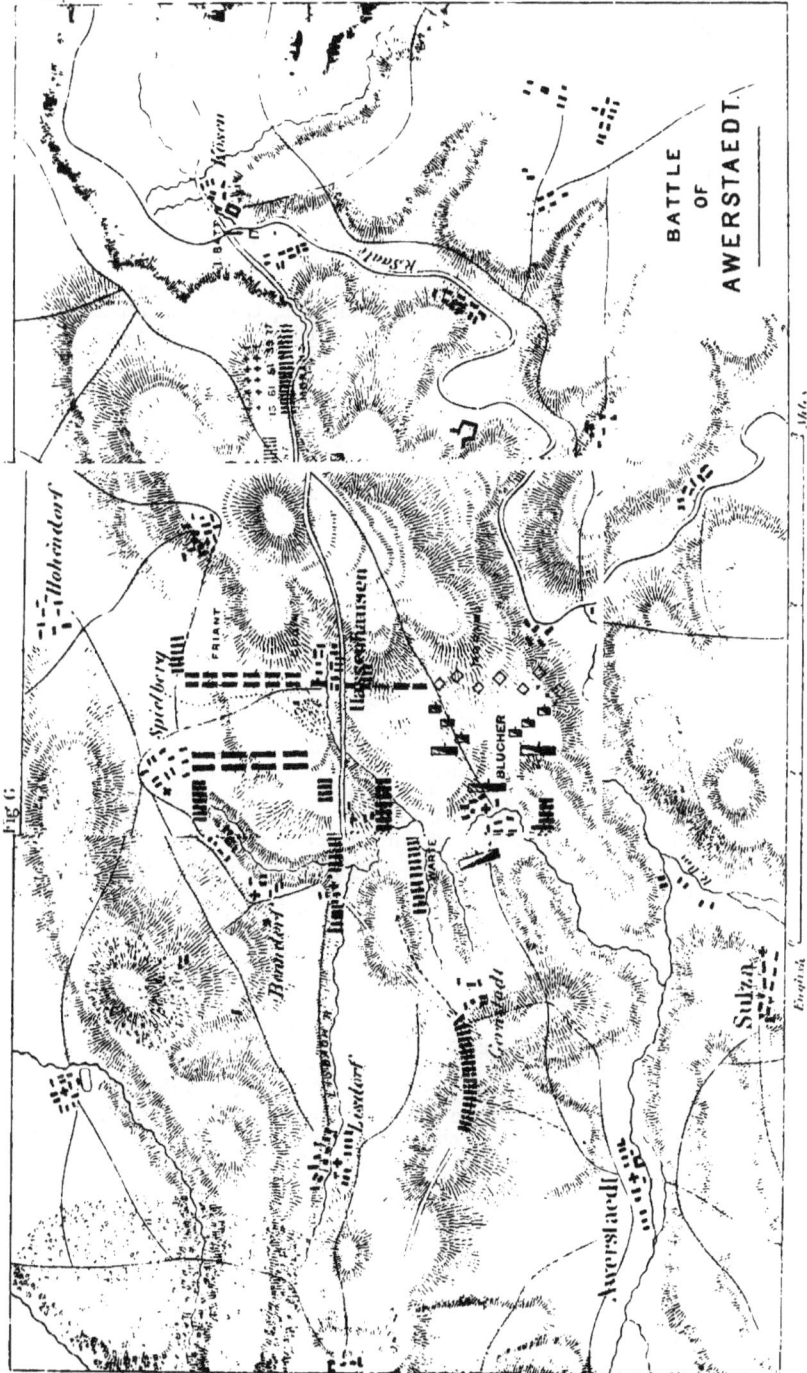

PLATE X.

BATTLE
OF
AWERSTAEDT.

the fortress of Magdeburg. One wing of the army, under the
Prince Hohenlohe, was left to cover the movement. The force
under the Prince Hohenlohe fought the battle of Jena, with the
main body of the French Army under the Emperor Napoleon.
Davoust's corps, which should have been supported by Bernadotte, but, for reasons which it is superfluous to mention, was
not, had to sustain the attack of the Prussian Army.

The main road from Weimar to Naumburg led through the
village of Hasenhausen, crossing the Saal at Kösen (*vide* Plate X).

Davoust had three infantry divisions, those of Gudin, Friant,
and Morand. Early on the morning of the 14th October, 1806,
he crossed the Saal at Kösen, and leaving a battalion to defend
the brid~~ advanced towards Hasenhausen, Gudin's division
leading.   '--- after a slight cavalry action,
Davous   ' ' -f th. 25th,
85th, 1!
six sqr
burg r<
1, Plat
    Th
body <
ploye<
secon
two l
on tl
prote
    I
infai
make
bodies
by forming the 12th Regiment ...
right battalion of the 21st into battalion square on its right
company, the right battalion of the 25th into battalion square
on its left company, the left battalions of these regiments,
partly covered by the wood, still remained in line. The Prussian cavalry were beaten back with great loss, and were charged
as they retired by the six squadrons of Gudin's division which,
up to this period, had been sheltered behind the infantry (Fig. 2).

Meantime Friant's division came up, and was pushed to the
right of Gudin's division, which, being thus supported on the
right, moved the 12th Regiment from that flank along the rear to
the south of Hasenhausen, when it deployed one battalion with
its right flank on the village, the left flank being covered by the
other battalion in double company column ready to form square
slightly in rear (*vide* Figs. 3 and 4).

The Prussians still attempted to force the French out of
Hasenhausen, and tried to turn their left flank, where the only
troops as yet in position consisted of the two battalions of the
12th Regiment formed as above described.

Wartensblen's division pushed well to the south of Hasen-

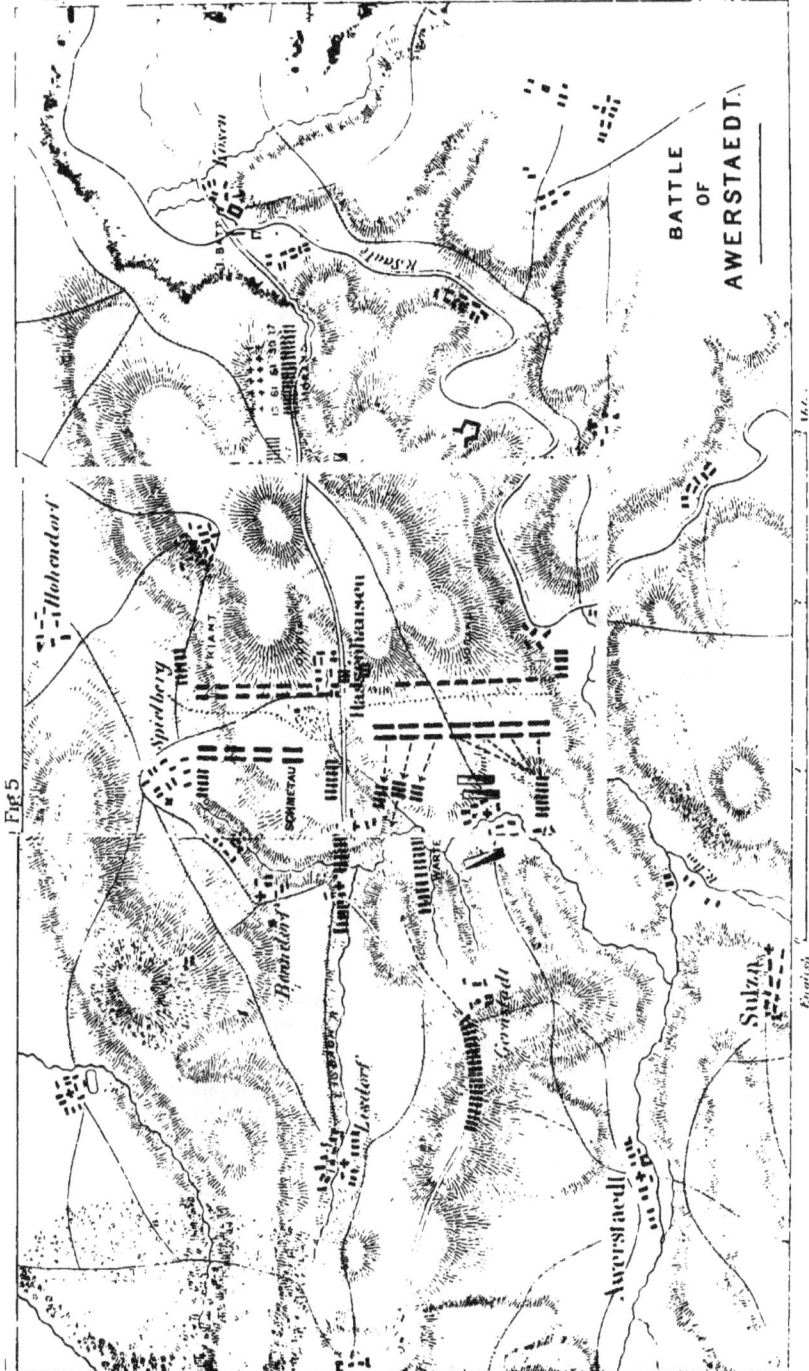

PLATE X.

BATTLE
OF
AWERSTAEDT.

Fig 5

Hohendorf
Spielberg
Hassenhausen
SONNETAU
Beaullieu
Poppel
Sulza
Awerstaedt

the fortress of Magdeburg. One wing of the army, under the Prince Hohenlohe, was left to cover the movement. The force under the Prince Hohenlohe fought the battle of Jena, with the main body of the French Army under the Emperor Napoleon. Davoust's corps, which should have been supported by Bernadotte, but, for reasons which it is superfluous to mention, was not, had to sustain the attack of the Prussian Army.

The main road from Weimar to Naumburg led through the village of Hasenhausen, crossing the Saal at Kösen (*vide* Plate X).

Davoust had three infantry divisions, those of Gudin, Friant, and Morand. Early on the morning of the 14th October, 1806, he crossed the Saal at Kösen, and leaving a battalion to defend the bridge, advanced towards Hasenhausen, Gudin's division leading ········· ······ ·······: after a slight cavalry action, Davous ······ ····· ····· ······ ····· ··· ···· of the 25th, 85th, 1

six squ

burg r

1, Plat

Th

body

ploye

secon

two l

on tl

prote

I

infan

mak

bodies

by forming ··· ···· ··· right battalion of the 21st into battalion square on its right company, the right battalion of the 25th into battalion square on its left company, the left battalions of these regiments, partly covered by the wood, still remained in line. The Prussian cavalry were beaten back with great loss, and were charged as they retired by the six squadrons of Gudin's division which, up to this period, had been sheltered behind the infantry (Fig. 2).

Meantime Friant's division came up, and was pushed to the right of Gudin's division, which, being thus supported on the right, moved the 12th Regiment from that flank along the rear to the south of Hasenhausen, when it deployed one battalion with its right flank on the village, the left flank being covered by the other battalion in double company column ready to form square slightly in rear (*vide* Figs. 3 and 4).

The Prussians still attempted to force the French out of Hasenhausen, and tried to turn their left flank, where the only troops as yet in position consisted of the two battalions of the 12th Regiment formed as above described.

Wartensbleu's division pushed well to the south of Hasen-

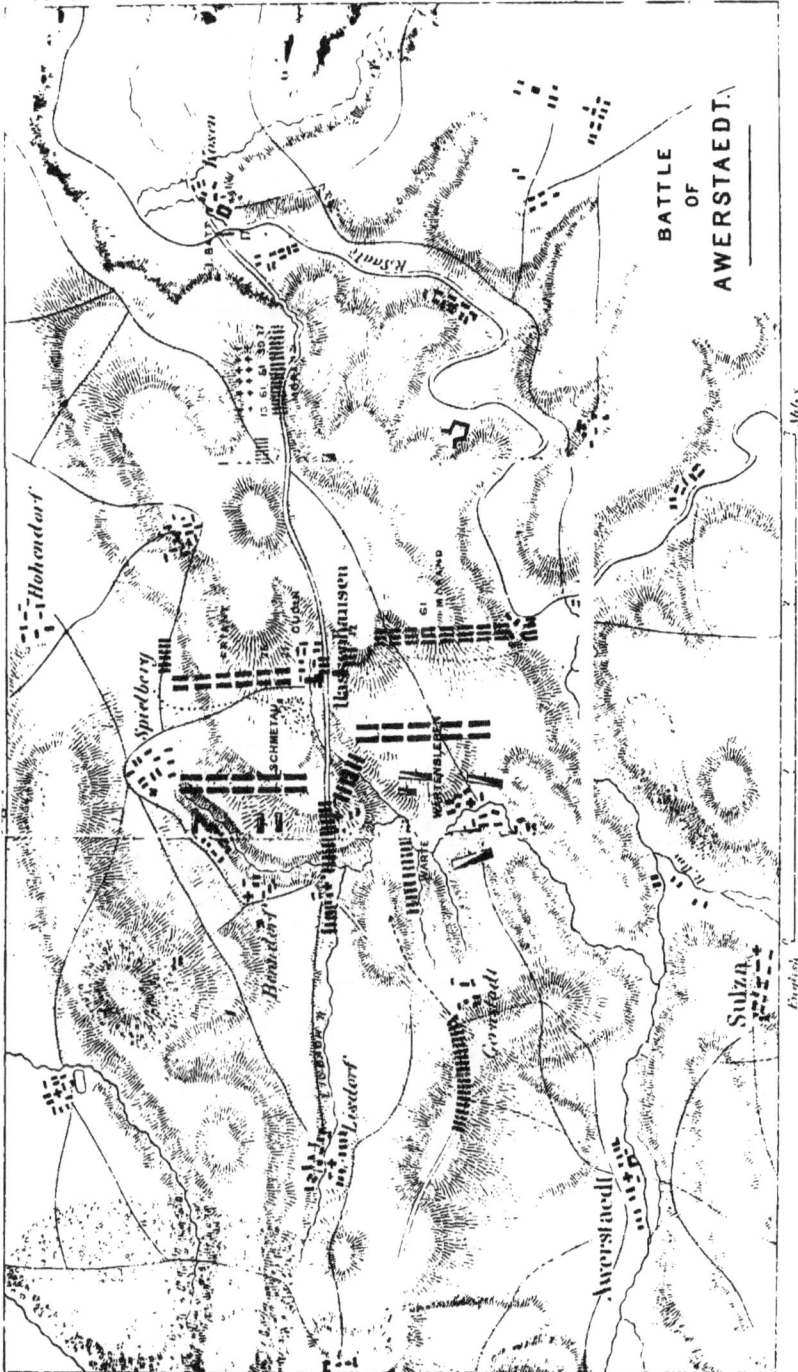

PLATE X.

BATTLE
OF
AWERSTAEDT.

the fortress of Magdeburg. One wing of the army, under the Prince Hohenlohe, was left to cover the movement. The force under the Prince Hohenlohe fought the battle of Jena, with the main body of the French Army under the Emperor Napoleon. Davoust's corps, which should have been supported by Berna-dotte, but, for reasons which it is superfluous to mention, was not, had to sustain the attack of the Prussian Army.

The main road from Weimar to Naumburg led through the village of Hasenhausen, crossing the Saal at Kösen (*vide* Plate X).

Davoust had three infantry divisions, those of Gudin, Friant, and Morand. Early on the morning of the 14th October, 1806, he crossed the Saal at Kösen, and leaving a battalion to defend the bridge, advanced towards Hasenhausen, Gudin's division leading ———— after a slight cavalry action, Davous ———— of the 25th, 85th, 1
six squ
burg r
1, Plat
Th
body
ploye
secon
two l
on tl
prote
infa
mak
bodies
by form
right battalion of the 21st into battalion square on its right company, the right battalion of the 25th into battalion square on its left company, the left battalions of these regiments, partly covered by the wood, still remained in line. The Prussian cavalry were beaten back with great loss, and were charged as they retired by the six squadrons of Gudin's division which, up to this period, had been sheltered behind the infantry (Fig. 2).

Meantime Friant's division came up, and was pushed to the right of Gudin's division. which, being thus supported on the right, moved the 12th Regiment from that flank along the rear to the south of Hasenhausen, when it deployed one battalion with its right flank on the village. the left flank being covered by the other battalion in double company column ready to form square slightly in rear (*vide* Figs. 3 and 4).

The Prussians still attempted to force the French out of Hasenhausen, and tried to turn their left flank, where the only troops as yet in position consisted of the two battalions of the 12th Regiment formed as above described.

Wartensblen's division pushed well to the south of Hasen-

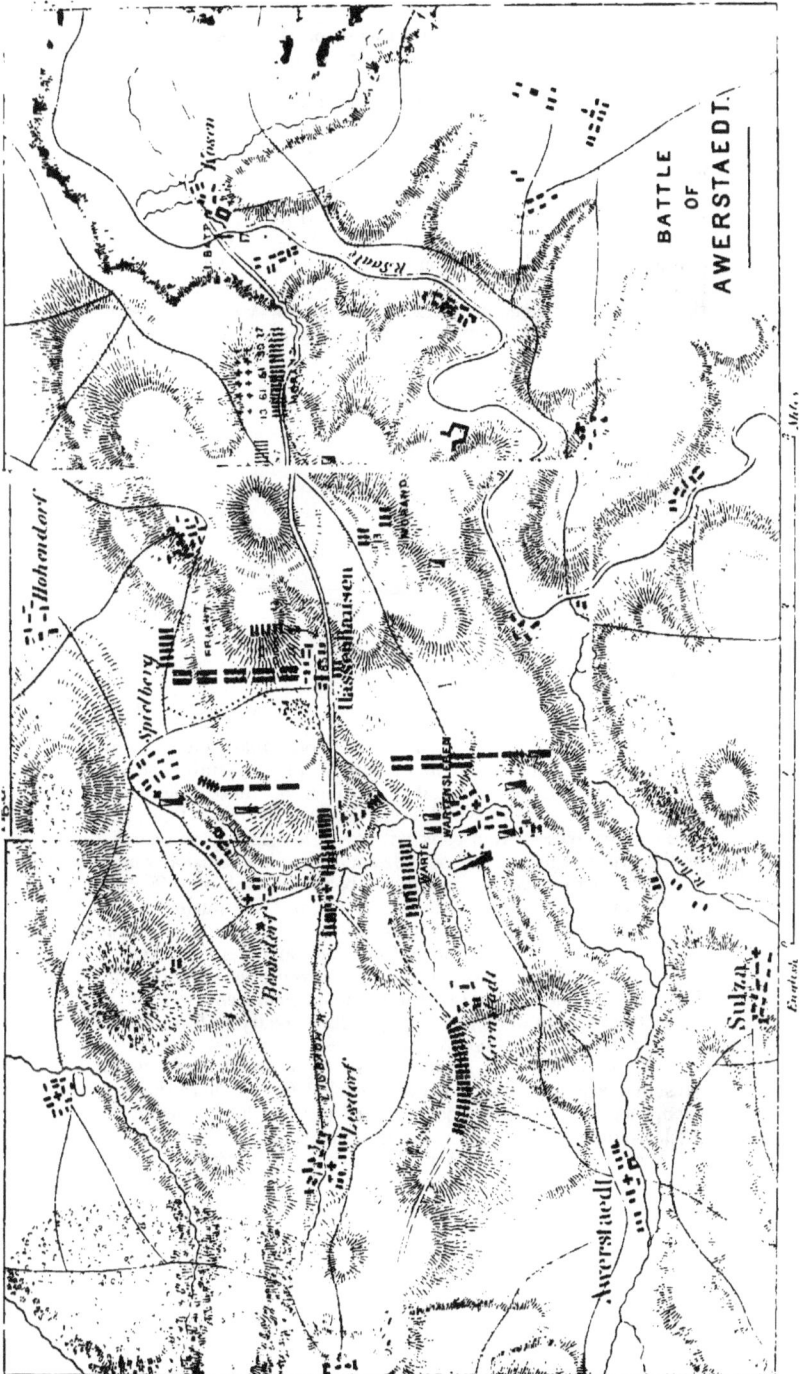

PLATE X.

BATTLE
OF
AWERSTAEDT.

the fortress of Magdeburg. One wing of the army, under the
Prince Hohenlohe, was left to cover the movement. The force
under the Prince Hohenlohe fought the battle of Jena, with the
main body of the French Army under the Emperor Napoleon.
Davoust's corps, which should have been supported by Bernadotte, but, for reasons which it is superfluous to mention, was
not, had to sustain the attack of the Prussian Army.

The main road from Weimar to Naumburg led through the
village of Hasenhausen, crossing the Saal at Kösen (vide Plate X).

Davoust had three infantry divisions, those of Gudin, Friant,
and Morand. Early on the morning of the 14th October, 1806,
he crossed the Saal at Kösen, and leaving a battalion to defend
the bridge, advanced towards Hasenhausen, Gudin's division
leading   —— after a slight cavalry action,
Davous   · of the 25th,
85th, 1'
six sqi
burg r
1, Plat
Th
body
ploye
secon
two l
on tl
prote
I'
infai
mak
bodies
by forn.

right battalion of the 21st into battalion square on its right
company, the right battalion of the 25th into battalion square
on its left company, the left battalions of these regiments,
partly covered by the wood, still remained in line. The Prussian cavalry were beaten back with great loss, and were charged
as they retired by the six squadrons of Gudin's division which,
up to this period, had been sheltered behind the infantry (Fig. 2).

Meantime Friant's division came up, and was pushed to the
right of Gudin's division. which, being thus supported on the
right, moved the 12th Regiment from that flank along the rear to
the south of Hasenhausen, when it deployed one battalion with
its right flank on the village. the left flank being covered by the
other battalion in double company column ready to form square
slightly in rear (vide Figs. 3 and 4).

The Prussians still attempted to force the French out of
Hasenhausen, and tried to turn their left flank, where the only
troops as yet in position consisted of the two battalions of the
12th Regiment formed as above described.

Wartensblen's division pushed well to the south of Hasen-

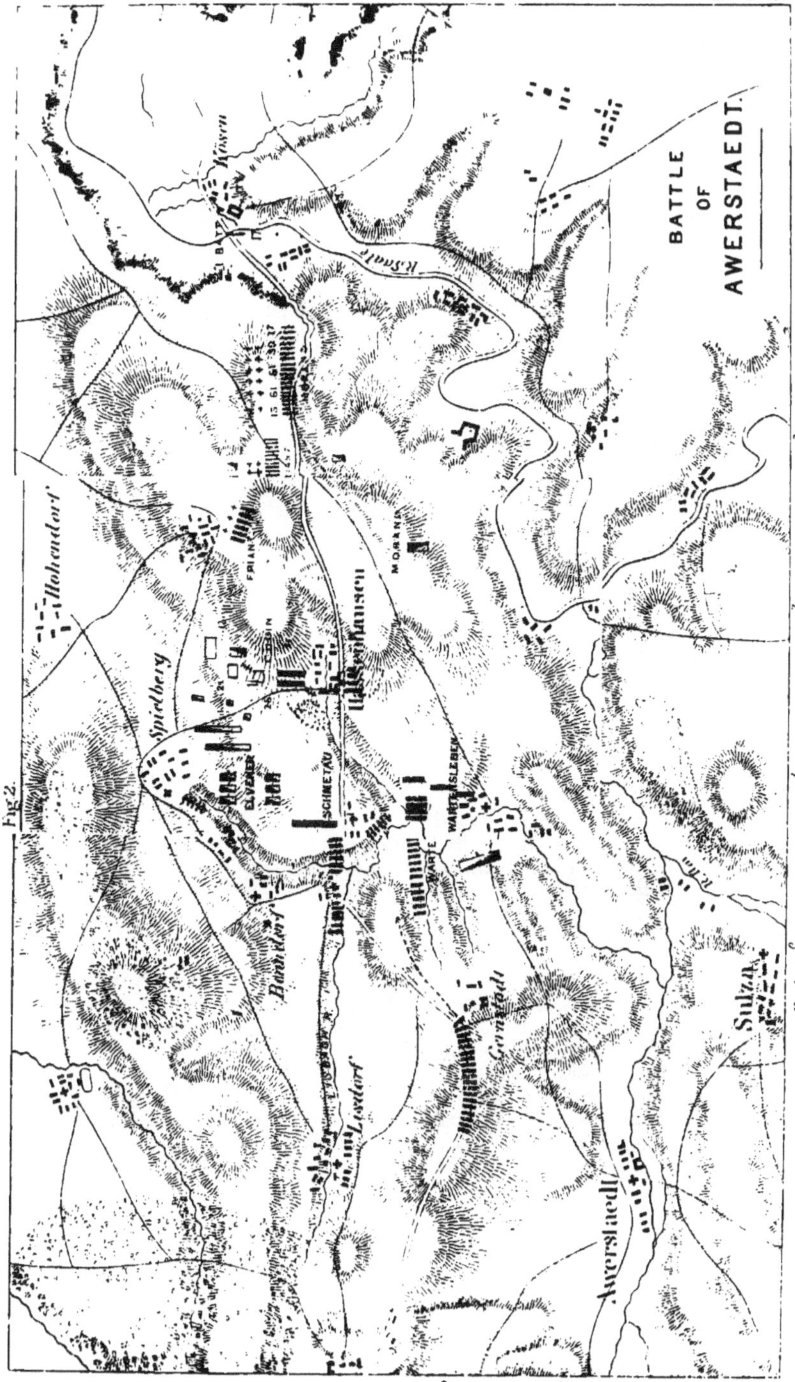

PLATE X.

BATTLE
OF
AWERSTAEDT.

Fig. 2.

the fortress of Magdeburg. One wing of the army, under the Prince Hohenlohe, was left to cover the movement. The force under the Prince Hohenlohe fought the battle of Jena, with the main body of the French Army under the Emperor Napoleon. Davoust's corps, which should have been supported by Berna-dotte, but, for reasons which it is superfluous to mention, was not, had to sustain the attack of the Prussian Army.

The main road from Weimar to Naumburg led through the village of Hasenhausen, crossing the Saal at Kösen (*ride* Plate X).

Davoust had three infantry divisions, those of Gudin, Friant, and Morand. Early on the morning of the 14th October, 1806, he crossed the Saal at Kösen, and leaving a battalion to defend the bridge, advanced towards Hasenhausen, Gudin's division leading   ——. after a slight cavalry action, Davous   · ' · 1 of the 25th, 85th, 1'

six sq1

burg r

1, Plat

Th

body

ploye

secon

two l

on tl

prote

I

infai

make

bodies

by form.

right battalion of t

company, the right .... of the 25th into battalion square on its left company, the left battalions of these regiments, partly covered by the wood, still remained in line. The Prus-sian cavalry were beaten back with great loss, and were charged as they retired by the six squadrons of Gudin's division which, up to this period, had been sheltered behind the infantry (Fig. 2).

Meantime Friant's division came up, and was pushed to the right of Gudin's division, which, being thus supported on the right, moved the 12th Regiment from that flank along the rear to the south of Hasenhausen, when it deployed one battalion with its right flank on the village, the left flank being covered by the other battalion in double company column ready to form square slightly in rear (*ride* Figs. 3 and 4).

The Prussians still attempted to force the French out of Hasenhausen, and tried to turn their left flank, where the only troops as yet in position consisted of the two battalions of the 12th Regiment formed as above described.

Wartensblen's division pushed well to the south of Hasen-

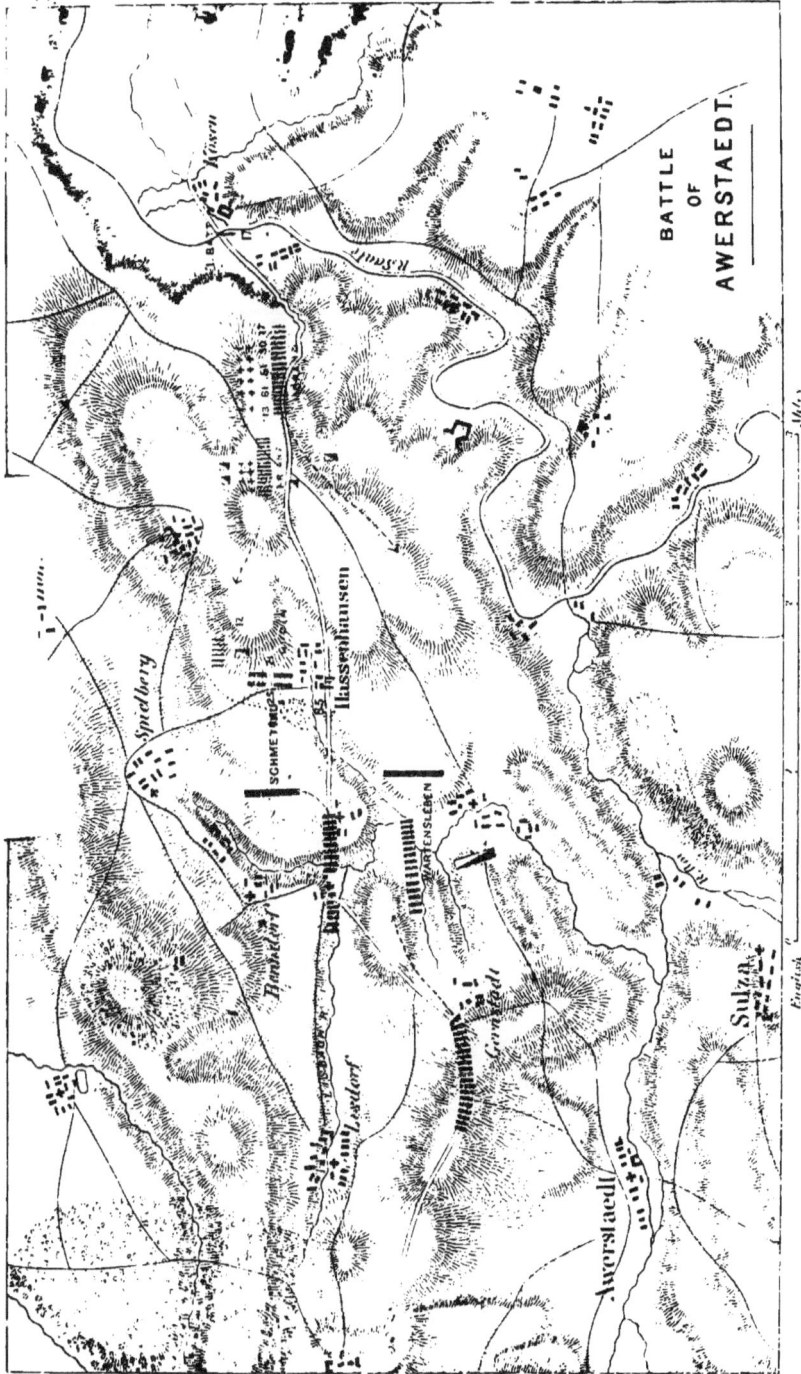

PLATE X.

BATTLE
OF
AWERSTAEDT.

hausen, threatened to turn and take Gudin's and Friant's divisions
in rear; at this moment Morand's division, composed of five
regiments, arrived on the ground, it brought, however, only nine
battalions, one being left at the bridge of Kösen; it had 12 guns
and some cavalry. This division advanced in mass of double
company columns with the artillery on its right, the 13th Light
Infantry leading, followed by the 61st, 51st, 30th, and 17th
Regiments of the Line (the latter having but one battalion).
Arrived near Wartensblen's advanced troops, Morand threw out
a great mass of skirmishers, checking Wartensblen's advance,
and deployed the mass of double company columns into line of
double company columns at deploying intervals with artillery
on the flanks; in this order the division advanced a short distance (vide Fig. 4), thus relieving the left of the 12th Regiment.
Morland now deployed all his battalions, except the battalion
of the 17th, on the left, and drove back the Prussians by a
heavy fire (Fig. 5). The Prussians, hoping to destroy the
French, deployed in single line, and without reserves or supports, formed a mass of some 8,000 cavalry behind Wartensblen's division, and charged Morand, who formed his division
with the exception of the two battalions of the 13th Light
Infantry, into an echelon of battalion squares, with the artillery
at the angles (Fig. 6). On the cavalry retiring Morand reformed
his division into line of battalion double company columns, at
deploying intervals, covered by skirmishers, and advanced (Fig.
7). The Prussians were finally defeated and fell back. The
Prussians invariably advanced in open column of companies,
marching in two or more lines, and sought to form line, by
changing directions to the right or left and wheeling into line;
they then attacked in echelons of battalions in line, but without
a single skirmisher.

The French marched in mass of double company columns at
close order, threw out a number of skirmishers to the front,
who sought to overwhelm the enemy with fire; they deployed
the mass into line of battalion double company columns at
deploying intervals, and finally into line. The advantages of
these columns, both in rapidity of deployment and also in
rapidity of forming square to resist cavalry, are apparent, and
their combination with skirmishers produce unity between fire
and shock tactics.

The tactics of the French Army had now established their
superiority over the Prussian or linear tactics. But tactics, such
as have been described, require for their complete development
thoroughly trained and well-educated officers in the position of
company and battalion leaders, thoroughly trained and well-
disciplined troops, zeal, enthusiasm, skill and activity on the part
of the individual men.

Long wars sap discipline, trained men who fall from wounds
or disease are replaced by untrained or partially trained recruits,
officers of experience are killed or wounded, and their places

E 2

taken by men of less experience and intelligence, and the more ignorant and undisciplined the men are the more must the officers exert themselves and consequently the more they suffer.

These causes began to tell on the French Army, and though two great Powers of Europe,—Austria and Prussia,—had been overturned, yet war was not popular in France, the vast number of substitutes purchased deteriorated the *morale* of the raw material composing the armies, and showed that the mass of the French nation did not desire war.

The natural result of these things was that the moral value of the French armies began to deteriorate, the supply of men competent to command isolated bodies fighting, as the small French battalion had hitherto fought, is unfortunately limited. It takes years of careful study or practice to make such men, and the enormous development of the French armies fighting both in Eastern Europe, on the Danube, or in Russia, and at the same time supporting a terrible struggle in Spain, enabled men to become battalion and company leaders who were entirely unfitted for such posts, men who perhaps could move a battalion about, but who wanted that nerve and self-confidence that distinguished those who preceded them. The terrible losses sustained in war, and the consequent anticipation of the various classes of conscripts, further tended to reduce the value of the French armies by filling them with young boys, whose half-grown bodies gave way to hardship and crowded the hospitals.

Consequent on, and following from, these changes in the composition of the army, changes in tactics took place, changes which are worthy of notice. These changes were chiefly the concentration of great masses of artillery to crush a portion of the enemy's troops in position, the advance of heavy columns composed of entire divisions formed in mass of battalion columns. Such formations were chiefly adopted to keep the troops under the eye and control of superior officers, and partly to produce that feeling of confidence which the thronging together of masses of men in such columns is supposed to give.

One of the first instances of the use of these heavy columns, was Eylau, and the battle of Eylau followed not only the two campaigns of Austerlitz and Jena, but the terrible hardships the French Army endured after its hasty march across Central Europe to Poland. The difficulties of feeding the army and looking after the sick and wounded had been much increased by the enormous distance from France and the severity of the climate. On this point, Napoleon, writing to Joseph at Naples, gives an account of his army as follows:—

" The officers of the Staff have not undressed for two months, many not for four months. I, myself, have not taken off my boots for a fortnight. We are in the midst of snow and mud, without wine, brandy, or bread. We have nothing but potatoes to eat; we make long marches and counter-marches, without anything being pleasant; we have to fight with the bayonet under a tremendous fire of grape; the wounded have then to be carried back 150 miles on open sleighs. We make war with all its vigour, but with all its horrors. In the midst of such great hardships everyone is more or less sick."

Davoust's corps numbered only 15,000 men : Soult's, which had been the strongest, was reduced by dysentery and fever, to 16,000 ; that of Angereau, weakened by a great number of stragglers and marauders, who had dispersed to seek food, was only 7.000 strong.

At the battle of Eylau, Napoleon formed the whole of the Artillery, including that of the guard, in front of the general line of battle and after a heavy fire, Davoust's Corps on the right and Angereau's Corps in the centre, were ordered to advance. The latter formed each of the two divisions composing his corps in mass of close columns, and attempted to advance under a heavy fire from the Russian Artillery ; his column suffered terribly from the fire, and being charged by the Russian Cavalry, it was destroyed, losing nearly 5,000 men. Eylau, 8th Feb.,1807.

After the peace of Tilsit, the Prussian, Austrian, and Russian armies gave up the formation of troops in line, and formed their troops on the French model.

The battles of Essling and Wagram are very remarkable. They show how from the deterioration of the French Army, and the introduction of large bodies of allied troops, who were by no means eager for French success, and who in many cases were a very inferior class of soldier, Napoleon was compelled to alter the whole of his tactics, and adapt them to the raw and motley force he commanded.

At Essling, Napoleon, wishing to break the Austrian centre, which was composed of the Hohenzollern Corps of 22 battalions, formed in two lines of battalions in close columns at deploying intervals, ordered Lannes to advance with Oudinot's three divisions on Breitenlee. The advance was made in an echelon of divisions, each division being formed in mass of regimental close columns.* When the French had to retreat the divisions commanded by Tharreau and Claparède suffered terribly from the Austrian fire, because, when retreating, the Generals were afraid to deploy such raw troops ; formed in these dense masses entire companies were swept away by the Austrian fire. These divisions were composed of 16 battalions and were respectively 6,000 and 7,000 strong, or the battalions were about 400 men. Compelled to retire into the Island of Lobau by the breaking of the bridges over the Danube, which prevented ammunition coming over, the French army received large reinforcements and supplies, and throwing seven bridges over the branch of the Danube which separated them from the left bank, crossed and turned the whole of the works erected by the Austrians between the villages of Aspern and Essling. The battle of Wagram is remarkable in many points of view, especially as marking the Essling, 21st-22nd May, 1809. Wagram, 6th July, 1809.

---

* The Regiment consisted of three Battalions at this period.

decadence of French tactics, and also the cause of that decadence. It is further remarkable for the many manœuvres executed under fire, and also for the influence that the General-in-Chief exercised over every portion of a very large sphere of operations ; it is also remarkable not only for an enormous concentration of artillery fire, but also, what is by no means so well known, a great dispersion of guns. Napoleon observing that each regiment, then three battalions, required a considerable number of horses and wagons, ordered guns to be also supplied. Thus each regiment really equivalent to a British Brigade, had a small battery of artillery attached to it.*

Although this curious return to battalion guns was never completely carried out in the French Army, it was, however, to a considerable extent at the battle now under consideration.

5th July.

As the French Army issued from the small loop of the Danube where it had been formed in the closest order, after the passage, it deployed across the Marchfeldt Plain, each corps being formed in two lines of regiments in mass of battalion columns at deploying intervals—(that is, there was space between the regimental columns to deploy into line of contiguous battalion columns, not for the battalions to deploy into line), with Artillery in the intervals. After the French Army had taken up its position an attempt was made to force the passage of the little river Rusbach. The Austrians opposed this attack in line of battalion columns at deploying distance, covered by a

---

* The following is the Imperial Decree ordering this formation :—

"*In Our Imperial Camp, Schoënbrun, 9th January*, 1809.

"Napoleon, Emperor of the French, King of Italy, Protector of the Confederation of the Rhine, We have decreed and We do decree as follows :—

"Article 1.—Each regiment of infantry of the line or light infantry will have 2 guns, 3 or 4-pounders, attached to it, 3 ammunition wagons, a field forge, 1 ambulance wagon, 1 officers' wagon. These 8 carriages will, on the line of march, more with the battalion where the eagle of the regiment is.

"Article 2.—There will be further attached to each battalion 1 small-arm ammunition wagon and 1 provision wagon, which for four battalions will be 8 wagons.

"Article 3.—These 16 carriages will be looked after, horsed, and driven by a company of Regimental Artillery. This company will be commanded by a Lieutenant, a Sub-Lieutenant, 3 Serjeants, and 3 Corporals, and will be divided into 3 squads.

"The 1st squad will consist of 1 Serjeant, 1 Corporal, 20 Gunners, and 2 Artificers. The Corporal will perform the duties of Storekeeper, and will have the key of the wagons ; he will be chiefly charged with the consumption of the ammunition.

"The 2nd squad will be composed of 1 Serjeant, 1 Corporal, and 20 train soldiers, whose duty it will be to horse the 8 wagons which move with the battalion carrying the eagle.

"The 3rd squad will be the same as the 2nd squad, and will horse the 8 other wagons, the Lieutenant will command the whole, but especially the Artillery—the Sub-Lieutenant will have special charge of the train. Both these officers will be mounted.

"Article 4.—Our War Minister will fix the amount to be granted for outfit, repair, and maintenance of the wagons.

"Article 5.—Our War Minister and Our Minister of Finance are charged with the execution of this Decree. It will be sent to Our Chief of the Staff, who will order its execution for all the battalions composing the army.

"NAPOLEON."

cloud of skirmishers in front. The French attempted to advance in mass of Divisional columns. The Divisions of General Dupas, Grenier, and La Marque, which attacked the Austrian position, being so formed. These columns got into confusion at the passage of the Rusbach, which flows along the foot of the plateau of Wagram, fired into one another and were forced to fall back.

The following day, the Austrians attempted to advance 6th July. between the French left and the Danube, so as to cut them off from their bridges. Boudet's Division of Massena's corps had been left at Essling to cover this point, the other three divisions were in line of battalions at deploying intervals extending from the river towards Aderklau in the centre, where Bernadotte's corps was posted.

The Austrians, holding the plateau of Wagram as a pivot, and wheeling their right forward, drove Bernadotte back, and advanced in great force on the left.

Napoleon, whose whole plan was to crush the Austrian left, before the Archduke John, who was hourly expected with large reinforcements, could come up, directed Davoust's and Oudinot's corps to cross the Rusbach, push in between the Austrian reinforcements on the march and the Austrian left, and ascend the plateau. Finding, however, that the Austrians were making great progress on his left, and that Boudet's Division was hard pressed near Aspern, he directed the whole of Massena's corps, then in line of battalion columns at deploying intervals, to wheel into mass of columns, and take ground to its left and support Boudet, covering the movement by cavalry (vide Fig. 2, Plate IX).

This movement left a large gap in the centre of the French line which was filled first with cavalry, who checked the Austrian advance, then with the 60 guns of the guard, composed of four horse and six field batteries, and subsequently with 40 more guns drawn from the adjacent corps; these guns came up in columns of batteries and deployed into line, filling up the great gap formed by Massena's movement to the left. Under cover of the fire from these guns, Napoleon formed Macdonald's corps into a column as follows (vide Fig. 3, Plate IX):— He deployed 8 battalions into line one behind the other at short distances, 13 other battalions were formed in mass of columns on the wings with cavalry closing the hollow square so formed: in this order, this extraordinary column advanced, and penetrated the Austrian centre, although suffering terrible losses.

While this attack was being made on the centre the turning movement made by Davoust and Oudinot on the Austrian left was successful. It is curious to observe the various formations of the French divisional Generals, who were the same who had fought at Auerstadt. Friant advanced with his regiments in line of contiguous battalion columns, Morand in two lines of battalion columns at deploying intervals. Gudin advanced with his first brigade in mass of regimental columns, his second brigade in line of battalion columns. Puthod attacked in two masses of brigade columns.

The Austrians, who were formed in one line of battalions at deploying intervals, retired by alternate battalions.

General Oudinot's corps was formed in three lines, each line being composed of a division, and each division being formed in line of battalion columns at deploying intervals.

The deployment of the battalions forming the head of Macdonald's column was very peculiar, and it is difficult to see what advantage was gained by this kind of formation. Troops belonging to different battalions and different regiments were placed close behind one another, and formed a dense mass, which must have got into confusion—men of all battalions mixed up with one another—before it had gone very far. Further, the deployment of the battalions must have rendered the power of command of each regimental and battalion officer so much the less. Why the battalions were not formed in line of contiguous columns it is very difficult to say.

Similarly, Oudinot's formation of each division in line of columns behind the other offers the objection that in a short time men of the various divisions got mixed together, which would not be the case if each division had been formed in two lines of columns.

It is, however, of more especial importance to notice how the French formations had all become deeper, less dependence being placed on the individual intelligence and firmness of the soldier. Morand, Friant, and Gudin were men who had tried and knew the value of the old formation. The connection that must exist between the individual capacity of soldiers, their military training, and the tactical formation in which bodies of soldiers fight, is clearly shown by a comparison of the method of fighting adopted by Davoust's corps at Auerstadt and Wagram.

The Austrian Army had completely given up the linear tactics of Frederick the Great, and had adopted the old French tactics of battalion columns at deploying intervals covered by skirmishers. The quality of the French troops had much fallen off since Austerlitz and Jena; Napoleon himself said in comparing the Austerlitz Army with that of Wagram, that he could risk manœuvres with the former which he dare not try with the latter. In the subsequent advance in pursuit of the Austrians, in many regiments the killed and wounded amounted to 500, while the missing men, that is the maurauders, were upwards of 1,000, three-fourths of the men falling out to pillage. That Napoleon could obtain such results with such an army, larger no doubt, but far inferior to former armies he commanded, is surprising.

The attack of a position in a mass of brigade or divisional columns of eight or sixteen battalions, one behind the other, against troops occupying a position, whether those troops are deployed or in battalion columns, tends to produce the same results as those that followed Soubise's movement at Rossbach. Forming troops for an attack on an enemy in position, in such a manner appears, almost tantamount to wilfully exposing a flank perpendicularly to an enemy.

The formation of the great battery of the centre, and the introduction of regimental guns, conjoined with heavy columns, marks an era in French tactics. It being an attempt to trust to the fire of artillery alone, to demoralize and shake the enemy, and use the infantry merely to advance and occupy their position. Such tactics are those that a leader, having a raw, undisciplined army composed of various nations, would adopt, trusting to the accuracy of the fire of his artillery, and the gallantry of certain specially selected regiments who might be placed to lead the long columns. The adoption by the Austrians of the formation of battalion double company columns at deploying intervals marks the abandonment by the German Powers of the linear tactics of Frederick the Great.

Prior to the Russian Campaign, the French regiments* were increased to four and five battalions, and the formations during that campaign were more in consonance with the old French tactics than they had been at Wagram. In the advance on Moscow, Davoust, who occupied Mogilew on Bagarthion's line 1812. of retreat, drew up his corps as follows:—The 85th deployed into line with four battalions behind the bridge of Saltanowka, the 108th, composed of five battalions, formed in rear in line of columns at deploying intervals, with the 61st in echelon, on the right: in this formation, the French resisted and drove back the Russians, who advanced in heavy brigade columns.

At Moskowa, the French Army was formed in two lines, each division having one brigade in the first line, one in the second. The attack on the great redoubt was made in two lines of battalion columns at deploying intervals.

After the retreat from Russia, Prussia declared war against France. During the interval that succeeded the battle of Jena, the Prussians had abandoned the linear tactics. The King of Prussia, in an order to his army, writes as follows—

Our enemy uses his infantry to delay and sustain the fight as long as possible; he occupies villages, woods, houses, and hides himself behind hollows in the ground and in ditches. He causes us much loss with few men; when we advance against him with large bodies, then he reinforces his troops with fresh men, and if we have no fresh troops to send to the front we have to retire. We must therefore follow the example set by the enemy; we must husband our fire, feed the battle with fresh troops until the decisive moment arrives when we can make our chief attack.

On account of the great number of volunteers who are armed with rifles, skirmishers must be largely increased; the advantage these rifles possess is, they have a greater range and are more accurate. The duty of the Volunteer

* The French regiments preserved their regimental Artillery, two guns per regiment.

58

so armed is to keep the enemy at such a distance that the rifle fire shall be effective, and the smooth-bore fire ineffective. To send forward skirmishers to attack a village occupied by an enemy, with the bayonet, is to lose one of the advantages of rifles ; men so armed must be posted in woods or placed in defensive positions.

These words are very remarkable, as foreshadowing the direction which tactics of the present day are taking.

The hatred of French rule produced the same results in Prussia that the revolution had done in France, it increased largely the amount of intelligence in the ranks, or, in other words, raised the moral value of the army.

Prior to this period, the Prussians always advanced with deployed battalions occupying two long lines; after this period, 1813, they broke their lines up into brigades, acting independently for one common object, and attacked in battalion columns. At Lutzen the French were generally formed in regimental columns, and occasionally in brigade columns.

At Bautzen, Ney's corps, which made a long turning movement, advanced in columns of divisions. The French corps in front of the allies were in two lines of battalion columns at deploying intervals.

At Leipzic, Napoleon directed all the French battalions to be formed two deep instead of three deep, giving as his reason that this would largely increase the front of fire. Such changes, however, on the eve of a great battle are to be deprecated.

In 1814, during the struggle in France, the French almost always fought with battalion columns at deploying intervals, covered by skirmishers.

In Spain, whenever the French and English came into contact, and also at Waterloo, the deployed line met and invariably overcame the heavy columns of the French infantry. The tactics adopted by the English were perfectly natural, and invariably succeeded; selecting a good position, they withdrew their infantry, deployed a little behind the crest, covered the front with skirmishers, and waited the attack. The French advanced to the attack in mass of columns, sometimes a whole division so formed, each company three deep, and company behind company; these columns, covered by skirmishers, advanced, suffering severely from the English artillery; as they came near the infantry line, the latter fired into them, the flank companies lapped round the flanks of the columns, charged them in front and on both flanks, and invariably beat them back. The battle of Busaco is an admirable instance of these tactics (Plate XI).

Napier.

Crawford, in a happy mood for command, made masterly dispositions. The table land between him and the convent was sufficiently scooped to conceal the 43rd and 52nd Regiments drawn up in line ; and a quarter of a mile behind them, on higher ground and close to the convent, the German infantry appeared to be the only solid line of resistance on this part of the position. In front of the British regiments some rocks overhanging the descent furnished natural embrasures, in which Ross's guns were placed, and beyond them the Riflemen and Caçadores were placed as skirmishers, covering

PLATE XI.

BATTLE OF BUSACO

THE ATTACK OF

LOISON'S DIVISION

27th Sept. 1810

REPULSED BY THE

LIGHT (MAJOR GEN! CRAWFORD) DIV!

Scale.

0   500   1000

References.

A. Forward movement of the Light Division after having repulsed the attack made upon its original position by a part of the 6th Corps of the French Army.

a. Forward movement and deployment of Colemans Portuguese Brigade when the attack was made upon the position of the Light Division.

b. Forward movement of support made by the German Legion when the Light Division advanced driving the enemy down the hill.

c. Movement to the Right made by B! Gen! Campbell's Portuguese Brigade when the Light Division was attacked.

D. That part of the 6th French Corps d'Armée which was most immediately engaged in the attack on the Position of the Light Division.

E. The 6th French Corps d'Armée in reserve.

DANCERFIELD LITH 22 BEDFORD S? COVENT GARDEN

the slope of the mountain. While it was still dark a straggling musketry fire was heard in the deep valley, and when the light broke, three heavy masses, detached from the 6th Corps, were seen to enter the wood below and throw forward a profusion of skirmishers. One of them, under General Marchand, emerging from the dark chasm and following the main road, seemed intent to turn the right of the light Division ; a second, under Loison, made straight up the face of the mountain against the front ; the third remained in reserve, Simon's Brigade, leading Loison's attack, ascended with a wonderful alacrity, and though the light troops plied it unceasingly with musketry, and the artillery swept through it from the first to the last section, its order was never disturbed nor its speed in the least abated. Ross's guns were worked with incredible quickness, yet the range was palpably contracted every round. The enemy's shot came singing up in a sharper key ; the English skirmishers, breathless and begrimed with powder, rushed over the edge of the ascent, the artillery drew back, and the victorious cries of the French were heard within a few yards of the summit.

Crawford, standing alone on one of the rocks, had been intently watching the progress of the attack, and now with a shrill tone ordered the two regiments in reserve to charge. The next moment a horrid shout startled the French column and 1,800 British bayonets went sparkling over the brow of the hill. Yet so brave, so hardy, were the leading French, that each man of the first section raised his musket and two officers and ten men fell before them —not a Frenchman had missed his mark, they could do no more. The head of the column was violently thrown back on the rear, both flanks were over-lapped at the same moment by the English wings, then terrible discharges at five yards distance shattered the waving mass, and a long track of broken arms and bleeding carcasses marked the line of flight.

The battle of Albuera affords a still more remarkable instance of how helpless a column of great size is when attacked by steady infantry in line. At the crisis of the battle the Divisions of Generals Girard and Darrican were in mass of close columns of double companies, that is to say, the whole of these two Divisions stood right in front, one behind the other, showing a front only of two companies. They ascended the hill in this formation, and fought in this order, covered by numerous skirmishers. The fire of the English lines, three battalions deployed, threw these great masses into disorder, the ranks got broken and mixed, and they became a mob, and when an attempt was made to deploy them they were completely out of hand. The reserve sent to support them only added to the confusion.

It will be observed that at Albuera the English attacked a mass of columns on a hill; at Busaco the English were in line on a hill and were attacked by a column coming up the hill.

At Salamanca, the 3rd, Pakenham's Division, sent to attack Thomier's Division (which was moving in columns to outflank the English army in columns), advanced in quarter distance columns, deployed, and attacking in line the head of the French Division, overlapped it on both flanks, and drove it back in confusion.

At Waterloo almost the same thing occurred. The French, under Ney, attacked the English left, the whole of Ney's Corps being formed in four masses of columns of double companies. In this formation they attacked the English, these four great columns advancing in echelon, preceded by a number of skirmishers. The Divisional Artillery limbered up and followed the Divisions after they had passed the guns. The fire of the English inflicted great losses on the heavy columns, the battalions in rear being useless to support the front. The head of the 3rd echelon charged by the 42nd and 92nd in line, shaken by fire, and unable to deploy, was broken, and the English Cavalry completed the defeat of the whole mass. "The columns were far too few, they were formed in deep masses, which are always difficult to deploy under fire, when all manoeuvres are difficult, and when, if order be preserved, it is fortunate."

The Imperial Guard attacked in precisely the same formation, and with similar results, on the right of the English line.

Upon this subject General Jomini remarks :—

Jomini.

In discussion on these subjects I remark a fatal tendency in the clearest minds to reduce every system of war to absolute forms, and to cast in the same mould all the tactical formations a General may arrange, without taking into consideration localities, moral circumstances, national characteristics, or the abilities of the commanders.

I propose to use lines of small columns, especially in the attack. I never intended to make it an exclusive system especially for the defence.

The Archduke Charles told me that such small columns resisted admirably the furious charges of the French Cuirassiers under General d'Espagne.

At the Battle of Wagram the greater part of the Austrian army was so formed. Wellington, in 1823, told me that he was convinced the manner of the attack of the French upon him in column, more or less deep, was very dangerous against a solid, well-armed infantry, having confidence in its fire and well supported by artillery and cavalry. I observed that these deep columns were very different from the small columns I proposed, a formation which ensured in the attack—steadiness, force, and mobility, while deep masses are much more exposed to the ravages of artillery, and afford no greater mobility than a deployed line.

I asked the Duke of Wellington if he had not formed the foreign troops under his command in columns at Waterloo. He said, "Yes, because I could not depend upon them as well as upon the English."

I said, "This admission proves that you think a line so formed firmer, than a deployed line." He replied, "They are certainly good also; but their use must depend on the ground and the spirit of the troops. A General cannot act in the same way always."

Napoleon, in 1813, ordered his infantry to be formed in column of double companies two deep.

The Duke of Wellington admitted that the French columns at Waterloo, particularly those of the right wing, were not small battalion columns, but enormous masses of columns. The Prussians say that Ney's four divisions were formed in four columns extending from La Haye Sainte to Papelotte. I was not present, but several officers have assured me that at one time the troops were formed in columns, each column composed of an entire division, the battalions being deployed one behind the other at six paces interval.*

I conclude—

1st. That Wellington's system was certainly good for the defensive.

2nd. That the system of one battalion deployed and one in double company columns on each flank is as good for the offensive as for the defensive as used by Napoleon at the Tagliamento.

3rd. That the most skilful tactician would experience great difficulty in marching forty or fifty deployed battalions in two or three ranks over an interval of twelve to fifteen hundred yards, preserving

---

* This differs from the French accounts.

sufficient order to attack an enemy in position with any chance of success, the front all the while being played on by artillery and musketry.

I have never seen anything of the kind, and I regard it as impossible, and am convinced that such a line could not advance to the attack in sufficiently good order to have the force requisite for success.

It has been pointed out how, after the campaign of Austerlitz, the Austrians adopted the formation of double company battalion columns, and how, after the retreat from Russia, the Prussians adopted the same formation.

The battalions were at that time usually weak, from 500 to 600 men, formed in eight companies.

Subsequent to the Waterloo campaign, the Prussian Army adopted a battalion of 500 men on a peace footing, having the power to draw 500 men from the Landwehr to complete the battalion in case of war.

With the view of economising the cost of the army as much as possible, this peace battalion was formed into four companies, so that in war time each company was 250 men, or really a small battalion; thus the Prussian company column followed as a natural consequence of the small battalion double company column introduced during the revolutionary wars, and subsequently so often used with success. It was not originally a formation devised for tactical purposes, but one that arose partly from economical reasons, and partly from the old weak battalion column.

When rifles began to take the place of smooth-bore arms, many proposals were made for altering tactical formations, and the effect of these weapons was much discussed. It became apparent that infantry fire had become of much more importance than formerly, and that as the value of fire increased, so the formation of troops must be altered, to give a greater development of fire than formerly on the one hand, and greater protection to the men when advancing on the other.

The first battle after the introduction of rifles was the Alma, there the British troops were, with the exception of the 4th Division, armed with rifles, the French had certain picked corps so armed, and the Russians had very few rifles.

At the Alma the 1st, 2nd, 3rd, and light divisions advanced in mass of brigade columns (*vide* Plates XII and XIIA) from the centre of divisions, the right brigade of each division being left in front, the left brigade right in front; consequently, when the divisions were ordered to deploy, each brigade deployed outwards on the two centre or leading companies. The deployment took place at a distance of about one mile, or 1,700 yards from the Russian battery of 18 guns.

The advance in line was made on ground covered with vineyards, across a river with steep banks, and on the right through a burning village, the advance being covered by a portion of the 2nd Battalion of the Rifle Brigade as skirmishers.

The distance between the columns of the light and 2nd divisions had been over-estimated, and when the deployment took place the 95th Regiment was obliged to form in second line. The first line, therefore, consisted of 11 battalions, deployed with one doubled behind. The second line of six battalions deployed in line, and six more slightly in echelon on the right rear; an entire division, the 4th, being in reserve.

In this order the army advanced. The Russians appear to have been formed in heavy regimental columns of three and four battalions,

A reference to the sketch will show the nature of the movements. It will be seen that the 95th got split in two, a portion attacking the main battery with the right brigade of the light division, a part rejoining its proper brigade, the 2nd brigade of the 2nd division.

To pass through the village of Bourliouk, the 1st brigade of the 2nd division had to get into a column formation, and crossing the river were reformed in mass of quarter-distance columns, they then formed line obliquely to the Russian front.

The 2nd brigade of the 2nd division also wheeled into open column and took ground to its right, marching up a ravine on the advance of the 1st division.

The heavy columns of the Russians advanced and attempted to drive back the Guards and Highland brigade, but were unable to do so, one column being much maltreated by being fired into in front by the Scots Fusilier Guards, and in flank by a portion of the Grenadiers thrown back for that purpose.

But little use seems to have been made of skirmishers, the Russians seem to have trusted to their powerful artillery fire and the weight of their massive columns, and not to have used their infantry fire to any great extent.

It will be observed that each of the English lines consisted of two entire divisions deployed, or each line was about 2,400 yards in length, each division occupying about 1,200 yards. To cover this front with skirmishers there was one battalion of the Rifle Brigade. The troops in the first line were not under the same command as those in the second line, and each General of Division had a considerable length of line to supervise. The skirmishing line, first line, and supports, thus formed perfectly distinct bodies.

Moltke.
(Translated
by Crawford.)
Of late years columns have never been actually opposed to lines except in the Crimea. At the Alma the Russians, occupying a purely defensive position, had formed all their battalions into deep columns of attack. The English adopted that line formation in which they had fought in the Peninsula, and in which they had withstood the shock of Ney's veteran columns at Waterloo. They now employed the same system on the offensive and experienced all its advantages and disadvantages. Owing to the want of practice they found great difficulty in simply making a forward march of about a mile, and then required several hours to deploy into two lines, the necessary space having been under estimated by nearly 1,000 yards. The front of the first line extended two miles, and it was but two deep.

PLAN OF THE
BATTLE OF THE ALMA.
Sketched by the
Officers of Royal Engineers.

The Positions & Movements of the British Troops inserted by Col. Hamilton C.B. Cᵗ 9ᵗʰ

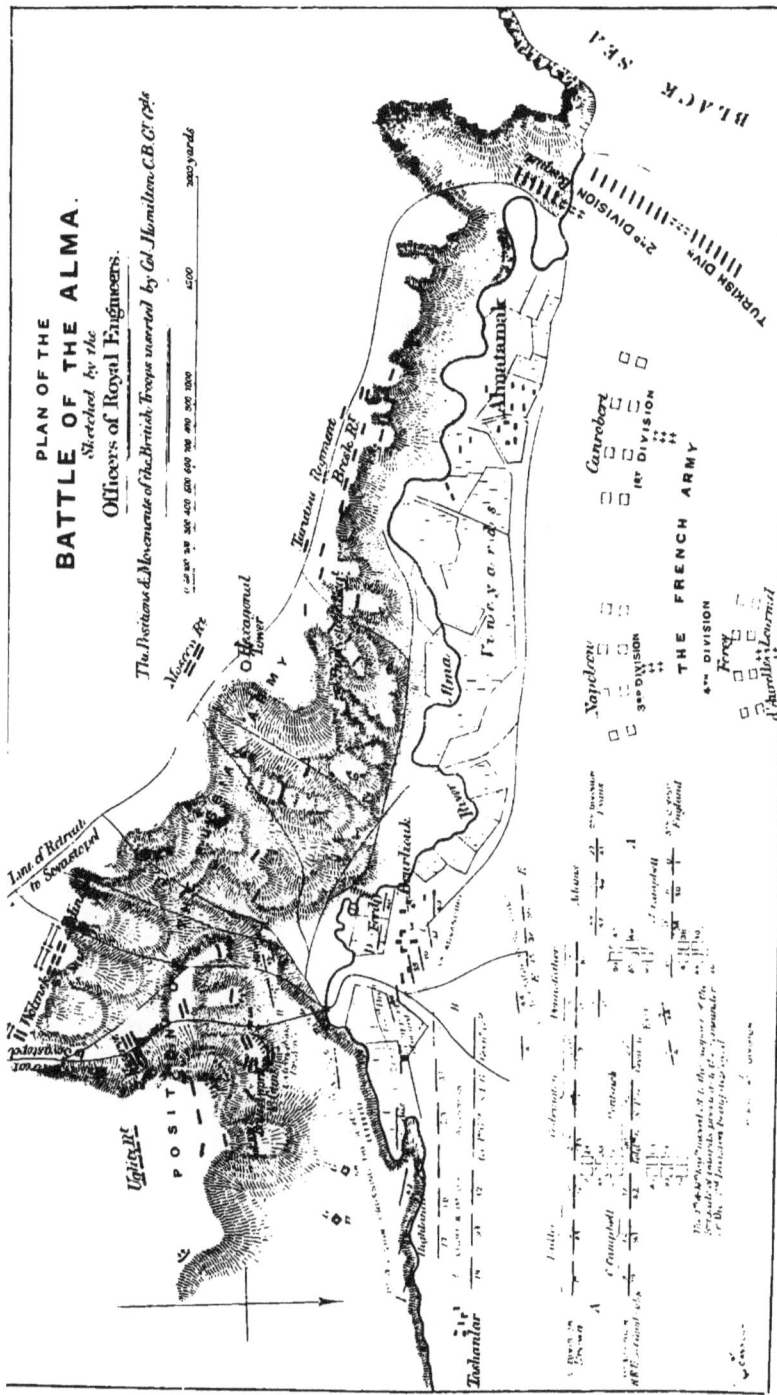

BLACK SEA

TURKISH DIV.

2ᵈ DIVISION

Alma mouth

Almatamak

THE FRENCH ARMY

Canrobert
1ˢᵗ DIVISION

Napoleon
3ᵈ DIVISION

4ᵗʰ DIVISION
Forey

Hamilton & Lourmel

Vineyards

Alma

Alma River

Mouscow Rᵈ

Ortacapaul Tower

Telegraph Monument

Break Rᵈ

ARMY

Line of Retreat
to Sevastopol

POSITION

Ulukul Rᵗ

Trahardar

DANCERFIELD. LITH. 22. BEDFORD Sᵗ COVENT GARDEN.

PLAN SHEWING 2ND PERIOD OF THE BATTLE

Section of the ground in front of 18 Gun Battery, stormed by the British Troops.

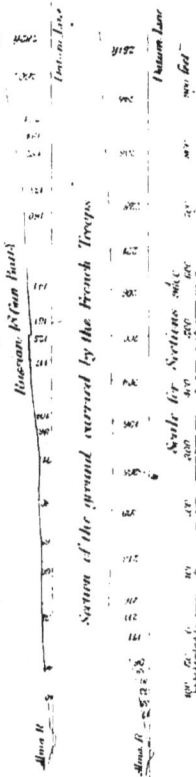

Russian 18 Gun Batt.y

Section of the ground carried by the French Troops

Scale for Sections

REFERENCE
Movements of the British Army.

A.A. English Army deployed preparatory to the attack covered by Skirmishers & 2nd Batt.n Rifle Brigade

B.B. Light & 1st Divisions advancing towards the River.

C.C. 2nd Div.n advancing Pennefather's Brigade &the 47th by the left of the Village the 41st and 49th through the Village: the 41st leading

D.D.D. 47th & 49th Regiments reforming under cover of a wall after passing the Village the 41st crosses the river by a ford

E.E.E. Campbell's Brigade 3rd Div.n & the 20th Reg.t of Eyre's Brigade advancing in support of the 2nd Division.

F.F. Codrington's Brigade with part of the 19th and 95th storming the great Battery

G.G. The 77th and 88th forming square after crossing the River on the appearance of Russian Cavalry on their left flank.

H.H. Pennefather's Brigade during the attack of the Battery by Codrington's Brigade and 19th and 95th Regiments

I.I. 1st Division crossing the river in support of Light Division.

N.B. The numbers & names below the lines show the numbers & names of the Regiments. The numbers above the lines denote the Casualties in those Regiments.

NOTE. The left bank of the river varies in height from 8 to 15 feet and is perpendicular. The right bank is not quite so high. The ground on the North side of the river slopes very gently to the bank and is nearly flat about the Villages. The ground about the Vineyards is very much broken and intersected with stone walls and fences.

REFERENCE
To Plan shewing 2nd Period of the Battle.

K.K. Minié's Brigade of Guards in reserve to attack the Battery

L.L. The Fusilier Guards and Codrington's Brigade reforming near the Battery

M. Russian Columns issuing from the Battery and advancing on Fuseliers.

N. The left Sub division of Gren.r Guards thrown back to pour a flanking fire into the advancing Columns of Russians.

O.O. Advance of Brigade of Guards and capture of the Battery

P.P. Deployment into line of 77th & 88th from square

Q.Q. Highland Brigade relieving Buller's Brigade the centre of 33rd passing through No 5 Co. of 77th.

R.R.R. Advance of the 1st Division after capture of the Battery

S.S. 4th & 44th Reg.ts of 3rd Div.n under cover of the embankment in support of Guards Brigade

T.T. Flank movement of Brandshaw's Brigade to the right on the advance of the Brigade of Guards

U.U.U. Adams's Brigade crossing the river advancing in Chasms and forming line to the left near the two guns brought up by order of Lord Raglan

W.W. 1st Division after the Action.

T.T.U. 2nd Division after the Action

Y.Y. 3rd Division after the Action.

X.X. Light Division after the Action.

The Light Cavalry were on the left flank: the 1st or Golden Brigade 4th Division was about 2 Miles in rear of the Field of battle.
The 2nd or Torrens's Brigade 4th Division was on the heights of the Bulganac and reached the bivouac of the British Army at night

DANGERFIELD, LITH. 22, BEDFORD ST COVENT GARDEN.

In this formation they had to cross a river with steep banks and to ascend a rocky slope in close proximity to a burning village, and among enclosed vineyards. Opposed to the English stood at least two-thirds of the Russian force ; so soon as the first line had ascended the opposite bank the 2nd and light divisions formed an irregular chain of skirmishers in which the men of not only different companies, but even of different regiments, got so mixed up together that it became no longer possible to fire volleys, or to make any regular movements.

The Russians felt confident of breaking this line at any point with their massive and powerful columns, but here the same thing occurred, as later on in the advance of the 1st division, and the same results were obtained everywhere

The Russian army, formed into columns composed of several battalions one behind the other, advanced with a resolute and imposing bearing, but without firing, and the thin, weak-looking line of the English held its ground and directed its firing on the dense mass at a range at which bullets could not fail to take effect.

Before they could come to close quarters or deploy, so as to deliver their own fire, the attacking columns halted and a few badly-aimed shots were fired from the centre of the leading battalion, which, of course, was the only one that could be employed.

Most of the officers, some of whom were of the highest rank, had fallen, but still for a short time the columns stood firm ; soon, however, it lost its wall-like appearance, and becoming more of the form of an irregular cloud, at length gave way slowly and unwillingly, and with a proportionally great loss.

On this occasion, according to the account of Anitschkoff, the Vladimir Regiment lost 49 officers and 1,500 men, but this is probably an exaggerated statement.

In these ever-recurring encounters of column against line the Russians lost in barely three hours 5,700 men, or nearly one-fifth of their whole force. The English, advancing in line, and keeping up their fire, twice broke into the principal intrenchment of the Russians, which was defended by 16 guns.

Their total loss did not amount to 2,000 men, and, as the loss of the French must have been very much less, this part of the engagement cost the Russians at least twice as much as it did their opponents, and mainly decided the battle. An actual hand-to-hand-fight occured at Inkermann, when the animosity was at its highest ; on this occasion a thick fog greatly facilitated the near approach of the Russian columns, and enabled them to surprise their enemy. Yet here again, they admit that they suffered enormous losses from the fire of the latter.

From these experiences, we infer that now, as heretofore, the column formation affords the best means of handling troops, both in an attack and in an actual fight.

Although the fire of artillery at long ranges forces a column into an early deployment, yet it does not prevent the approach of a line of columns so small as to be able frequently to obtain cover from the inequalities of the ground, and to advance with great rapidity.

On the other hand, that portion of an army which is to sustain the immediate attack of an enemy should receive that attack in line, for the success of the defence depends on the fire of the deployed battalions, and it is only by fully employing the fire that the possibility at last arises of deciding the issue with the bayonet. Our system of company columns, and the instruction given in our schools of musketry, are adapted to meet all these contingencies.

CHAPTER III.

INFANTRY TACTICS.

When what is meant by the word a "battle," between armies provided with the weapons now used, is considered, it cannot be denied that powerful influences must be brought to bear on men to get them to face the dangers that have to be encountered.

The animal instinct of self-preservation is strong in men as it is in other animals, and his superior knowledge and intellect point out dangers more clearly to him, and it is by appealing to moral faculties only, that men can be induced to meet the dangers that they must face in war. Thus the very intellect which gives man a clearer knowledge of approaching dangers than other animals, is that which enables him to meet and grapple with those dangers as no other animal can.

Captain May.
Tactical retro-
spect.
(Translated
by Ourry.)

He who considers that our men are all heroes because they are derived from a brave class is very considerably mistaken. If only all soldiers of their own accord would simply do their duty in battle, an army would be perfectly invincible, and would not require any tactical instruction at all.

But man has in his composition a natural desire of self-preservation, an egotism and indolence united with many sensual desires, but at the same time capable of being developed into higher qualities.

Who would ever maintain that death was indifferent to him? for in the tumult of battle danger is not so much despised as forgotten or ignored. The less the powers of the mind have attained to this freedom of development of its spiritual powers, so much the more will its sense hold sway. The man of the people who is accustomed to rough or dangerous work has rather deadened this sense by custom than conquered it.

Thus in war we often find the most extraordinary instances of the victory of small bodies of men over large forces, produced by moral causes. The most numerous army is by no means the most likely to conquer, but that which is the most highly endowed with moral and physical qualities and the best trained and disciplined. There are many different motives which tend to produce the moral power that enables men to overcome the natural instinct of self-preservation; feelings of duty, fanaticism, enthusiasm for some object or some leader, love of country, pride, with perhaps even more sordid motives, as desire for promotion, self-interest, love of plunder, or even, perhaps, in rare instances, love of actual bloodshed.

These passions, working in different proportions in different men's minds, produce that feeling which is termed bravery.

And men with these passions excited and influenced by feelings of discipline or obedience to a superior, become formidable troops.

Napier.

The possession of Badajos had become a point of personal honour with the soldiers of each nation, but the desire of glory with the British was dashed by hatred of the citizens on an old grudge ; and recent toil and hardship, with much spilling of blood, had made many incredibly savage, for these things render the noble-minded, indeed, averse to cruelty, but harden the vulgar spirit. Numbers also, like Cæsar's Centurion, who could not forget the plunder of Avaricum, were heated with the recollection of Ciudad Rodrigo and thirsted for spoil. Thus every spirit found a cause of excitement, the wondrous power of discipline bound the whole together, as with a band of iron, and in the pride of arms none doubted their might to bear down any obstacle that man could oppose to the fury.

Experience has shown that these feelings are by no means constant, that the bravest and most warlike troops have, when exposed to unexpected and unknown danger, yielded almost without a struggle.

Some of the soldiers called out "a mine." At that word such is the *Napier.* power of imagination, those troops who had not been stopped by the strong barrier, the deep ditch, the high walls, and the deadly fire of the enemy, staggered back appalled by a chimera of their own raising.*

Consequently it a leader desires to obtain great exertions from those under his orders, he must seek to work on and excite their feelings, he must carefully watch against any sudden or unexpected action of the enemy, and be careful that nothing shakes the men's confidence in themselves. The object of the leader of bodies of men, whether great or small, should be to inspire those under his command with the greatest moral force before an action, to preserve that moral power during the action, and to seek to demoralise the enemy.

There is nothing that tends to raise the moral power of an army more than education ; the consciousness of possessing superior knowledge adds greatly to the power of an army.

When, said the Prussian officers, our men came in contact with the *Stoffel.* Austrian prisoners, and on speaking to them found that they hardly knew their *(Translated* right hand from their left, there was not one who did not look on himself as a *by Home.)* god, in comparison with such ignorant beings, and this conviction increased our force tenfold.

Many Asiatic races far exceed Europeans in their contempt for death, but they are invariably defeated by the moral power that superior education, civilization, training and discipline give. Men who are accustomed to obey their superiors, look to them in danger and take their ideas from them by a kind of sympathy. If a leader be firm, clearheaded, and understands what he is about, he will, from the mere fact of there being danger, be more readily obeyed ; but if he is vacillating, uncertain in his action, and appears to doubt and hesitate in the presence of danger, his men will mistrust and disobey him.

Two Mamelooks could defeat three French horsemen, because they were *Napoleon.* better armed, better mounted, and more skilful. 100 French horse have nothing to fear from 100 Mamelooks, 300 would defeat a similar number, and 1,000 French would defeat 1,500 Mamelooks. So great is the influence of tactics, order, and the power of manœuvring.

This moral power is much increased by the feeling of security

---

* Students of Napier will recall the description of the panic that occurred to the light division in the middle of the night, when no enemy was near.

F

which men have, when they are conscious of being well-armed and know how to use their weapons. The results produced by the possession of superior arms, and being confident in their use, is well shown by the following extract, describing an event in the war of 1866.

Stoffel.
(Translated
by Home.)

Our soldiers, said General Kessel, had rarely recourse to a rapid fire, and the proof of this is the small number of rounds per man expended during the campaign ; but for many years we have lost no opportunity of convincing the men that they carried a weapon superior to that of all other European armies, and the pains we took with rifle practice only strengthened this conviction. This confidence was increased and strengthened after the first action, when they found the security afforded by an arm which loads rapidly. People speak continually of rapid fire, the expression is not correct and gives a false notion, they should rather say rapid loading. The 29th June, 1866, at Königenhof, the Prussians had a sharp action with the enemy. After the action, which took place in fields covered with high corn, Colonel Kessel went over the ground, and what was his astonishment to find five or six Austrian bodies for every Prussian. The Austrians killed had been mostly hit in the head. His men, far from firing fast, had hardly fired as many rounds as the enemy. The Austrian officers who were made prisoners said to the Prussians, our soldiers are demoralized, not by the rapidity of your fire, for we could find some means, perhaps, to counterbalance that, but because you are always ready to fire. This morning your men, like ours, were concealed in the corn ; but in this position yours could, without being seen, load their rifles easily and rapidly ; ours, on the other hand, were compelled to stand up and show themselves when they loaded, and you then took the opportunity of firing at them ; thus we had the greatest difficulty in getting our men to stand up at all, and such was their terror when they did stand up to load that their hands trembled and they could hardly put the cartridges into the barrel. Our men fear the advantage the quick and easy loading of the needle gun gives you ; it is this which demoralizes them. In action they feel themselves disarmed the greater part of the time, whereas you are always ready to fire.

In the first chapter, the advantage that constant intercourse with the men gives a company leader, has been pointed out, but if men learn to respect, follow, and trust a leader, in whose knowledge of his profession they have confidence, they will from that very intercourse learn to doubt and distrust one who is ignorant of his duty ; and no matter how personally they may like him, will never obey his orders as completely as he in whose knowledge they confide.

When actually engaged, the noise of artillery and small-arms, the effect produced by seeing killed and wounded men drop continually, causes a kind of nervous excitement ; at such moments men are peculiarly apt to be affected by trivial things, and at such moments coolness, decision, and confidence in the leader of small bodies, are of the highest importance.

The direction of great masses of troops, getting them into position, or forming them in line of battle—such movements, in short, as those by which Napoleon debouched from the Island of Loban and deployed his army on the Marchfeldt, or that by which the Prussian army, after the battle of Mars-la-Tour, facing north advanced in direct echelon of corps from its left, and pivoting on its right, changed front to the east, may be termed "Manœuvre Tactics," in contradistinction to the actual fighting, which really is often nothing more than the struggle for certain positions on the battle-field, which may be termed "Fighting Tactics." It is to the latter that the following observations bear special reference; and it must be remembered that all the operations of war, the direction given to great masses of troops, moving over large areas of country, and concentrating on certain places, termed strategy, the movement of these masses, so as to place them in line of battle, and attack certain definite points of the enemy on his flank or centre, termed manœuvre tactics, are closely linked together and are really subordinate to fighting tactics, or the actual collision of troops, by which victories alone can be won.

The first troops that come into contact with one another before battles are fought, are small detachments. Military history necessarily passes over much that is done by these small bodies; but there can be no doubt that the correct leading and handling of these small bodies conduces greatly to bringing the action of larger bodies to a successful conclusion. At the beginning of any great battle, there are numerous struggles for important points, indeed great battles are often brought about by the necessity for supporting small detachments seeking thus to obtain some advantageous ground.

Now it is undoubtedly one of the consequences that flow from the use of modern arms, that troops once actually engaged can rarely, if ever, move to the right or left. Manœuvring under fire, always difficult, may now be deemed almost impossible; once troops are really engaged it would appear that their movements must be either forward or backward. Fresh troops may be brought up from the rear to feed the fight in front, but such movements as those made by Massena at Wagram, are at the present day impossible. As an example, at the battle of the Alma, the Russian battery was stormed by a confused mass, composed of four battalions and a portion of a fifth; one of these battalions did not belong to the brigade actually employed on that part of the field and the odd portion belonged to another division.

Death loves a crowd, and in some places our soldiers were pressing so close together that when a round shot cut its way into the midst, it dealt a sure havoc. Some of the clusters into which our men had gathered were eight or ten deep, and the round shot, tearing cruelly through and through, mowed down the men.   *Kinglake.*

Moving to the attack, without being ordered to move to any given spot, almost every officer and man had instinctively proposed to himself the same goal, and that goal was the great Redoubt.

This description proves clearly that manœuvres under a heavy artillery fire, even of old guns, much more so with modern artillery backed by breach-loaders, are impossible. Who could have turned that body of men, pushing on, either to right or left? Similarly at St. Privat, the Prussian Guards, when attacking, could only advance, halt, or retire. Under the tremendous fire that modern arms enable troops acting on the defensive, to pour in, all movements to the right and left are vain. He who gives the order is the next moment down, and another pushes to the front.

It becomes therefore apparent that the actual success of operations in war, must primarily rest on the action of small bodies, good previous strategical movements, a correct formation of the order of battle, a proper selection of the points to be attacked, will make the success when obtained, of far greater importance; but the actual success must ultimately depend on the correct handling of small bodies of men. The question how a small body of men should be handled in actual fighting has now become of far greater importance than formerly. Important as affecting the individuals concerned, perhaps more so, as reacting on larger bodies. This is one of the features of modern fighting, and one which must be carefully considered. A battle under existing circumstances is a series of small battles or fights in which bodies of troops, perhaps not greater than a brigade, are engaged, and each of these bodies must be tactically complete, must work for one object, and seek to carry one point. From this fact several consequences flow which have to be carefully considered (*see* page 153).

It follows that it is difficult to assign to several battalions the same definite object of attack—house, village, wood, &c. In general it is to one and only one battalion that the duty of attacking and carrying a definite point can be entrusted.

The first thing to conduce to the proper leading or handling of a small body, is a clear understanding of the various conditions of the problem. A definite object to attain, a clear understanding of the difficulties, and the best means of meeting those difficulties, are the first essentials to success. It has been said that for the future no direct attack can possibly be made on troops occupying a position, and that all attacks must be made on the flanks; but experience shows that attacks on the flank, unless supported by a front attack, can always be met and defeated. The battle of Wagram, and perhaps still more, the counter strokes delivered at Rossbach and Salamanca, show, that unless front attacks are made at the same time, flank attacks are unlikely to succeed; consequently, however difficult and dangerous such attacks may be, yet it is requisite that they should be made, in order that the change of front, which any well-disciplined army can make if unopposed, may be prevented.

Boguslauski. (Translated by Graham.) We said that on the German side the intention was generally evident of attempting to turn the enemy. But the fight often developed itself in such a manner that, after preparing the way by artillery fire, the Germans made a vigorous attack upon the French centre, without waiting for the effect of the movement on the flanks. This mode of action has often been criticised, and attention has been called to the enormous sacrifices which it has generally entailed; but these critics forget that, when you wish to force the enemy to fight, a fairly sharp attack in front is necessary to hold him fast, otherwise he would avoid the turning movement which is meanwhile going on, either by a timely retreat, or by throwing himself upon the turning column and attacking it, whilst executing its movement.

A great deal has been written on the subject of flank attacks, and it has been pointed out that troops, when ordered to attack, invariably spread out to the flanks, thinning the line in the centre. This may be, and undoubtedly is the case, looking to the attack of brigades and divisions on isolated portions of a battle-field : but it would not be the case if the centre of the enemy's position was that from which the least fire came, or that which afforded the greatest cover or the greatest facilities for attack.* In looking at the actions of the recent war, it is absolutely requisite to bear in mind that the army which made the flank attacks was either far superior in numbers to that it attacked, or was dealing with troops (as in the latter battles) that could not manœuvre. This subject is dealt with in more detail at page 155. We must not assume that in all future battles such superiority on one side will exist. If it does exist, then the attacker may really do pretty much as he thinks fit ; attack both flanks and leave strong forces in the centre. What is meant is this—if A B (Fig. 1, Plate XIII) be an army opposed to another (C D) of equal strength, it is manifest that if C D attempts to turn the flank A of A B, it may be met either by a change of front as $A_1 B_1$, or by a counter movement $A_2 B_2$; and if a flank be thus threatened when forces are equal, the army threatening the flank either places itself in the position of being caught in a flank movement, or simply making a toilsome march to find its enemy still before it.

It is hardly safe to generalise on recent experience and lay down a rule that front attacks must not be made.

French tactics were entirely deficient of the offensive element on a large scale, by which, with inferior numbers even, you may gain great advantages if you are in a position to make rapid concentrations and advances on desired points. *Boguslauski. (Translated by Graham.)*

Partial counter-strokes on isolated points of a battle-field, such as the French made frequently and with great bravery at Sedan, can only have a momentary effect.

The attempt to turn the flank of an enemy can only be justified by a great superiority, this superiority may be either actual superiority of numbers, or it may follow from the way the lines of communication are placed. *Clausewitz.*

When an army endeavours to attack another by making a flank movement, and a corresponding change of front is made by its adversary, the manœuvring powers of the two armies come into play, and each leader watches for, and seeks to profit, by the mistakes of his opponents.

The movements of the French and British armies prior to the battle of Salamanca afford a good example of this.

The two armies were for some days in close proximity to one another, each seeking to take the other at disadvantage ; for some time the French out-marched the British, and had the best of it until Marmont made the fatal error of extending his left too much, an error which Wellington seized, and thereby won a great victory.

---

* This spreading out appears to be caused by an instinctive feeling that the surest way to avoid an enemy's fire is to equal or exceed his front.

Ultimately a flank attack becomes locally a front attack, or the troops whose flank is attacked must meet or try to meet the attack by forming a *crochet*, throwing back a portion of the line, or bringing up a reserve; in any of which cases the attack, although a flank attack as regards the general line of battle becomes locally in that place a front attack.

Thus the Prussians at Waterloo made an attack on the right flank of the French army, although it was locally a front attack on the young guard under Lobau.

Similarly, the Saxons made a flank attack at the battle of Gravelotte, on the French line of battle, although a front attack on the troops at Roncourt, forming the right of the VIth Corps, but these troops would have been in greater force had the Prussian guard not held the French fast in front by a formidable attack. It is quite true that the front formed to resist the flank attack will not be posted as strongly as the troops holding the true front; but still the attack will, in the locality where made, be a front and not a flank attack.

It is not meant that there are no circumstances under which an army of equal or inferior strength should not attempt to turn the flank of another. Such circumstances may undoubtedly occur. Fig. 2, Plate XIII, shows an ideal case. An army, A B, on the defensive has one wing strongly posted at A. It is induced to spread the other out towards B by a demonstration in its front. The attacking army, occupying the wood in its front strongly, places a portion in a state of defence, so as to check any advance of the enemy to the front, and seeing that the nature of the ground at A is such that a counter-movement in that direction cannot be easily made, moves round to that flank, preserving the line of communication towards D, and by concentrating a fire on A, the attackers are enabled to carry that point; such a case is not an unfrequent one, and the power of the breech-loader on the defensive, enabling a small body of determined men well posted to delay a large force, appears to have given increased facilities for making concentric attacks. The effect of the breech-loader in this respect appears to have introduced the greatest modification in modern fighting. *Vide* page 155.

It is desirable to review the problem as it at present stands. If a reference be made to the battle of the Alma, it must be acknowledged that the heavy guns used by the Russians compelled the British troops to deploy into line earlier than they would have done had the Russians been provided with the usual field artillery. This is exactly what rifled artillery now does, only to a greater extent; it compels troops attacking to quit their column formation (in which marches must be made) and open out sooner than formerly. Breech-loading rifles also produce effects at longer ranges than formerly. Hence the problem resolves itself into the following: A certain space of from 1,500 to 2,500 yards swept by fire, the intensity of which increases as troops

PLATE XIII.

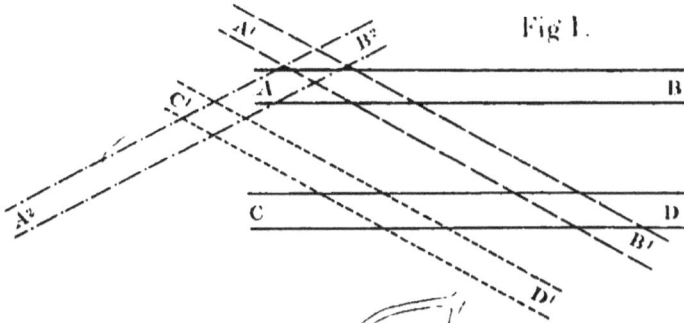

Fig 1.

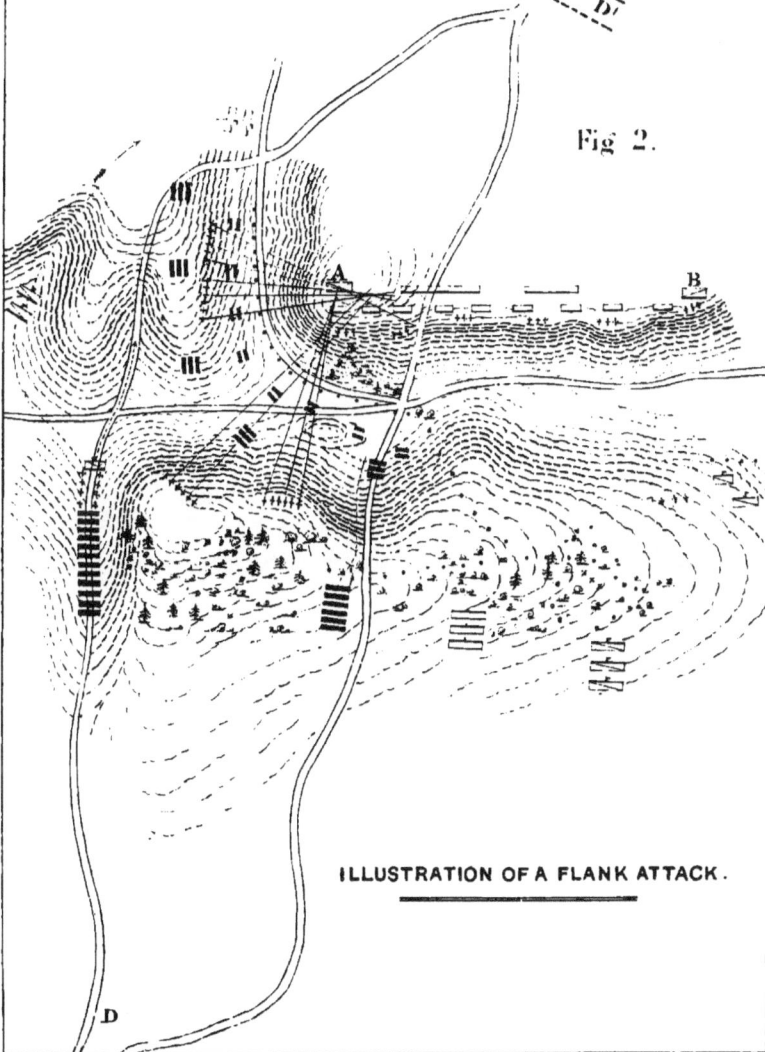

Fig 2.

ILLUSTRATION OF A FLANK ATTACK.

Dancerfield. Lith 22 Bedford St Covent Garden

approach the position from which that fire is delivered, has to be passed over. How shall it be crossed?

It is requisite here to consider what the peculiar nature of the breech-loader is, as distinguished from the muzzle-loader, assuming both to possess equal accuracy and range. It can be loaded with greater ease and rapidity, hence its defensive power is greater than that of the muzzle-loader, but if the position of men advancing to an attack be considered, it will be found that the breech-loader (from the very great ease with which it may be loaded) enables a well-sustained, well-directed fire to be kept up from troops advancing in extended order, the operation of loading being performed when lying down or in confined places with much greater ease than with the muzzle-loader. Hence the *offensive* power of the breech-loader is very much greater than that of the muzzle-loader.* The defence has gained greatly, but the offensive has, relatively speaking, gained still more, or, in other words, the superiority of the defence over the attack is not now so marked as it was with muzzle-loading rifles.

It is desirable that those who read this statement should understand *that it was until recently contested in Prussia; and it is believed that it will meet with much opposition in this country.* The following extract shows the latest, and what is believed to be the generally accepted opinion abroad.

Every improvement in firearms produces a powerful impression that the *Defensive* has thereby gained an accession of strength. This feeling is all the more natural because a purely defensive attitude in the open field was first rendered possible by the invention of firearms and of gunpowder. In earlier days battles took the form of encounters in which both sides took the offensive, or else the defender was driven to make use of fortification to an extent far surpassing the practice of the present day. [Scherff. (Translated by Graham.)]

Firearms and the Defensive are as much allied in our minds as are "*l'arme blanche*" and the Offensive; in neither case can we well imagine the allies separated. "The better the firearm, the stronger the defence" is, therefore, a maxim the justice of which has always exerted its influence upon military operations since firearms have become general, and which has not yet quite lost its power.

So it was after the Crimean War, when the rifled musket, and so after the Bohemian Campaign, when the breech-loader, respectively made their *début* in the field. In each case theory raised its voice very loudly in favor of the principle of the *Defence*, and if the book-tacticians of those days had been worthy of credit, the war of 1870–71 should have bloomed into one of the finest specimens of a war of positions, in which, as is well known, the art of *beating* gives place to that of *not being beaten.*

This theory was deduced in a curious manner from our latest war experience, each time in an indirect way, that is to say, the new arm was in both campaigns victorious in *Offence;* nevertheless we are told that it should properly give more power to the *Defence.* The fact that in 1859 the Austrian rifle did not hold its own against the smooth-bore with which the French were still mostly armed, was accounted for by the action of the French rifled cannon. But, as was still maintained, "rifled guns and muskets must infallibly make the Defensive invincible."

---

* What is meant is, *Now the fire of the assailant's infantry is of far greater importance than it ever was, the defenders suffer far more from this fire than formerly,* consequently every means must be taken, when attacking, to increase and develop that fire.

It is a remarkable and interesting fact that at a time when these defensive theories had obtained pretty general approval, both in literature and even in other ways, the Austrians in 1866 would have nothing to say to them, and setting at naught the dictates of nature and tradition, rushed almost fanatically into the *Offensive*—to be everywhere beaten ; and that when the tables were turned and many voices were raised against that one-sided theory to reject it, the French in 1870 went upon the opposite tack, and like the Austrians, acting contrary to their nature and traditions, servilely followed a Defensive system—to be in like manner everywhere beaten !

These striking contradictions show plainly enough that the formula of the "certain shot" is not infallible, when we have to decide upon the absolute merit of this or that tactical formation.

It must be confessed that the critics recovered themselves pretty soon from the first panic, so to say, which was created by the general introduction of rifled arms, and resting upon the experiences of 1859, they met the theory of the absolute *Defensive* with the argument that it was not so much the accuracy of the new arms as their low trajectory, which rendered them such valuable allies to the Defence. With regard to breech-loaders, it was asserted even before 1866 that their rapidity of fire would serve the assailant at least as well as it would the defender.

In fact, the more portable, moveable, handy, and quick-firing a gun is, so much the more suited is it to the attacking party which is compelled to be constantly in movement, a condition unfavourable to the use of firearms. The development of Artillery from the gun of position to its present degree of perfection was a consequence of this conviction, just as the rapid-firing infantry of Frederick the Great, acting as it did on the offensive, was an example of its justice.

Thus a very decided opposition to the defensive hobby grew out of purely technical considerations. Is it necessary to enlarge upon the decisive question of *morale ?*

We think not, after 1870, after 1866, after the whole of Prussia's history. Indeed it may appear superfluous to moot the question at all at the present day, and in our country ! The theory of the superiority of the *Offensive* is for the time being so firmly rooted that a reaction is not much to be feared.

And yet even with us, the time of the doubters has not long passed away ; a single instance of failure on the part of the *Offensive*—always a possible event—would again wake up these theorists, who in accordance with their critical German nature, would once more produce their coldly-reasoned "*demonstrations founded upon the nature of the arm.*"

Reverting to the battle of the Alma, the British advanced firing, and it is quite evident that such a fire must be heavier and more deadly from an advancing body of men armed with breech-loaders, than from a similar body armed with muzzle-loaders ; and further, that the time a given number of men advancing across a given space take to discharge a given number of bullets, must be much less than formerly, or in other words a body of men armed with breech-loaders, and advancing to attack a position defended by men similarly armed, will inflict greater loss, although suffering more, than if both were armed with muzzle-loaders.* This is the chief peculiarity of the breech-loader, and to it must be subordinated the formation of the troops ; or, whatever formation be adopted, it must be such as will enable the soldier to use his weapon, loading and firing as he moves ; at the same time that by the formation adopted the undoubted power of the breech-loader on the defensive may be

---

* *Vide* the description of the action at Königenhof, page 66, as an illustration.

reduced, that is to say, the offensive power of the weapon must be developed, while at the same time every means must be adopted to reduce its destructive effects. The following description brings this point out clearly :—

The intensely effective and continuing rolling fire of the Chassepôt made it clear to all our commanders that a strong deployment of skirmishers was absolutely necessary, so as to answer the enemy's fire in an effective manner, not to expose too strong supports to its effects, and at the same time to prepare the way for our attack.

Boguslauski. (Translated by Graham.)

Or, in other words, the power of the breech-loader as an offensive weapon had to be brought into play.

The French fire was at times so murderous that it was impossible to bring up detachments in close order near, that is to say, within 100 to 150 paces of the skirmishers, or to keep them in close order if they were there. There was, therefore, the choice of either keeping further back, or of extending the supports.

The latter course was followed all the more frequently, because the line of skirmishers soon required strengthening in different parts, and gaps caused by the enemy's fire required filling up. In broken ground affording more cover, it was often possible to bring the supports nearer to the skirmishers, but in moving up they frequently scattered, in consequence of the necessarily cautious nature of their advance, partly extending and joining the skirmishers.

What contributed to this was that it was very difficult for officers to keep their men together, because the noise of a close conflict between breech-loader and breech-loader often drowns the sound of the human voice, so that a great part of the men cannot hear the word of command, and the officer can only influence by his example and conduct, and this leads him also to the front, even up to the line of skirmishers. Meanwhile the German line of skirmishers was approaching the enemy by a succession of rushes. This was done either by taking advantage of cover, or else they would advance, throw themselves down, and then run on again.

Much address was displayed in this manœuvre. In this manner the line of skirmishers got part to within 400 paces, part to within 150 to 300 paces of the enemy, according to the nature of the ground, seldom without suffering great and inevitable loss.

This advance would occasion separate strokes and counter-strokes which naturally caused the tide of battle to roll backwards and forwards. At this period the fight would attain its highest pitch of intensity. The fire of the breech-loaders on both sides resounded unceasingly, and the work of commanding became more and more difficult. These were doubtless the right tactics, and suited to the present arms, because one should use the offensive power of the needle gun before attacking an enemy in position.

Neither French nor German ever succeeded in bringing troops in close order into front line, in a fight such as that described, or in pushing battalions or companies forward to fire volleys. If fresh detachments came up from the rear during a stationary musketry fight, whether to strengthen the line of fire or made an attack, it was necessary to double them up with the old skirmishers, because closing the latter to a flank was usually not to be thought of; thus men of many different battalions and regiments were intermingled.

To attain victory, it is requisite to be the strongest at a given moment on a given point. In order that troops attacking may have and utilise the maximum amount of force, they must be guaranteed—

Scherff.

1. The greatest amount of mobility, which alone allows offensive movements to be undertaken.
2. The greatest amount of protection from the enemy's fire.
3. The most efficient use of their own fire.

The masses used in the Napoleonic wars satisfied, more or less, the conditions above referred to, and so long as arms were not improved, the individual order was only an accessory; improved arms made that order daily more important. 1859 placed it on a level with the compact or massive order. 1870–71 gave it the superiority. Everywhere in 1870 the real assault of positions was with swarms of skirmishers followed more or less closely with troops in line or column. The individual order has now become the only practical means for infantry fighting.

When skirmishing with muzzle-loading rifles, the rule was that two men, a file, should act together, one man being always loaded. This rule was based on perfectly correct principles; the time it took to load rendered it absolutely requisite that the soldier pushed out in front should have a support and protection while he loaded; this protection was afforded to him by the fact that two men acted together. With a weapon that, practically speaking, is always loaded, this is not now required. With a weapon that loads and fires as fast as the breech-loader, the same amount of fire may be obtained from a far smaller number of men than formerly. If one man with a breech-loader can load and fire four times as fast as formerly, the effect he can produce is, in *some* respects, four times as great as formerly.

This is not the case, however, in all respects, for there is a certain moral security given by the close contact of men with one another; and also men working close together excite one another, and a certain amount of emulation ensues. Hence it follows that a line of skirmishers may now be thinner than formerly, and yet produce a greater effect, and the thinner the line the less likely is there to be great loss, fewer objects being exposed to be hit on the ground swept by fire.

Thus it follows, not only that greater use must be made of skirmishers, and that a smaller number of skirmishers may produce a greater effect than formerly; but it also follows that the chief portion of the fighting must be done by the men fighting in extended not close order. It will be seen hereafter that although a thinner line of skirmishers than that formerly used may produce greater effect, yet it is requisite that the skirmishing line should be thicker not thinner, in order that the offensive power of the weapon may be fully developed.

The expression "loose order" has been often employed to describe the mode of attack, but the expression is an inaccurate one. The attack is not loose, which rather means a careless haphazard action, but it is the individual action of the soldier fighting in extended lines; the real facts being that such a method of fighting demands not only greater individual exertion and intelligence, but far higher and more complete instruction on the part both of officers and men. In the chapter on the history of tactics it has been shown how, as the moral value of the French army diminished, their formations became more compact and denser from the necessity of keeping the men more immediately under the supervision of the superior officers. The converse of this is equally true, that to enable men to fight in individual order, not only must the captains and subalterns be better trained, but also the privates themselves.

The word " loose " is one that has a very dangerous application, its use should be carefully avoided. Continually the expressions are used, " No troops can live under fire unless in " *loose* order," and " troops must attack in *loose* swarms of " skirmishers," and the celebrated instance of the slaughter of the Prussian Guard at St. Privat is quoted, as affording clear proof that troops must advance in loose order. Further, the word " loose " gives an impression to young officers that any kind or description of drill is good enough, and that neither thought, care, nor study are required. Now, the moment when troops are hotly engaged, and suffering much from fire, is the very time that looseness, or anything like irregularity, must be as much as possible avoided ; then is the time that discipline and training enable men to obey and follow their leaders ; to introduce anything that savours of irregularity at such a time is more than dangerous. If discipline, and the system of acting under control, is to fail at the supreme moment, *cui bono*, why have it all ? The passage in the Duke of Wurtemberg's pamphlet, descriptive of the attack at St. Privat, is well worthy of study.

During the action at St. Marie aux Chênes, Prince Hohenlohe, commanding the Artillery of the Guard, had collected 84 guns opposite St. Privat, and cannonaded the French position with great effect, at first at 2,640 paces and afterwards at 2,000 paces. *About five o'clock in the afternoon the Commander of the Guard considered the enemy to be sufficiently shaken for him to risk an assault across the open and gently ascending ground,* [Duke of Wurtemburg. (Translated by Robinson.)]

The 4th Brigade of the Guard (Kessel) first moved forward from Habonville in the direction of St. Privat in line of columns in two lines, with skirmishers thrown out in front ; and a quarter of an hour later the advance of the 1st Division of the Guard (Pape) commenced in the same formation from St. Marie aux Chênes, distant about 2,640 paces from the main French position. Habonville is about 3,960 paces, therefore the three Brigades came about the same time within the effective reach of the enemy's fire. The front of attack including little more than 2,000 paces, so that there were about 10 men to the pace : this was, however, the closest formation of attack employed by the Prussians in the campaign.

The effect of the enemy's fire, even at a distance of more than 1,500 paces, was so murderous, that according to the accounts received nearly 6,000 men fell in 10 minutes, and the advance had to be immediately discontinued.

The attack in line of columns over open ground was, in spite of the final success of this one, marked out as an impossibility, and a useless loss of men, and definitely rejected.

Now what does this amount to ? First, the words italicised show a clear error of judgment. Troops who could pour in such a fire as the French infantry did, could not have been " sufficiently shaken" to render it justifiable "to risk an assault " over such a glacis as the ground in front of St. Privat. Next, if a little consideration is given to the moral circumstances attending this attack, it will be found that the Prussian Guard is a peculiar body of men selected from all Prussia, not a local force as the other corps are ; that it includes the chief aristocracy of the country, and, like the Guard of other nations, has certain privileges, real or imaginary. Now there had been four considerable actions with the French during the previous 14 days, the battles of Woerth, Spicheren, Borny, and the very bloody contest at Mars-la-Tour but two days previously.

At none of these actions had the Guard been engaged. Perhaps the Army did not expect more from the Guard than from other corps, but the Guard most certainly did, and a certain feeling of regret that they had not been engaged, undoubtedly was felt throughout this body.

The Prussians, on the day of Gravelotte, were pivoting on their right, and circling their left round. On the right flank (Von Steinmetz) the first attacks were made by the 33rd Fusiliers (Von Weltzien's Division), on the Bois de Vaux, about 1.30 p.m., at the same time a brigade passed to the north of Gravelotte to attack the Bois de Genevaux. Frossard's foremost detachments were driven in at 2 o'clock, and a very severe fight raged along the line from Gravelotte towards Amanvilliers. Now, while all this was passing, the Guard were marching, hearing the noise of the battle, perhaps getting a stray shot now and then; the feelings of these men, wrought up as they must have been to the greatest tension on arriving about 5 o'clock opposite their enemy at St. Privat may be imagined. Hence we conceive that the earnest desire to be in the fight and doing; the strong feeling that the mere weight of such splendid troops would bear all opposition down, joined perhaps to strong feelings of exultation at their own recent victories, and a certain amount of contempt for their enemy, may have carried even the leaders away, and produced a premature attack, which this confessedly was, an attack in a formation well adapted for a rapid advance to seize a position feebly held by demoralized troops, but not equally well adapted to attack a position determinedly defended.

Upon this subject, General Walker writes :—

General Walker, C.B.

I repeat, with even more emphasis than when I made the same statement at the United Service Institution, that the dense formation of the attacking troops was but *one* of the causes which led to the loss of between 6,000 to 7,000 officers and men of the Prussian Guard that day. The arguments, based on a false appreciation of the causes of that failure, have led to very erroneous and hurtful conclusions, and as one of the most earnest advocates for improvement in infantry formations and modes of attack, I am anxious at the same time to combat the wild passion for disorder which thoughtless men consider to be the only alternative and substitute for too great rigidity of formation.

The fact that the denseness of the formation (battalion columns) was not the only cause, is clearly shown by the following Prussian army order on the subject, issued three days after: and it should be clearly understood that battalion columns were not the proper Prussian formation for such attacks, but company columns, or columns composed of one-fourth of a battalion.

ARMY ORDER.

I have gathered from the reports on the detail of the recent victorious combats that the serious losses arose partly from the fact that the troops frequently advanced to the assault in battalion columns following too closely on their skirmishers.

I therefore point out the fact that the assault on a hostile position must in the first instance be sufficiently prepared by the artillery and a well-directed fire of skirmishers ; and that in the infrequent cases when turning or outflanking the enemy is not possible, and a frontal attack over open ground is therefore absolutely necessary, the formation of company columns and half battalions, as laid down by regulation and applied on the practice ground, must be employed.

I bestow the fullest acknowledgment on the gallant forwardness of the infantry, to whom hitherto nothing has been too difficult, but expect from the intelligence of the officers, that they will be able, by taking closer advantage of the ground, by a more thorough preparation for the attack, and by the employment of suitable formations, to obtain in future the same results with inferior losses.

(Signed)   WILLIAM.

Head-Quarters, Pont à Mousson,
  21st August, 1870, 11 *a.m.*

In this order there is no counselling of loose formation, no urging of wild swarms of skirmishers out of hand, but there is a word of warning against premature attack, against pushing battalion columns on the top of skirmishers, and a gentle admonition to adhere to the company column, the proper recognised Prussian formation for such attacks. Further, the necessity of making all formations subservient to the ground, and the necessity of rapidly taking the formation suitable to the ground, are clearly pointed out.

And the king points out that the intelligence of the individual officers must be exercised : within certain limits, each man must have individual freedom, it must be not a careless, reckless, loose order of attack, but a careful "individual" order of attack.

It cannot be too often repeated that words convey ideas, and ideas govern actions. If officers think and speak of loose order of fighting, the whole bonds of union that bind armed bodies of men together, may become relaxed, and the whole machine incapable of putting out its force when called on. Modern fighting is not *loose* although it may be *individual.*

We must contrast the expressions "individual" with that of "close" order. We mean by the latter that formation of troops when each man has a fixed place which he must not leave, while by the former we mean a formation that assigns each man his place only in a general way, leaving to the man a latitude within certain limits on his own initiative to modify or alter it. *Scherff.*

Perhaps one of the most common and unsuspected causes of failure in such attacks as that made on St. Privat by the Prussian Guard is to be found in the fact that troops are often trained in confined positions, in barrack squares, or in small spaces, the effect of which is that the proper distance between the supports, main body, and skirmishers is not given, but is reduced to suit the ground ; the result being that in action men eager to do what is right, do what they have always seen done, they act at such moments of intense excitement from instinct more than from reason, and they do what they have done in peace, forgetting that they are no longer confined by ground. This is but another instance of the necessity of training men on large areas.

A further source of failure arises from the fact that at instructional drill the long periods required for preparing the attack are rarely given; a manœuvre, especially if it be one on a large scale, is looked on too much as a show, too little as instruction, and the time spent in the preparation of attack in peace time is rarely one-fourth of what it is in reality ; thus the tendency on the part of men to act by instinct rather than reason induces premature attacks.

Habits of action become instinctive : some men may have undoubtedly peculiar gifts and powers in certain directions. But there is no talent or gift required in doing things that are done each day, because men do these things so continually that the habit becomes second nature, becomes a portion of the men themselves. This peculiarity of human nature to be governed by habit should be enlisted as an aid to the man on the field of battle; far too often, from the circumstances we have tried to describe, it is allowed to act against the successful result rather than in its favour.

But no matter how devoted a skirmishing line may be, and no matter how gallantly it may be led, it will in a short time expend its force.

It appears that in action, any body of troops pushed out to the front, has stored up in it a certain amount of energy, *vis viva*, which will carry it forward over a certain space, be it great or small. This energy is due to various causes, either the personal power of the leader, or the inherent pluck of the men; but once that distance has been reached, once its energy has been expended, it can do little more; it has a tendency to halt, consider it has done enough, and look less to the front than the supports behind it.

This is the moment when those supports must be forthcoming; they can see their own men in front, so far as they have gone the supports can go; and the mere natural emulation of men will carry both on further. Thus it is that the fight in the front must be incessantly fed from the rear; and hence it follows that the troops first pushed on must be composed of a portion of the same body in rear; gradually working on in this way, men may reach a point sufficiently near the enemy to make their fire tell heavily on him; and what is of still greater importance, be so close that any attempt at a change of position on his part, which means a diminution of fire, will enable a forward movement to be made, or a greater number of the supports in a closer formation, to be brought up.

The front, therefore, of all attacks must not only be covered now as formerly by skirmishers to feel the way and drive back the enemy's skirmishers, but the fight must be fed by continuous waves of skirmishers pushing on in advance of one another, and so passing over the ground swept by fire.

Yet the tendency to converge towards the Redoubt, as this goal had so closely compressed the assailing mass that its front now hardly outflanked the parapet,* and all the assailants of the Redoubt were either within the work or closely gathered round it. They were, perhaps, 2,000 men; our soldiers were well inclined to rest and make themselves at home. But they were only a crowd; and they, all of them, wise and simple, now began to learn in the great school of action that the most brilliant achievements of a disordered mass of soldiers require the speedy support of formed troops; then, as it is said, for the first time the men cast back a look towards the quarter from which they might hope to see supports advancing. `Kinglake.`

Although troops must now fight in extended order,—and for the future, on such lines of closed skirmishers or opened files the brunt of fighting must fall; and although small bodies of men, perhaps rarely exceeding a brigade, often perhaps a battalion, must attack definite positions or places, yet it is absolutely requisite that the number of men sent forward must not be sent in driblets. If a handful of men be pushed on, then another handful, when the first is beginning to be demoralized or losing many men, it will simply subject the troops attacking in such a fashion to be beaten in detail. Such a system is one that courts disaster. It must invariably be borne in mind that whatever attack is determined on should be made with a force sufficient to give a reasonable hope of success, except indeed in cases where false attacks or demonstrations for a particular object have to be made. The first consideration in all military actions is success. A successful attack always saves life, for the men making it have to cross the shot-swept zone only *once*. If beaten they must cross it *twice*, once in advance and again when retreating.† Hence the losses caused by employing too small a force to attack will really be far greater than by employing a sufficient number, and these losses will not be confined to the actual loss in killed and wounded of the actual attackers, but will infallibly entail demoralization on the army generally, perhaps a lavish expenditure of life in the future to recover the lost ground.

Sir John Burgoyne, speaking of the assault of Burgos, says:—

When the ladders were placed, an officer and 20 men were to advance from the cover and mount them, and when they were well up, 20 more were to follow them, and so on, until the 200 men were in. By this mode the first small party has in fact taken the work by itself without the encouragement of a close and strong support: and if they do not succeed, the next party, who coolly from behind their cover see them bayonetted, are valiantly to jump up, and proceed to be served in the same way; the argument in its favour was, "Why expose more men that can ascend the ladders, or enter the work at `Field-Marshal Sir John Burgoyne.`

---

* About 300 yards.
† This fact cannot be too closely impressed on men; *once well under fire it is much safer to go forward than backward.*

" one time, when by this mode the support is ordered to be up in time, to
" follow the tail of the preceding party close ?"

My answer is because large bodies encourage one another, and carry with
them the confidence of success ; because there is more chance of a few brave
men to lead.

The miserable doubting unmilitary policy of small storming parties, on
the plea that, " if we fail we can't lose many men," causes more mischief, loss,
and disgrace than any other proceeding in war.

These words, though referring to assaulting parties at sieges,
are just as true of all attacking parties. The point is to determine of how many men " a sufficient number" really consists?

The answer to this is to be found by considering that the
attacking force must move over rough ground at a rapid pace,
and must be able to load and to keep up a continuous fire. Can
this be done with a deployed line? Assume a battalion 800
strong in line, advancing for 250 or 300 yards over rough
ground, how many men would be squeezed out of the ranks,
doubled behind one another, or placed in such situation that
they could only fire in the air? In the advance of the Light
Division on the 16-gun battery at the Alma, the men were eight
and ten deep, the leading men only could fire, and thus the
attackers were deprived of a large number of rifles, and those
that could be used were not so efficiently used as they might
have been if there had been more room. The subject is very
clearly dealt with in the following extract :—

Scherff.

Experience has demonstrated that the principle hitherto considered
important of reinforcing a line of skirmishers only little by little, is more
dangerous, and costs more men, than the use of a sufficient force from the
moment the troops are within easy range.

The moment this new rule is substituted for the old one, the question
arises, " What is meant by a sufficient force ?" Taking into consideration the
increase of the defensive power, we may reply, *as many men as the ground will
permit to be placed in line, so that they may use their weapons efficiently.* In
order that the preparation for the attack may be really efficacious, that is to
say, that it may shatter the enemy both physically and morally, the chief
condition is that it should continue uninterruptedly from the beginning to the
end ; if the final assault follows the cessation of fire only after the lapse of
some time, the fire may have materially weakened the defenders, but as for
moral effect, in so far as good troops are concerned, it will have died out, and
on the other hand, the moment the attacking fire ceases, either really or apparently, the spirits of the defenders rise.

Now, with the firearms in use, the action of each man may be considered
to be continuous, and since each man, to use his rifle freely, requires one yard
and a half of space, it follows that the maximum number of men, that can be
placed in the line of skirmishers, should not exceed one man per yard and a
half. At this period of the action there is nothing to be considered but the
development of fire. Every man in the skirmisher line who on account of a
want of space cannot take his share of the firing is absolutely hurtful, at the
same time that he increases uselessly the chances of loss.

It is desirable to determine what ought to be the extent of the front of
attack of a given number of men. We have already pointed out that it is
desirable to continue the preparatory fire uninterruptedly from the moment it
begins until the moment for the actual assault arrives, it becomes requisite to
fix the exact time when the preparatory fire should begin. The object of
preparing the attack is to shatter the enemy ; the moment when this preparation can begin, must be that when the attacking troops will be sufficiently

near to make their fire tell heavily. With the arms at present used this distance will be when the attackers are about* 400 to 200 yards from the place where the line is to be pierced. It follows from human nature itself that the best troops in the world can sustain such a heavy and uninterrupted fire for only a few minutes, the defenders being assumed as good troops, and as well armed as the attackers. Leaving out of consideration the actual losses, which rarely bear any proportion to the number of rounds fired, the effect on the nerves is such that in a short time some decisive action must follow so great excitement.

As regards the attackers, although it must be conceded that the defenders, despite the advantage of the situation, have been preparing the attack, have less moral power than the attackers, and are more disposed to retire, yet they cannot do so until after the lapse of some short time during which some impulse may carry the attackers (skirmishing line) forward or backward.

In either case the main body, whose function it is to carry the position, must arrive exactly at the moment, or rather a little before, to support the skirmishing line, who without this support would be quite incapable of making the final assault.

It is evident that the main body is naturally interested in not closing on the skirmishing line, who have been preparing the attack, that is to say, of not entering into the zone where they will experience heavy losses, until the fire of the skirmishing line has acted for a certain time, a length of time which, if possible, ought to be prolonged until the moment when the crisis arrives.

Until that moment the main body should remain as much as possible out of the zone rendered dangerous by the enemy's fire. This main body must then fulfil two distinct and contradictory conditions, and from an examination of these conditions we may deduce the distance which should exist between the skirmishing or preparatory line, and the troops who have to complete the business.

Experience has shown during the recent war that, when there is a rapid fire on both sides, such as we have just described, that it cannot be prolonged more than five minutes before a crisis arrives. Hence we arrive at the conclusion that the main body must not be further from the skirmish or preparatory line at the moment it begins to act than about 500 yards. If the ground is perfectly open, the main body can only reach this distance about the time that the quick fire begins in front of it.

But then, although even if it follows the line of skirmishers at 300 yards distance, it is requisite to have an intermediate line between it and the skirmisher line, which, in accordance with the principles we have just enunciated, should be extended at one yard to a yard and a half intervals. Further, a line of skirmishers advancing, as we have supposed, cannot advance to effective range without suffering losses, perhaps very heavy losses ; if then the preparatory fire is to be continued without interruption, there must be at hand a support with which to fill up the gaps.

According as the ground offers shelter, more or less good, to approach the enemy, this support or intermediate line ought to be stronger or weaker ; it may, however, be admitted, as a practicable principle which is justified by experience, and accepted in all theories, that the support should vary from one-half to the whole number of the skirmishers. Now, in addition to these two bodies, which from the beginning we may consider as acting on the offensive, and which really both serve only to prepare the attack, it is absolutely requisite to have a third force or main body at least equal to the other two.

From the digression we have made to describe the various phases of the attack, we are again led to our first question, "What is to determine the extent of front to a fixed number of men ?"

The distance may be arrived at as follows : one-half or two-thirds of the whole force as main body, and one-half or one-third as preparing the attack,

---

* This is with needle guns of course. The distance with an improved rifle would perhaps be greater.

G

one-half of the last number spaced at one yard to one and a half yards, will give the required front.

Or, in other words : if we take a battalion of 1,000 men, it will, cadres and absent men being deducted, put 800 rifles on parade. Hence the normal front of such a battalion in open ground should not exceed 300 yards ; there being 200 rifles to prepare the attack, 200 in support, to fill up gaps, and 400 as the main body.

It is very desirable that the reason why extended order offers a protection from *aimed* fire should be clearly understood, and the distinction in this respect between close and individual order as regards aimed fire is clearly put in the following extract :—

Col. Gawler

Because the more open order invites the more direct or even divergent fire, *i.e.*, less intense fire ; the close order, as the men form an object, invites the convergent or more intense fire. Thus, if 100 men in line are firing at 25 advancing towards them, the fire will be *convergent or intense* if the 25 are formed in a body ; but if the latter extend themselves, say four paces, they will occupy a front rather wider than the enemy. They then offer no special attraction, and therefore invite a direct or less intense fire. One great safeguard for those exposed to aimed fire is to equal the enemy's front.

"It has been said that the troops first pushed on must be composed of a portion of the same tactical body as those immediately in rear." Page 78.

This immediately brings up the question, What is meant by "lines"? It has been seen that Frederick formed his army in two lines, each three deep, and that at the Alma the English advanced in two lines, two deep, with a reserve.

From a two-deep line it is impossible to feed a fight or support the skirmishers, for a two-deep line is little more than a compressed line of skirmishers. Hence the word "first line," "second line," must not be taken as meaning either a line of skirmishers or two-deep lines, but the troops actually fighting in the front line ; and if a brigade of three battalions be taken as an example, one battalion skirmishers, one in support, in two columns of half battalions, and one again behind it at a further distance, collectively the whole form the first line, the General Officer's command extending from front to rear, over a far greater extent of ground than formerly.

Although from the fact that the breech-loader enables the same amount of fire to be procured from a much smaller number of men than formerly, or in other words, enables a smaller number of men to occupy a given space than formerly, it may follow that the front occupied by a brigade of three battalions, formed in *some such way* as described above, may be quite as great as formerly.*

The second line of troops may be formed, until required, in almost any formation that may be best suited for the ground and most convenient. The action of the General Officer Commanding a Brigade or Division can no longer be that of accom-

* Such a method of formation is by no means suggested as a good one, it is only intended as an illustration of a change.

panying a line in its advance, which he can from its length hardly supervise; he must watch the action of the troops in front, and support them by ordering up fresh men from the rear. Continually it has been shown, that ground is won to the front by some company officer who has taken advantage of the folds of the ground, and pushed up where he is sheltered from fire, or where the artillery and rifle fire has told heavily and consequently reduced the number of defenders and shaken their morale, and has so found an opening somehow where he can enter.

Generally the skirmishers, the moment they saw that a superiority was gained on a certain point, rushed to it from all directions, and concentrated their fire on it. *Militärische Gedanken und Betrachtungen.*

Watching for these movements the Brigade Commander can push up fresh troops to keep the ground already won, and support the troops who have won it.

The more the different parts of an army have a disposition to fight separately the greater will be the strength of hand required to hold them together and arrange matters so that all the unchained power, instead of following their own ideas eccentrically and without plan, shall finally work towards a point fixed upon by the eye of the Commander. A mere mechanical leading will produce no result, because the leader would then not understand how to use his precious instrument; a faulty leading is still worse, for it would ruin it. *Tactical retrospect. Captain May. (Translated by Ouvry.)*

This loose individual mode of attack requires a counterpoise which must be twofold; the first and most important is the Commander-in-Chief, who remains out of the range of fire. He watches over and has by him a strong reserve to reinforce the front line, when requisite. The other counterpoise is the officer commanding the front line, whose essential duty it is to execute all necessary movements in the same.

The necessity of working the first or fighting line, so that it shall have in itself and under its own commander, a body which may serve as a support and reserve, is all the more requisite, as any sudden action on the part of the enemy, the sudden advance of troops of all arms, the bringing up of a reserve, or some unexpected action on the flanks, may suddenly drive the fighting line back, if it be not at once supported; if the commander has nothing in hand to steady the fight, the support from the second line can hardly arrive in time; hurrying up from the rear it can hardly re-establish, although it may renew the fight, and the probability is that what has been won already will be lost and have to be again fought for: fortunate if the retiring line does not throw the advancing troops into confusion.

Many are the instances in war when a part of the defensive position of an army, ranged on a long line, has been for the moment carried; but the success not being properly followed by support, or the defenders having brought up reserves more quickly than the assailants, the latter have been cast out again perhaps with heavy loss. Such was the fate of the advance of Junot's corps at Busaco, after it had fairly penetrated the English position on the west of the hill. No less unfortunate was the issue of the bold attack made by the centre of the allies on Napoleon's works at Dresden, although it succeeded for a time. But as striking an instance of the uselessness of this kind of temporary advan- *Campaign in Virginia. Chesney.*

G 2

tage occurred more recently at the hill held by the allies at Inkermann. There a Russian battalion having crowned the heights unopposed, at an unguarded point, deployed, halted, and melted away again down the slope, without any pressure, being timid and distrustful of their advantage from sheer want of support.

Kinglake

We saw that whilst the Grenadiers and the Coldstreams were still forming under the bank, the battalion called the Scots Fusilier Guards had been hurried forward by the appeal from the troops, then still clinging to the Redoubt, had incurred the fire of the Vladimir column, and had afterwards encountered a mass of our men retreating, which broke the formation of its left companies by sheer bodily force, and compelled them to fall back in disorder.

Napier.

In the excitement of success the English guards followed with reckless ardour, but the French reserves of infantry and dragoons advanced, the repulsed men faced about, the batteries smote the guards in flank and front so heavily they drew back, and at the same time the Germans being sorely pressed, got into confusion. Hill and Campbell stood fast on the extremities of the line, yet the British centre was absolutely broken, and fortune seemed to incline to the French. Suddenly the 48th, led by Colonel Donellan, was seen advancing through the vast disordered masses, which seemed sufficient to carry it away bodily; but wheeling back by companies, that regiment let the crowds pass through, and then resumed its proud and beautiful line. Then the Guards and Germans rallied. In all actions there is a critical moment, which will give the victory to the General who knows how to seize it. When the Guards first made their rash charge, Sir Arthur foreseeing the issue of it had ordered the 48th down from the hill. These dispositions gained the day. The British became the strongest at the decisive point.

The first or fighting line must then be formed so that it carries its own reserve or support with it, and when spoken of as the first line, it is not to be regarded as a deployed line of infantry.

From what has been said, it appears therefore that the formation most suitable for the attack is one which, while occupying a front quite as long as that formerly held by a deployed line, will do so with fewer men, and will give commanding officers means of feeding the front, or in other words, *the area of action of a commanding officer will be as long and far deeper than formerly.*

And it also follows that the skill and intelligence of individual officers of every grade, more especially their aptitude for seizing favourable places for an advance, are now of more value than they have ever been in war.

The foregoing are the general principles on which the formation of troops for an attack should be made. But it is manifest that there can be no definite or determinate rule laid down, and the words of Jomini, quoted at page 60, must be borne in mind, and "the fatal tendency to systematize," to seek for "absolute forms," and "to cast all tactical formation in one mould," must be struggled against.

To recapitulate, it appears generally that troops formed for attack, should be formed in at least three bodies, and that these bodies should under one direction work for one object, and be closely linked together, and be of such strength, that each shall be a considerable force. It is evident (*vide* page 5) that a company is far too small a body to be so split up, hence the battalion must be taken as the attacking unit if any real work has to be done. We thus arrive at the formation of a skirmishing line, a supporting line, and a main body. Taken together these three form the first line.

It further appears that the men placed in the skirmishing line should be extended so as to diminish loss, increase accuracy and rapidity of fire, while at the same time a heavy and destructive fire is maintained. The functions of the skirmishing line being to crush and overwhelm the enemy with bullets. The object of the supports being to fill up gaps among the skirmishers, and so sustain the intensity of their fire. The duty of the main body being to advance the moment the enemy is sufficiently shaken, and drive him out of his position.

The distance between these three bodies must be governed partly by the work they have to do, partly by the trajectory of the arms in use, partly by the ground; to effectively support the skirmishers, that is to say, to be able to feed them with fresh men, the supports should be about 200 to 250 yards in rear. The main body must be able to cross the interval that divides them from the skirmishers in about five minutes, or they must be 500 to 600 yards off. And consistent with the due performance of these functions the supports and main body may be in any formation that from the shape of the ground, or other circumstances, will protect them best from loss, whether that formation be extended order, line, or columns, and they must change from one formation to another as quickly as possible. The principles which govern the formation of troops for attack can only be given, their application must depend on the knowledge and ability of the Commander in adjusting his formation to suit the ground he is working over.

Thus the more cover there is, to take advantage of, naturally the smaller will be the loss, and consequently the supporting body, whose function is to supply the losses of the skirmishers, may be reduced, and the length of the skirmishing line increased, at the same time that the intervals between the lines may be diminished. But the original question embraced more than the formation of the troops. It was, How shall the shot-swept zone be crossed?

Putting irregularities of ground out of consideration, this zone is swept by fire of different kinds, in different places—

1. The artillery fire which may be said generally to begin at about 2,500 yards.
2. The unaimed or random fire of the infantry which may begin to tell at about 1,100 yards.
3. The aimed fire of the infantry, which will begin to tell at about 600 to 700 yards.

Artillery employed in defending a position do not fire so much on advancing infantry in the early stage as on the attacking artillery, in addition to which the actual loss by artillery fire is in action comparatively small, being from $\frac{1}{12}$th to $\frac{1}{7}$th of the loss caused by the musketry fire.* Hence it may, speaking in general terms, be disregarded.†

The unaimed infantry fire produces many losses, but it appears that the effects of such fire may be mitigated by observing where it falls most, and avoiding those places.

Tellenbach.
(Translated by Robinson.)

Projectiles must not be considered only in relation to their mark, they sweep and command the battle-field. There are certain portions in the shot sphere, varying in situation and with time, where the shot fall more or less thickly; and we can partly gather from general rules, and partly observe those where they fall least thickly. Therefore, apart from the question of increasing the difficulty of aiming, there are means even on the open plain of lessening the effect of the enemy's fire. These means consist in the attitude of the men, the formation of the troops, the selection of the position to remain in, of the direction, and the manner of advancing, and they vary with circumstances.

The fire that causes heavy losses, and checks advancing troops, is undoubtedly the aimed or directed fire of infantry. The sooner and the quicker the space between, where the deployment of the troops takes place, and the enemy's position is crossed the better; but if crossed at the double, one of the objects of the skirmishing line, crushing the enemy with bullets, would not be accomplished, hence, such a method of advance, even if it were possible to run over the 2,000 yards without stopping, would be undesirable. But it seems desirable that the first 1,000 yards should be crossed without firing, and as rapidly as possible. It will be shown hereafter, that the attacker's artillery usually fires on the enemy's infantry, not on his guns, hence, until the attacking troops reach the zone of dangerous infantry fire, or about 1,100 yards from the position, if possible they should advance without firing, and as quickly as they can without being disordered, once the dangerous zone of infantry fire is reached, not only will they begin to suffer, but the power of inflicting loss on the enemy by means of their own fire begins, and about this stage of the advance the skirmishers must begin to fire. How should they then advance? Bearing in mind that the function of the skirmishing line is to keep up a continuous rain of shot on the enemy, and expose themselves as little as possible, or to develope the offensive power of the breach-loader, while reducing the destructive effect it has when used on the defensive. Bearing this in mind, it appears that the advance may best be made in a succession of short rushes, lying down, firing rapidly, and again running on, as described at page 73. This manœuvre may be performed in several ways; the whole line may so act, or alternate men

---

* At Gravelotte, where the French were in position, 94 per cent. of the Prussian killed and wounded was from infantry fire, 5 per cent. from artillery, and 1 per cent. from bayonet, sabre and lance. At Fredericksburg the Northern loss was about 78 per cent. by infantry fire.

† At 2,200 yards the guns in the English service will strike a deployed line of infantry once in three rounds, once in 10 rounds at 3,300 yards.

may so act, or alternate portions, sections, subdivisions, or companies may so act. The first method entails the disadvantage of there being a time, however short yet a small appreciable time, when the fire ceases.

The second method has this objection, that the party in advance are sure to mask the fire of those in rear more or less, and that soldiers are peculiarly apt to be discouraged by losing men from their comrades' fire and that the men are apt to get out of hand, and the officers find their control reduced.

The rush forward of a portion of an extended line invariably draws the enemy's attention, and consequently his fire on that portion; this is the moment for the other portion to seize and rush on too, hence there is an advantage in the alternate advance of portions.

It appears therefore advisable to adopt the third method, the alternate advance of fractions. But in what fractions? In such fractions as are best adapted to the ground, and are of such a nature as to constitute a definite command accustomed to work together, and are led by an officer whose position gives him influence with the men. If the formation of the British battalion be considered, by which two companies, a double company, or about 250 to 200 men will be in the skirmishing line, this alternate advance may be made by companies, each company being then led and commanded by the officers who know the men individually.

For what distance should these rushes be made? They should be of such a length that the men should not be exhausted and out of breath after making them, even when the distance is run over as rapidly as possible; for this reason, it would appear that these rushes should not exceed about 60 yards, but should be adjusted so as to obtain cover; if cover exists, the rush should be from cover to cover. Before advancing, the officer commanding the body about to make the rush should select the place he is going to, point it out to his subordinates, and at a given signal (a shrill whistle is the easiest to hear) he should dash to the front, his subaltern and men following;* on getting into his new position he will get his men under cover as quickly as possible, kneeling, lying down, or standing, as may best cover them, and will open fire at once, and fire steadily and deliberately until the company on his flank is rushing, when he should fire a few rounds as quickly as he possibly can, to cover its advance.

It should be a standing rule that when any body of skirmishers is rushing to the front, those on its immediate flank should fire rapidly to cover its advance and reduce the effect produced by the cessation of its fire.

From the foregoing, it would appear that about 2 companies would form the supports and 4 companies the main body. It

---

* An officer, or a steady non-commissioned officer, should be left to see that the men follow.

is the function of the supports to fill up the gaps in the skirmishing line, hence, companies must get mixed up together, it is perfectly impossible to prevent it. But it is possible, by careful training, to obviate, or rather to mitigate, the evils that may ensue The Emperor of Germany has recently issued an order on this subject, of which the following is an extract :—

19th March, Cabinet Order, 1873.

The foregoing general principles are intended to meet the requirements of the tactics of the present day ; I must however bring prominently to notice, that in training companies, battalions, regiments, and brigades, according to Sections 43, 88, 98, 99, 112 to 115, and 130 of the Field Exercise, particular care must be taken that the frequent dispersion and development of strong lines of skirmishers, which is demanded by the present mode of warfare, may not lead to a pernicious loosening of the tactical connection. This danger can alone be met by great intimacy on the part of officers with battle formation, and by a high state of discipline in action and in firing, combined with a thorough and strict system of drill. In thus making increased demands on the training of the infantry, I will also give relief, by abolishing some of the formation in the field exercise, and putting restrictions on others.

Various proposals have been made to obviate the mixing up of companies in the skirmishing line.* One of these is that each of the four companies forming the skirmishers and supports should be formed in column of sections, and that the feeding of the skirmishers should be carried out by each company feeding its own leading sections.†

It is manifest that the objection to this arises from the fact that each company will thus be about 200 to 300 yards deep, and supposing it to consist of 100 men extended at one yard and a half interval, its front section will cover 35 yards, or each captain will have his command scattered over a wide area—too wide to allow him to lead in front, command in the centre, and judiciously support from the rear. Further, the skirmishers would want that cohesion which having whole companies in front gives ; and a similar difficulty would occur with supports. Each line must have a definite commander and leader, and removing the captain from the skirmishers removes the nerve from the place where it is most wanting. But, it may be argued, if the captain is killed the nerve is wanting. Hardly so, for the subaltern then commands the skirmishers as captain on his own responsibility, not as the subordinate of another, which is a very different thing.

Companies *will* get mixed up. Long-range weapons compel an advance in extended order for long distances, and do what officers may, men under such circumstances, exposed to a heavy fire, do get out of order. There is no use blinking this fact ; it is impossible that it can be otherwise, so long as human beings possess different physical and moral endowments. Some men will be eager and anxious for the work, others will hang back,

---

* This subject is dealt with more in detail in Appendix I, when describing the new Italian infantry tactics.

† It should be understood that this proposal to skirmish by sections, is one that meets with support, and the best method of formation, whether by sections or companies, is an open question. *Vide* Appendix, Italian formations, for a further statement of both sides of the question.

and their courage gradually ooze away. Some can be influenced by example and encouragement, others cannot; some are stronger, and better able to keep up than others, consequently we must expect such a mixing up of companies amongst the skirmishing line. It is better to foresee and provide by training that an evil which *will* take place may be as little of an evil as possible, than attempt to guard against what all experience shows cannot be guarded against. No army ever went into action with better drilled or steadier troops than the English did at the Alma; they were the results of years of careful drill and the finest and most perfect regimental organization and system that any army ever had, and yet what was the force that first carried the battery at the Alma but a mob, composed of various regiments, brigades, and divisions mixed up together, and such must ever be the case where a rapid advance under a heavy fire is made by a body of troops for any distance. When line formations were introduced into the British army, advances under fire, of the length of that made at the Alma, were unknown, being quite needless; but even in the Peninsula, with the short distances there moved over, such mixing up of companies was recognised as an evil to be mitigated, but still one that would exist. The wisdom of introducing any complication with the object of preventing companies being mixed, is at least questionable.

The principles on which troops should be formed, and which govern their advance, being such as have been described, it is desirable to endeavour to realise as clearly as possible the circumstances under which, and the reasons why an attack is at the present day possible.

At a distance from the enemy's position, varying according to the nature of the ground, and the state of the atmosphere, but perhaps lying within the limits of 2,500 to 3,000 yards, troops will have to deploy and quit the close order in which they have previously been formed. *Now an attack on an enemy presupposes a superiority of force at the place where the attack is made.*[*] War, whether viewed tactically or strategically, is but the art of being the strongest at the right place at the right time. This superiority of force may be numerical, moral, or local, or it may be composed partly of all three, but for an attack to have a reasonable hope of success, *the attackers at the point the attack takes place must be superior.*

Now, when the first deployment takes place, the attacker's infantry will suffer but slightly from artillery fire. But the assailant's artillery will shake down the walls of villages, farms, or houses in which the defenders are posted, thus driving the infantry out. Their artillery will consequently become the object for the defender's guns to fire at, as it will be stationary, or only advancing occasionally, and in masses of several batteries.

---

[*] To obtain this superiority is one of the chief objects of the manœuvres that precede the actual collision of armies.

Hence the infantry will, in this the first stage, suffer but little from the direct or aimed fire, although a few losses may be occasioned by stray shots. As the infantry advances, a large portion of the artillery will advance also, not together, but by alternate batteries, or brigades of batteries, so that a fire will be always kept up. It will probably advance thus, until it gets near to the extreme range of the infantry fire, or about 1,200 to 1,400 yards from the enemy's position. The moment the first or skirmishing line of the infantry comes near enough to the enemy's position to become a mark for its aimed or direct fire, say about 600 to 700 yards, the troops in rear, that is to say, the supports and main body, will suffer but little, except from the unaimed or random fire. It is desirable that this point should be clearly understood. The fire of the assailant's artillery and the fire of his skirmishing line will have the effect of drawing on them both the enemy's artillery and infantry fire, *and hence it becomes possible to bring up the main body in a much closer formation than is often supposed.*

The frontal attack of Infantry. (Translated by Colonel Newdegate.)

When the skirmishers are once involved in a fire action with the enemy, close detachments can come forward with insignificant losses. On the 19th January, at St. Quintin, two companies 1st Rhenish Infantry Regiment, No. 70, upon the right wing of the 16th Division, were brought forward to protect the batteries of the division from the enemy's infantry fire. One zug of each company was sent out to skirmish with two close züge following in support at 100 paces; these suffered heavy losses at a distance of 800 yards while passing over a hill, one-sixth of the effective state in a very few minutes. On the other hand, the two remaining companies of the battalion which were brought over the same height an hour later hardly suffered at all, although no change had taken place in the French position. The attention of the French was now completely directed upon the fire action at a distance of about 400 paces.

Now here is one of the strong points of the attack, and *vice versâ* one of the weak points of the defence. The defenders, do what they will, instinctively fire on the troops that are doing them an injury and consequently the main body of the attack escapes, or nearly escapes, from all but the unaimed or stray shots that have missed the skirmishing line. Hence in every attack the fire both of the artillery supporting the attack, and of the infantry skirmishing line, must be continuous, carefully directed and brought to bear on the portion of the enemy's position where an entrance is to be forced.

Scherff.

From this moment (the first deployment) until that of the actual collision, the attackers are exposed to the fire of the defenders, and they may be struck by two classes of projectiles, those which strike the mark, and those which miss the mark and do injury by chance.

This circumstance has not yet been sufficiently appreciated in the various essays and theories that have been put forward by various writers, it deserves to be most carefully considered, if the questions regarding the formation of troops are to be resolved.

The artillery and in a short time the infantry of the defenders becomes the object of the attackers fire. It follows that their fire will be diverted from that portion of the attacking force which composes the main body (or the true assaulting party). The more the troops charged with the preparation of the attack succeed in drawing on themselves the defenders fire, the better they will do their work ; a defence properly conducted will seek not to be so led.

But it cannot help itself, it may perhaps avoid the direction of all its fire on the skirmishing line, and may direct a portion on the supports and the batteries. But the fire on the main body will be much diminished, and its action on it will be merely accidental. If on the one hand the fire of the defenders does not check the advanced or skirmishing line of the attackers, it will be destroyed by its fire (united to that of the attacking artillery). If on the other the defenders concentrate their fire on the skirmishing line, they indirectly facilitate the advance of the main body of the attackers.

And this is the dilemma on which the possibility of attack mainly rests. And hence the necessity of giving the troops engaged in preparing the way a considerable force.

We consider that the most advanced portion of the attacking troops will thus become the mark of the defender's fire, and the main body will thus receive a far less efficacious fire, that of random projectiles.

But no fire, however heavy, well-directed, and continuous, will drive good troops out of a position. A heavy cross-fire of musketry and artillery may shake the *morale*, and disorganise the defenders, may kill and wound many, may induce many of the less brave individuals to seek some excuse to leave the position either by assisting wounded men to the rear, or otherwise, but still the men whose heart is in the work, the really brave men, will remain to fight it out. So long as they have ammunition these men will hold their position, and it is only the actual advance of *superior numbers* that will finally compel them to retire. It is not meant that they will remain to be bayonetted. But they will not go until the forward rush of the main body of the assailant warns them that two hostile bodies of men cannot stand on the same piece of ground. Hence all fire must be looked on as paving the way for the object of getting possession of the enemy's position, and in this respect modern weapons have made no difference whatever; a formed body of the assailants must be placed in the enemy's position and must maintain themselves there, in order that victory may be achieved. The attack of an enemy's position is based entirely on the science of the attack of a fortress. A mass of artillery fire is concentrated on certain points; under cover of that fire the infantry advance until checked by infantry fire. Again, the infantry fire is subdued by the infantry fire added to the artillery fire of the attackers, a breach is made in the enemy's position, and through that breach a formed body of men is pushed, who make a lodgement there. Such in general terms is the attack of a fortress, such in general terms is the attack of a position, with this difference, the former is the work of days, the latter that of hours. The necessity of bringing up a sufficiently strong body formed, in hand and under control, to drive out the defenders, occupy their positions, and reap the results of the fire, is manifest, and the question arises: How shall this body be brought up? It must conform more or less to the movement of the skirmishers; at what distance from them should it be, and in what formation? The answers to these questions have been generally given at page 85, but it is desirable to state the case somewhat more in detail.

The three distinct zones of fire, through which troops must pass in moving to the attack, have been already described; these zones, or rather the nature of the fire in these zones, must govern the formation of the main body.

When entering the zone of artillery fire, which may be said to begin at from 2,500 to 3,000 yards, from the enemy's guns, the main bodies should be so formed as not to offer a mark sufficiently large to induce the enemy to turn his guns on them.* This formation will probably be found to be that of half-battalion quarter or double-company columns, at deploying intervals or perhaps somewhat less, as many men will be lost during the advance, and the number of men per yard thus diminished.

The great object of the defence is to retard the attack, and as the attacking artillery will at this, the first stage, be partly in action, partly moving up with the skirmishing line, the defenders must, if this force be, as it should be, a powerful one, direct all their attention to it and not to the main body. Formed in such a way, and kept at from 550 to 650 yards behind the skirmishers, the main body may advance and experience but little loss. On arriving at from 1,200 to 1,400 yards, the unaimed fire of the infantry will begin to tell; beyond this point, the guns cannot advance, and at this point the formation of the main body may be again extended. But at this stage the extension will not reduce the actual loss so much as the moral effects of those losses.

Scherff.

At this stage (the second zone), if the artillery of the defence does not direct its attention exclusively upon the artillery and troops engaged in preparing the attack, it will begin to direct a portion of its fire on the main body, which will then receive fire of two kinds, aimed and random. The whole ground will thus be swept by a nearly evenly divided fire, the effect therefore, unless the attackers be very badly handled, and so formed as to induce the defenders to concentrate their fire on certain points, will be nearly the same, no matter in what formation they are. The more a mass of men is concentrated, the more confidence is given in its force, and the greater the number of men likely to be able to show a good example. Further, the greater the number of men to exert this influence, the easier will it be to impress a motive power on the whole mass. These are the views which in former days fixed columns as the proper formation for attack, and it cannot be denied that these views are sound.

But it must be equally admitted that a heavy loss occurring unexpectedly, and all at once, demoralises the minds of men, more than if the same loss is distributed over some time, and in different places. Hence we must conclude that the more a mass of men is disseminated, the less it will require examples to lead it on. Let us assume a column of 400 men, 20 in front and 20 deep; a shell falling in the middle will knock over 8 or 10 men; the moral effect produced will be far greater than if the men were ranged two deep at two paces interval, and 3 or 4 shells fell at the same time, but at different places, although in the latter case the shells might produce even a greater

---

* It may be most fairly questioned whether troops formed in small columns, with intervals equal to their front or double their front, are not much safer from artillery fire than if in line. One shot in three will hit a line of infantry at 2,200 yards, but the probability of striking the small columns is very much less.

loss. Because if the formation be a shallow one, and moving to the front, the men who fall will be left behind, and the loss will be thus concealed. The question then is, What front must we, what depth can we, give the troops of the principal body at this moment?

The size of the fractions into which the main body must now be divided, must be such that the leader (who has at this stage of the advance to dismount) can exercise a personal influence, that they can move easily to the front and yet be sufficiently compact to give the soldier the idea of solidity : this is found in a front of from 30 to 40 yards, and a depth of 6 to 8 men.

It is important to observe, that in passing through the "unaimed shot sphere," speed alone can diminish the risk of loss, avoid it or cross the least intense portion of it, if such be possible, but formation can affect the question in no way whatever, except as it may affect the speed. Bullets are flying at a given rate within certain limits, and if all must pass through those limits, the individual chances are not affected by being in company. It would be otherwise reasonable to assert that a body of men marching in skirmishing order, would be reached by fewer drops of rain, *i.e.*, would get less wet, than if they passed through at the same pace in column, or that you would get less wet walking alone in the rain, than you would do in company with a friend. *Colonel Gawler.*

The formation requires to be such as will enable the men to advance with speed without being demoralised; and this appears to be more likely to be attained by small columns than by either a line or extended formation.

At the point, therefore, that the main body enters the second zone, at some 1,000 to 1,200 yards from the enemy, the half-battalion columns, if at quarter distance, at deploying intervals, or slightly less than deploying intervals, should deploy into columns of two companies at deploying intervals.

This can be most easily effected if the half-battalion columns have been formed in double-company columns on the centre, as the right and left wings can then incline to the right and left without stopping their advance, moving to a flank diagonally, by the leading of their officers. It is desirable that the reason why these small columns are preferable to a line for this purpose should be clearly understood. A line is the formation for firing— the main body cannot fire, the supports and skirmishers being in front of it. It is further requisite to remember that in any attempt to advance in line over rough ground the inequalities are proportional to the length of the line. The best drilled troops in the world cannot advance 300 yards over rough ground without being disordered—many men being squeezed out, while the attention of both officers and men is devoted to an attempt to preserve the straightness of the line and its true direction. Any one who observes a line of 400 infantry advancing over rough ground will see fluctuations running through all its length, and wearing themselves out at the ends; by splitting up the line into several portions these fluctuations are diminished, precisely as bracing a long bar or dividing it into a number of short bars reduces its vibration; and further, the action of such small columns affords some protection to the weak points—the flanks.

The action of the supports during the time that elapses from the troops coming under fire should be now considered.

The duty of the supports is essentially to keep up the fire of the first line, and fill gaps. It is not so much for reinforcing the skirmishers that they are requisite, the skirmishing line should originally consist of a "sufficient number," their function is to keep that line up to "the sufficient number," feeding it to fill up the gaps caused by the enemy's bullets. Hence the officer commanding the supports (two companies), must watch the front, or skirmishing line, and send up men when he sees they are requisite. The nearer to the skirmishers the supports are the more they will suffer, but if too far off they will cease to act as supports. It appears that the supports will suffer less, that is to say, they will attract the enemy's fire less if they advance in small groups; and it would appear desirable that the two companies forming the supports should be formed into as many sections as there are officers available, that is to say, each company into two or three sections. The distance at which the supports are from the skirmishers must be left chiefly to the officer commanding those supports, but it should rarely exceed 300 yards. As the skirmishing line advances towards the enemy, and begins to get into the zone of aimed fire, or some 600 to 700 yards from the enemy, the supports must be freely pushed on, and take their places in the skirmishing line, and as the advance of the skirmishers will, from the fact of their moving in successive rushes, be somewhat slower than that of the supports, the latter will close on them, and the main body will also close somewhat on the supports (as if will experience less loss, and consequently be less retarded). *Vide* page 90.)

Scherff.

The Commander of the supports must during his advance seek to find out the places where his assistance may be most usefully sent. The best points for the attack may be found when about 80 to 100 yards from the enemy.

As the fire is kept up the main body will advance, and when it comes near the line of supports the latter should rush to the front and join the skirmishers.

Scherff.

The following rule should be absolute, the moment the main body arrives near what is left of the line of supports, they should dash to the front and join the line of skirmishers, in order to give the impulsion requisite to cross the last and most dangerous zone of all, and finally give the assault.

If an attempt be made to realise the state of affairs at this period of the attack, it will be seen that the skirmishers, reinforced by the supports, are within 250 to 300 yards of the enemy; that the main body is some 300 yards in rear of the skirmishers; the divisional artillery perhaps some 1,200 to 1,400 yards off, supported by a portion of the corps artillery, the remainder of the corps artillery occupying advantageous places up to 2,000 yards off, and all bringing a heavy cross-fire on the enemy's position; the second line of troops following up in rear of the main body of the first line, and perhaps some 500 to 600 yards in rear of it, a tremendous fire being maintained by the now thickened skirmishers, and the whole front covered with clouds of smoke. Such a state of things cannot last long; the skirmishers may get a hundred yards nearer, and the main body getting closer to them, must prepare to carry the position; gradually converging, the various portions of the main body must push rapidly to the front and drive the enemy out. While the second line, seeing the advance and hearing the cheers which accompany it, should push rapidly on also, ready to support the attack, meet the enemy's reserves, and confirm the success.

What should the skirmishers do when the main body advances? The skirmishers, who have borne the heaviest portion of the fighting, will undoubtedly have got much excited, and heated; they will have been brought close up to the enemy's position, and by that time all the men whose heart is not in the work will have disappeared, officers and men who have worked through the zones of fire that have been described, who have seen comrades and friends dropping, will be in such a state of nervous excitement that the cheer and advance of the main body will, no matter what orders are given, carry them to the front. In all likelihood their cartridges are exhausted, or nearly so, for they have done most of the firing, and the last few minutes they must fire as fast as they can load and aim. In addition to which their fire would be completely masked by the main body advancing in front of them.

The idea of leaving the skirmishers lying down is contrary to the fundamental principle of the attack, which is that all the disposable forces should be applied, leaving them behind really leads to nothing. This line left behind cannot fire effectively on the enemy, it cannot collect and reform the *débris* of the troops crushed by the enemy's fire, it will have done enough, and suffered too much arleady to do that. Judging by all experience, what it must do, is to push on with the rest. To leave it lying down is in the most favourable case a useless theoretical course to pursue, generally it will be a dangerous one. *Scherff.*

The moment the position is carried every effort must be made to hold it. The troops should be reformed. A heavy fire should be poured on the enemy as he retires, and the second line following rapidly, must endeavour to occupy the ground, and coming up in regular order can do so far better than troops whose nerves have been wrought up to the highest pitch of excitement by a successful attack.

The troops taking part in an energetically carried out attack are thrown into the completest loose order. In this state they can certainly still follow up the existing object of the fight, but they are unavailable for action in any other direction. *Frontal Attack of Infantry. (Translated by Colonel Newdegate.)*

The nature of the attack described is illustrated by plates XIV.-XVIII., but although such sketches are useful as giving expression to ideas, it should be clearly understood as regards the supports and main body, that there can *by no possibility be any definite or fixed formation.* The formation to be adopted should be entirely suited to the ground, thus one company of the supports may be in column of sections, another in line, and after advancing 100 yards the formations may be entirely altered, the company in column being extended, and that formerly in line now in column : similarly for the main bodies. The plates cannot therefore be taken as recommending any special formation.

It is perhaps fortunate in one sense for our country that the direction which improvements in tactics are taking, is one peculiarly adapted to the genius and temperament of her people.

For years British troops, formed in lines two deep, have met and defeated the best armies in Europe. *Extended order is but an extension of the two-deep line.* British troops have for hundreds of years been famed for their steadiness and coolness under fire, the influence of infantry fire is becoming every day more and more formidable, that influence to a great extent depends on the coolness of the soldier delivering the fire. The steadiness of the individual British soldier, his coolness, and his proverbial ignorance of the time when he is beaten, tend to make individual fighting simple and natural to him. Further, the reliance of the British soldier on his officer and his confidence in him, augurs well for the future, when British infantry have to meet a foreign enemy.

Napier.

The habitual French method of attacking in column cannot be praised. Against the Austrians, Russians, and Prussians it may have been successful ; against the British it must always fail. The English infantry is sufficiently firm, intelligent, and well-disciplined to wait calmly in lines for the adverse masses, and sufficiently bold to close upon them with the bayonet. The column is good for all movements short of the actual attack, but as the Macedonian phalanx was unable to resist the Roman Legion, so will the close column be unequal to sustain the fire and charge of a firm line aided by artillery. The repugnance of men to trample on their own dead and wounded, the cries and groans of the latter, and the whistling of cannon shots, as they tear open the ranks, produce disorder, especially in the centre of attacking columns, which, blinded by smoke, unsteadfast of footing, bewildered by words of command coming from a multitude of officers crowded together, can neither see what is taking place, nor advance nor retreat without increasing the confusion.

No example of courage can be useful, no moral effect produced by the spirit of individuals, except upon the head, which is often firm and even victorious when the rear is flying in terror. Nevertheless, columns are the soul of military operations ; in them is the victory, and in them is safety to be found after a defeat. *The secret consists in knowing when and where to extend the front.*

Bugeaud.

The English generally occupied well-chosen defensive positions, having a certain command, and they showed only a portion of their force. The usual artillery action first took place. Soon, in great haste, without studying the position, without taking time to examine if there were means to make a flank attack, we marched straight on, taking the bull by the horns. About 1,000 yards from the English line the men became excited, spoke to one another and hurried their march ; the column began to be a little confused.

The English remained quite silent, with ordered arms, and from their steadiness appeared to be a long red wall. This steadiness invariably produced an effect on the young soldiers.

Very soon we got nearer, shouting "Vive l'Empereur ! en avant ! à la baïonette !" Shakos were raised on the muzzles of the muskets ; the column began to double, the ranks got into confusion, the agitation produced a tumult ; shots were fired as we advanced.

Skirmishers two Companies.

300

300

Supports two Companies.

800

Main Body four Companies.

Skirmisher Line 3500 yards from the main position of the enemy.

N.B. No absolute formation for the Supports and Main body can be given, they should be extended in line or columns as may be best adapted to the ground they are advancing over.

PLATE XV.

Second Stage.

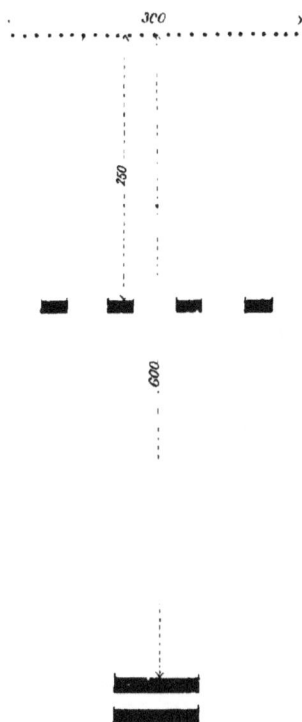

Skirmisher Line 1200 yards from the main position of the enemy.

N.B.—No absolute formation for the Supports and Main body can be given, they should be extended in line or columns, as may be best adapted to the ground they are advancing over.

PLATE XVI.

Third Stage.

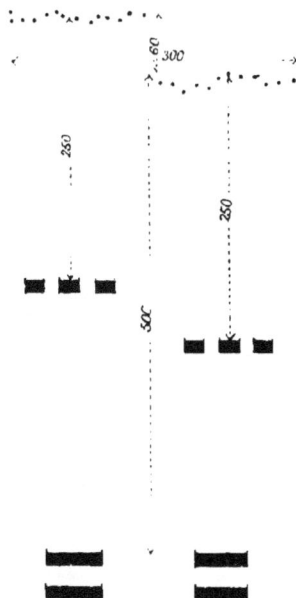

Skirmisher Line 800 yards from main position of the enemy

N.B. No absolute formation for the Supports and Main body can be given, they should be extended in line or columns, as may be best adapted to the ground they are advancing over

PLATE XVII

Fourth Stage.

300

300

Skirmisher Line 300 yards from the

enemy's main position

600

Second Line

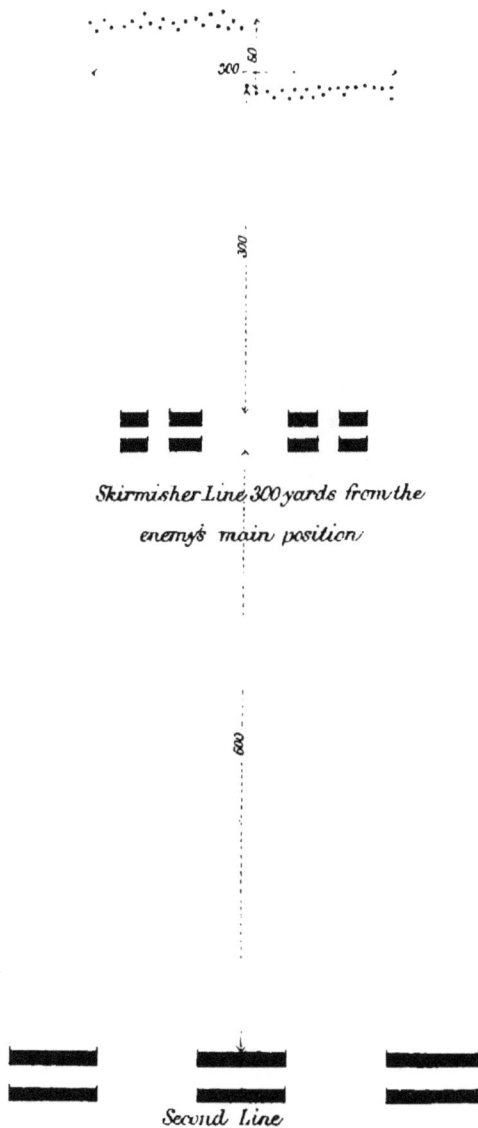

Half Battalion Double Company, columns at deploying intervals.

N.B. No absolute formation for the Supports and Main body can be given, they should be extended
in line or columns, as may be best adapted to the ground they are advancing over.

PLATE XVII.

PLATE XVIII

Fifth Stage.

< ...... 300 ...... >

- 300 -

General advance
The Skirmisher Line 200 yards from the enemy's position

- 600 -

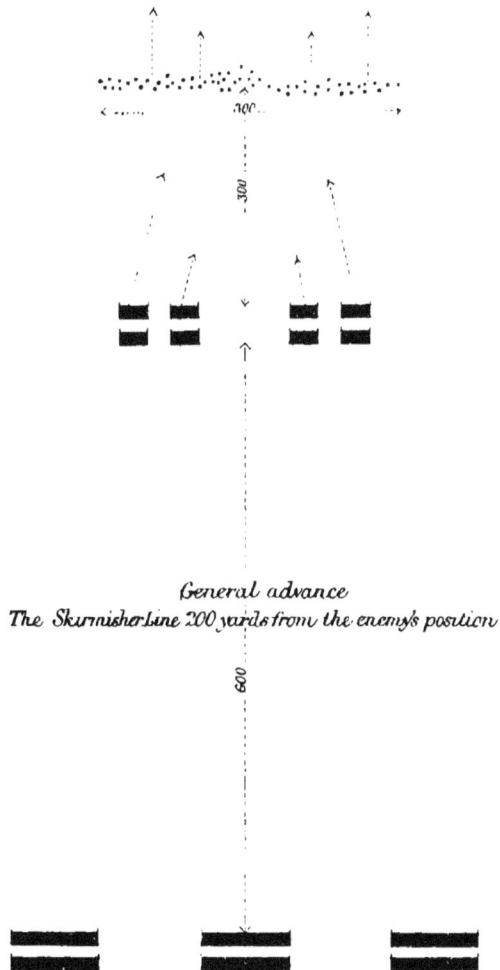

N.B. No absolute formation for the Supports and Main body can be given; they should be extended in line or Columns as may be best adapted to the ground they are advancing over.

The English line remained still, silent and immovable, with ordered arms, even when we were only 300 paces distant, and it appeared to ignore the storm about to break.

The contrast was striking; in our inmost thoughts, each felt that the enemy was a long time in firing, and that this fire reserved for so long, would be very unpleasant when it did come. Our ardour cooled. The moral power of steadiness, which nothing shakes (even if it be only in appearance), over disorder which stupifies itself with noise, overcame our minds. At this moment of intense excitement, the English wall shouldered arms, an indescribable feeling rooted many of our men to the spot, they began to fire. The enemy's steady concentrated volleys swept our ranks; decimated we turned round seeking to recover our equilibrium; then three deafening cheers broke the silence of our opponents, at the third they were on us pushing our disorganized flight. But to our great surprise, they did not push their advantage beyond a hundred yards, retiring calmly to their lines to await a second attack.

The British army, from its tradition and history, is in a position better adapted for grasping, and appropriating, the development of tactics caused by the introduction of breech-loading arms than the army of any other nation. All that is requisite is to develop and carry out the identical principles which led the British leaders to adopt a line formation in the peninsula.

This point is one that must not be lost sight of, the peculiar genius of a nation invariably comes out on the battle-field, and it is essential that it should be clearly understood that the British army, with its historic training, and traditions of advancing and fighting never more than two deep, possesses qualifications for modern fighting that the army of no nation in the world does. As the line was an advance on the column, giving greater power and effect to improved arms, and producing far less loss than the denser formation, so the extended line, giving full effect to the offensive power of the breech-loader, and enabling troops to attack with less loss, is an advance on the two-deep line. An advance which it is much easier for British troops, who have never fought in columns, and whose ideas and tactics have always turned on a large development of infantry fire, to make, than for those who have had to step from the deep column to the individual or extended order at one stride.

We were all astonished at the extraordinary firmness with which the red jackets, having crossed the river, opened a heavy fire in line upon the redoubt. This was the most extraordinary thing to us, as we had never before seen troops fight in lines two deep, nor did we think it possible for men to be found with sufficient firmness of morale to be able to attack in this apparently weak formation our massive columns. *Choda Seiwitz.*

"The terrible English column which, advancing under a murderous fire in front and flank, all but won the battle of Fontenoy;" the victories of the British line on many fields, mark two distinct phases in the tactics of this country; the latter being due to a clear appreciation of the effects of improved arms. Following the same natural development, the individual order will still further bring out the coolness, the self-reliance, and courage of the British soldier.

H

We have said that the direction tactics are taking *is fortunate in one sense* for this country. It is desirable, however, that a disadvantage should not be lost sight of, speaking *in general terms;* when we formerly defeated foreign armies we did so because the front of fire we directed against them was larger than what they brought to bear on us, *our lines outflanked their columns.* But now that foreign armies fight with as wide a front as we can hope to do, and that extension of the front has become general in every army, and with every nation. the small numerical strength of a British army no longer compensated by its comparatively wide front of fire will be felt, and felt severely. It is manifest that extension of front is limited, that there is a point below which it is impossible to reduce the number of men per yard of position. That point once reached by the troops composing two armies, the weaker must always suffer: although the temperament of the British soldier is perhaps better adapted for individual fighting than that of the soldiers of any other nation: yet modern arms have undoubtedly placed armies more on a footing of equality and consequently given to numbers an element of superiority they previously did not possess. The greater the effect of the weapon the greater the results produced by putting large numbers of such weapons in action. Improved arms will undoubtedly enable a small number of men so armed to resist a large body of men armed with inferior weapons, but when the weapons are of equal power, then it appears that the effect of numbers must preponderate.

An unquestionable advantage is possessed by the British army in its small companies, and consequently the number of officers in the battalion. It should be remembered that the Prussian company was the result not so much of tactical, as of economical motives, and that the Prussian army, formed from the results of universal compulsory service, and education, possesses an amount of intelligence in the ranks that other armies do not, Hence, to follow Prussian customs as regards companies without following them in other things would be absurd. It is impossible to adopt one portion of a nation's customs and ignore the basis on which the whole superstructure is built.

Much has been recently said and written of the advisability of altering the formation of a British, and assimilating it to that of a Prussian battalion. To do so would be to blindly copy Prussian customs, and we might just as well copy Prussian uniforms or Prussian words of command. Undoubtedly there is much to be obtained by a careful study of the Prussian system, but that study must be an intelligent study, which will enable us to graft on our own framework what is good, and suitable to our peculiar temperament. And the formation of the Prussian battalion is not only not suitable to British infantry. but it may be fairly questioned if it is not one of the weakest points of the Prussian system, which, on account of the success attending Prussian armies, is so much admired.

Heavy were the losses with which we paid for our victorious attacks. The diminution of the capitation however is not the only consequence of such sanguinary battles.

The notion of the excellence of war-seasoned battalions has vanished from our army. According to general experience, the men went into action with the greatest ardour, and without dread of the fire, until they had once suffered very severe losses.

Then even the exhilarating consciousness of victory cannot dissipate the impression which such sanguinary experience has made upon the spirits of the troops. Months afterwards this feeling has still not quite disappeared.

It is true that other causes contribute to produce this; those who had fallen were just the bravest men, because they exposed themselves most in the skirmisher line ; *and above all there were very few officers still remaining.* *

Frontal Attack of Infantry. (Translated by Newdegate.)

After these great losses, how would this army have stood the effects of a defeat, and consequent demoralising retreat? True the losses in this case purchased victory, but it might have been otherwise. To organise, as if victory were always certain, is really to organise disaster.

Hence the necessity of not destroying, but modifying, our existing arrangements; the one and only one advantage of a strong company appears to be that it is a force of sufficient strength to make an attack. 200 men extended in front of a battalion will give a sufficient force to begin an attack; 200 more will be sufficient to act as supports ; and each of these being under one command, form a tactical body accustomed to work together. But to obtain this advantage it is surely not requisite to sacrifice the British battalion.

It has been pointed out (page 74) that the use of the breech-loader enables troops to be more extended than formerly, hence more supervision is required. The difficulties of command are consequently greater than formerly. The necessity of proper leading, of seizing points where cover exists, making them bases for further advances and getting the men out of cover again, are now of the highest importance. These reasons, and the necessity of forming small groups, and seeking with them to penetrate the enemy's line, clearly demonstrate the advantages of small companies and many officers.

Further, as movements to the right or left to close-in skirmishers, and so make room for fresh skirmishers coming up to fill up gaps, would reduce the fire, compel men who had won certain advantageous places to leave them, not to advance on the enemy, but merely to take ground to the right or left, a thing very difficult to do with any troops, more especially with those like British troops, possessing, as all Anglo-Saxons do, a strong individuality, sure to come out under fire ; so com-

* The Prussians lost 1 officer to 8 men at Wissembourg ; 1 to 20 at Wœerth ; at Mars-la-Tour and Gravelotte, 1 to 18 or 19. The 16th Regiment and the Rifle Battalion of the Guard lost all their officers-- (General Zeddeler).

panies must get mixed up, precisely as brigades and even divisions did at the Alma. Hence the more points of support, and the greater the number of men accustomed to command and lead, the greater will be the success of the troops.

Officers in action must command, not their own companies only, but any men who they can get together and take command of.

Boguslauski.
(Translated
by Graham.)
In order to work with tolerable readiness in such lines of skirmishers as we meet now a days in battle, a man should have gone through something like it in peace time. He should have gained as good an idea of this sort of thing as possible ; he should not merely know by hearsay, but experience in his own person, that if separated from his own company and unable to rejoin it, he at once comes under command of the officer who may happen to be where he is. He should be prepared to get quickly at home amongst new comrades. An officer, on the other hand, when he sees stray soldiers in action, should take them under his command, either forming them into a compact body or leading them into the line of skirmishers.

It may, perhaps, be argued that this kind of fighting makes troops unsteady; but it may be fairly replied, that unsteady troops cannot fight as described, that they would inevitably get into confusion and loose their heads. It is only really well-disciplined, well-commanded bodies of men, which can turn apparent disorder into real order, and it consequently follows, that the training and careful intelligent training of troops, is now more than ever requisite.

The real result of the introduction of the breech-loader is not to introduce a loose, careless method of action. Its introduction has rendered fighting far more difficult,—rendered it requisite that much of the care formerly bestowed on the *ensemble* of a dressed line, or perfect column, should be now devoted to the individual man, that the knowledge of each individual, from the general to the private, must be greater than formerly, while at the same moment the *ensemble* is still preserved.

It is often said that, if troops do not change front and manœuvre under fire, it is needless to teach them more, than what they do when actually engaged. This is founded on an entire misconception of what the duties of troops really are. These things are but means to an end, and most important means; for one day's fighting troops have 30 days' marching and manœuvring, and the power of marching and manœuvring is of the utmost importance, not only as giving that training which enables the men to be placed in front of their enemies, but producing that discipline without which everything else is useless.

But although men must be taught to manœuvre, it is essential that manœuvre tactics, important as they are, should not be rated above their proper value, but that fighting tactics should be practised, and studied, and carefully thought over by officers. The Emperor of Germany's order of the 19th March, 1873, shows clearly the necessity of both fighting and manœuvre tactics, and as the former have become more difficult, the Emperor gives " relief " to his troops by reducing the latter. The different kinds of formation in which troops can advance best over different kinds of ground, can only be thought out by officers who keep their minds continually bent on the subject, and who in default of real experience endeavour to realise the power of the arms in use and the effect of ground in modifying that power. By such thought and by study alone can the really difficult art of handling troops under fire be acquired, Tactics are often defined to be and generally considered inferior to strategy, but for one man who really requires to practice strategy 500 are needed who can handle troops. The General but gives the order to attack ; the serious responsibility of making the dispositions for attack. fixing and modifying the formation of the troops to suit the ground, so that they shall suffer as little as possible, rests, and must rest, with the field and company officers; and when it is remembered that neglecting to change from a close to an extended formation at the right moment may cost the lives of many men, the necessity for careful painstaking study really becomes a solemn duty, and a duty that the more it is studied the more difficult it appears to be. It cannot be too often stated that there is great danger of officers being induced to consider that now-a-days anything in the shape of drill is sufficient if the men only can shoot. The drill book may be made very simple by leaving out three-fourths of it. But doing so will not render the soldiers', much less the officers' duties the easier, and it is important that those who advocate sweeping reductions in the size of the drill book, and imagine that when the officer or soldier has mastered what is contained between its covers, his education will be complete, should remember that the great difficulty is, the drill book, whatever its size, now, far less than ever, can be taken as a *rule ;* it is merely a guide, which points out the general direction. A knowledge of drill, and the power of adjusting the formation of troops to ground, is at the present day more requisite and more difficult than ever it was, and this fact should be recognised ; and met by a thorough practical training, on the part of the company officers to adapt not only the formation of companies, but also of small bodies of men to the ground worked over. Such training is not acquired in a day, such knowledge cannot be learned from a drill serjeant, in a barrack square or a drill shed, but must be imparted by men, who have carefully and practically worked out these questions, and it must be taught on diversified ground, of some extent.

Improved arms, far from reducing the labour of the infantry officer and giving him more time to devote to kindred branches of the military art, have really increased it a hundredfold, and converted what at one time might perhaps have been termed machine-like action, into what at the present day most certainly requires study, and ability of no mean order. In instructing infantry soldiers, a defensive, as well as an attacking party, however small, should be used, and should continually be made to change places, so that each man may see how a formation altered to suit the ground tends to conceal the attackers from the defenders, and so reduce loss.

It has been proposed to extend not only the skirmishing line but the supports and also the main body; advancing in the latter case, either in a deployed line or in a line with intervals of one to three feet between the men. What is the object of such a formation? It is evidently proposed with the view of preventing loss among the supports and main body; but until troops come within infantry range, say 1,100 yards, it is theoretically certain, that formed in small columns, provided the columns are not too deep, they will suffer much less from artillery than if in line. After getting under infantry fire, it has been shown that the formation of the men has within certain limits, really very little to do with loss. Further, such a formation tends not to prevent but rather to produce and perpetuate what is the great danger of this kind of fighting, viz., a gradual cessation of all the elements of regular order, and a gradual dissolution of the whole force into the skirmishing line.

The formation of troops when they have to deliver a fire is undoubtedly a line or extended order, but the duty of the supports and main body is not to fire, they cannot fire without endangering those in front of them, consequently the formation should be such as is best suited for the work they have to perform i.e., to march over a certain space of ground; during this advance the troops in front of them will, as has been shown, draw most of the fire, and that formation should be adopted which will enable the leaders to hold the men most thoroughly in hand, keep them completely under their eye, and at the same time advance as rapidly and with as little confusion as possible.

Assume a support composed of two companies of 100 men each extended at one and a half yards apart, the companies would cover 150 yards, it is manifest that in an advance over rough ground for a considerable distance, such a line will become disordered, get out of hand, and not be a steady support to the troops in front of it. It is manifest that if the two companies be formed in two columns, each column composed of two subdivisions, that the captains can superintend their men better, check irregularites, and serpentine the companies they command better out of fire, take greater advantage of the sinuosities of the ground and be ready at all times to support the skirmishing line if it be checked or threatened by a few cavalry. It is desirable that the functions of the main body be kept clearly in view its duty is not to fire during the advance, but it is under cover of the fire of other troops to which it acts as a reserve to gain a place sufficiently near the enemy to make a rush, to drive him out. Also it may be fairly asked, looking to the great length of the advance required at the present day (2,500 yards) how will a support or main body, if deployed into a long extended line,

afford support to the flanks of the attack?—the weakest point,
and that consequently sure to be assailed. A small column may
afford such protection, an extended line cannot, and would be
perfectly helpless if suddenly attacked by a small body of horse.
The word column is one which gives the idea of a mass of men
one behind the other, but this disappears if it be considered that
the columns are either double company columns of a half battalion, or columns composed of two subdivisions. Further, it is to
the formed body of men acting behind the skirmishing line that
that line looks for support, and its moral effect is very great.

In all the accounts we see depicted the uneasy feeling with which skirmishing lines advanced when there were no closed detachments following in
reserve; and on the other hand the exhilaration of spirits, as soon as the
bayonets of the latter were seen, although only in the distance.

*Frontal
Attack of
Infantry.
(Translated
by Colonel
Newdegate.)*

To advance with this main body in a deployed or extended
line would be really to remove all the moral effect that formation
has on the skirmishing line. Further, if any slight change of
direction, such as converging towards a point, or a change of
direction to suit the nature of the ground, advanced over, has
to be made, the main body in a long spread out line, will
infallibly get into disorder. Hence, such a formation is not one
that meets the requirements of the case.

II.

THE DEFENCE.

The foregoing remarks have been chiefly confined to the
attack, or to troops acting on the offensive.

A pure defence can never win a battle, it may perhaps enable
the troops acting on the defensive to preserve their position, but
the most that can be hoped for from a pure defence is a drawn
battle, not a victory. The improvements in modern arms have
undoubtedly added much to the power of the defence, but the
attack has benefited also.

At first sight, it would appear that the defence would gain more from the
peculiarities of improved fire-arms, than the attack. An army acting on the
defensive, may have it in its power to choose such a position, as to oblige
the enemy to cross an open plain; it will also probably have time to ascertain
the distance of certain fixed points, so as to produce the greatest effect from
its fire. On the other hand, the advantages that an attacking force possesses
are also very considerable. As its commander has only to consult his own
judgment, he regulates his movements according to the dispositions of the
enemy. He, being the assailant, has a definite object before him, and chooses
his own way of attaining it; while the defender has first to find out his
adversary's intentions, and then to make the best arrangements for frustrating
them. On the one side, confidence and resolution, on the other, uncertainty
and anxiety. The defender, if he wish to bring about a decisive result, must
eventually himself become the assailant; but here the question arises, whether
before advancing to the attack, he should not exhaust all the material

*Von Moltke.
(Translated
by Crawford.)*

advantages to be gained from stationary fire, by employing it to the very last moment.

One phase of this superiority has already been discussed, page 90. But there is another which is deserving of attention. When two armies come in contact, the one that acts on the offensive or takes the initiative has the power of selecting the point for attack, and of arraying against that point a superior force. The defender does not know where he may be attacked, and has to provide for several possible, nay probable contingencies. He is liable to be deceived, induced to disseminate his force, and seek to be strong at all the threatened points, while the assailant need be strong at one and that the decisive point. Increased range and accuracy in weapons have given the attacker the power of selecting far more advantageous positions for covering and supporting his attack than formerly. Ground which in the days of old artillery might be simply ignored must now be held by the defender, thus compelling him to extend and therefore weaken his whole line; or it must be abandoned to the enemy, who will quickly make use of it as a *point d'appui* for an attack; and as the area operated over has thus increased at a much quicker rate than the actual effective range of the weapons, the assailant benefits considerably. Let any person examine a piece of ground and consider how he would occupy it with a given body of troops and he will find that a continued tendency exists in his own mind to occupy certain advantageous positions in front of what must be his main line. Let him imagine troops placed on these advantageous positions and he will find certain places in front tempting him on to them too, and this without end, until he will find himself compelled from the limited number of his troops to abandon all hope of holding many points, which he nevertheless can distinctly see must be most beneficial to an attacker. If this problem be worked out it will be found that the question will at last resolve itself into, not what is *best* to be held, but what it is *possible* to occupy. Further, the actual space, or neutral ground, between the outposts of armies closing on one another, a space which acts as a kind of curtain between them, through which neither can penetrate, must, from the increased range of arms, be now far wider, and offer more concealment than formerly. This space is really more dependant on the action of musketry than artillery, and the army acting on the offensive will usually, if not always, appropriate the greater portion of it.

Field-Marshal Sir John Burgoyne

It is of great advantage to an army in the field to push its advanced posts as far forward as it can in safety, in order to cover as much of the country and its resources as possible, to have longer and more precise warning of any movement of the enemy, and to impede his reconnaissances and proceedings generally.

It is still of more importance to restrict the enemy to the narrowest limits. Under ordinary circumstances midway between the respective forces may be considered a reasonable line of demarcation that each ought to insist upon, but several circumstances may give a superior power to one side.

1. The opposing armies may be very unequal in force, or one may have gained a marked ascendancy over the other ; in which case, the superior will be able to press the inferior into smaller limits.

2. One may hold some peculiarly strong, defensible post or batteries, in a salient position, that may give him a command over the neighbouring ground, in which case the line of demarcation will be midway between those parts and the position of the other army.

3. There may be a river not fordable, or other essential obstacle between the two which will naturally form the line of demarcation, although nearer to one than the other.

Subject to those sort of contingencies, it is very essential that no encroachment should be allowed ; the greatest efforts in particular should be made to prevent an enemy from holding parts, or even temporary possession of the foot of the heights on which part of an army is posted ; distant fire of artillery is not sufficient to justify submitting to the disadvantage ; and if the enemy's circumstances are such as really to enable him to enforce it ; the army which is subject to it must be in a very insecure position.

There is a great deal of brag in the matter of keeping possession of a greater extent of ground than a party is entitled to ; old campaigners know the value of it, and will take all the liberties they are allowed, returning however as soon as they are opposed.

There is a great moral power in the offensive ; the assailants are moving—doing something behind a mysterious curtain that the defenders know nothing of, there is something peculiarly demoralizing to men in waiting anxiously with nerves at a high state of tension, for something they know not what, to begin somewhere. In these respects improved arms have not increased the power of the defence.

No kind of fire tends so much to shake the *morale* of troops as a cross fire, and this from the great extension of the area of operations is the very fire that, increased range enables artillery to pour into villages, houses, or intrenchments. Men acting on the defensive may make up their minds to a fire coming in one direction, they may so dispose themselves as to mitigate its effects. But the moment shells and bullets come from other directions the whole thing is changed, and a feeling of inability to resist or maintain a position so attacked makes itself felt. The power that improved arms has given to the defence is that of keeping the attackers for a longer time under a heavy fire than formerly ; it is also stated that the defenders derive much advantage from the following causes :—

1st. Their fire is delivered by men in position, who can take a better and more correct aim

2nd. That the force acting on the defensive may be better covered and protected than that acting on the offensive, suffer less loss, and consequently be cooler and less excited.

3rd. That the ground may be better studied by the defensive than by the attacking force, and not only can advantage be thus taken of its conformation, but also additional force may be obtained by removing men from where they are of no use to important places.

If, however, these advantages, or supposed advantages, be analysed, they will be found to have hardly the importance that they at first sight appear to possess. With reference to the first, it must not be forgotten that the assailants move rapidly and by rushes of alternate fractions, which tends to disconcert the aim of the defenders, who are ever firing at a running target, while the attackers are firing at a fixed target; therefore the superiority of the defence in this case does not seem to be very great.

With reference to the second, page 89 states the circumstances under which an attack is possible, and it appears that the concentration of fire on one spot so demoralises a defender that he can be neither cool nor calm. The fire of the attacker is always convergent, that of the defender divergent.* Further, the advance of troops takes them away from the dead and wounded who are left behind. The defenders must remain in one place, and the dead and wounded can with difficulty be removed, hence the *morale* of the defenders will suffer the most.

With reference to the third, there can be no doubt that the defence will benefit greatly from its superiority in this respect; and it is not only to its fire, but the power of bringing that fire to bear on proper places, that the defender owes his superiority.

How then should a defensive position be occupied? It would appear that for the correct holding of a defensive position, arrangements should be made to bring a heavy artillery and infantry fire on the attackers at the very beginning of the action, and to hold a few powerful reserves in hand, to attack and drive out any troops that may obtain a lodgment within the general line.

It has been pointed out at page 89 that the assailant to have a reasonable hope of success must be superior at the point where the attack is made. Now to counteract this superiority there must be on the side of the defence large reserves kept ready in hand to be moved the moment the attacker's project is developed, and sufficiently near to be brought up in time to drive the enemy back; not merely to check his advance after he has penetrated the position. Such reserves must be in the hands of the Generals commanding the Divisions and Corps, rather than those of the General in Chief, and hence it follows that these bodies should each form their own reserve.

On the defensive it may fairly be questioned if a deployed line is now requisite. The breech-loader enables an extended line to deliver more fire now than a closed line in former days. It will perhaps be wiser, therefore, to keep back a large portion of the first line until the attack has developed itself, and then to use it in thickening the line of skirmishers where most threatened. Such a method gives much additional power to

* The comparison between a siege and an attack here holds good, the assailants working on a wider front, direct their whole fire on one portion of the defender's position, their fire is thus convergent; if the defender replies his fire must be divergent.

the men who see themselves supported by those behind, and who feel that they are not left alone to cope with the attackers.

The sudden increase of the defender's fire, by a large reinforcement of the supports, has a powerful effect in checking the enemy's advance.

It appears, from the testimony of all continental writers, to be the experience of recent war, that volley firing cannot be used, and that independent firing, which enables each man to judge his own time and aim, is far more effective.

Even when on the defensive, to which, according to theory, volley firing is peculiarly applicable, it could so seldom be employed, that the few exceptions only serve to prove the rule. Even behind cover, field walls, barricades the fire of dense crowds of skirmishers was preferred to bringing forward parties in close order to fire volleys. To fire a volley always takes up a certain amount of time, which will be made use of by the enemy's skirmishers to pour a heavy fire into the compact body then showing itself, causing serious loss and in part hindering the volley. Boguslauski. (Translated by Graham.)

The chief argument against volleys at such a moment is that they have little effect upon skirmishers who are the first to come up. But if you wait till the enemy's supports are visible, the party in close order which is intended to fire the volleys would be for some time exposed to the skirmishers' fire, and would be a heap of corpses before it got a chance of acting.

It would appear, therefore, that in holding a defensive position, the skirmishing line in front should be supported exactly as in the attack, and this all the more so, as in most defensive positions, the supports which feed the front line may be much closer than in the attack. In occupying any defensive position, small bodies of troops of all arms should be told off at favourable places to make an advance on the enemy and check his movement. Such a force advancing a short distance from the main position disconcerts the assailant, compels him to direct his fire on the new opponent, relieving the actual defenders from fire, and enables them to act with renewed vigour. For this purpose small posts in front of a position are of great value, but they should not be surrendered or evacuated at the first attack, they should be firmly held, and to do this they must be supported from the rear. The old rule, "Salients should be few and marked" is as good now as ever it was.

But no defence has a chance of ultimately succeeding that is not based on the offensive, or that does not contemplate taking the offensive when an opportunity offers.

An army acting on the defensive should never altogether give up the idea of itself assuming the offensive. Von Moltke. (Translated by Crawford.)

It has been already stated that there is a tendency on the part of the assailants to avoid the centre of the defender's position as being that where usually the fire is heaviest, and to turn off to the flanks, and to cover their advance by seeking out places unswept or only partly swept by fire, Such movements must leave gaps in their line, and these gaps, if not filled up from the supports at once, are the very points favourable for the defenders to attack, and by so doing threaten the assailant's advance on the flanks. But in making such forward movements, the greatest care is requisite that the main position be not lost, and hence arises another necessity for reserves. Generally, both supports and main body may be much nearer the skirmishing, or firing line, than when attacking. The only thing is to place them so that they shall escape fire as much as possible; but especially in the defence it must be remembered a small reserve that arrives when it is wanted, is infinitely superior to a strong one that arrives too late. Early deployment and a long march over ground, in extended order, exhausts an assailant; the defender should therefore seek to make the attacker deploy as soon as possible. But it is questionable if this should not be rather done by bodies of cavalry and artillery, pushed well out to the front, and supported by infantry, who, using the containing power of the breech-loader, will make the attacker deploy; rather than by long shots from the main positions which are not very efficacious, and mark the position held, better perhaps than anything else.*

Scherff.

The basis of a pure defence should be to fight the attack only at the distance where its fire produces the greatest effects. But though this is so, it is requisite to profit by the extreme range of arms and by the aid of small detachments entrusted to selected officers, to keep up a fire on the general advance of the enemy. The first line (*skirmishing or firing line*) will seek, by means of the most rapid fire, to keep the last halt of the enemy's skirmishers, or that preceding the assault, as far off as possible. All the intensity, all the power of the fire, will be developed against the real assault for 300 to 400 paces. The defence should be convinced, that despite its fire, it may become necessary to use the bayonet, and that this resort is less dangerous than a retreat.

It appears, therefore, that both in defensive and offensive fighting tactics, one great object is to develop the individual action of the man, whether in the use of his weapons or as a unit. For officers this development of independent action is the power of leading and handling small groups or bodies of from 10 to 200 men; but while this independence is developed, it must be held in hand and directed, it must be freedom, not license. It must be carefully watched by a commander who has reserves in hand to support it, either by completing the victory or checking defeat; and above all it necessitates most careful training on the part of the soldier. It further appears, that a general acting on the offensive, must (to secure his flanks and protect his line of battle partially denuded of troops to concentrate a superior force on the point of attack) never lose sight of defensive operations. That a general acting on the defensive must impart to his defence as much of an offensive character as is possible.

The foregoing pages give a general statement of what may be termed the tactical problem of the present day, and some general ideas as to how that problem may be dealt with.

* The effect of artillery fire is three times as great at 2,200 yards as it is at 3,300 yards.

Manœuvre tactics are essentially different from fighting tactics, the former admit of certain definite rules being laid down. Time and distance, both of which are known factors, enter largely into such questions, and therefore it is most desirable that manœuvre tactics should be governed by rule; but when fighting tactics are dealt with, such indeterminate factors as human passions, the ground, the weather, and the enemy, complicate the problem to such an extent that it would be as dangerous as it is impossible to lay down fixed rules. It is therefore desirable that officers should see these subjects from as many stand points as possible.

The Italian army have recently modified their tactics to a great extent, and a *précis* of the report of the committee entrusted with this duty is appended. It will be observed that the problem is stated in almost identical language to that used in the foregoing pages, but the conclusions are slightly different.

III.

CAVALRY.

At the close of the War of 1866, the action of the Prussian military authorities was carefully watched, they had tried their army on which years of careful thought and study had been bestowed, they had tested its capabilities, gauged its powers and seen its weaknesses. What they then, after seeing the machine in motion, did, when an opportunity for repairing and overhauling it took place, was of peculiar interest.

Amongst other things, they largely increased their cavalry. This of itself was the most effectual contradiction that could be given to the statement so constantly made, that the breech-loader had numbered cavalry amongst things of the past.

Recent events have shown that the duties of Cavalry, not only as covering the advance of an army, as outposts or reconnoiterers, but also on the actual field of battle, is perhaps more brilliant than ever. True it is that the qualities and knowledge now required of cavalry are different from what they were, or to put it more correctly, the same qualities and a great deal more besides are needed. Quickness, coolness and gallantry are now as always requisite in a cavalry soldier. But more still is needed, knowledge of country, knowledge of what the requirements of other troops are, power of observation and description, ability to seize instinctively the object of the Commander-in-Chief, a certain acquaintance with engineering, all these are now necessities for a cavalry officer. His sphere is greatly enlarged, and to fill it properly his military knowledge must be far more extensive than that involved in leading a squadron and keeping it effective, all important as the latter is, as the basis of everything else. Far from doing away with cavalry, modern events have clearly shown that there is no arm of the service from the correct management of which the army can reap more benefit.

If its action be paralysed, from any cause, there is none the want of which will be more severely felt.

Von Moltke.
(Translated
by Crawford.)

Because in modern warfare the long range and destructive fire of artillery necessitates a scattered formation, there will be more frequent opportunities for those brilliant dashes of small bodies of cavalry, in which, by taking advantage of the critical moment, the cavalry of division so often distinguish themselves.

Tactical
retrospect.
Captain May.
(Translated
by Ourry.)

So long as rapidity, boldness, and dash are active agents in war, cavalry will retain its importance. A cavalry devoid of these qualities, but merely possessing good intentions, obedience, with ordinary bravery, and a laudable modesty, is worse than none at all.

The duties of cavalry in the field may be divided into two classes. These duties although similar, are sufficiently distinct to produce a real division.

They are:—

1st. The duties of the cavalry attached to a Division of the army.

2nd. The duties of the cavalry Division.

A reference to page 8 shows that in the Prussian Army a regiment of cavalry is attached to each Division. The duties of this cavalry is to cover the head of the Division, examine the country, provide small parties to look out for the enemy in various directions, feel for and communicate with troops marching on roads parallel to that its own Division is marching on, keep up the communication with troops in front and rear, and thus link the component portions of the army-corps together, and lastly to provide orderlies and escorts.

The duties of the cavalry Division are similar, but on a far larger scale; it has to keep the army acquainted with every movement of the enemy, to harrass him and conceal the movements on their own side by keeping a strong curtain of posts constantly in advance, so that the enemy shall know nothing of what goes on within that curtain, to connect the various army-corps moving together, and keep each informed of the action of the other.

Tactical
retrospect.
Captain May.
(Translated
by Ourry.)

In speaking of the action of cavalry, we must distinguish between divisional cavalry and the cavalry division. The first has to work in immediate connection with the other branches of its division, the latter, the cavalry division, as an independent tactical body stands more frequently in a strategical rather than a tactical connection with the rest of the army.

It may be questioned if the charges of masses of cavalry, as executed during the wars of the early part of this century, such as those at Essling, by General d'Espagne's cavalry, those at Echmühl, or at Waterloo, can now be carried out, except for some very special object which warrants the great loss that must ensue.

It appears that the action of cavalry on an actual battle-field must now be generally limited to watching the flanks, checking the action of the hostile cavalry, attacking broken and repulsed infantry. There are, however, many instances when an able cavalry leader can seize opportunities to use his arm with great effect. Such opportunities do not often occur, but when they do, the success achieved will generally be very great. The opportune and unexpected charge of a small body of cavalry, under Kellerman at Marengo, is an instance of such an opportunity.

The charge of a small body of English cavalry, under Colonel Taylor at Vimeiro, is another instance. And a similar opportunity occured at the defence of St. Privat, when the Prussian guard halted staggering under the terrible effect of the French fire. Had the French cavalry been on the right in place of the left, and had it circled out from behind the woods in rear of St. Privat, and swept across the front, it would doubtless have suffered terribly, but would have rolled up the Prussian attack. Such attacks can however generally be best made by small bodies of cavalry. Another use to which cavalry can be put on the battle-field is to charge infantry which have gained a position and are disordered by their own success. Such, for instance, as when the attackers have penetrated into the defenders' position. Moments like these will doubtless always occur on every battle-field, but if not immediately seized they quickly pass away.

The gallant charges made by the French cavalry against the Prussian infantry when the latter were not disordered were perfectly useless and effected nothing, although the fact that the German cavalry did succeed on one occasion shows that the successful attack of cavalry against breech-loaders and rifled artillery, although exceedingly dangerous, is by no means impossible.

On the 16th of August, the French army was seeking to retreat on Verdun from Metz, a small portion of the Prussian infantry only was up on the south of the Verdun road, and it became a matter of the utmost necessity to pin the French to the ground and keep them there until the remainder of the Prussian army could come up.

The Third Army Corps had fought since 9 a.m. against threefold numbers and closed the road to Verdun, along which Bazaine's army was retreating. About one o'clock both the strength and the cartridges of the brave men of Brandenburg began to fail, when an attack of several cavalry regiments, ordered between one and two o'clock, gave them breathing time. The ground on which the attack took place is chiefly flat, therefore favourable to cavalry. The French first line was, like ours, extended into a long line of skirmishers; as a scarcity of ammunition had shown itself with the third Corps, it is probable that the enemy was no better off. *Boguslauski. (Translated by Graham.)*

Several brigades charging on various points at full gallop and with the most reckless bravery, overwhelmed the first line; then coming upon the supports broke several battalions, rode through several batteries, were at length repulsed by the masses which they encountered further on, and, being attacked by French cavalry, retired under a fearful fire.

Some of the regiments had indeed sounded the rally before coming upon the third line. A similar attack was made some hours later, now was this a success? Certainly it was; the French, surprised by the impetuous onset of the German squadrons, paused in their advance, time was gained: the German reinforcements, which eventually decided the victory, came into line. The charge at Mars-la-Tour, was doubtless an exquisite stroke of higher tactics on the part of the General who gave the order, and a brilliant feat of arms on the part of the cavalry brigade which executed it.

The attack had a great effect on the fate of the day. Our cavalry sacrificed a third, some regiments indeed half their men, to bring the French to a stand-still. But here lies the difference between this charge and the great cavalry attacks of former days, that the latter themselves decided the victory.

The following is another description of this charge :—

Borbstaedt.

The French Sixth Corps still remained in its old position on the right, opposed to Buddenbrock's division, which it completely overlapped, and threatened to roll up with a flank attack. Lieutenant-General Von Alven-sleben received a report that one of the French corps, which had been marching from Gravelotte towards Doncourt, had halted, reversed its columns, and was about to climb up the plateau to the south of Bruville. It was requisite that Buddenbrock should be enabled to hold his ground till reinforce-ments came up. In order to secure this, if possible, Bredow's Cavalry Brigade, which had been previously withdrawn from the right wing and sent to the main road, Mars-la-Tour and Vionville, was now ordered to advance between the high road and the wood, against this formidable position of the enemy. It was of course to be apprehended that a cavalry attack, undertaken against intact infantry and powerful lines of artillery, neither of which had been previously shaken by artillery fire, must prove a total failure, or at least cause immense losses. Still it had become necessary to demand the sacrifice from the cavalry for the good of the army, and above all, in order to check the enemy's advance and gain time.

Bredow's Cavalry Brigade had present, at the moment it was ordered to effect a breach in the front of the Sixth French Corps, only six squadrons, viz., three of the 7th Cuirassiers and three of the 16th Uhlans.

These six squadrons crossed the high road to the west of Vionville, taking at first a northerly direction formed in a close column, the Cuirassiers leading till they arrived near the wood.

Here the head of the column wheeled to the right, and when the new direction had been gained, the word was given to deploy to the right, first into squadrons and then into line of the brigade, all of which was done under a heavy fire of the enemy's artillery.

The three Cuirassier squadrons, which being on the left first got into line, commenced the charge forthwith the 16th Lancers having to wait until its right squadron came into line, followed immediately, so that at first a charge in echelons took place unintentionally.

In a moment the batteries were reached and the gunners cut down at their guns, when the whole brigade then in one line, charged the infantry in the rear, who received the rush of the cavalry with a heavy fire.

These lines were broken through too, and at such speed, that few of the French had time to fire a second shot. The main object of the charge had been attained beyond all expectation, but carried away by the ardour of combat, the impetuous band of horsemen swept irresistibly forward, despite of all endeavours of the officers to rally and reform the men. The latter pounced on a line of mitrailleuses drawn up in rear of the infantry. Some of the foremost horsemen had reached the line of mitrailleuses with the last efforts of their horses, and begun to cut and stab at the artillerymen, when, quite unexpectedly, the French 7th Cuirassiers of Forton's Division issued forth from the wood on the old Roman road. One of its squadrons penetrated at once into the intervals between the disordered Prussian squadrons, the remainder of the regiment and a Dragoon Brigade followed at a trot. At the same moment French Hussars and Chasseurs, passing through the intervals of the second line of their own infantry, fell upon the right of the Uhlans, so that the six hitherto victorious Prussian squadrons, finding themselves attacked on all sides, were compelled to retreat, and with their blown horses to force a way through the enemy's masses of infantry.

Of the 7th Cuirassiers only 7 officers and 70 men, of the 16th Uhlans only 6 officers and 80 men, came out of this sanguinary hand-to-hand combat.

It is quite certain that the sacrifice demanded from the cavalry in a most critical moment of the engagement was repaid by the complete success of the manœuvre.

For the fatal attack of the 6th French corps against the left wing of Buddenbrock's Division was completely checked and never resumed, a proof how much the French troops were shaken by the vehement attack of a few Prussian squadrons.

The graves of horses and men which remain on the ground mark distinctly the course taken by the Prussian cavalry in its advance, and show the terrible effects of the breech-loader and rifled guns.

These descriptions prove the absolute necessity of cavalry when it charges being supported by fresh cavalry.

The rapid advance over ground, often heavy, tends to blow the horses to such an extent that no matter what may be the success of a charge, if the cavalry making it are, when the horses are blown, charged by fresh cavalry they must suffer much. Hence the rule which has been laid down for many years that cavalry should attack in lines, the second line being ready to advance to the support of the first line when its energies are spent.

It is so desirable that a reserve should be kept in all cases in which the cavalry is desired to charge, that it appears to be a matter of necessity ; and the officers and men should be accustomed to form and conduct the reserve at exercise.   *Wellington.*

The reserve of a body of cavalry charging is intended to answer two purposes. 1st. To improve and complete the success of the charge ; 2nd. To protect the retreat of the troops retiring, supposing those who charge are unsuccessful, or possibly to acquire success after their failure.

The proportion of the body of cavalry to be kept in reserve must depend upon the nature of the ground and of the body of troops to be attacked. It should not be less than one-half of the body formed for the operation, nor should it exceed two-thirds. It follows that every body of cavalry should be formed in two or three lines. The second line should be deployed, the third might be in columns of such a size as that they could be readily formed into line.

The next point for consideration is the distance at which these lines should be placed, and should precede one another : and it will be observed that this must depend upon the nature of the enemy to be attacked, and in some degree upon the nature of the ground, and what may be the object of the operation. It has been already stated that one of the objects of the reserve is to protect the retreat of the body charging which has failed, or possibly to turn the fortunes of the day by a fresh attack upon the enemy engaged in his pursuit, and it is therefore obvious that the reserve or second line of the cavalry should not be so near the first, as to be at all affected by the confusion into which the first will naturally fall in its retreat from the charge.

Wellington then lays down the distance of the lines when the attack is on cavalry, to be about 450 yards ; that being sufficient to allow the beaten line to pass through the intervals of the second line, and yet near enough for the second line to support the first. He adds, in the attack of infantry and artillery, the encounters are different, and the distances between the lines should be altered accordingly. In this case the object should be for the second line to strike its blow as soon as possible after the first shall have failed ; as there is no chance of either the infantry or the artillery pursuing a line of cavalry, whose attack it may have repulsed, there appears no reason for guarding so cautiously against the confusion into which the second line may be thrown

I

by the retreat of the first. 200 yards appears to be the distance between lines of cavalry attacking bodies of infantry and artillery.

At Mars-la-Tour the Prussians appear to have attacked in one line, without supports of any kind. The object of the attack was perfectly clear, and justified the sacrifice. But the retreating squadrons would have been far less roughly handled had there been a second line in support.

The French Cavalry. Colonel Bonie. On the side of the Germans as well as our own, charges were invariably made at a gallop over too great an extent of ground ; horses get blown after galloping 1,000 to 1,500 yards. When horses get blown, and lose their wind, on reaching the object of attack they become quite incapable of resisting an attack or securing success. Look at the attack of Bredow's brigade. Taken in flank by our cavalry, it was so exhausted that the men could get no more out of their horses ; they were entirely at the mercy of our men, who cut them down like sheep. This attack proves the absolute necessity of a reserve, which, following the movement of the attackers without pressing on them, and arriving fresh, completes the success, and profits by the exhaustion, of the enemy. The *échelons* of Bredow's brigade obtained a first success, but could not preserve it ; having no supports, they were at our mercy.

Judging from the latter account, but six squadrons were employed, and the success achieved by these squadrons shows that cavalry used with decison, and at the right moment, will still effect much on the actual battle-field; and that its effective action may be secured perhaps, more by small bodies, than by large divisions. The six squadrons which charged at Mars-la-Tour were hardly more than the cavalry attached to a single division. It is quite true that breech-loaders, placing the soldier in the position of being always ready to fire, have given to small bodies of infantry acting together a far greater defensive power than formerly, but the extended order in which troops fight makes them peculiarly liable to be thrown into confusion and driven back by charges of small bodies of cavalry, more especially if the ground is such that cavalry can come out unexpectedly on the extended infantry line. And this effect will be all the greater that infantry so advancing can rarely be supported by cavalry to meet such attacks, which it would appear should be made by a lightly-equipped active cavalry, never seeking to pursue too far, but rather to drive the attacking infantry into compact bodies, retiring as rapidly as possible to leave those bodies exposed to fire before they can again open out.

The Prussians in their new Cavalry Instructions have made some alterations bearing on these points. By the old regulations the charge was supposed to be made over 600 yards, it is now supposed to be made over about 1,150 yards, of which 750 are supposed to be crossed at a trot, 325 at a gallop, and 75 at full speed. The whole of that portion of the book bearing on the movement of cavalry in two or more lines has been rewritten. The following is an extract.

Prussian Regulations. The object of the second line when working in the presence of an enemy, is to relieve the first line of all anxiety as to its flanks or rear. When an attack is made it has to support the first line by attacking itself if requisite.

It aids the first line in driving back the enemy and pursuing him. A reserve drawn from the second line should be held in hand as long as possible, for other conditions of the fight being equal, victory falls to him who at the last moment, and when all the enemy's troops are engaged, can produce a reserve, no matter how small, provided only it is *fresh*. In such cases also, the principle directing that as far as possible charges should be made on the flank, must be followed.

Leading the second line is more difficult than leading the first, and much more is required from regiments in second line, both as regards manœuvring power and speed, than from those in first line.

Cavalry cannot ride about within a few hundred yards of the enemy under his rifle fire. If that were possible, you would not see infantry mounted officers dismount. In spite of the powerful effect of fire, we cannot assert that the square has become absolutely useless. If cavalry in extended order attack skirmishers in flank the latter will often have nothing left but to form square ; but if cavalry attacks in front or even obliquely, the skirmishers will find it quite sufficient to draw up in line, if there be not sufficiently good cover for them to remain extended. *Boguslawski (Translated by Graham.)*

In such attacks the cavalry leader, having compelled the extended line of the enemy to run together, must remember that his object should then be to get away as quickly as possible, and leave those masses to the fire of the infantry and artillery which his presence in front of the general line masks.

Rifled guns will effect cavalry at far greater ranges than formerly, but it may be questioned if (within certain limits of fire) they will have as much effect as smooth-bore guns, and although cavalry advancing to attack will be longer under fire, yet from the rapidity of their motion, the continually altering range, and the fact that with rifled projectiles those that graze short of the mark usually deflect, and do not, as is the case with spherical projectiles, follow the original path, it would seem that the attack of artillery by cavalry has not been rendered much more difficult than formerly. But whether this be the case or not, such attacks should be exceedingly rare and only for very special objects ; they are sure to put the cavalry making them *hors de combat*, and the value of cavalry in the field is too great to allow it to be thus used, except for some reason of paramount importance.

The thin and extended lines of formation in battle will, in future, afford the cavalry opportunities of acting in a new aspect, by giving it occasions for energetic and immediate co-operation with the infantry and artillery in action. If the infantry attacks with the cavalry at hand, the latter will then be in a position to take advantage of the decisive movement, which has been prepared for it by the artillery, and the present tactics with regard to skirmishers which requires swarms of men in loose order, will reap the richest advantages. *Tactical retrospect. Captain May. (Translated by Ouvry.)*

It will not be impossible for them to throw themselves in gaps through the enemy's line on their reserve ; and even if no success were to follow, they would still spread terror and consternation. Indeed the moral effect that an efficient fire of musketry or shell always makes, even on the best infantry, causes a favourable opportunity to arise for the use of cavalry.

The following proposals for the attack of cavalry are well worthy of being considered. But it should be observed that they make no provision for what is really the grand danger of cavalry, viz., being charged when the horses are blown by fresh cavalry, in which case the cavalry on the blown horses are perfectly helpless, and no gallantry or leading can help them.

Boguslauski.
(Translated by Graham.)

Prussian cavalry has for a long time adopted the échelon form of attack. The principle is correct, for the squadrons follow one another at intervals, one drawing the fire, the next breaking in. But the present fire-arms are so quickly loaded, that there is really no cessation of fire. You may, however, mislead infantry into dealing its fire with precipitation and want of regularity. The attack in skirmishing order seems to us here preferable to that of compact squadrons.

Thus we will imagine the charge of a cavalry regiment to be executed as follows : Two squadrons in extended order, throw themselves upon the infantry two following at a trot, about 300 paces in rear. The leading squadrons rush at, or perhaps ride through the enemy's skirmishers, wheeling off before his masses, or galloping past them.

The Officer Commanding the two squadrons in close order, who with his trumpeter accompanies those in advance, until pretty close to the enemy's infantry, sounds the gallop for his own squadrons, as soon as those in front have felt the first effective fire, and makes his charge.

This plan may be the most likely to induce the enemy's infantry to blaze away in a hurry, thus affording greater chances of success to the real charge which follows. We repeat, it *may* have the effect, but we are far from setting it forth as an absolute recipe for restoring to cavalry its old power in battle At all events this appears to us to be the best method, particularly as the horsemen, in extended order, would suffer less than if they were in compact bodies.

The Austrian cavalry regulations are very precise on the subject of attacks, and are in some respects peculiar. The following is a précis of the rules on this subject :—

Austrian Regulations.
(Translated by Captain Cooke, 22nd Regt.)

In war, the attack is the decisive, therefore the most important *rôle* of cavalry. The main conditions for success are rapidity and surprise in the advance, vigor and momentum in the shock. The men must therefore be practised in advancing over considerable distances, against the enemy, at speed, without in consequence losing steadiness, order (*i.e.* close formation), and force. "These essentials they seek to gain in peace, by invariably throwing out a "skeleton enemy; it is distinctly laid down that on no account is an attack "to be delivered, no matter how small the unit, without showing a skeleton "enemy.

"According as a section, squadron, regiment, or larger unit forms the "attacking body, a corresponding unit or number of units is used ; each "squadron being marked by the four section-leaders and the squadron leader, "the whole under an officer or commander of the enemy." In practising the attack, the attacking body should break into a gallop at from 800 to 1,000 paces from the skeleton enemy ; after sounding the "gallop," the commander gives the word "attack," which is the signal for the men to draw their swords ; when at 60 to 80 paces from the enemy, he orders the "charge" ; after pursuing about 200 or 300 paces, he orders the "rally," when the men fall into a trot and collect behind their leaders ; when all are quietly at a trot, the line is halted. In presence of a real enemy, the commander must judge the right moment for ordering the "attack." In open ground, *e.g.*, he should give the order when about 1,000 paces from the enemy ; in a close country as soon as the enemy is discovered or his proximity is reported by the patrols. The moment for breaking into the gallop must depend upon circumstances, in which the condition of the horses, the nature of the ground over which the attack must be delivered, and the object for which it is made. must be considered. When within 60 or 80 paces of the enemy the "charge" must be ordered, the horses put to their full speed and the rush made with shouts of "Hurrah." The charge must not be ordered at a greater distance than from 60 to 80 yards, for the charging pace, if made over too great a distance, would tend to open out the files, and consequently to diminish the overwhelming force of a closed cavalry attack.

* * * * *

Every attacking body whose front is greater than a squadron, must always detach parties for the protection of its flanks, which should follow in échelon at from 50 to 80 paces to the flank and rear ; these defensive flanks, if composed of two or more sections, should be formed in column. As a rule, both flanks of the attacking line should be followed by "defensive flanks," but if one flank is covered by the ground, the exposed flank only should detach a "defensive flank."

There must always be a reserve, which should follow the attacking line in column, at from 200 to 400 paces to the flank and rear. If the attack is delivered against the enemy's front, the nature of the ground, the enemy's formation for attack, etc., must determine in rear of which flank the reserve should follow ; if the attack is delivered against the enemy's flank, the reserve should, as a rule, protect the flank which is most exposed to the counter attack of the enemy's reserve.

* * * * *

It may sometimes be more advisable to attack in "swarms" than in a closed body, e.g., when attacking guns, in order to suffer as little as possible from their fire, or when attacking advancing infantry, when the object is rather to check their advance than actually to charge them ; or to attract their fire, so as to give greater chances for a closed body following in rear ; or when the appearance only of cavalry would be sufficient, or when the ground would not permit of the advance of a closed body. A squadron attacking in "swarms," should always leave a section behind in reserve.

* * * * *

Cavalry should be surprised, if possible, while deploying ; if deployed, it should be attacked, if possible, in flank. A small body may attack a considerably larger body in flank with every chance of success. Relative numbers in this case are of minor importance, but the flank attack, in order to succeed, must be executed with the greatest possible promptitude, so that the enemy may have no time to change front. Carefully observing and taking advantage of ground, i.e., forming and advancing under cover, is the main essential for the success of a flank attack.

Infantry should if possible be attacked when in motion, or be surprised, so that they have no time to form squares. If this cannot be effected, and it is necessary to actually charge the squares, the attack should be delivered against the faces of the squares with successive bodies, following each other at from 80 to 100 paces.

Artillery should, if possible, be attacked in motion, when limbering up or unlimbering, or in flank. The attack on the guns should be executed in "swarms," while a closed and strong body attacks the escort ; if the attacking body is a squadron, one section in swarms should go against the guns, the remaining sections in a closed body against the escort.

It is a matter of the greatest importance, that before any forward movement of cavalry is made, the ground over which it is to act should be reconnoitred. This reconnaissance may be of the most rapid character ; two or three men, if well trained and with quick eyes, riding rapidly over the ground, will bring back intelligence as to its state, whether marshy or not, and whether there are fences or hedges unseen from the main position, where the enemy can place his infantry. A few men galloping rapidly out in this way for intelligence, will rarely be hit, if some are, one at all events will come back for information. The moment a body of cavalry halts in a position from which they may be called on to advance rapidly to the front, the officers should at once seek to learn all they can of the ground over which they are likely to act; and such knowledge must not be a general knowledge, but one obtained by actual observation of the ground.

It may be added that a really powerful telescope, mounted so as to be carried in a lance bucket, would be a most useful article of equipment for a cavalry regiment.

The French Cavalry.
Colonel Bonie.

The cavalry in this charge* came close to the Prussians and without great loss, when it was completely disordered by the numerous obstacles strewn on the ground, biscuit cases, baggage wagons, and camp equipment hurriedly abandoned by the troops in their retreat. 22 officers, 208 men, and 243 horses were lost in this charge by the regiment of cuirassiers. This would not have been the case if the artillery had been in action a little longer, and we must also deduce that it is indispensable at all times to reconnoitre the ground, for if the obstacles on the ground had been known the cuirassiers would have taken another direction.

Campaign of 1866; official account.
Translated by Hozier and Wright.
Napier.

In their eagerness to meet the enemy as soon as possible, the Hussars omitted to throw out éclaireurs in their front, and when they were already in full gallop they unexpectedly came upon a deep gully which had been hidden from view in the high corn ; part of them pulled up in time, some got over to the other side, but the greater part fell into the ravine.

Sir Arthur Wellesley immediately ordered Anson's Brigade of Cavalry, composed of the 23rd Light Dragoons and 1st German Hussars, to charge the head of these columns. These regiments, coming on at a canter, and increasing the speed as they advanced, rode headlong against the enemy, but in a few moments came upon the brink of a hollow cleft, which was not perceptible at a distance.

The action of cavalry on the actual battle-field is by no means a thing of the past. The use of cavalry with skill at the right moment and in the right numbers has always been considered one os the most difficult problems in war ; modern arms have increased this difficulty many fold, but to say that the day of cavalry on the field of battle if past, is merely another way of saying that the knowledge of how it should be used is wanting.

The question of how flanks are to be protected during an attack in extended order is one that continually crops up, and one to which as yet, no satisfactory answer has been given. This weak point of the infantry attack is precisely that on which the cavalry should fasten, and it is that where knowledge of ground, quickness and decision will continually afford to young officers in command of small bodies, an opportunity of performing brilliant feats. The action of cavalry supported by horse artillery on the flanks of an army will be of the greatest importance by extending the line occupied by the troops on the defensive, the enemy if he attempts a flank movement must consequently be thrown further off, and compelled to make a longer

---

* Charge of Cavalry of the Imperial Guard at Mars-la-Tour.

march. And the action of a powerful cavalry supported by artillery on the head of the columns moving to a flank will at all times delay their progress, and give time for the army on the defensive to manœuvre. But to work cavalry and horse artillery in this manner it is requisite that they should be boldly used, and advantage taken of the rapidity of their movement, they must not be kept close to or hanging on the infantry for support, but must act boldly, seek to find out the enemy's flank movement, and once those movements have declared themselves, the cavalry must act on the head of his columns ; whenever troops move to outflank an enemy in position they must always move in long columns, for they attack to a flank not to their front. Hence, the front being narrow, they themselves may be overlapped and taken on the flanks.

During the battle of Gravelotte the *rôle* of our cavalry was without importance, because the divisions Desvaux of the guard, Forton of the reserve, Valabrègue of the second corps, or in other words the mass of cavalry, was halted in the ravines of Less, Châtel Saint Germain, and Moulin Longeau, where they received shell without being able to do anything. Could they have been usefully used on the open ground in the front of St. Privat and Roncourt? The right wing of the army was the only place where the ground was sufficiently open to allow the action of cavalry. There the previous day our cavalry should have been assembled upon the banks of the Orne, in the villages of St. Marie Aux Chénes, Saint Batilly, Habouville, it would have found excellent bivouacs, a large open space, and ground sufficiently hard to work over.

Thus disposed it would have warned us of the great turning movement made by the enemy under cover of his cavalry. This cavalry did not charge our line of battle, but it preceded the artillery and protected it in the great change of front to the right, it covered the infantry columns in the Batilly and Saint Ail ravines before the attack on Saint Privat.

Used in such a way our cavalry, with the help of its horse artillery, would have checked the enemy's advance, and might have prevented him from reaching the right wing until the close of the battle. If the cavalry divisions we have named, useless where they were, had been placed on the right, they might have enabled that wing to take the offensive, supported as it would have been by the two cavalry divisions of 3rd and 4th corps which remained on the defensive, and consequently were useless all day.

The French Cavalry. Colonel l'onie.

No army that is able to manœuvre, and the cavalry of which is properly posted, and does its duty, should ever, under any circumstances whatsoever, be surprised by a flank attack.

But the great use of cavalry undoubtedly is in advance of the Army. Not a few miles only, but several marches ahead feeling for and obtaining information of the enemy, and it is in such operations that the skill and boldness of officers of comparatively lower grades comes so prominently to the front. The action of good cavalry in thus protecting an army is invaluable, in giving the main body rest and repose, free from the disturbance caused by vague rumours or alarms. Similarly, the constant annoyance which such cavalry can give an enemy, demoralises his troops, and spreads an uneasy feeling of insecurity through the best army in the world.

This duty of cavalry to the army generally, is well explained, in the following words.

Von Mirus.
(Translated
by Russel.)
De Brack.

It is a noble and right feeling for the soldier to think that my comrades can sleep as I am awake : my comrades have nothing to fear ; I watch the enemy.

The mechanics of war really consist of two things, *fighting* and *sleeping*, using and producing physical power ; to keep both in perfect equilibrium is the science of war, it often takes far more skill to produce force than to use it.

In presence of an enemy the science of procuring repose is given to few, no duty requires an officer to possess a surer, quicker, or better trained *coup d'œil militaire.*

The numerous surprises of the French troops, such as that of Forton's Cavalry Division, on the 16th August, a Division specially sent out to feel the way of the army, and protect it from all surprises, and the similar surprise that took place at Beaumont, are inexcusable, and are good examples of the uselessness of cavalry to an army, if it hangs on the infantry for support and protection.

The action of cavalry in spreading a curtain round an army, hiding its movements and seeking to obtain information of the enemy's position and intention is not the consequence so much of improved arms, as it is a consequence of railways, telegraphs, improved roads, increased cultivation, and large armies. To develop the full power of railways and telegraphs an army must be a large one operating over a large area. A small army of 30,000 to 60,000 in Europe will by no means reap the same proportionate advantages from rapid means of communication as an army of 300,000 to 400,000 men. But such an army cannot work at all, unless it operates over a large area ; an area again which is not proportionate to the size of the army, but which increases at a rate much greater than the size of the army does. Now, no troops using railways even for supplies, can be considered safe if those railways are subject to destruction by small bodies passing through the columns and getting in rear of them, consequently troops must be used to cover the whole front and close the openings between the columns. Cavalry, from their more rapid means of locomotion, are evidently the troops to whom this duty must fall ; and the telegraph has given them a power of being useful by enabling them to receive orders or send information more rapidly than formerly. The object of cavalry employed for such a purpose is not to fight, their object is to watch and report ; once the enemy is felt, the touch should never be let go, and this cannot be better kept up than by a number of horsemen in two's and three's scattered all over the country, feeling along every road, ready to retreat the moment the enemy turns on them, never pressing or attacking him, but always watching him.

The custom in former days for an army acting on the defensive was to retreat by one or more roads, "covering its line of retreat by cavalry." Now what is meant by the words " covering the line of retreat by cavalry?" We continually find that the covering simply meant that when an army retired along one or more roads, a mass of cavalry was placed on the road or roads used by the army, and that they closed the columns, the object of putting cavalry there being that the enemy in pursuit headed his columns with cavalry, his fastest moving force, and that therefore cavalry were requisite to meet and check that cavalry. Similarly the pursuing army "advanced covered by cavalry," or in other words the heads of its columns were composed of cavalry. Such a system of covering either the advance or retreat of an army is manifestly an improper use of one of the chief weapons of cavalry, the speed and power of the horses.

It requires but a slight amount of thought to perceive that the leader who follows with even a small force, and pushes on as rapidly as possible, small parties of cavalry to hang upon the flank of the column in retreat, to turn any obstacles they may prepare, and show themselves past the actual tail of the retreating force, will reap great benefits.

Such a system will not only harass the retreating army, far more than a system of useless attacks on its rear-guard, but will speedily demoralise it, by producing a constant feeling of uncertainty, and will compel the retiring force to hurry its march, send out strong bodies to its flanks, and so weary the men.

It is manifest that a cavalry very inferior in number, but skillfully directed, may, if the men composing it be well trained, cope easily with a superior force badly handled. Light rifled guns have in this respect altered the part of cavalry; for the pursuer, using a light and mobile horse artillery, may cut in on the flanks of heavy masses of cavalry and speedily throw them into disorder. Once that disorder makes itself felt the troops lose confidence in their leaders, and want of confidence in their leaders is a great step towards demoralisation. This use of cavalry and horse artillery to check troops retreating is one capable of great development, but like all such operations in war, is dependent on the skill of the leader.

The position of cavalry should be on the flanks; that is to say, there should be no mass of cavalry on the roads, following or leading the army, but the whole country should be filled with horsemen, working on a broad front, pushing on at all times, if checked simply halting, while those on the right and left turn whatever stops the advance. In the rear of those feelers must be the supports on which they retire, and again in rear the main bodies. All information from a wide front is brought into the main bodies, there collated, tabulated, and telegraphed back to the directing head in rear. Thus the cavalry of an army resembles more than anything else the feelers of some insect, pushed out in front, and conveying impressions to the animal, which guide its movements. To accomplish this duty thoroughly and completely the cavalry soldier must be trained as an individual, not merely as a unit of a large mass. His individual knowledge and ability must be continually improved and strengthened while at the same time his power of acting as a fraction in large masses should be kept steadily in view. Thus, as previously said, the cavalry soldier requires to be all he has ever been, together with a great deal more he has hitherto not been.

There are few things more remarkable than the contrast of the French and Prussian cavalry during the recent war; the former guided entirely by old rules and ideas, the latter guided not only by new ideas suitable to altered circumstances, but with those ideas carefully based on the old customs.

The French Cavalry.
Colonel Bonie.

If an army is retreating the place of the cavalry can no longer be in the rear as formerly laid down. This arm is incapable of struggling against a long ranging artillery, and it would be speedily crushed were it to be taken in flank by many batteries, and fatal results would ensue to the army in retreat, from a panic on the part of a mass of cavalry in its rear.

On the 7th August, Clèrembault's cavalry division received the order to cover the retreat of the 3rd Corps, which was to march on Metz from St. Avold *viâ* Longeville. From St. Avold to Longeville, a distance of 4½ miles, the road passes through woods, which at some places almost touch it on each side and leave a space where only a very small force can deploy. At Longeville the road forks, and that to the left runs on an elevated plateau of some extent.

Clèrembault's division consisted of 6 regiments. The general seeing that the least disorder in the rear guard would produce fatal consequences, as he could not act on the sides of the road, pointed out to Marshal Bazaine that so large a force of cavalry was likely to be more dangerous than useful.

The Marshal did not change his arrangements, and in conformity with the first order, at half past three a.m. the retreat commenced.

The infantry divisions moved in heavy columns on the road, followed by an interminable convoy of requisitioned carts, which tailed out unceasingly, owing to their interrupted, slow and irregular march.

While this column was defiling, the cavalry had to remain in the hollow at St. Avold, thus the men and horses were much fatigued without being able to be of any use, as they could not prevent the enemy from attacking the flanks of the column, if he wished to do so.

At one p.m. the cavalry division received orders to move. The general formed it in *échelons* to the right and left of the road; towards the frontier the ground did not allow more than one squadron to be deployed.

A 4-pounder battery, placed under the General's orders was posted so as to command the Valley of St. Avold; at 2 p.m. Decaen's division moved out of its position in admirable order.

The cavalry alone remained behind to protect the retreat, and very soon, owing to the shape of the ground, it had to form a column on the road of great length, as there were 24 squadrons.

It should be used on the flanks to prevent the enemy from advancing, cutting in on the convoys or infantry columns.

It is interesting to remark the action of the Prussian cavalry during this retreat; they threatened the rear of the column with a small force, thereby inducing the French to keep these 24 squadrons fixed there, while small parties were pushed up on the flanks of the column, exciting terror and confusion by their sudden apparition amongst the convoys.

The engineer train of the 3rd corps marched with the baggage of the leading infantry division, and the following is from the journal of the officer in command of the train.

123

We saw on a hill about 1,000 to 2,000 yards off, on our left, three small groups, one mounted, the other in advance dismounted; on the slopes of the little valley that divided us, we saw a single horseman entirely exposed alone in the fields near a hamlet, the inhabitants of which stared at him with surprise. We could not deceive ourselves, it was the enemy. One of the dismounted parties mounted and disappeared followed by the others, the single horseman after carefully watching us, vanished also.

Three Months with the Army of the Rhine. By an Officer of Engineers.

These scouts had passed not only the 24 French squadrons but two divisions of infantry, the reserve artillery and baggage, and were making their presence felt close in rear of the leading infantry division, unchecked and unmolested.

The action of the Prussian cavalry in watching, feeling, and hanging on to the French troops retreating from Wöerth on Chalons, and the result thus produced by a mere handful of men in demoralising an army, and the very small number of men required for that purpose, if only they be properly handled, are well shown in the accompanying extract, which is descriptive of the French retreat from Wöerth. The writer was an actor in the scenes he describes.

Arrived at Sarrebourg the regiments were reformed, and we then were able to furnish the lists of killed, wounded and missing, which were truly frightful.

The French Cavalry. Colonel Bonie.

The generals resumed command of their brigades and divisions, and thinking Alsace would not be abandoned, without further resistance, we looked for orders to take the offensive. We received in the middle of the day of the 8th August, orders to saddle and mount, because the enemy's cavalry was in view. Some scouts were mistaken for the head of numerous columns; we then retired.

From that moment until we reached Luneville their scouts watched us unceasingly. Linked to their army by horsemen, they gave an exact account of our positions, of our halts, of our movements; and as they watched us from some little distance, incessantly appearing and disappearing, they spread uneasiness.

In place of acting in a similar way, we kept our cavalry in masses difficult to move, which did not protect the army, and rendered no service whatever.

The 10th August we arrived at Luneville, hoping to have time to procure there, those articles of camp equipment which we still wanted.

We were informed that regular rations both for horses and men would be issued, a luxury which we had not known for some days, and we were supplied with meat, sugar, coffee, oats, and hay. The soldiers recovered their good humour, lit their fires, made their soup, and looked forward to a rest for one day. Suddenly we were ordered to march. The kettles were emptied, the nose bags taken from the horses, and we bridled in haste. Why this sudden alarm? It was again the enemy's cavalry. Hitherto it had only acted the prologue, but now the real play began.

Prussia, by a terrible blow, had made a breach in our line of corps scattered along the frontier. The line being cut in two she sought to beat each portion separately, and consequently strove to prevent their junction.

The cavalry undertook this important duty, operating over a great space, two regiments were pushed into Nancy. They stated that resistance was useless, as they were followed by a considerable force. This news was sent to us at Luneville, and the line of our retreat was consequently thrown off to the left by Colombey, Beaumont, Neufchateau, and Joinville.

This cavalry was that which destroyed the railway junction near Nancy, and so prevented the VIth French Corps receiving its reserve artillery, ammunition, and its engineers. It will be remembered that the VIth Corps was that which defended St. Privat, and much of the French disaster at that place is to be traced to the fact that this corps was tactically incomplete. The trains, with artillery and engineers, had left Chalons and actually arrived close to Nancy, before the news of the destruction of the railway compelled them to return.* Indirectly the cavalry excited great influence on the results of the battle of Gravelotte.

Similar action of Prussian cavalry is also noted by General Vinoy in his retreat from Mezieres.

Vinoy. From that moment we became the object of continual and rapid inspection from the enemy's scouts. They kept galloping on our flank, just out of range, seeking to see the head of our column and so calculate its force and report to their supports.

But why did the French not copy the Prussians? Baron Stoffel, a shrewd observer, and one who by no means deemed his countrymen perfect, in his comparison of the French and Prussian cavalry, gives to the former the praise of being better swordsmen, better mounted, and acting together quite as well as the Prussians. The Prussians, he thought, rode better. Courage was most assuredly not wanting among the French cavalry, but old customs and old prejudices are not to be dismissed on the battlefield. We train men in peace, for what we wish them to do in war. When war comes we must be satisfied if they do what we have taught them. If the instruction is faulty, the country whose armies have been badly trained suffers. When war is declared, the time of preparation, the time for training is past, the day of action has come. If the weapon is not well tempered, wants edge, and is useless, the responsibility rests with those who have allowed it to become so.

The French Cavalry. Colonel Bonie. In place of pushing the cavalry out to a distance, it was kept compact. It marched in divisions of 5 or 6 regiments, hampered with its baggage wagons; it never sent out a vedette, it followed the great roads, and it was well contented if it accomplished its day's march. In short, the rôle of our cavalry during this long retreat was simply nil, it neither fought nor scouted.

Why could we not imitate this cavalry, and why did we allow this hundred-eyed Argus to ride round and round us as he wished?

The answer to this question is, war is the harvest of peace. The seed sown in peace is then reaped.

But it was not only in the pursuit of the enemy that the careful individual training of the Prussian cavalry soldier told, it told equally when feeling the French advance. In Prussia the necessity of teaching cavalry completely, has been so recognised, and the labour entailed in that instruction so clearly appreciated

* Forty trains started, conveying the artillery, engineers, and reserves of the VIth Corps, on the 10th August, on the 11th the Uhlans cut the telegraph at Pont à Mousson; the trains however pushed on close to one another, some troops got out of the carriages to fire on the Prussian cavalry, and the greater part of the trains might have reached Metz if the Germans had not seized and torn up the rails between Pont à Mousson and Metz: the trains were then compelled to return to Chalons (Jacqmin).

that every effort is made to retain men in the cavalry for a fourth year, it is well known that practically infantry in Prussia are trained only for about 2½ years, but the cavalry generally received their 3 years' training, and the men were in many ways induced to re-engage for a fourth year.

This shows that the leaders of the Prussian army do not think the day of cavalry over, and that the difficulties of teaching men to ride, use their arms on horseback, and scout properly are fairly faced. Scouting cannot be taught on a parade ground nor on a Champ de Mars. The perfection to which the Prussians reduced this system is shown by the following:—

> For one moment the Prussian Staff lost our track in the plains of Champaigne, because we suddenly changed our plans. But they quickly found us again by means of their cavalry, which never lost the touch, and marched on our flank,* spreading out a curtain behind which their army worked.
>
> When he arrived at Chêne Populeux, the enemy was 30 miles† behind his cavalry; as we advanced we met groups of five or six horsemen who retired slowly after examining our arrangements and informing those who followed them. If we wished to pursue, each fraction fell back on a support capable of resisting us and keeping us from penetrating the curtain. This service was so well performed by the Prussian cavalry, that we marched, so to speak, within a net which enclosed us in its meshes.

The French Cavalry. Colonel Bonie

Four years before the Prussian Cavalry perhaps scouted no better than the French did.

For we read just before the Battle of Königgrätz.

> Thus the outposts of both armies faced each other on this day within a distance of 4½ miles, without either army suspecting the near and concentrated presence of the other.

Campaign of 1866; official account. (Translated by Hozier and Wright.)

The war of 1866 taught the lesson: it was carefully learned, it was brilliantly applied. An army will never fail so long as it can learn and apply a lesson.

IV.

ARTILLERY.

The introduction of rifled artillery and breech-loading arms has caused considerable modifications in the action of artillery in the field. These modifications are based partly on the nature of the infantry fighting, partly on the peculiarity of the rifled gun itself.

It is undoubtedly true that rifled artillery is far more powerful in accuracy and effect at long ranges than smooth-bore guns. But at short ranges it is very questionable if such advantages exist, and this is all the more the case that at short ranges the effect of rifles on artillery is now very greatly increased.

With smooth-bore guns, accuracy of laying at short ranges was hardly required, the gun even badly laid was sure to produce a good effect. With rifle projectiles this is not the case; to produce the full effects of a rifled artillery, careful attention is at

* McMahon's march on Sedan.
† Two long marches.

all times required, and this attention can hardly be given at short ranges, when the gunners are suffering much from infantry fire.

Two things follow from this:—1st. That if the full value of rifled artillery is to be brought out, it must come into action much sooner than formerly, it must continue in action much longer. 2nd. That it must move about far less than formerly. Mobility is an essential for good artillery, as it is for all arms, but it is the power to move rapidly when required, not continual movement, that is requisite. Artillery when moving is useless, suffers injury, and does no good. Breech-loaders have enabled infantry to advance firing if required, such is not the case with artillery, which can only fire when halted.

If the problem of the proper use of artillery on the field of battle be considered, it becomes at once apparent that its chief function is to pave the way for an attack. It may be accepted as an axiom that the success of an infantry attack, on a body of infantry favourably posted, is, with anything like equal numbers, very doubtful. The position taken up by troops on the defensive is sure to be always more or less difficult of approach, and there are sure to be houses, walls, farmyards, villages, used as points of support; in such places, or behind even the smallest shelter trench, or in rifle pits, an enemy usually suffers but little from the fire of attacking infantry, and at the same time can inflict loss all the more that he is sheltered and preserves coolness and can use his weapons deliberately.

It is then the province of artillery to drive the defenders out of such places, and shake their *morale* by a heavy concentrated fire, which will enable the infantry to advance to the attack.

It has been said that in an attack on an enemy in position, the spaces unseen or partially unseen by fire in front of his position must be sought for, and it is the duty of artillery to increase such dead spaces by concentrating a heavy fire on a portion of the enemy's position, breaching it in fact, and thus making an opening through which the infantry can advance.

There is nothing which tends to produce so great a moral effect as a heavy cross-fire of artillery. The best troops in the world get shaken and demoralized by such fire. Loopholed houses or walls rapidly become untenable, and the shells search out the trenches or rifle pits. The effect of a given number of guns placed so as to bring a converging fire on a portion of the defender's position is very much greater than if they merely brought a direct fire. A direct fire may be more or less guarded against, but a cross-fire on a position produces the moral effect of an attack both on a flank and in front.

There are therefore two general rules for the use of artillery: it must act in large bodies, and must seek to bring a converging fire on the point aimed at.

Except in certain special cases, it is doubtful if less than two

batteries should act together. A battery acting singly has full
work in its management and direction for all the officers belonging to it. It can spare none to remain with the Commander of
the attacking force. It can spare neither men nor horses to
carry or receive orders. Two batteries are usually provided
with a staff who can perform this duty, and the Lieutenant-
Colonel in command remaining with the Commander can receive
his orders, and see the effect of the guns and so direct them,
that they shall support the infantry properly.

It may perhaps be urged that if the two batteries are separated
some distance they can bring a more convergent fire to bear on
the point aimed at. This is doubtless the case; but on the field
of battle there are many batteries, and the additional effect
produced by separating two by no means makes up for the
greatly increased difficulty of direction.

It is essentially requisite that unity of action should be preserved amongst batteries of artillery, and that they should act
together, in bodies which have some cohesion, and are under
some definite command. If this be not carefully observed,
much of the advantage of massing artillery is lost.

The artillery engagement south of the Sadowa wood did not proceed so
favourably; a want of unity in the direction of the artillery was painfully
evident on this part of the field. Two commandants of regiments were on
the spot, but the eleven batteries then present belonged to five different
artillery divisions, some of them to the Divisional Artillery and some to the
Reserve. This accounts for the want of unity of action at this spot; some
batteries advanced perfectly isolated, whilst others retired behind the
Bistritz at the same time

*Campaign of
1866; official
account.
(Translated
by Hozier and
Wright.)*

Exactly a similar complaint was made by one of the French
corps leaders in 1870. His artillery belonged to seven different
regiments, and there was only one field officer who had ever
done duty with any of the batteries before.

The advantage that rifled artillery possess in its great range,
in the greatly increased choice of positions available, is immense—the area on which possible emplacements exist being
proportional to the square of the range; hence guns are more
likely to find cover than was formerly the case. On a field of
battle every effort should be made to get large numbers of
batteries into line under one command, especially during the
earlier stages. These masses of artillery acting in concert with
one another, will, by the very weight of their fire, crush what is
opposed to them, and the various points to be so attacked
should be selected in the order of their importance. An example of this occured at the battle of Noisseville.

General Woyna (7th Corps) opened fire on Flanville, situated at a distance
of about 1,200 yards; the French infantry held this position strongly, and a
close musketry fire had no effect on them; after a very short time the two
batteries detailed for this purpose overwhelmed the village with shells, the
houses took fire and the infantry abandoned them; the 53rd regiment then
advanced and took it. The guns were next turned on Coincy, which in a
short time also became untenable, and the French retired. The German
infantry during these operations remained with ordered arms.

*Militair
Wochenblatt.*

The sphere of action of artillery is twofold, viz., that of the Divisional artillery, and that of the Corps improperly termed reserve artillery. The action of these two kinds of artillery presents many points of similarity, and for certain purposes both may be used for the same object, precisely as the Divisional cavalry and Cavalry Divisions may on occasions both work together for one object.

The distinction between their duties may perhaps be best described by saying that the duties of the Divisional artillery are special, and generally confined to support the Division to which it belongs, while the action of the corps artillery is less restricted, and directed to more general objects.

Names that do not express duties, or rather that express a duty or function that no longer exists, are very pernicious. *Reserve* artillery has become so much an expression in military books, that it is desirable that it should be got rid of entirely, as conveying a false idea.

After 1868, the *Reserve* Artillery was termed *Corps* Artillery. Far from being a reserve, this artillery is really like the Divisional artillery, an advanced guard. Its duties are really those of an advanced guard. The duty of an advanced guard is to see the enemy first and come first into action. Artillery from its range ought to be the first arm to attack the enemy. An advanced guard cannot perform its duty of covering the deployment of the army, unless it be powerfully supported by artillery.

The greatest fault a General can commit, is to have Reserve artillery at all; the preparation of an attack is the function of artillery. Looking to the enormous power of its fire, nothing should prevent the concentration of all available means, every battery, every gun should be in position, one gun may even make a difference. It is by acting in accordance with these principles, and placing in line as many batteries as possible, that we have won all our victories.

It is one of the special duties of the Divisional artillery to support the infantry of the Division to which it belongs, whether that infantry be acting on the offensive or defensive.

The necessity for artillery to perform these functions was plainly evidenced by Napoleon's attaching 2 guns to each regiment, or to 3 battalions of infantry, and this at the very time and occasion when he developed the power of artillery in masses to an extent that never previously had been attempted.

The close continuous support that Divisional artillery should give to the infantry of the Division to which it belongs is a marked feature of British tactics.

Todleben.

It should be remarked that the English artillery always thoroughly supported its infantry. It followed it everywhere, and opened a close fire upon the Russian columns. On the one hand the artillery of Codrington's Brigade established on the left side of the careening ravine, swept our reserves and took in flank the troops who advanced to attack the left wing of the English army.

Battle of Inkerman.

On the other, our artillery which continuously preserved its first position upon the slope of Cossack Hill, remained always in the same place, and did not support the attack of our battalions. We must again reiterate what we had previously said, that the English infantry was always opportunely supported by its artillery, which swept the Russian columns and skirmishers with ease, whilst our troops unfortunately were deprived of the co-operation of their artillery.

After occupying the Cossack Hill, our artillery acted independently with much skill and coolness against the enemy's artillery, but it hardly at all supported the infantry. At the beginning of the battle it opened its fire, and thus to a certain extent paved the way for success; but later, when the infantry advanced to attack, the artillery continued to fire without altering its position, until at last our own troops marched into its fire as they advanced.

The importance of close continuous artillery support is here clearly shown, and that by the testimony of an enemy who felt its value; although as already stated the different nature of rifled artillery will render movements much less frequent than formerly, and enable batteries to effectually support infantry when considerably in rear of them. Thus, the support of a Division of infantry by its artillery does not mean that the guns are to move about with the infantry following it wherever it goes. But it means that the fire of the Divisional guns is to be directed to crush what is in front of the Division, to subdue the enemy's infantry, and facilitate the attacks of the Division; in so doing, the Divisional artillery may or may not be supported by the corps artillery. But it must be directed by the Divisional General as a portion of the tactical force he is handling. This point is one of considerable importance. If by the tactical independence of artillery is meant that each battery is to engage what it thinks fit, to halt and fire, or limber up and move as its commander deems well, then the independence of artillery is nothing but a loosening of the tactical union of the different parts of an army, a loosening which will infalliby entail weakness, if not disaster. But if by the independence of artillery is meant that batteries are not to be treated as battalions of infantry, but as an entirely different arm, belonging, however, to the same tactical force although using a different weapon, and requiring different arrangments; and working conjointly at all times for one object, then the independence of artillery is an advantage.

It is only when the infantry come within about 800 to 900 yards of the enemy that the best point for effecting an entrance into his position becomes quite clear. The Divisional artillery must watch for any movement on the part of the infantry, seeming to indicate the point of attack, and conform to it. When dealing with the various zones of fire into which a battlefield may be divided, it has been pointed out that the artillery of the attack may come up to within some 1,000 to 1,200 yards of the enemy's infantry, and this appears to be one of the special duties of the Divisional artillery; the Corps artillery, perhaps, keeping a little further off, and taking up such a position that it can at the proper moment reinforce with its fire (without moving) the Divisional artillery. The moment that this may be best done can be determined only by the Commanding Officer

K

of the Corps artillery, after a careful study of the progress and phases of the attack.

Becker.

He should be always well acquainted with the object of the action, and the views of the general, all the batteries of the artillery should be at his disposal to carry out his orders completely.

The corps artillery is directed entirely by the Officer Commanding the artillery of the corps, under the orders of the Officer Commanding the Army-Corps, and its object is to reinforce the Divisional artillery where requisite, or united to the corps artillery of other corps to form a mass of artillery sufficiently powerful to crush everything in front of it.

Artillery have been usually supported by special escorts told off to the various batteries, composed of either cavalry or infantry; on the actual battle-field, and indeed in general. it may be questioned if such escorts are really requisite. The true escort for artillery would appear to be the troops it is tactically acting with. Sending squadrons or companies with batteries breaks up units, and it may be fairly asked would a squadron or company constitute a real defence against any force that could seriously threaten a battery? To attach a company to a battery is really to compel the battery to conform to a foot's pace when it can go faster; and very often should go faster; or to forego the advantage of the escort by leaving it behind. The position of artillery, owing to its great range, will generally be sufficiently near to the second line to enable it to receive effective support from it. A few active, well-mounted, intelligent men attached to a battery as a portion of its establishment, who could watch the front and flanks, look into hollows and unseen ground, and bring back an intelligible and trustworthy account of what is in front, would appear to be all that is really required.

This by no means assumes that artillery should be left on a flank unsupported, which it may be. if a long line of guns has been formed prior to any other troops coming up. But such a support which the artillery commander should see that he has, is not a battery escort, it is a tactical support, and should be on the flank some hundreds of yards in front.

The practice of sending artillery well to the front, which has become a necessity at present, appears to render the escort system still more undesirable. as it will frequently happen that a mass of artillery will be up, and in action, with such a meagre force of cavalry and infantry to support it as would entirely forbid escorts. Had the Prussians at Mars-la-Tour told off a company or a squadron to each battery they would have kept a large proportion of their weak force out of action, and broken up their brigades, and tactical formation entirely; companies and squadrons as escorts to batteries, are very often so many sabres and rifles lost to the army, for neither the one nor the other, except in special cases, can help the general result of the day. The infantry being at too great a range, the cavalry being in too small a force to have any useful effect. In addition to which, such escorts increase the size of the mark to be fired at; and in case the batteries have to limber up, advance or retire rapidly, they are very likely to get in the way.

When artillery appeared on the field of battle in small numbers, and short range guns only existed, such escorts were decidedly requisite, but now that the effective range and accuracy of weapons has been largely increased, and the proportion of artillery nearly doubled, it appears that these escorts, except in special cases, are not requisite.

On the line of march, if the advance guard has done its duty properly, there should be little fear of an attack on artillery, although in such a case, more especially in a close country, an infantry escort will doubtless be useful.

It has been said that artillery in action should move rarely, and rather alter their elevation within certain limits than limber up. Whatever movements artillery make under fire should be rapid; not only is artillery so moving out of action a shorter time, but it suffers far less when moving rapidly than when moving slowly.

At about 2,000 to 3,000 yards from us was the Conflans Road; we saw a Prussian battery gallop up, halt, unlimber and open fire in a manner that excited our admiration. It set the farm of Malmaison on fire; at this moment our sappers were very thick and attracted the enemy's attention, who sent a shower of shell on them; two of our guns then came up to fire on the enemy's battery, but these guns came up at a foot's pace, in addition to which, being able to conceal themselves behind a row of poplars before coming into action, they disregarded the shelter and marched in the open; they then halted, hesitated, and being fired at, retired at a trot without firing one shot. *Three months with the Army of the Rhine. By an Officer of Engineers.*

Artillery fire is far more effective when it is calmly delivered, when every shot is carefully made to tell, than by hurried or wild shooting. To shoot calmly, there must be a certain amount of security, and hence, the actual position occupied by the guns is one of the greatest importance. A common error is to place guns on the most commanding positions, such positions are often unsuitable, as not only are the guns better seen, but often cannot themselves see the ground in front of the battery, and consequently lose the benefit of their low trajectory.

The most favourable position for guns is a gentle hillock, sloping gradually to the front and more abruptly to the rear, with a command over the ground occupied by the enemy, of about 1 in 100. As regards the ground in plan, guns may be drawn up with good effect behind a marsh, a pond, a river, or a ravine, provided that such obstacles do not render an advance to the front impossible. *Lieut. Hime, R.A., Prize Essay.*

The most obvious lesson to be learned from the campaigns of 1866 to 1870 is, that it is not alone desirable but necessary to cover the guns and horses of a battery from the enemy's fire, either by field intrenchments or by the accidents of the ground; for it is only when so covered that the battery can be ensured against destruction from the enemy's infantry and artillery fire, and that the men can preserve that *sang froid* which is essential for carying on an effective fire.

The importance of a thorough knowledge of a position cannot be overestimated by officers of the field artillery; for the security of a battery depends almost entirely, and the effect of its fire to a large extent, upon the use that is made of the accidents of the ground.

This last is quite as true of the ground in rear as that on the flanks, and it is very requisite that the communication between the guns and the wagons should be carefully seen to. The Prussian artillery has been often reproached by Prussian writers for not supporting the infantry effectively at Königgrätz. A great deal of this was due to the fact that the guns came into action on one side of a small muddy stream over which there were very few bridges, and across which bridges might have been put with ease, while the wagons remained on the other.

Campaign of 1866: official account. (Translated by Hozier and Wright.)

The difficulty of keeping up the communication between the batteries and their ammunition wagons was universally felt to be a very great inconvenience.

It arose from the scarcity of available passages over the Bistritz, only one of the serjeant-majors succeeded in bringing his wagons up to their battery and in supplying it, as well as some of the neighbouring 4-pounder batteries, with ammunition.

It is evident that artillery must, on the march, move very near the head of the column, for nothing causes greater confusion or delay than the attempt to pass troops up from the rear of a long column to the front; artillery being required early in the action must be placed where it can be got at. To have long trains of guns in reserve if they exercise no influence on the battle-field, is worse than useless. The evils of the system of having guns in reserve is shown by the fact that the very moment the French troops at St. Privat were being crushed by the Prussian artillery, there were many French guns in reserve which never came into action at all. To place guns in reserve is voluntarily to deprive oneself of a most powerful auxiliary at the very moment its aid is most urgently required. *Vide* page 157.

Tactical retrospect. Captain May. (Translated by Ourry.)

We brought a numerous and imposing artillery into the field it is true, but how many guns ever came into action? They planted themselves here and there among the reserves and never found places anywhere to engage. Artillery without tactical training and daring, who have merely a knowledge of technical gunnery, will always find excuses and make impossibilities. What is the use of an artillery that makes capital practice indeed, but which is never in the right place? much better one that blazes away cheerily, that at any rate rejoices the heart of the men.

The effective range of field artillery may be taken as from 2,000 to 3,000 paces. At the former distance and up to 2,500 paces its effect is very considerable, beyond that range, unless in special states of the weather, or under peculiar circumstances, the effects of the shot cannot be detected, and it becomes consequently impossible to correct the gun. Down to 800 yards the action of artillery is very destructive, within that distance its effect may be considered to diminish, and within that distance the effect of the breech-loading rifle begins to get very formidable, consequently the effective fire of the artillery may be said to begin just at the range that musketry becomes wild. Hence it should be borne in mind that artillery should rarely or never come within 1,000 or 1,200 yards of infantry, and conversely, infantry should not be allowed to come within that distance of guns, except in special cases, when it may be

judged requisite to sacrifice the guns to the necessity of checking the enemy's advance.

When a mass of artillery is deployed it will be well to have the
batteries not in one great line, but, so far as the ground admits,
in échelons of two or three batteries, so as to allow troops to pass
through if requisite.

The placing and forming of such lines of guns are amongst the most
difficult things in the tactics of the three arms. What difficulties are often pre-
sented by the ground, and how seldom have commanding officers the time to
reconnoitre it thoroughly before ordering up their batteries? The question is
not only to take position, but also to choose one whence the enemy can be
effectively cannonaded. They must further provide for the possible advance
of the line either in échelon or by batteries, and, lastly, for retreat. If,
however, artillery wishes to cover effectively the advance and deployment of
infantry masses, and to render their attack possible in the shortest time, it
will often find it necessary to go very much to the front, and perhaps to come
into action very badly protected against an attack from the enemy.

It was a grand, inspiriting spectacle to see the German batteries overcome
all obstacles, form their line, and open fire. After allowing this a short time
to work, and one had not to wait long for the effect to show itself, the long
line broke into sections, each of which advanced in turn towards the enemy's
position.

Boguslauski.
(Translated
by Graham.)

Artillery once engaged, even if many of the guns under fire are *hors de
combat*, must not be relieved, although it may be supported by other artillery :
a superiority of guns gives great advantages in an artillery action.

Hohenlohe.

The question what artillery should engage is a very important one. If two armies are engaged with equal forces of artillery, and the guns engage one another, the artillery is simply
eliminated, and the other arms left to fight it out between them.
Fighting under such circumstances ceases to be a scientific combination of various military bodies, possessing different powers
and means of working, to mutually support and remove one
another's deficiencies; it becomes a mere struggle of brute force.
If used in such a way, for all practical purposes both parties
might have left their artillery at home; as infantry cannot advance and carry a position properly defended, if the defence be
not first shaken by artillery fire, it follows that for artillery
to simply engage artillery would be to deprive the attacking
army of many of its chances of success.

It has been said that guns must come early into action, and
when acting on the offensive the guns must fire at woods, villages,
houses, and the enemy's infantry; when the guns are acting on
the defensive, then they must fire on the attacking artillery from
the moment it shows itself.

If the attacking side shall have succeeded in establishing a superior
artillery, that is, as many batteries as it has at its disposition, the first question
to be asked is, Which is the point to be attacked?

If one battery exchanges shots with one of the enemy's batteries, another
with another, and the third fires on an occupied field work, while the fourth
thinks that it has discovered the position of the enemy's reserve, we cannot call
this an artillery action having a common purpose. To silence the artillery of
the enemy cannot be the most important object of the side which takes the
offensive. Even if this should be done, the advance of the infantry on a
position defended by breech-loaders is not possible. To silence the attacking

Tactical
retrospect.
Captain May.
(Translated
by Onvry.)

guns is the essential object of the artillery on the defensive, then the infantry will know how to repulse the attack of the enemy's infantry. But artillery, on the offensive, should, on the contrary, make it the principal object to play upon the infantry of the enemy. An attack can only be thought of when this has been weakened ; it has only to engage with the artillery of the defensive in so far as is absolutely necessary, always having the principal object in view.

Consequently the fire of artillery on the defensive must be steady, careful, and every shot must be so aimed as to do mischief to the enemy's guns. But although the attacker's artillery must be one of the chief objects aimed at by the defender's artillery, yet it is erroneous to suppose that the advancing infantry should be neglected. One of the objects of the defenders is to compel an early deployment; this can be best managed by a fire on the attacker's infantry, thereby compelling him to deploy from heavy masses to an open formation, and this is such an important object with the defender, that small detachments of all arms pushed out in front should be used for this purpose. The artillery of the defenders actually in position should therefore direct there fire on the infantry, the moment it is within range sufficient to allow an efficacious fire. But it should also watch the moment any battery or brigade of batteries attempt to move to the front, and should endeavour to crush it when limbering up, moving, or unlimbering. It should rarely fire at the skirmishing line, but rather at the supports and main body. Such questions as these have really to be settled to a great extent by the amount of command the artillery has, and how the ground in front is seen, the nature of the ground that has to be crossed, and how the defending infantry are covered.

The moment a battery takes up a defensive position its commander must ask himself—Where is the enemy most likely to place his guns first? and as he advances. Where will he place them next ? Having answered these questions, he must at once measure his range, and carefully study the problem before him, which is to place the attacking guns *hors de combat*. Artillery on the offensive should, on the contrary, while striving to keep up as accurate a fire as possible, fire more rapidly, its object being to overwhelm a certain space with projectiles prior to the infantry attack.

Von Walder-see.

During the crisis of the action the artillery fire should be directed on the attacking columns, this principle has no exception, unless some of the attacking batteries are doing much harm to the defenders, when they may be fired at also.

A new weapon, the mitrailleuse, has been introduced recently, about the value of which opinions are divided. It may be justly questioned if the Prussian opinion that they are useless is correct. This weapon was concealed and only brought out by the French just before the war; its action was little understood and its true position entirely misunderstood ; even artillery officers of the highest rank in the French service appeared to be utterly ignorant of its weaknesses. Fire was often opened with these weapons at a range of 3,000 yards, when the mitrailleuses were useless.

The German have, in their more recent books, acknowledged the power of the mitrailleuse, more especially in the last portion of the attack, when its effect on infantry is very great, and when the nerves of the defenders are somewhat shaken. To be brought out, however, at this stage of the attack, the mitrailleuse must be carefully protected during the earlier portion of the action.

The French still adhere to it, and few who have seen the graves in the hollow road above Wöerth, or near Gravelotte, will question its power in certain places.

It has been seen how Napoleon attached two guns to each regiment of three battalions, thereby giving it a powerful support if ordered to hold a village or wood, or to act on the defensive. May not this be the true place of the mitrailleuse, to support infantry when closely pressed, to be kept back until the advance of the hostile infantry to a certain extent masks its artillery, and then to be used on the advancing infantry? The range of the mitrailleuse but very slightly exceeds that of the rifle. But its effect in flanking positions and firing down hollow roads or ravines must be very great; attached to infantry brigades in small numbers it might do good service without being in the way.

V.

ENGINEERS.

The introduction of modern weapons has caused the development of tactics to take a peculiar direction, and has produced changes in the action of the various arms of the service, but nowhere are the changes more marked than in the art of the Engineer.

Looking at the subject generally, we find that one of the first consequences of the development of fire-arms at the end of the 16th and beginning of the 17th centuries, was a large increase of the offensive power of arms, a reduction of defensive armour; and following from this a large increase of field-works. A history of war at this period would be the history of entrenchments, one army seizing a position, entrenching it and holding it, the other watching it and afraid to attack.

The increase in roads, the opening up of the country, and the greatly increased size of armies under Napoleon, united to his peculiar strategy, the suddenness of action with which he sought to overcome an enemy, and the great development which the offensive received, all tended to the disuse of field-works and entrenchments.

Although the rapidity of Napoleon's marches tended to develop other branches of the engineers art, that of bridging and that of the pioneer, to a far greater extent than had previously been known, yet Napoleon was clearly alive to the evils produced by the neglect of field-works.

Napoleon.

Field fortifications are always useful, never injurious when they are rightly understood. The principles of field fortification stand in need of improvement. This branch of the art of war is susceptible of great progress.

And in discussing this subject he points out one of the causes why field fortification has made such little progress.

Napoleon.

Engineer officers give up all their time to study permanent works; infantry officers are ignorant of engineering.

It is often said that war is now so offensive in its character, that in the field the use of earthworks is impossible, and except in so far as the pioneer's duties are concerned, modern war finds no room for field engineers. There is a great fallacy contained in this statement, because the introduction of the breech-loader has added so much to the power of the defence, that every means should be taken to increase and develop it still more.

The campaigns of 1866 and 1870 are examples, on the part of the Prussians, of the pure offensive being kept from the beginning to the end. And yet we find a critic of the former writing as follows :—

Tactical retrospect. Captain May. (Translated by Ouvry.)

If we take a review of the battles of the campaign in this point of view we shall find that there were frequent occasions when the action of the engineers might have been useful. The reasons why that branch of the service was less active than the others may be found in the remark that both were equally at fault. But, perhaps, the soldiers were not sufficiently engineers, or the engineers soldiers enough, for this consideration to have entered their thoughts.

The history of this century shows that field fortification, when it has been judiciously used, has invariably produced the greatest results, and these results were produced by the application of the same ideas, viz., the use of field-works to cover the front of a large extended position, one considerably larger than the troops could hold in line of battle, the flanks being protected and the communication for supplies being open to the rear.

The celebrated lines of Torres Vedras are an instance of this. The English army with its flanks resting on the Tagus and the sea, occupied with about 50,000 men a line of some 25 miles in length; it had its internal communications perfectly open, its supplies were brought up by the sea and the French general could do nothing; he was unable to outflank the lines, turn, or attack them. They were so strong that any attack in front would have failed; the defenders could not be starved out, and unless they were regularly attacked by siege works there was no means of dealing with them. *From those lines the tide of conquest of the French armies first began to recede.*

Many years later the same thing happened at Sebastopol. The Russians holding a straight line of weak field-works with their communications open, actually advanced from their works, threw up fresh trenches and works, and almost besieged the allies in their positions. Both these cases were brilliant examples of what field-works properly adapted to tactics can produce.

There were great opportunities in the blockades of Paris and Metz for the tactics displayed by the Russians to be repeated; and it is no exaggeration to say that had the garrison of Paris been composed of good troops it might really have dug itself out of Paris and through the German lines.

The French put a singular, new and promising mode of attack in practice against Le Bourget and also against Chateau Ladonchamps, north of Metz. They advanced from Drancy and Woippy respectively, against these places by flying sap. The armistice, and in the other case the capitulation, interrupted this work which had already progressed far.

Duke of Wurtemberg. (Translated by Robinson.)

Hitherto the French corps of engineers has been rarely employed in line of battle, but has been used almost entirely for the attack and defence of a fortress, or fortifying some point, the preservation of which is of vital importance. The recent campaigns have demonstrated the necessity of using this arm in battle as well as at sieges. With long-range guns and the masses of troops now put in the field, battles become the work of days, not hours. It follows from the many complicated combinations, that the result will not declare itself for 24 hours; in order to work out these conditions troops must be enabled to hold certain points at any cost, this can only be done by giving the troops a certain amount of security. The engineer arm has thus become an essential to security.

Viollet le Duc.

There are many things which point at present to a largely extended use of field-works in the future, and one of them is the enormous extension of the great military powers of continental Europe have given to field engineering, and the much larger bodies of sappers that they now keep on foot than formerly. History not unfrequently repeats itself, and the same causes that produced the development of field-works in the days of the Duke of Parma, and subsequently, appear to be again at work.

It further appears at the present day the necessity of making flank attacks has given a fresh importance to field-works. When speaking of this subject previously, the ease with which an army having its flank threatened can change front and attack was pointed out, and it was further pointed out that to prevent such a change of front, an attack in front as well as on flank was needed. Now, is not it possible to check any attempted change of front by the construction of field-works? The Americans in the civil war made a very extensive use of entrenchments for this purpose; they covered their front, and then moved round to a flank.

Lee, with two divisions of Longstreet's Corps, determined to keep the enemy's front occupied for a time, whilst Jackson should make the circuit of the Federal right. The Federal work of entrenching consisting, as usual, chiefly of making breastworks of felled trees, was continued through the night and following morning, and Hooker strenuously pressed this labour on as necessary to the success of the design he had lately formed of remaining still and receiving the attack which he expected. But Lee, as we know, was purposely deceiving him as to its direction, and continued on the morning of the 2nd, as on the day before, to cover his own weak line by similar means. Meanwhile, Jackson began at dawn, with his wonted skill, to execute the movement which crowned the brilliant successes of his life.

Campaign in Virginia. Chesney.

Flank attacks are alarming to the best troops, and are especially applicable to the case of a forest engagement, when the enemy's line, broken

"Edinburgh Review."

into skirmishers each covered by a tree, could be forced back from the front only by slow degrees, and with considerable sacrifice of men ; and yet may be approached without observation at either extremity. At the period of the war of which we are writing it had become a fixed habit of the armies to cover every hundred yards gained by a breastwork wherever the materials could be found.

Many similar quotations could be given as illustrating the system by which the commanders on both sides in the American war sought to use field fortification for its legitimate purpose, viz., that of enabling a small body of men to resist a large one, or in other words to secure a portion of an army from a front attack, while the remainder was used to strike on the flanks.

The whole spirit of modern war is to reduce everything to calculation, to leave nothing to chance, to provide for and foresee all possible combinations, whether arising from moral causes, such as panics amongst the men, or from actual physical causes, such as the enemy's fire, or the configuration of the ground : whatever then increases the security of certain places or their defensive power, is of the highest importance.

The duties of the engineers in the field may be divided into two classes :—

> 1st. The duties of making, repairing, or destroying com-
> munications, including, in the word communication,
> roads, bridges railways, and telegraphs. *These may*
> *be classed together as pioneer duties.*
> 2nd. The preparation of positions for attack or defence,
> *which is the higher duty of the military engineer*, and
> where the art of fortification must be considered
> entirely in a tactical point of view.

With reference to the first class of duties, the men and means must be invariably present when required. The engineers should march with the advance guard, and must be sufficiently supplied with tools and materials, although the fact that they must be mobile, should keep the number of carriages or other transport accompanying them at the minimum. It is hopeless to bring troops wanted at the head of a column all the way up from the rear, and like the artillery the engineers must march in front if they are really to be useful. In an advance on the track of a retreating army, the destruction of large bridges does not entail so much delay as the destruction of many small bridges, and the formation of numerous small obstacles, all of which cause halts to be made, necessitate the deployment of a certain amount of force, and in many cases the repair of roads, bridges, and removal of obstacles. Hence it is desirable that all troops forming advanced or rear-guards should be provided with engineers; and as advanced and rear-guards are usually formed of cavalry, some military writers have advocated the employment of mounted sappers. When Napoleon advanced on Charleroi in 1815, his light cavalry advance was detained for a long time at the bridge over the Sambre which was only cleared by the sappers of the guard being sent across country on horseback.

If the importance of the works, which form the speciality of engineer soldiers, be taken into account, it must be acknowledged that in most armies there are too few of them. The strength of these troops, is by no means proportioned to the duty they have to perform. The Duke of Wellington considered that an army could not have too many. The engineer soldier can at all times, when not employed executing the work for which he has special training, act as an infantry soldier. Brailmont.

A good organization would be that which attaches to each division of infantry a battalion of engineers composed of four companies, or a company to each regiment.

We think it would be also useful to attach to each division of cavalry a company of mounted sappers to destroy or re-establish communication, create ambuscades, intrench posts; operations which an advanced or rear-guard has frequently to perform, or when a cavalry corps operates on the flank of an enemy. The War of the Secession (in America) has shown that it is often requisite to destroy at great distances from the army railways useful to an enemy, or to re-establish a line which has been cut.

The idea of having mounted sappers is by no means a new one, it is referred to by Frederick the Great in the following terms:—

There is an idea which has just struck me, it is quite new; I would like to give to the advanced guard mounted sappers to break up the enemy's road, cut down small woods, which might interfere with the vedettes, make a small bridge, mark a ford, make communications or an emplacement for guns when they come up, a parapet for the outposts, a retrenchment for infantry, loop-hole houses, sink wells, make trous-de-loup, remove or place stones, pull down masonry, scarp or cut down the banks of a rivulet. To do this an officer should be with the advanced guard; he should be well-mounted and intelligent. Frederick.

In all such operations time is of the greatest importance, and unless engineers are so equipped that they can be in the place required at the proper time, the army must suffer by delays. The organization of the engineers should therefore be such as will admit of small bodies being detached if requisite, and yet allow the whole to be reunited rapidly when necessary. Such operations, however, belong rather to the subject of marches than to tactics.

It is the second class of duties, or those of the *military engineer* as distinguished from the *pioneer* where the tactical relation of field-works to the other arms is fully developed, although at times the line between the two kinds of work may be difficult to draw. In a tactical point of view every field of battle may be divided into distinct portions, the defensive and offensive portions. The former is usually that which embraces the key of the position. And it should be the object of all field-works to strengthen such positions as shall enable them to be held by a small force, and release the mass of the troops to strike an offensive blow where it can be best delivered. No defence can possibly be successful that has not an offensive as its basis. The mere fact of field works being constructed is far too often considered as limiting the action of the troops to a strick defensive; viewed in such a light, entrenchments are useless, if not hurtful, and hence arises the absolute necessity of viewing all such works in their tactical relation to troops.

Napoleon. Those who neglect the support which the art of the engineer can give in the field gratuitously deprive themselves of a power and an auxiliary never hurtful, always useful, and often indispensable. To maintain that victory falls to him who can advance and manœuvre, and that it is not requisite to work, is to say what tends to produce error, and is false.

Field-works must not be scattered about irrespective of the plan of action of the general commanding in chief; they must at all times be made subservient to the action of the troops.

Brailmont. It is manifest *à priori*, that the defences of a position must be in accordance with the plan of the battle. Works must not be constructed or ordered, except by the General Commanding.

A skilful General will always choose positions in such a way as to give him the advantage of ground, or, in other words, those that enable him to reinforce a portion of his front, occupying one position with a smaller number of men and concentrating his principal force on the other, ready to take the offensive.

Victory can only be the result of a successful attack ; it is requisite to have the maximum force ready on the point and at the decisive moment of attack.

In the opinion of some, shock tactics, for a long time in favour, must now yield to fire tactics. This is an error. Neither one nor the other are good by themselves, or absolutely. The shock must be prepared by the fire, and the fire without shock cannot give victory.

In organizing the defence of a position held by an army capable of taking the offensive, the Engineer must keep clearly in view that the attack must be helped. This may be done by strengthening a portion of the position of an army which is on the defensive, so as to render a large number of men disposable for an attack at the right moment. When, therefore, a position offers this double field, the offensive and the defensive, it is the best that can be found.

The defensive zone is that part the attack of which offers the most difficulty, either because the ground is covered with obstacles, or because the artillery can take favourable positions.

The offensive zone is that where large bodies of troops can act freely and decisively.

The object of fortifications on the former should be to stop the enemy as long as possible, with as few men as possible.

The object of fortification on the latter should be twofold,—

1. To shelter the troops of the first line until the moment everything is ready for attack.

2. To support the troops, if driven back after an unsuccessful attack, to stop the progress of the invader and prevent him establishing himself in the position he has won.

Upon the offensive zone shelter trenches and epaulments only should be constructed for a portion of the battalions in first line, with large intervals for the troops to advance through.

The hedges in front should be cut and passages opened through the woods.

Intrenchments on this zone are most useful ; they mark the limit of any retrograde movement, they give confidence and enable the troops to be reformed. On the defensive zone, batteries should be established to take the enemy in flank as he advances towards the offensive zone. With the same object posts, houses, and farms should be held in advance, which will be of great use in supporting a retreat.

Works, which are the real points of support of an army, should be closed at the gorge otherwise, once the enemy passes them the defenders will retire, and experience proves that no reliance can be placed on troops which retreat; in danger, everyone thinks of himself.

The foregoing is a clear definition of the principles on which works should be constructed, and it is of great importance that only such as can really be completed should be attempted; in almost every case in war 6 or 7 hours may be calculated on to put a position in a state of defence, and if the engineers and tools are where they should be, this period is ample; in six hours works of a very powerful nature may be constructed which will effectually support an army.* It is generally allowed that an entrenchment occupied by 200 men offers as much resistance as a battalion not so covered, and that the labour of 1,000 men for 6 hours on the position occupied by a division is equivalent to the reinforcement of a brigade. The whole history of war is filled with examples of these truths.

The villages of Aspern and Essling, linked by a river embankment, saved the French army in 1809. The neglect of the defences of the villages in front of Leipzig ruined the same army in 1814.

The Archduke Charles, speaking of field-works says, "Like "any weapon, they lose their value when badly used, that is to "say when constructed without an object, without intelligence, "and defended without bravery."

The engineer, in virtue of the character which is particular to his branch of the Service, may hold an equilibrium in military operations. He may render the success gained by an impetuous attack secure by quickly throwing up field works behind the attaching force, and in the same manner stop a retreat by hastily-constructed entrenchments, the holding of which then concerns the honour of the troops.

Tactical retrospect. Captain May. (Translated by Ourry.)

At Königrätz the Austrians appear to have thrown up a good many entrenchments, but there was no tactical connection between the works and the troops; that is to say, the Austrian engineers, acting under the orders of the Commanding Engineer of the army, made a number of works on the ground, ordered by the General in Chief, Benedeck, to be occupied, but it seems that the corps leaders and Division leaders knew nothing whatever of these works, or of the exact position they were to hold; they extended far beyond the position intended, and the Commanding Engineer riding round, some hours after the battle had begun, found there were no troops near the works at all, and when they were occupied the Prussian tide of victory was rising too fast for anything to stop it. This is another of the many proofs that the proper means of working the auxiliary arms of the service is not by making them independent of the others, and thus forming an *imperium in imperio*, but by preserving a close tactical connection between all arms, which can only be done by working through the Generals commanding the tactical bodies. Thus if a Division be ordered to entrench a position, the Divisional General should, on receiving the order,

---

* At Gravelotte, the French had certainly double this time at their disposal.

give his instructions thereon to the Divisional Engineers, who may, if requisite, be strengthened by the Engineer Reserves, precisely as the Divisional Artillery is worked under the Divisional General, but supported, if requisite, by the Corps Artillery. To form works under orders from the General in chief command, without reference to the Generals who command the troops to occupy the works, is an evident abandonment of the principle of individual responsibility.

We often read in military history of villages being taken and retaken several times in the course of the day; these are the moments when success may be secured, and when the companies of engineers should be forthcoming.

Tactical retrospect. Captain May. (Translated by Ouvry.) We were aware that as far to the rear as the Aupa there was no reserve worth mentioning to relieve the hard pressed troops. An intrenched battery on the Kapellenberg (for the construction of which there was ample time), would have supplied the want of these reserves, and have re-established the battle, but there were no pioneers, we had left them behind.

Time for the construction of works in the field does not so often fail, as the presence of the engineers and tools at the right time on the right place.

According to Prussian ideas intrenchments had fallen into disrepute; they were thought to be detrimental to that offensive spirit, which was the leading principle in our conduct in the war. The example of that of the Austrians led us to scout the idea, but we rejected that good with the bad. The fault of the Austrians was, that they threw up their intrenchments beforehand and then expected that the fight would take such a course as would render them useful. Instead of making the fight dependent on the intrenchments, we would make the intrenchments dependent on the fight.

The same writer observes, in concluding his remarks on the engineers: "the next campaign will show us this fourth arm acting in rivalry with the others in the battle." His prophecy was fulfilled, for not only were the pioneer duties of the Prussian army admirably performed, but the true spirit of the use of field engineering was in many cases seized; one remarkable instance was at Mars-la-Tour,—early in the day the Prussians gained possession of Vionville, on the Verdun road; the instant the infantry got in, two companies of engineers supplied with 6 wagons of tools were pushed on; they were charged by a regiment of French hussars and lost some of the wagons and a section of one of the companies, but the remainder got in to the village, and so strengthened it that all the attempts made to retake it failed. And although at the close of the day the Prussian right and left wings were forced back by the French, yet the village of Vionville, forming the apex of the Prussian position, was never lost, and effectually barred the road to Verdun. Here fortification was used correctly; it confirmed and established the success of the infantry, and secured the object for which the Prussians struggled so hard on the 16th.

That night the French determined to hold the position extending from Gravelotte to the north, and, pivoting on their left, they threw back their line a quarter of a circle on the 17th. An examination of the ground shows that the position they occupied was susceptible of division into an offensive and a defensive zone. The latter extended from the high ground above Gravelotte to the centre of the 3rd Corps near the farmhouse of Leipzig. The former from that point to near the River Orne, with numerous farm-yards, houses, woods, and posts in the front. But the French system of having almost all their tools with the reserve baggage prevented advantage being taken of this; the mass of carriages belonging to the army were parked at the back of their position in the St. Germain ravine, the steep sides of which perfectly precluded the engineers from getting at their tools.

The 2nd Corps, which was on the extreme left, entrenched its position, and their entrenchments, united to the many shallow quarries made for road-metal, enabled General Frossard to hold this position with comparatively little loss, although it was continually attacked by the 1st Army under Steinmetz, which suffered much. Writing of this, General Frossard says :—

If the losses of the 2nd Army-Corps, at the Battle of Gravelotte, were comparatively slight, this is undoubtedly owing to the precautions taken in sheltering the men behind earth and epaulments, and to the care taken in profiting be all depressions in or excavations of the ground, not by allowing the troops to hide behind such things, but by using them to protect the men when firing. We have never seen so remarkable an instance of the advantages which this method of entrenchment affords. We point it out for the attention of those who will hereafter exercise commands. *Frossard.*

It was quite feasible for the French, knowing the natural and artificial strength of this portion of the position, to have diminished the force holding it considerably, and so reinforced the right or the portion of the army acting on the offensive zone, either by extending the troops in that direction, or sending the whole of the reserve to support it. But on the extreme right the weakest corps in the army was placed, one that had not a single engineer or tool with it. If the positions at St. Privat and Roncourt had been strengthened with shelter trenches, those villages properly placed in a state of defence, and a powerful reserve with a second line of entrenchments placed in rear, near the Jaumont woods, not only would this portion of the position have been almost impregnable, but an admirable field for taking the offensive and sweeping down with the right covered by the Orne, would have been afforded. No one who examines the history of this battle but must feel that had fortifications been used to support the troops, with judgment, a different result might have followed.

The want of tools was sorely felt all along the French line, from the fact of the tools not being in the front but in the rear. In the centre, the 3rd Corps had to use its railway section to make works.

I was sent to try and bring up the corps supplies. I was told that doing so would be of great use. These were mere words ; the order was impossible anybody who looks at a map can see that wagons could not come up the slopes. About 7 o'clock the general sent for the railway section to do some *3 Months with the Army of the Rhine. Officier de Génie.*

work in the first line ; as it descended the hill the enemy doubtless took it for a fresh battery, for they covered it with a shower of shells, but the little column broke into a trot, and not a shell struck the sappers or their wagons.

The moment the Prussians carried St. Privat their engineers strengthened it, and formed a shelter trench between it and the crest of the hill. with an epaulment on its right flank threatening that portion of the French position still defended. It is requisite, however, as was stated in the first chapter, that if the full advantages of armies carefully trained in peace is desired by the State that maintains them, officers must know more than their own special arm of the service ; and this is perhaps more essential for officers of those arms of the service, cavalry, artillery. and engineers, which are auxiliaries to the main force,—infantry,—than for infantry officers themselves. And this is all the more requisite now, when the power breech-loaders has given to infantry is considered.

Wright.

The conclusion I draw, says an American general, is that a simple trench, defended by two ranks of infantry, covered by abattis or other obstacle, and placed on ground which allows the range of their arms to develop itself, is absolutely impregnable except by surprise.

This was before the days of breech-loaders, and undoubtedly the power of musketry has since been increased many fold. The following remarks are worthy of attention.

Boguslauski. (Translated by Graham.)

The works directed by Engineer Officers, however excellent they may have been with regard to their technical execution, did not always show that those Officers had, so to speak, understood how to reduce to practice the tactical ideas of the present time.

One might not only often remark that they had missed a just comprehension of existing infantry tactics, particularly of the effects of fire of the breech-loaders and other arms lately introduced, but also that they had not understood the ground or made use of it according to correct defensive tactical principles. Field fortifications must be based upon tactics, and especially upon defensive tactics, and must keep pace with their progress.

The art of planning works of this description is evidently quite different from that of an engineer attack on a fortress.

In order to instruct Engineer Officers in tactics, it would appear advisable to attach them to infantry for some weeks in summer in the same manner, although on a larger scale, as they now are to pioneer battalions.

It is further desirable that the latter should take a larger share in our field manœuvres, and that detachments of them should be furnished to commands of the other arms.

CHAPTER IV.

COMBINED TACTICS.

However desirable it is that officers should know more than their own branch of the service, and should understand the nature and action of other arms, yet it is a mischevours error for any arm of the service to seek to undertake the duties of others.

A correct tactical action is one in which the powers and peculiarities of each arm of the service shall be developed to attain one object. A general looks on the different arms as instruments for attaining his object, precisely as a carpenter regards his tools; but no good carpenter would use his chisel as a saw, or his mallet as a hammer.

Therefore, although officers must know and understand something of the duties of the various branches of the army, any attempt to make these branches interchangeable, to make artillery work as cavalry, infantry as artillery or engineers, is to use a thing for a purpose it is not intended for, at all times a slow and costly operation, producing a minimum amount of result with a maximum expenditure. In armies, infantry undoubtedly takes the lead, and to its action that of the other arms must be subordinated. An intimate knowledge of infantry tactics consequently becomes most essential for officers of the auxiliary arms,—cavalry, artillery, and engineers, it being their duty to aid and facilitate the action of the infantry, and they must seek, not what is most advantageous and best viewed from a cavalry, artillery, or engineer point of view, but what is best viewed from an infantry point of view.

Invariably the action of the auxiliary arms is either preparatory, or supporting, and good results can only be obtained when this tactical relation between the arms is clearly understood and appreciated.

Hence it is that we find modern tactical writers laying great stress on the fact, that commanding officers of artillery and engineers should be first-rate tacticians and strategists, and that commands of these important auxiliary arms should in the field be held by men who possess a good deal more than a technical knowledge of their profession, which, however valuable in peace time cannot in the field compensate for ignorance of the points of contact between their own and the other arms.

The relative position of the officer commanding the artillery and engineers as regards the Divisional and Corps generals, and the Divisional and Corps artillery and engineers, should be clearly understood. Nothing can be worse than the attempt to centralize the direction of these arms in the hands of the senior officer attached to the army, such a system entirely destroys the tactical relation of the forces commanded by the Divisional and Corps generals. On those officers rests the responsibility of success, it can be shifted on no one else. If the artillery and engineers under their command are interfered with by the senior officer of the arm, then responsibility must cease, and where there is no power there can be no responsibility.

The Division being the tactical unit, its component portions should never be interfered with. It has been pointed out, page 141, that disastrous consequences ensued to the Austrian army at Königgrätz by this system of interference; the same results appear to have followed at Paris.

L

Vinoy.

The concentration of the various military departments, despite the great zeal of each, produced everywhere difficulties and delays which were irritating and much to be regretted. As regards the artillery and engineers it followed from these arrangements that during the siege they were entirely distinct from and independent of the commanding officers of corps and Divisions, and the confusion consequent on these arrangements caused disastrous consequences. Batteries were often built, armed, and even opened fire without the commandant of the troops in the immediate vicinity being informed, thus these batteries were unsupported and in danger of capture. Friction of this kind has the great disadvantage that when the hour for action arrives, each commander thinks only of his special arm without any reference to the functions of others, and from this want of co-operation far too often results inferior to what might fairly have been anticipated under a better system are obtained. The fire of artillery undoubtedly paves the way for an infantry attack, but it also may hamper it. Artillery must receive support from infantry, but by our new regulations this cannot be done, the two arms working quite independently of one another. This subject is a most important one ; a conflict of authority in action is so much to be deprecated that it is absolutely requisite that the faults of our organization should be remedied. Although the commandant of the 13th corps could not agree with the views of the Governor of Paris, he cheerfully obeyed his orders. No serious action is possible without the most complete subordination of the artillery and engineers to the officers commanding corps and Divisions, and our regulations must be altered.

The best way of obtaining the results which General Vinoy considers, and justly considers, so absolutely requisite, is to send all correspondence and orders for the Divisional artillery and engineers, to and from the senior officers of those arms, through the Divisional or corps generals. By these means the artillery and engineers will be always properly *en rapport* with the other arms.

An army is composed of the various arms of the service in proportions suitable for the work it has to perform.

If a campaign in a hilly difficult country is to be undertaken, the cavalry and artillery would be diminished, the engineers increased. If a war was to be carried out in which frequent sieges were anticipated, the artillery and engineers would be increased. Further, the nature of the climate and the quality of the enemy, the means of communication, and the possibility of getting supplies, must be taken into account.

A campaign in New Zealand differs from one in Europe, and a war in India from an Abyssinian campaign.

Certain definite proportions have been laid down by writers as a general or normal proportion for the various arms.

Napoleon.

If the infantry of an army be represented by unity, the cavalry should be $\frac{1}{4}$, the artillery $\frac{1}{4}$, the engineers $\frac{1}{16}$, the train $\frac{1}{16}$. But if the country be mountainous the cavalry need be only $\frac{1}{8}$.

Thus, if the infantry of an army be 30,000 men, the whole force on this assumption would be :—

Infantry..	..	..	..	..	..	30,000
Cavalry ..	..	..	..	..	..	7,500
Artillery	..	..	..	..	..	3,750
Engineers	..	..	..	..	..	750
Train ..	..	..	..	..	..	1,000
	Total	..	..	..	..	43,000

These proportions seem to require revision, the cavalry force being very large, the artillery and engineers small. At the time Napoleon wrote, there were no telegraphs or railways, and the pontoon train in the French service formed a portion of the artillery, not the engineer service.

The proportions of the different arms in a German army corps are :—

Infantry..	..	..	..	..	..	26,486
Cavalry ..	..	..	..	..	..	4,128
Artillery	..	..	..	..	..	4,026
Engineers	..	..	..	..	..	1,254
Train ..	..	..	..	..	..	2,177
Administrative Services		..	..	..	..	1,054
Staff ..	..	..	..	..	..	223
	Total	..	..		..	39,341

This would give the following proportions: infantry 1, cavalry $\frac{1}{6}$, artillery $\frac{1}{7}$, engineers $\frac{1}{21}$, train $\frac{1}{13}$, administrative corps $\frac{1}{30}$. If the totals of the IInd Army in the last war be taken, it will appear that the whole force was composed as follows :

Infantry	..	..	..	..	..	177,942
Corps Cavalry ..	..	..	..	24,768	
Divisional Cavalry	..	..	..	9,478	
						34,246
Artillery	..	..	..	..	..	23,214
Engineers	..	..	..	..	..	7,524
Train ..	..	..	..	..	..	13,062
Administrative Services		..	..	..	..	6,324
Telegraph and Railway Corps		..	about			500

The proportions, therefore, between the different arms in the army-corps and the army remain unaltered, except the cavalry, which is increased from $\frac{1}{6}$ to between $\frac{1}{5}$ and $\frac{1}{6}$, and the engineers slightly increased by the addition of the railway and telegraph corps. These proportions are of course those of field troops ; as is well known, the whole of the Prussian lines of communication are kept up by special bodies,* and the siege corps are also formed specially. If these numbers for the North German army-corps be compared with Napoleon's, it will be found that the proportion of Cavalry is slightly reduced, the proportion of artillery, engineers, and train, increased.

---

* This fact is often forgotten when speaking of the Prussian Army. The number of officers and the various arms of the service are calculated from the army-corps, forgetting that the whole " Etappen," a force destined for the lines of communication, are not included, and that staff officers and soldiers for these necessary duties are in other armies drawn from the fighting bodies, which are consequently weakened.

Clausewitz.

Artillery being the 'most powerful arm for destruction, cavalry the weakest, the question should be asked how much artillery can an army have? What is the necessary number of cavalry?

But whatever be the proportion of the different arms of the service, in fixing them, the manner in which the army is raised, whether by universal service, conscription, or voluntary enlistment must be considered, and the nature of the service the army is to be engaged on, should be well weighed before they are definitely laid down.

Infantry is undoubtedly the main stay and the backbone of all armies, whether it be viewed in the light of numbers, or its action on the field of battle. Its fire is more deadly than that of artillery, its action is sure, while that of cavalry is fitful.

On the infantry of an army the brunt of the fighting falls,[*] it suffers more in action and more on the line of march, and to it the action of all other arms are subordinate. Artillery fire but to pave the way for an infantry attack, or to check an infantry advance. Cavalry charge but to confirm an infantry victory or to check a pursuit. Engineers open roads and make bridges, to allow infantry to pass; they strengthen positions, and throw up earthworks, but to protect and cover the infantry, or to enable a small body to resist a superior force. On infantry tactics the whole superstructure of military operations must be built.

But it must be borne in mind that in any tactical action, one arm of the service without the others is really incomplete, and the true function of tactics, is to so apply the action of each arm, that not only its special power shall be developed, but that it shall be developed at the time and place requisite for the support of the other arms.

Napoleon.

A good infantry is doubtless the nerve of an army, but if it has to struggle for any length of time against a very superior artillery it gets demoralised and will be destroyed.

Tactical retrospect. Captain May. (Translated by Ouvry.)

The expression, 'infantry tactics,' is essentially a scientific abstraction, necessary for the fixing of scientific ideas, elementary forms. In a battle there is no such thing as infantry tactics. Tactics are for the handling of the branches of the army united. It cannot be said at any moment during a battle,—here the artillery tactics cease, and those of the infantry commence ; both of whom are constantly interwoven one with the other.

There are really only two ways in which a battle can arise:

1. When one army is on the defensive, and occupies a strong position, the other moving forward to attack it.

2. When the two armies meet, both being in movement. Auerstadt, Solferino, Mars-la-Tour, are all examples of this

---

* The loss of the various arms of the Service during the recent war are given for the German army as follows :—

Infantry ..	4,458	officers,	112,029	men, or	17·6	per cent. of the whole force.
Cavalry ..	279	„	4,342	„	6·3	„ „
Artillery ..	422	„	5,597	„	6·5	„ „
Engineers	48	„	533	„	2·8	„ „
Train ..	7	„	105	„	·3	„ „

latter kind of battle, but in every case the *rôle* of attacker or defender falls to one side, sometimes to each side alternately, and it may vary in different portions of the field, the same army being on the defensive in one place, and on the offensive in another. However a battle may actually come about, the order of march of the troops forming the army must be intimately connected with the action of the troops in line of battle; consequently the order of march must be invariably detailed so as to allow of the arms first required being near the head of the column. If the way in which battles begin is considered, it will be found that the cavalry of the advanced guard usually find the enemy and report his position: if he is in a defensive position, they report the circumstance, if on the move they report the force immediately in front of them. In all probability they will be driven in on the main body of the advanced guard, the commander of which must then take up the best defensive position he can, to cover the deployment of the troops in his rear. If the enemy are holding a defensive position, he will not be much troubled, because few generals will like to leave a carefully prepared position, and to give up too soon the advantage of acting on the defensive, or to move until the plans of the attacker have declared themselves.

In such a case the commander of the advanced guard, knowing that the enemy is to be attacked, must take up such a position that he may protect and cover the advance of the main body to the attack.

If the enemy are not holding a defensive position, he will in all likelihood be hardly pressed, and have some difficulty in maintaining a *point d'appui* on which the troops in rear are to form up to the right or left, such as Hassenhausen, held by Gudin at the battle of Auerstadt. Consequently it follows that those arms of the service which can facilitate the formation, should be near the head of the column. Hence there is a very close connection between the tactical action of troops on a field of battle, and their order of march, and it is essentially requisite that the order of march be subordinated to the deployment of the army into line of battle.

It is manifestly the object of the officer commanding the advanced guard to find a position such as will compel the enemy to develop a considerable force to attack him, and at the same time enable him to make head against such an attack.

Such a position can generally be found; it is often desirable to occupy a small village or town, loop-hole some houses or buildings, or form some trenches, which will enable the advanced guard to remain in possession of the ground. It is requisite in many cases to open passages to the right and left for troops to move through and facilitate the formation; a strong body of engineers should therefore move with the advanced guard. If the enemy is in position, and does not show any inclination to attack, a portion of the engineers may be detailed to remove obstacles, form any small bridges that may be required, such as those that were needed for the passage of the Bistritz and Sauer, and facilitate the advance of the troops beyond the position taken up by the main body of the advanced guard. But as the line of advance of an army acting on the offensive will, if defeated, be generally its line of retreat, it will be always well to strengthen some points which in case of disaster may afford a rallying place to troops that are worsted. But no position can be properly defended without artillery, consequently the commander of the advanced guard should have a strong force of artillery with him, which he must use boldly, to search out the enemy's position, compel him to unmask his guns, and declare himself. The commander of the artillery of the advanced guard has a very responsible office thrown on him. He must not only find positions for his own guns, but he should, from the fire of the enemy, be able to select places for the corps batteries as they come up, and to facilitate this object he should place his batteries so as to leave room for others to come up in support of them.

The battle of Mars-la-Tour offers an excellent example of the action of an advanced guard on a large scale, when meeting an army on the move. The object of the Germans was to hold the French fast, and prevent their retreat on Verdun, while the remainder of their army came up. Thus the troops that first attacked the French were really acting like all other advanced guards, they were covering the front and giving time for the deployment of the army.

The German general, Alvensleben, learning from his reconnoitring officers that the French were encamped between Vionville and Rezonville, determined to attack them with his own corps, the IIIrd, and what other troops were near.

At 9 A.M. the Germans established between Tronville and the road by which the French were retreating, four horse artillery batteries and three cavalry regiments, which surprised the French encampments, compelled the French to retire and deploy, facing west across, and at right angles to, the Verdun road.

At 11, Vionville was taken by the Prussian infantry, and immediately strengthened by two companies of Engineers, and it at once became a *point d'appui*, round which the whole Prussian line pivotted throughout the day.

The four horse artillery batteries were soon supported with four other batteries, which fired on the French infantry masses, causing them to suffer severely; soon, however, the German ammunition began to be exhausted, and the ammunition columns left at Gorze, although ordered up in time, could only come up the ravine with great difficulty, and under a shower of French shells. Then the corps artillery came into action to the east of

Tartleville. The operation was no easy one. Once in position it was received with a terrible infantry fire from Flavigny. But the batteries held their ground, being shortly supported by four more batteries, which extended the line of guns to the left towards Vionville. The fire of the French infantry, although at 900 to 1,200 yards, caused great loss, covering the batteries with a rain of bullets.

The eight batteries in position near Vionville, and the seven near Flavigny, now concentrated their fire on Flavigny and the Cistern wood; these 15 batteries completely cleared that important position, which fell to the Germans about 12 o'clock without any serious infantry fighting. The 2nd French Corps, shaken by the terrible artillery fire, called on its cavalry for support, and a sharp cavalry action ensued, under cover of which nine of the 15 German batteries advanced beyond the Flavigny road so as to embrace that place in the German line of battle: three other batteries advanced almost simultaneously along the main road between Rezonville and Vionville; but these movements were only executed at the cost of heavy losses; some batteries losing all their officers, others many of their horses.

It will be seen by this abridged account, that the German guns were not advancing in line with or following in rear of the infantry. But the movements of the artillery, far from being rigidly tied down to conform to those of the infantry, were tactically independent, that is to say, both arms were working each according to its own special peculiarities for the attainment of one object. Long before the Prussian infantry could come on the ground in any force, the artillery was in position, preparing the way for it, protected on its flanks by cavalry and a small force of infantry. The manner in which the German artillery was used to extend the line of battle, fill up a great gap in its centre, and so not only occupy a longer front themselves, but attack their enemy over a larger front, is well worthy of notice; they were working tactically together with the cavalry and infantry to debar the French from the Verdun road, and give time for the deployment of the German army. The attack of the French cavalry on the German batteries was at once met by the German cavalry, and the fire of the guns being then masked, both as regards their own, and to a certain extent their opponents' fire by the cavalry fight, the batteries seized the opportunity and dashed to the front. At one o'clock the Prussians had two cavalry divisions, one corps, and 21 batteries in action, the French had one cavalry division, two corps, and 26 batteries. The whole of the Prussian guns were really in three batteries, of nine, seven, and five guns respectively, while the French guns were scattered about. After one o'clock the French took the offensive, and drove back the Prussian wings; the centre, however, held fast to Vionville.

In this action the use made of the artillery and engineers to check the French and gain time,—the action of the artillery, especially, in seizing advantageous places, and rapidly bringing up fresh batteries, and in concentrating masses of fire on certain points, are well worthy of close examination. If the guns had not been with the advance, the same result could never have been obtained. It is worth noticing where the guns marched. It appears that the four horse artillery batteries attached to Rheinbaben's cavalry, and which having bivouacked at Vionville, first attacked the French, belonged three to the Xth, and one to the IVth Corps, and were attached to the cavalry division. The artillery had no special escorts, one battery marching with the cavalry brigade forming the advanced guard, and the other three with the main body of the division ; the divisional artillery of the IIIrd Corps marched between the brigades of the leading division, the corps artillery between the divisions. Although the VIIIth Prussian Corps hardly came into the action at all, a large number of its batteries coming up towards the close of the day, supported the exhausted artillery of the Xth and IIIrd Corps.*

It is evident that the order of march must be intimately connected with the deployment of the troops, and this becomes all the more important as the troops approach the actual point of collision. As they do so, the number of roads on which they are moving must be reduced, by the mere convergence of the columns, and hence, the order of the troops in those columns becomes of the utmost importance. It is further manifest that there should be no definite order of march, but the actual order in which the troops stand should be regulated by the work to be done, and the nature of the country.

We have said that no matter how a battle may begin, the *rôle* of attacker and defender will usually fall to one side, and perhaps change several times during the course of the day, depending on the number of men engaged at each place, the strength of the positions, the mode of handling the reserves, and the number of men defending the position.

There has been a gradual tendency for many years to extend the front of an army occupying a given position, or to reduce the number of men occupying a given piece of ground. This has been evinced by the reduction of the number of ranks in most armies.† Concentration is undoubtedly strength, but we must clearly understand what concentration of force, in its military sense, means. It means the assembling on a given point, of a mass of military units *sufficient* to deny the use of

---

* At this action the Prussian artillrey fired 19,638 rounds, or an average of 531 rounds per battery, or 89 rounds per gun ; the greatest number of rounds fired was by a horse battery, which fired 1,164 rounds or 194 rounds per gun.

† Napoleon's reasons for reducing the depth of the French army at Leipzig from three to two ranks,—viz., it enabled him to increase his front,—is a case in point.

that point to the enemy if acting on the defensive, sufficient to drive the enemy out if acting on the offensive.

But if the *sufficient number* be exceeded, concentration becomes dangerous, becomes unwieldly accumulation, and it deprives other places of their proper defence. Further, when military units are massed together, or concentrated, it must be borne in mind that if that concentration exceeds certain limits it prevents the proper use of the men's arms; hence under certain circumstances concentration and disorder may become convertible terms. The *sufficient number* must be concentrated in such a way that they can use their arms so as to produce a maximum effect; hence we arrive at one limit to concentration incident on the action of one side. But it is further limited by the effects of the fire of the opposite side upon densely concentrated masses; hence it follows that a certain number of military units are sufficient for the attack or defence of any position, and to exceed or reduce that number is undesirable.

The result of the gradual appreciation of these facts is, that the number of troops considered requisite to occupy a position of given length is now much less than formerly; because the power of the individual firearm is now so much greater.

The tendency to which we refer has been gradual and has been going on for more than 200 years, but during the last seven or eight years, however, the rapid strides made in improving arms have produced a sudden expansion of the front occupied by armies.

There has also been developed, especially of recent years, a tendency to occupy long lines by holding certain points strongly and leaving others, comparatively speaking, weak. This tendency was first shown in permanent fortification, which, standing on the same basis (arms and contour of ground) as tactics, often takes the lead in tactical questions. Of recent years the curtains of fortifications have disappeared, the bastions have been pushed far apart, in fact have been converted into "detached forts." This tendency has been much strengthened by the power of resistance that the breech-loader gives troops when acting on the defensive, and the fact that even a small body of men cannot be turned out of a position until regularly attacked, thoroughly shaken, and their *morale* destroyed by fire. From this tendency to form lines of battle with certain decisive points strongly held, and others comparatively speaking undefended, arises the fact referred to at page 68, that battles at the present day tend to become a series of independent combats or small battles. At page 68 we said several consequences resulted from this breaking up of a great battle into many small ones; some of the results we have referred to, but to prevent confusing the subject, others have been left to this part of the work.

It follows from this division of battles into numerous small combats that the losses are very disproportionate; a glance at the table in the Appendix shows that the relative proportion of killed and wounded to the total force engaged has by no means increased since the introduction of improved weapons. But if modern battles be analysed, it will be found that the great mass of the loss takes place at one place and in one corps, to whose lot it has fallen to capture certain special and decisive points in the field of battle. Thus the great proportion of the Prussian losses at Königgrätz took place in Fransecky's division, which captured the Maslowed wood, a most important point, as linking the 1st and 2nd Armies together. Similarly the greatest proportion of losses at Gravelotte was sustained by the guards, who captured St. Privat, the key of the French position, and it is a consequence of improved weapons that once a lodgement is made on the key of the defender's position, the results extend to the flank more rapidly and to a greater extent than formerly. Hence every effort should be used to discover such points and to strengthen and maintain them so long as they are held. Attacks on the places of minor importance, the intervals between what may be termed the "detached forts," produce but little effect; another consequence is, that numerous flank attacks may be made; at first sight it appears that an army having only two flanks, can only be subject to two such attacks. The fact being that each distinct portion of the field will offer such points for attack, which become more marked by the swaying backwards and forwards of the general line according as either side gains or loses ground.

It further results that the formation of a large reserve for the whole army is now no longer admissible. The extension of front is so great that the reserve, even if placed in the centre, could hardly reach the flanks in time to be of use.

We therefore arrive at a general rule that no body of troops should ever engage without forming its own reserve; thus if a battalion engages, as already pointed out, the main body is the reserve. The Division should form its own reserve, also the corps, while the use of an army reserve, except under special circumstances, may be fairly questioned.

The containing power of the breech-loader used on the defensive, and the number of small battles, into which a great battle divides itself, produces other remarkable results.

Great concentration destroys mobility, and the paradox appears of armies widely spread, with external lines of communication, defeating a concentrated force with interior lines. Jomini, many years ago, pointed out that this might be the case, but it has become so now in a marked degree. Take the battle of Königgrätz as an example. The Austrian army offered, perhaps, the maximum amount of concentration that was possible, the Prussians were spread over a wide front, and were on exterior lines.

Campaign of 1866; official account. (Translated by Hozier and Wright.)

The whole Austrian Army of the North (*about* 206,000 *men*) was assembled behind the small river Bistritz, with the fortress of Königgrätz and the Elbe in its rear. It extended over a space of about five miles (or about 41,000 men to a mile).

A state of concentration like that in which the army had been for the last five days renders the subsistence of the troops extremely difficult, and only admits of bivouacking, thereby weakening the strength of the troops and opposing the greatest obstacles to all further movements ; under these circumstances the march of the army on the 1st of July, although only nine miles long, lasted 24 hours. The Prussian armies had voluntarily kept a front of nearly 23 miles breadth.

Generally speaking it will be remembered that the Prussian armies, advancing from two different directions, were converging on Königgrätz.

Now why could not a concentrated force like the Austrian army leap on and crush one of the Prussian armies, each about one-half its own strength, before it could be helped by the other ; it had the advantages of being well in hand, completly concentrated, and had internal lines.

It is desirable that this question should be carefully considered. Writers and speakers sometimes write and speak as if Prussia had discovered something new in the form of strategy and tactics, and they point to the division of force in Bohemia and France, and the double external lines of operation, as being a contradiction to the Napoleonic experience, and speak of the Prussian attack as being like "a pair of nut-crackers" or "a pair of tongs." There is much danger in these ideas, as there is in the general application of any law to every instance. Jomini pointed out that with very large forces, the benefits of concentration disappeared, and he says 100,000 men holding a central position will have a better chance against three armies of 30,000 or 35,000 men, than an army of 400,000 in the same position against three armies of 135,000.

A concentrated army of large size moves so slowly, and meets with such resistance if it attacks a force say of one-half or one-third its size, that it cannot crush it before the arrival of the other forces. This was precisely the Austrian case at Königgrätz; concentration had made them too unwieldly to attack either Prussian army.

And it appears that the resisting force of the breech-loader on the defensive has still further reduced the advantages of the army occupying the central position and closely concentrated, when it attempts to attack one of two or three scattered detachments.

An army that is concentrated too much is really as feeble as one that is too much disseminated, and generally suffers more, as it becomes the mark of a convergent fire from the attackers, who quickly outflank it.

It is well known that the Austrian General Benedek intended * to form his line of battle on two sides of a square, of which

* His orders were only partially carried out.

Chulm was about the salient, and he detained as a reserve, to act under his sole orders, the Ist and IVth army-corps with five cavalry divisions and the artillery reserve. At an early stage of the battle the reserve behind the centre, near Sweti, was swept by Prussian shells.

Campaign of 1866 : official account. (Translated by Hozier and Wright.)

The left wing had a reserve of three weak brigades behind it on the right wing, only one brigade covered the ground between the right flank and the Elbe. On the other hand a main reserve of two corps and five cavalry divisions, stood ready for action, full two miles behind the centre of the whole line of battle.

The battle of Königgrätz affords also an example of the value of numerous small reserves, as used by the Prussians, and the comparative feebleness of huge reserves as formed by the Austrians.

De Looze.

In the attack on the wood of Maslowed, the Prussians formed company columns, but very soon lost all tactical order, but their constant care to keep small reserves formed of every man that they could rally as quickly as possible, enabled them to sustain an heroic struggle for eight hours with 14 battalions against 51 Austrian battalions.

At Gravelotte, the French reserve and their splendid reserve artillery hardly fired a shot. Judging from these facts, reserves must not be massed together but must be numerous; of a size proportionate to the object to be attained, and must be so disposed as to be able to act without delay when needed.

In addition to a reserve there should be a second line. In small affairs, or when the attack is made with a narrow front, not exceeding effective rifle range, the second line and the reserve would become the same body, but no commander should ever be without a force held in hand. The moment that his second line and reserves have passed out of his hands, his power of directing and ruling the fight is gone, and has passed to his subordinates, perhaps to the enemy.

A remarkable instance of this occured at Langensalza. The Prussian army was inferior to the Hanoverian; in their endeavour to show an equal front they extended to the right and left. The reserve came into action in the interval between the wings, a single line of battle was formed, which was penetrated by the Hanoverians, and once penetrated the Prussians were unable to retrieve the day, being without any troops to make the effort. A second line is therefore indispensable, but it may be composed of much fewer men than the first line, speaking in very general terms, for no rule can be given as an absolute guide, the second line and reserve may perhaps be equal to the first line.

If a position be held by 6,400, or 8 battalions of 800 men each, and the position be a mile in extent, or $3\frac{1}{2}$ men to the yard, the formation *might* be—

Skirmishers, 8 Companies..	..	..	=	800 men
Supports, 8 Companies ..	..	..	=	800 „
Main Body, 16 Companies	..	..	=	1,600 „
Total of First Line, 4 Battalions			=	3,200 „

157

Second Line, 2 Battalions	..	=	1,600 men
Reserve, 2 Battalions	.. ..	=	1,600 ,,
Total, 8 Battalions ..	..	=	6,400 ,,

In many such cases the reserve and second line might really constitute one force, and would remain together, the second line battalions being those first called on. The question of keeping artillery in reserve is one that demands some consideration; it has been already referred to at page 132.

Owing to the great range and accuracy of rifled guns it is possible to concentrate the fire of a great number of guns upon a given spot; this is of course favourable to the defence, but although this is the case, the attack is also benefited in a similar way, and as the action of an attack is enveloping to a great extent, the range and accuracy of rifled guns allows them to support infantry making an attack until almost the moment of actual assault. And further, it would seem that there is no reason whatever, but rather the reverse, why all guns should not be brought into action as soon as possible and remain in action until the very close of the engagement. In considering the action of artillery it must be remembered that that arm differs from the others, inasmuch as it embraces more *matériel*, less *personnel*. *Within certain limits* it suffers less in both its efficiency and its *morale* from loss than infantry does.

Further, many of the losses it does suffer are not of a nature to make it inefficient for that day's work, and many may be repaired and put to rights even under fire. We allude to such damages as a wheel being struck, a carriage hit, &c., all of which really affect the fighting power of the battery but slightly, as they can be at once repaired. Consequently, to keep artillery of any kind in reserve, with the view of bringing it up fresh, at a critical moment, except under special cases, appears to be a doubtful policy. So long as the batteries have ammunition, the amount of loss they usually sustain, will rarely put them *hors de combat* as fighting bodies.

If a tactical body, such as a division or corps, is kept in reserve, there should be no hesitation in using its artillery freely. Prussian critics of the recent war invariably blame the arrangements by which the artillery of the Xth Prussian Corps, which was the reserve at the battle of Gravelotte, was not brought into action against St. Privat, "The affair would have been completed much sooner had these 90 additional guns been in position."

To keep artillery during an action in reserve is to neutralise a force, which from the beginning to the end, should produce an effect with its guns whenever they can see anything to fire at. Von Walder-see.

The great range of artillery enables it to be so placed that with little change of position it can support, while receiving a reciprocal support from both lines.

The whole essence of modern fighting, whether it be the attack or defence, lies in these words:—*Seek to overwhelm the enemy with fire, and shake his morale to such an extent that his fire becomes so feeble that he may be attacked.* Consequently every means that can augment the fire and so crush an opponent should be adopted.

If the combined action of the arms of the service are considered, it will be found that the side that attacks usually fixes on some portion of the enemy's position and establishes a cross-fire on it; if this point be a village, a heavy cross-fire will soon shake the buildings so as to render them indefensible; watching the moment when the enemy appear to be leaving the village, the infantry should advance, the function of the artillery here is to keep the enemy from returning to the village, and for this reason it should continue to fire until its fire is masked. The moment this is the case the guns, unable to do more in this direction, should turn their attention to the enemy's artillery, which has been, in all probability, playing chiefly on them, although the advancing infantry have undoubtedly come in for their share.

As the infantry advance, seeking to gain ground to the front in extended order, they must be not only carefully supported from the rear, but as they are peculiarly liable to the attack of small bodies of cavalry on the flanks, cavalry must be held in hand, under shelter in some convenient place, with orders to watch any attempted action of the enemy's cavalry, and move rapidly to the front if they show themselves. The cavalry must, in such a case, act by instinct not by orders, and their leader must be most careful to watch lest, in the smoke and dust, the hostile cavalry move to the front without being noticed. In such cases it is of great advantage to get as near the enemy as possible; often a small wood or inclosure will offer itself, or some fold of the ground, behind which the cavalry may shelter themselves, unseen from the enemy's position, and remain in readiness. The approaches to such places may be over ground heavily swept by artillery, and even musketry fire, but which it is quite possible to cross; so soon as a few infantry have got into the wood or enclosure, the cavalry officer may push some men rapidly out; riding fast a few men, in extended order, will usually escape; they may be followed by a few more, until the whole force is got over. But cavalry cannot remain in such positions without the support of some infantry, who will prevent the enemy's infantry from making a forward movement with a small body and harassing the cavalry. In such positions the cavalry must be prepared to venture everything to check a hostile movement.

The infantry with them will always give a point of support to rally on, and working thus a few cavalry may render very efficient service on the field of battle. But no large body can be so employed. If the ground enables cavalry to be thus pushed on in small bodies and kept covered from the enemy's fire, they will be of great value in checking any unexpected action on the flanks of the attack.

When acting against the enemy's cavalry they have little to dread from projectiles, as the enemy, on account of his own cavalry, will be afraid to fire much.

If the infantry are unable to make way in front, as is very likely to be the case, the battle will probably be decided by a flank attack; but it has been already pointed out that however, generally speaking, an attack may be termed a flank attack, it must invariably be, locally speaking, a front attack.

If the infantry penetrate the enemy's position they must be at once largely reinforced from the second line, and artillery and engineers should be pushed up to support them. The mere fact of the enemy's position being forced will have usually reduced the fire considerably, and left a dead space. Across this, guns, and some sappers furnished with tools, should be rapidly pushed, and every means taken to strengthen the position won. If the enemy means fighting, in a short time he will attempt to retake the ground won; the minutes that elapse between the capture of a position and the retaking of the offensive by the enemy are invaluable; no man should be allowed to stray or wander about, the confusion incident on all successful attacks must be rapidly remedied, the men's pouches seen to, and the engineers must work to form shelter and maintain the lodgment. As troops come on they must be pushed to the right and left, and extended in front, but nothing should interfere with the strengthening of the foothold gained. If the enemy has his reserves at hand he will shortly advance fresh troops to attempt to retake the position, and will endeavour to concentrate a fire of artillery on it. If guns have been brought up they should be covered as much as possible, and should open on the enemy's artillery when on the move, which it will in all probability be, at a moderate range. The position being held firmly, the defensive should not be simply taken, but a fresh advance made, which will usually enable large forces to brought up. The penetration of the enemy's position will thus place the attacker in the position of being on the flank of both of the two wings or portions into which the army is split, and if that position be maintained those wings must fall back. But supposing that a front attack fails, or that the troops making it are unable to advance owing to the heavy fire poured on them, or that for other reasons a flank attack has been resolved on, it then becomes requisite that the troops not employed in making the flank attack should occupy the enemy, threaten his front, and at the same time strengthen their position so as to check any forward movement the enemy may make. It being possible that when he finds a flank threatened he may refuse that flank by throwing it back, and strive to check the turning movement by an attack on the troops immediately in his front, or he may move large forces to the threatened flank; either of these operations would seriously interfere with the success of the flank movement, hence it becomes requisite that every means should be adopted to prevent the enemy leaving the position he has taken up or modifying his line of battle to any great extent. For such purposes as these, partial attacks on the enemy's position may be undertaken, and various expedients resorted to to detain and keep him in position, while the flank movement is being made.

The action of the Prussian Ist Army at Königgrätz offers a good example of this. It was well known that the Austrians could not hold their ground once the IInd (Crown Prince's) Army came well into action, and that its arrival would be decisive. The object then of the leaders of the Ist Army was to threaten the Austrians, keep them in position, and establish themselves firmly on the left in the Maslowed wood, so as to feel for the IInd Army, and link the two armies together. The fierce attack on the wood at Maslowed held the Austrians fast.

(Campaign of 1866: official account. (Translated by Hozier and Wright.) One fact, however, nobody could foresee, namely that by far, the greater part of those troops which the enemy should have employed to guard against an attack from the north were already engaged on the line, Cistowes-Maslowed-Horenowes, and that his main reserve was at that moment further from the latter place than the heads of the IInd Prussian Army.

The Prussians also used the line of the Bistritz to protect their right, the Ist Army, from any offensive movement of the Austrians, and placed the villages along its course in a state of defence.

Such flank movements, if the whole attacking army be concentrated, must, owing to the long range of modern weapons, be made on a circle of far greater radius than formerly, hence a concentric attack, if feasible, offers many advantages.

Cavalry will often be of great use in such movements, for it may be possible, from the more rapid movement of that arm, to throw an overwhelming force of cavalry on the rear of the threatened flank; the moral effect of a force of cavalry appearing there would undoubtedly exercise great influence on the stand made by the troops attacked, who would find their ammunition columns &c., assailed and taken in rear by the cavalry, while they themselves were being pressed in front. It is, perhaps, here that the tactical action of cavalry in large bodies may be of great importance; but if cavalry be so used, care must be taken that they do not separate to too great distance from the infantry moving to the flank; and the cavalry leader must keep up a tactical connexion with the infantry at all times, and warn it of all movements that the enemy may make to meet the flank attack.

CHAPTER V.

MARCHES.

The influences of marches over tactics and strategy cannot be over-rated; indeed, in the older books on the military art, logistics was placed, and correctly placed, on an equivalent footing to both, as a distinct and important branch of the science of war,

It is quite evident that as the success of strategy is mainly dependent on accurate calculation of the powers of marching, the most brilliant conceptions, and the most profound combinations, must fail if the troops do not move over the distances calculated on, and do not occupy the prescribed relative positions to each other.

Similarly, when the head of a column is attacked, the most skilful tactics will not help it, if the artillery, cavalry, or infantry that are required for any particular action cannot be found, if the roads are blocked, and reinforcements cannot be brought up, or ammunition be got at; consequently the art of marching forms a most important portion of the science of war.

It may generally be said that the direction of marches, and the rate of progress, are connected more with strategy than tactics, while the order of march, that is to say the position of the troops in the column, is more closely connected with tactics.

The objects for which a march is made, and the nature of the country through which it is undertaken, can alone decide the number of columns that there should be, and the actual composition of those columns.

The fewer the number of men and horses on a road the easier will they march, and the less will they suffer from checks, and that wave-like motion which pervades every long column, by which the intervals and delays increase in geometric progression towards its tail. Hence an army should march on as many roads as possible, and with as broad a front as possible, provided always that the distances apart of the various columns are not too great to allow them to support one another. Consequently every officer commanding a column must know the whereabouts of the columns to the right and left of him, and of what portion of the army they are composed, and he must keep up a touch with them by means of a few mounted men, who should communicate generally where in the columns the different arms are to be found, and where the commanders may be heard of.

It has been already stated that the increased power of weapons enables a small body of men, who know they will be supported, to hold a position longer than formerly, this enables an advanced guard to check an enemy, compel him to deploy, and bring up his artillery before he can make an impression; consequently the distance apart of columns on the march, or the front of an army moving in proximity to an

M

enemy, may now be enlarged to an extent that formerly would have been unsafe. This is a matter of no little importance as affecting rapidity of marching and punctuality of supply.

Guibert.

An army cannot march in a deployed line, even if the country were a complete and open plain, the extent of the front would make its movements too sluggish and difficult.

Neither can it move in a single column, because its immense length would retard the column, increase the fatigue of the troops, and render the army liable to be beaten in detail before it can deploy. To make a march at all, the army must divide itself into several corps or columns, which shall move in the same direction, and with the same object, and shall be ready by combined action to take up a general position for fighting.

Clausewitz.

It is requisite that the troops, marching by one road, constitute a complete unit ; suppose an order of battle with two lines, one Division in each line, and that an advance on the enemy on two roads is to be made, no one would dream of putting half of each Division on each road, but each Division would take one road, the Divisional generals being then responsible that they form their own reserves. Unity of command is of far greater importance than a stupid adherence to the original geometric arrangement. The Divisions may subsequently resume their proper places.

The number of columns in which troops march must depend chiefly on the number of good roads available. In almost every country there are certain main roads, the distance between which varies greatly, and between these roads are minor roads and lanes. As a rule troops should only move on the main roads, reserving the side roads and lanes for the flanking parties, and those keeping up the communications. Little or nothing is gained by using the side roads, they never go straight, but twist about to suit various farms, and troops marching on them are very apt to lose their way; they are narrow, and consequently if fenced the troops get jammed together. They are either not macadamized, or very badly, hence it is desirable, as far as possible, to adhere to the main roads of the country.

When the country admits, as it often does in continental Europe, it is advisable to march the troops on the fields at the side of the road, reserving the road for the wheeled traffic.

In some cases also, such as when many columns make a concentric movement on one spot, it becomes absolutely requisite to march right across country through high standing crops, over hedges, &c. But as a rule wheel carriages adhere to the roads until compelled to leave them.

Campaign of 1866: official account. (Translated by Hozier and Wright.)

The Division of Guards continued its march up and down hill, straight across country, in order not to cross the line of march which the Commander-in-Chief of the IInd Army had appointed for the advance of the 1st Corps. Soft and heavy as the rain had made the soil, the head of the column reached Chotoborek as early as 11 o'clock. On the heights of Daubrowitz the Reserve Artillery was ordered to place itself at the head of the main body of the 1st Division of Guards.

The guns trotted past the columns straight across country, and through the high standing corn, but the long straw mixed with the clayey soil, wound itself in thick wreaths round the wheels, and rendered such extreme exertion necessary that by the time they reached Jericek several horses had fallen dead before the guns from sheer fatigue.

De Ternay.

In general an army-corps should march by Divisions, one on each road, the advanced and rear guards being on the same road; the least stony road being reserved for the cavalry, and the firmest road for the artillery corps.

The strength of a column should not exceed 20,000 to 30,000 men. If a calculation is made of the distances occupied on the line of march of such a column it will be seen that in order to effect a deployment before the enemy arrives, that number should not be exceeded.

There are cases when an army must march in a single column, and cases when it must march in several.* An army does not usually confine itself to a path 12 feet wide, the main roads are 24 or 36 feet wide, and on them two lines of carriages, or 15 to 20 men abreast may march; almost always it is possible to march right and left of the main road. I have seen an army of 120,000 men, marching in one column, take up its line of battle in six hours. The advance guard should be composed of light cavalry, heavy cavalry, selected infantry, and a sufficient number of guns; its duties are to manœuvre, contain the enemy, and give the army time to come up. *Napoleon.*

The actual order of march is very important; each column should, as far as possible, be preceded by a detachment of engineers, with tools to level all obstacles which may retard the march; the engineers may be assisted by the people of the country or by infantry soldiers. This detachment should be divided into two sections; at the first obstacle the first section halts and works, the other proceeds until a fresh obstacle presents itself. An officer of engineers looks after the work.

It is desirable to consider the rates at which troops can march. A good walker can easily do four miles an hour, but this far exceeds the power of a soldier, moving as one of a mass of men, and carrying a heavy weight, in addition to which there is much fatigue from the necessity of sending out small parties to the flank; and further, the soldier on the completion of his march does not find a bed and comfortable dinner, but he often has to go on outpost duty at once, take his night duty, always sleep on the ground, and usually have a spare and ill-cooked meal. Consequently, exertions such as may be made by private individuals cannot be made by an army, except at the risk of destroying its efficiency, and leaving large numbers of stragglers behind. A few forced marches often reduce the effective strength of an army more than a lost battle. Under the influence of excitement, and urged by appeals to their higher nature, men can be got to perform considerable feats of marching, but a general who makes many forced marches may be likened to a man who spends his capital,—in a short time both will come to the end of their resources. The rate of marching of soldiers varies much from the state of their health, the state of weather, roads, and very often whether or not the roads are encumbered with traffic.

All nations allow about the same average rate of marching, viz., 2¾ to 3 miles an hour for infantry, 4 miles for field artillery, and 5 for cavalry and horse artillery. This includes short halts of five minutes or so, and represents the pace at which they can get over fair marches with least fatigue. But these rates apply to small bodies only. With large bodies the rate is slower, for every check is felt throughout the column, and multiplied by the length of *Lt.-Col.Colley, Lecture at U.S. Institution.*

* In 1866 two Prussian Corps, the 5th and 6th, advancing on Nachod, used but one road.

it. Thus a division of infantry can seldom accomplish more than $2\frac{1}{4}$ to $2\frac{1}{2}$ miles an hour, and a corps on one road even less—2 miles an hour ; the infantry, as the slowest marchers, regulating the rate of the whole ; and even this rate can only be depended on on good roads, and with good arrangements. If the roads are bad, or crowded, it is still further reduced. Thus, Vandamme, marching from Ligny to Wavre, and the Prussians marching from Wavre to Waterloo, could only accomplish about $1\frac{1}{2}$ miles an hour, owing to the bad state of the roads.

Napoleon's troops, trained marchers as they were, could only sometimes accomplish 8 or 9 miles in as many hours in the sands and mud of Poland.

At Magenta, when support was urgently required for the Guard, it took five hours to bring up Canrobert's corps from Novara, a distance of 9 miles. The road in this case was excellent, but encumbered. In 1866, before Sadowa, the 8th Austrian corps took 14 hours to do 12 miles. In 1870, when the Crown Prince was following MacMahon northwards his troops were sometimes on their legs from 4 A.M. until 8 P.M., yet it is doubtful if they ever did 24 miles in one day.

By comparing a number of marches, I arrived at the conclusion that 10 miles a day is as much as should be reckoned on in prolonged operations, and from 12 to 15 miles for actual marching days ; and these calculations agree curiously with the account of the operations of the 5th German corps in the late war. It appears the distance actually traversed by this corps between the Rhine and Paris was 520 miles in 50 days, or $10\frac{1}{2}$ miles a day. The average for actual marching days was $13\frac{1}{2}$, with a halt usually every fourth day ; the longest march was 21 miles, when in pursuit of MacMahon's army northwards.

When troops are closely concentrated, the distance marched is very much less ; in fact, where a large army is closely concentrated, a march of 8 miles takes a long time.

A long convoy of heavily laden wagons cannot march more than two miles an hour, the time taken up in putting on and removing the skids at hills being included.

The space occupied by troops on the line of march is very important. Lieut.-Colonel Colley gives a very good practical rule, viz., to allow one yard for every two infantry soldiers, one yard for each horseman, and 20 yards for a gun. The success of a march is less interfered with by the actual length of the columns of troops of the different arms, than by the continual tendency troops have to tail off, or open out; it is essentially requisite that this tailing off should be checked and the distance corrected at halts. A striking example of this tailing off occurred when the 2nd Prussian Army was advancing on the Austrian right at Königgrätz. The roads were so narrow that the infantry could only march in double file, the artillery in column of single guns.

General Von Hassenfeldt had given instructions that the close order of the columns should be carefully preserved, and a report should be sent forward as each single battalion passed the defile, or when its distance from the preceding battalion exceeded 300 paces. In spite of all these precautions it was impossible for the troops to keep close up. When they descended the hills, the guns had to put on the drag, and even if they themselves could regain their lost ground within the battery itself by increasing the pace, still the infantry behind them necessarily fell further and further to the rear.

The spaces left between troops on the line of march have for one of their objects that of absorbing such openings and preventing irregularities which may occur at the front of the column, being passed to its rear. All doubling on the part of men, or trotting on the part of horses or baggage-wagons, to recover distances so lost, should be discouraged as much as possible. If it is allowed it will be found that those at the end of a column will be either running or halting the whole time. When a halt has to be made in front it should be at once taken up along the whole column, so as to avoid any jamming. The amount to which troops will open out really depends on the discipline of the army and the care of its officers. With well drilled troops it may be perhaps one-sixth the length of the column ; with careless officers and undisciplined men the opening will increase to perhaps two-thirds, or even the whole length. The various rules to be observed in marches, and the details as to baggage, times of assembly, marching off, duties of various officers, and all similar matters, are perhaps more clearly given in General Crawford's orders for the Light Division in Spain, than in any other book, and as these orders are very valuable, and are out of print, they are given in the Appendix.

One march of a moderate length does not much affect an army, but several such marches will do so, *à fortiori*, if the marches are long the troops will suffer. *Clausewitz.*

Upon the theatre of war itself, the insufficiency of good nourishment and accommodation, united to bad roads, broken up by the passage of carriages, the incessant strain demanded by the necessity of being at all times ready to fight,—all these causes produce an expenditure of force which breaks down the men, the animals, the material, and the equipments.

A great deterioration of power must be expected in a war in which many movements are made ; plans must be carefully combined, and reinforcements must quickly follow. Unless under some pressing necessity a long march must not be made at first, because it strains the horses and men who are not in training, and often from such a cause an army finds itself deprived not only of private transport but even the commissariat and artillery draft cattle damaged.

A column of 20,000, composed of infantry, cavalry, and artillery, will, in line of battle, occupy some three miles of front, so that the troops on the wings will have to move about three miles daily to get into their places, if the operation is only done once, but often it must be done several times ; and this added to the distance gone over when defiling over bridges, through towns and woods, which are very fatiguing, although they do not help the column forward one bit, make 15 miles a day, the most that troops can do ; and often to march even this distance they must be 12 hours under arms. *Fallot Lagrange.*

Frequent halts should be made during a march, and such halts should, if possible, be made after passing a defile, to enable the troops to close up. It is absolutely requisite that such halts should be carefully regulated ; a Division must not halt when it is pleasant to do so, or when the troops are a little tired. The larger the army the more necessity for moving together, and the more requisite is it that the hours of departure and halting should be carefully regulated, especially if night marches are made. There should be a halt for 1½ hours in the middle of the march, half an hour at one-fourth and three-fourths the march, and a halt for five minutes every hour. *Thiebault.*

The necessity of having large numbers of engineers and artillery at the head of the columns has been already referred to. It is absolutely requisite that these engineers should be provided with light bridging materials, perfectly independent of the pontoon equipment of the army. The Prussians suffered much at Sadowa, owing to there being no bridges laid over the Bistritz. At Wœrth no less than 11 bridges were made over the Sauer, a little stream not 18 feet wide ; six companies were employed at the work, and yet there were not bridges enough : in such instances the more bridges the better, as it reduces the thronging, and consequent crowding.

De la Pierre.

The order of march of a column should be such that the various arms may take their places in line of battle as quickly as possible.

Now as the artillery is used first, then the infantry, then the cavalry, this should be the order of march. We would therefore place the divisional batteries in front, only to prevent their being captured by surprise some troops must be placed in front to cover them.

The infantry then follows, and lastly the cavalry ; its rapidity will enable it to come up when it is needed. The cavalry should be preceded by its horse artillery. The baggage and the reserve artillery march at the end of the column.*

So far as the position of the artillery is concerned, it may be stated as a *general* rule that the artillery of the advanced guard should march between the battalions composing it.

The artillery of the Division between the brigades composing it, and the corps artillery between the Divisions.

Von Walder-sée.

In a column composed of all arms, the point or extreme front should be formed of that arm that is the most mobile, because the regular advance of the main body, and the space it passes over, must depend to a great extent on the distances traversed in all directions by the advanced guard, which is charged with the duty of feeling the way,—a difficult office and one subject to many delays.

Everyone knows the fatigue, loss of time, and waste of power, entailed on infantry who perform this duty, as well as the fatiguing checks that the troops in rear suffer.

Consequently, with troops of the different arms of the service, whenever the ground will admit, mountains and woods not excepted, cavalry take the head of the column. and furnish the flankers ; behind these cavalry patrols, which precede the column at some distance, and are entrusted both with the duty of scouts and vedettes, some infantry should follow, forming the kernel of the vanguard.† This infantry itself furnishes an advanced guard and patrols. These must search all the hollows and inequalities in the ground which the cavalry has already rapidly gone over, without, however, checking the advance of the main column.

As regards the artillery, it should be sufficiently far forward to be immediately at hand to meet the first shock of the enemy ; experience proves that at least two guns must be in position at the beginning of the action if the enemy is to be attacked vigorously and the initiative kept. This is requisite if the column is not to be checked by a small force in front, if it has to gain any pre-determined position, or the enemy are to be severely dealt with before they can obtain cover.

This necessity of having guns at any moment at the front forbids that they should march in rear, to bring them up would occasion a very inconvenient loss of time, a loss of time a skilful enemy would quickly take advantage of to drive back the advanced guard, while the guns finding the road blocked by the troops seeking to get to the front, would have much difficulty in opening up a passage.

---

* One of the alterations made by the recent progress in tactics is that the reserve, or corps artillery, must be placed further to the front than is here stated.

† The word " Vanguard " is used here really as the advanced guard of the advanced guard—the extreme point.

PLATE. XIX

From 3th. Squad. 1st Huss.
4th Subdivn 1.2&3Subdivn

300 paces   300   300

Foster Batt.n 1st Regt
12th Co   3rd 9th 10th 11th Co   1st Light Batt.S
2 Guns
1st Light Batt.S

Engineer Co

Vanguard

1st Infantry Regt.
2nd Batt.n   1st Batt.n   1st Hussars   2nd Squadt
4 Guns
1st Light Batt.S   1 Section   Sanitary Detacht

Main Body

600

Advanced Guard

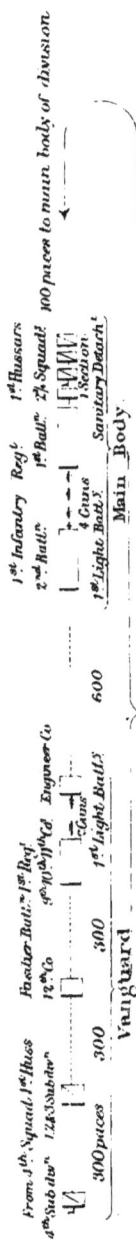

Distance occupied by troops 2.570
Interval of Formation 1.500
Total occupied by Advd Gd 4.070

1000 paces to advanced guard

From 2nd Squad.   2nd Infantry
1st Hussars   Regt.
1st subdivision

1.060

1st foot division of 1st
Artillery Regiment

1st light batt. 1 heavy batt 2nd heavy batt

1.420

4th Infantry Brigade

2.190

Section Wagons Field hospitals
Sanitary Det: exclusive of the Train of div.
100   640

Main Body of the Division

Total length of March.

Addd Gd.
to main body .... 4.070 paces
Main body 1.000
Main-body wagons, &c 5.000
.... 10.480

Add. Cavalry Brigs.
with horse battery } ... 2.350
.... 12.830

Addl Train of Column 1.220
Total 14.050

Distance occupied by troops   4.470
... wagons &c   640
1...ve occupied by Main Body 5.410

exclusive of interval between Train and rear of Division
taking this at 1 mile, the Grand Total. 16.650 paces

March of a Division.

100 paces to main body of division

2770

Consequently artillery officers are desirous that the advanced guard guns should be placed with the vanguard, either at its rear, or immediately after its first battalion if it be composed of more than one.

The following table shows the arrangements of two columns, one as proposed by Waldersée the other by Verdy du Vernois, with the length of the latter :—

Von Waldersée.	Verdy du Vernois.		Length of the latter Column.
1st. Vanguard.	**Vanguard.**		**Advanced Guard.**
Half Squadron.	4th Squadron, 1st Hussars.	4th Div., 300 yards. 3rd Div., 300 yards.	Length of Column 2,570 Intervals 1,500
Half Squadron.			
A Battalion.			Total .. 4,070
A Battery.		12th Company, 300 yards.	
2nd. Main Body of Advanced Guard.	Fusilier Battalion of 1st Regiment	11th Company.	**Main Body.**
Two Battalions.		10th Company.	Length of Column 4,770
A Section of Engineers.			Carriages 640
A Section of Pontoniers.			
	9th Company.		Total .. 5,440
3rd. Main Body of the Column.	Two guns of a 4-pounder Battery.		
A Battalion.	Company of Engineers. 600 yards.		**Total Length of March.**
Two Batteries.			Advanced Guard.. 4,070
Five Battalions.			Intervals 1,000
Two Squadrons.	**Main Body of the Advanced Guard.**		Main Body with Carriages .. 5,440
Hospital Detachment.			
Light Baggage.	2nd Battalion 1st Regiment.		Total .. 10,480
	Remainder of 4-pounder Battery.		
4th. Train.	1st Battalion 1st Regiment.		
Infantry Ammunition Column.	Hospital Detachment.		Cavalry Brigade with Horse Artillery 2,350
Artillery Ammunition Column.	2¾ Squadrons of Hussars, 1,000 yards.		
Field Hospital.			Total .. 12,830
Provision Columns.	**Main Body of the Division.**		
	100 yards	Half a Div. of Hussars. 2nd Infantry Regiment.	Add train.. .. 1,220 Add distance between Train and Column 2,600
	1,420 yards	2nd Battery of 4-pounders. 1st Battery of 6-pounders. 2nd Battery of 6-pounders.	Total length of the Division.. .. 16,650
	2,190 yards	4th Brigade of Infantry.	
	100 yards	Hospital Detachment.	
	640 yards	Hospital Wagons without the Divisional Train.	

Plate XIX. shows the arrangement of Verdy du Vernois, with the distances.*

* This plate is copied from that in Hildyard's translation of Verdy du Vernois' book

No normal order of march for a British Division or Corps has ever been authoritatively laid down; it is desirable, therefore, that some general idea of how a division or corps might be formed for a march should be here given. But in such a matter the normal form can only be considered as *the general* arrangement given, not so much to be followed, as to be altered to suit the nature of the country and the proximity of the enemy.

Lieut.-Colonel Colley, Professor of Military Administration, Staff College.

The cavalry should always, if possible, be pushed well to the front; it moves with greater freedom and ease for being independent, and covers the march of the army better than any regular advanced guard. In fact, the chief use of the advanced guard (providing against surprise) ceases. But the division into advanced guard and main body has also its advantages for fighting purposes—opening an engagement without compromising the main body, feeling the way, and making the enemy declare himself, hence it is usually retained. The subdivisions of the advanced guard and intervals between the fractions may however in such cases be dispensed with.

An army-corps so covered by cavalry would be preceded by engineers, with one or two companies of infantry, partly as escort and partly to furnish extra working parties if required, and a troop or squadron of cavalry to explore roads and maintain communications; then would follow an advanced guard comprised as usual, but moving in one compact body, and then at a moderate interval the main body. Intervals are necessary to prevent surprise, but when not required for that, are objectionable, on account of lengthening the column.

If the cavalry cannot push forward without support, and therefore collision may take place with very short warning, the advanced guard must be formed with a view to surprise. It is very difficult to draw up a normal formation, that best suited to England would be unsuited to most of the continent of Europe. Cavalry should always be used as much as possible, and unless the country is peculiarly unfavourable, should accompany the advanced guard if not lead it.

The following is a sort of compromise, it being understood that the cavalry always pushes to the front if it can :—

A BRITISH DIVISION.

Half Troop of Cavalry, with patrols at least 400 yards in front.
400 yards.
Remainder of squadron.
1 Company of Rifles.
300 yards.
3 Companies of Rifles.
2 Guns without Wagons.
Section of Engineers (pack horses only, if possible).
600 yards to ½ mile.
Officer commanding Advanced Guard.
4 Companies of Rifles.
4 Guns.
Half Battalion (1st Battalion) from 1st Brigade.
2½ Squadrons Cavalry (H. Q. of Regiment.)
Engineer Company with Section of Train.
Wagons of Artillery.
S. A. Carts and Tool Wagons of Infantry of Advanced Guard.
Section of Ambulance.

1,000 yards to 1 mile.
Officer commanding Division; and Staff.
Troop of Cavalry
Officer commanding 1st Brigade.
1st Battalion, 1st Brigade.
2 Batteries R.A., with one wagon per gun.
Remainder of 1st Brigade.
Officer commanding 2nd Brigade.
2nd Brigade.
Artillery Wagons (second line).
1st Brigade S. A. Carts and Tool Wagons.
2nd ditto, ditto.
Reserve Ammunition Column.
Ambulance.
1st Field Hospital.
500 yards.
Divisional Baggage Master and Detachment of Police.
Supply Wagons carrying day's supply.
(Regimental Wagons if such are issued).
Baggage of Division, Head-Quarters.

PLATE XIX

1st Squadron Engineer C°

1st Batt. 1st Brigade

2 Batteries

4 Guns

4 Companies of Rifles

Off'r Command'g advanced Guard

1st Brigade

Ambulance and Field Hospital

Interval

Ammunition Column

Off'r Command'g 1st Brigade

½ Troop of Cav?

Off'r Command'g Division

Small arm carts & tool Wagons 2nd Brigade

ditto 1st Brigade

Stores

Provision Column

Det't of Police

Comp'y of Inf'y from 2nd Bat.

Field Hospital

Interval

Sect'n of Engin'rs with Pack Horses

2 Guns

3 Companies of Rifles

Artillery Wagons 2nd Line

Baggage of Non Combatant Staff

Non Combatant Staff

Military Police

Interval

Comp'y of Rifles

1½ Troops of Cavalry

Baggage 2nd Brigade

Interval

½ Troop of Cavalry

Ambulance

Tools

Artillery Wagons

2nd Brigade

Baggage 1st Brigade

Baggage of Cav'y Reg't

Baggage Divisional Staff

Head Quarters Divisional

Baggage Mass & Det't of Police

Off'r Command'g 2nd Brigade

Vanguard. Troops	781	700
" Interval		
Main Body of Advanced Guard	1544	800
" Interval		
Main Body of Division	5989	1500
" Interval		
Total Troops	8314	
Intervals		3000
Grand Total		11314 yards

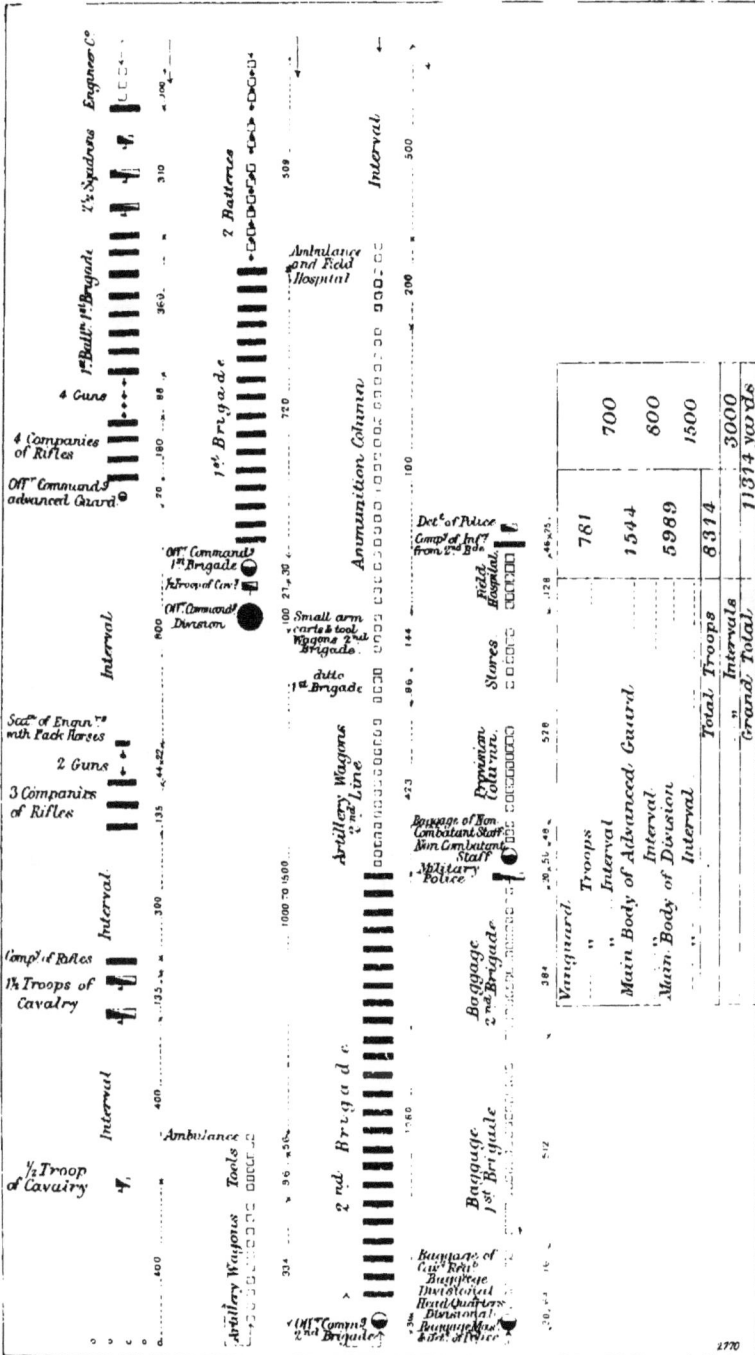

Order of March of a Division

1770

Baggage of Cavalry Regiment.	Baggage of ditto, and Transport Cols.
Baggage of Staff, 1st Brigade.	Provision Columns, Stores, &c.
" Regiments of 1st Brigade.	2 Field Hospitals.
" " 2nd Brigade.	1 Company Infantry from 2nd Brigade, as rear guard, assisted by detachment of Military Police.
Military Police.	
Non-Combatant Staff.	

BRITISH ARMY CORPS.

(*If Cavalry cannot be pushed forward.*)

Half Troop of Cavalry.
400 yards.
1½ Troop of Cavalry.
2 Companies of Rifles.
400 yards.
6 Companies of Rifles.
3 Guns.
Section of Engineers.
Half mile to 1,000 yards.
1 Battalion 1st Brigade.
1½ Batteries, R.A.
2 Battalions, 1st Brigade.
2½ Squadrons Cavalry.
Engineer Ammunition Wagons, Ambulance, &c.
1 to 1½ miles.
Officer Commanding Corps.
1 Battalion 2nd Brigade.
1 Battery R.A.
2 Battalions 2nd Brigade.
Ammunition Tool Wagons, Ambulance, and 1 Field Hospital.
Corps Artillery.
2nd Division.
- 1st Brigade 2nd Division.
- Artillery of "
- 2nd Brigade "
- Rifles "
- Engineers "
- Cavalry Regiment of 2nd Division.
- Ammunition and Tool Wagons.
- Ambulance.
- 1 Field Hospital.

3rd Division in same order.
500 yards interval.
Supply Wagons for Corps, for the day.
Staff and Regimental Baggage by Divisions.

Plate XIXA. shows the arrangement for a British Division.

It is always most useful and instructive to examine marches that have been really made, and to see how in face of actual war the theories which have been thought out in peace have been put in practice. The following orders for the march of the Crown Prince's Army, prior to the action of Wiessenburg, on the 4th August, are worthy of the closest study. At 4 P.M. on the 3rd August the following disposition was issued by the Commander-in-Chief of the Third Army:—

The Franco-German War. German Official Account. (Translated by Capt. Clarke.)

Head-Quarters, Landau, 3rd August.

It is my intention to-morrow to advance with the army as far as the Lauter, and to throw vanguards across it. With this object the Bienwald will be traversed on four roads, the enemy is to be driven back wherever he is found. The separate columns will march as follows:—

1. Bothmer's Bavarian Division will continue as advanced guard, move on Weissenburg, and endeavour to gain possession of the town; it will guard its right flank by moving a suitable detachment *viâ* Böllenborn to Bobenthal. It will break up from its bivouac at 6 A.M.

2. The remainder of Hartmann's Corps, inclusive of Walther's Division, will break up from its bivouac at 4 A.M. and move, avoiding Landau, *viâ* Impflingen and Bergzabern, upon Ober-Otterbach. The trains of the corps will be moved forward as far as Appenhofen in the course of the forenoon.

3. The 4th Cavalry Division will concentrate to the south of Mörlheim, at 6 A.M. and march *viâ* Insheim, Rohrbach, Billigheim, Barbelroth, Capellen, as far as the Otterbach, 4,000 paces eastward of Ober-Otterbach.

4. The Vth Corps will break up from its bivouac in Billigheim, at 4 A.M., and march *viâ* Barbelroth and Nieder-Otterbach, to Gross Steinfeld and Kapsweyer. It will form its own advanced guard, which will cross the Lauter

at St. Remy, and the Wooghäusern, and place outposts on the heights on the far side. Trains remain at Billigheim.

5. The XIth Corps will start at 4 A.M., and move *viâ* Steinweiler, Winden Schaidt, across the Bienwald to the Bienwald hut. It will form its own advanced guard, which will press forward over the Lauter, and place outposts on the heights on the further bank. Trains at Rohrbach.

6. Werder's corps will march along the main road to Lauterburg, and endeavour to gain possession of that town, and place outposts on the far bank Trains at Hagenbach.

7. Von der Tann's corps will break up from its bivouac at 4 A.M., and move along the main road *viâ* Rülzheim to Langenkandel, to the westward of which village it will bivouac. Trains remain at Rheinzabern. Head-quarters at Langenkandel.

8. My position in the forenoon will be on the heights between Kapsweyer and Schweigen, and as far as I can foresee, my head-quarters will be transferred to Nieder-Otterbach.

(Signed)   FREDERICK WILLIAM,
Crown Prince.

These orders are peculiar, they give in the first paragraph in few words, but very clearly, what is the object the leader had in view, and then detail generally the movements of each corps, but are most careful not to interfere with the independence of the Corps Commanders, who are expected, knowing the object in view, to help that object as much as possible. Such a system is undoubtedly a correct one, it enables officers to substitute intelligent co-operation for blind obedience. The last paragraph is of great importance, the position of the commander of any body should be known well by those who must seek him with reports or for orders.

On each of the paragraphs bearing reference to the movements of a corps, the corps-order for its movement was based. Major-General Walker, C.B., has been good enough to furnish us with the corps-order of the Vth Corps, based of course on paragraph 4 of the army order quoted, and it carries out the principles of the army order, detailing what is be done clearly, without interfering with the independent action of those responsible for the execution of the order.

Verdy du Vernois. (Translated by Hildyard.)

Such an interference is seldom useful, for the dispositions of the subordinate leaders are thwarted by it. Every commander, however, has the right, so long as he does not commit conspicuous errors, to carry out his duty according to his own ideas, and this can frequently be done in different ways; each chooses that which agrees most closely with his character and education. He has been placed in the position he holds in the confidence that he will fulfil the duties of it; should he not justify this trust he must be removed.

The duty of a commander is to impart the necessary orders clearly to his subordinate leaders, and to watch over their execution; he must only interfere when dispositions are made which endanger the attainment of the aim in view.

Billigheim, 3rd August, 1870, 4½ o'clock P.M.

To carry out the above army disposition the following orders are issued :—

Advanced Guard.

The 4th Regiment of Dragoons.
17th Infantry Brigade.
59th Regiment of Infantry.
1st Heavy, } Batteries, Lower Silesian
1st Light, } Regiment No. 5.
58th Regiment of Infantry.
5th Rifle Battalion.
Pontoon Company with Light Field Bridge Train.
Half the Sanitary Detachment No. 1.
The Light Baggage of the Advanced Guard.*
The second line of Battery Ammunition Wagons and the Ammunition Wagons of the Infantry of the Advanced Guard.

Main Body.

18th Infantry Brigade, with two Batteries (1 heavy and 1 light), half the Sanitary Detachment, No. 1, Field Hospital 1 and 2, Light Baggage of the remainder of the 9th Division.
The Corps Commander with the Staff, but without the Non-Combatant Staff.
Corps Artillery 6 Batteries:—2 Heavy, 2 Light, 2 Horse Artillery.
The 19th Infantry Brigade.
3rd Division Field Artillery.
20th Infantry Brigade.
14th Regiment of Dragoons.
Sapper and Miners Company, together with entrenching tool column.
Sanitary Detachment No. 2.
Field Hospitals Nos. 3 and 4.
Light Baggage of the 10th Division.
Staff of the 10th Division without the Non-Combatant Staff
The second line of Battery Ammunition Wagons, as well as the Ammunition Wagons of the Infantry. Those of the 9th Division in front, the 10th Division following.
Second line of Ammunition wagons of the Corps Artillery.
Sanitary Detachment No. 3.
Field Hospital No. 5.

Trains.

Provision Columns Nos. 1 and 2.
Heavy Baggage of the Advanced Guard.
Non-Combatant Head-Quarter Staff.
Heavy Baggage of the remainder of the 9th Division.
Heavy Baggage of the Corps Artillery.
Heavy Baggage of the 10th Division.

1. Advanced Guard, Major-General V. Sandrart. Formation and order of march as detailed opposite. This advanced guard will be formed ready to march off with the van at Billigheim at ½ before 4 A.M. to morrow, and will move off punctually at 4 o'clock. General V. Sandrart will designate the details of the order of march.

The advanced guard moves past Barbelroth and Neider Otterbach on Kopsweier, from whence it will cross the Lauter in two columns at St. Remy and at Wooghäusern, where further orders will be issued. Connexion must be kept up with detachments on the flanks.

2. The remainder of the Army Corps follows the advanced guard as main body, at a distance of 3,000 paces, in order of march as opposite, under the command of the Commander of the 10th Division, Lieut.-General V. Schmidt.

3. The train and columns of the Army Corps which are parked at Impflingen, as well as the heavy baggage of the Staffs and of the troops, will wait until the Bavarian Corps Hartmann, including the Division Walther,† have passed Impflingen, and move then in the order

---

* To the light baggage belonged the led horses, pack horses, company and squadron carts, and the wagon for the Regimental Staffs. The other carriages were considered as belonging to the heavy baggage.
† *Vide* Army Orders, par .2.

Remount Depôt.
Provision Columns 3, 4, and 5.
Field Hospitals 6 to 12.
Field Bakery Column.

given opposite from Impflingen to the northward of Billigheim, where they will be parked. Formation and order of march as opposite, each independent detachment of the train or of the heavy baggage, is to be under the command of an officer of the corresponding branch.

The Train Escort Squadron undertakes the convoy of the trains under the special orders from Major V. Herwarth.

Column Detachments.

1st échelon of Ammunition Columns.
Small-Arm Ammunition Columns No. 1.
Artillery Ammunition Columns Nos. 1 and 2.
2nd échelon of Ammunition Columns.
Small Arms Ammunition Columns Nos. 2 to 4.
Artillery Ammunition Columns Nos. 3 to 5.
Pontoon Columns.

4. Afterwards the ammunition column will follow at a distance of about half a mile,* with the pontoon column under the command of the commander of the detachments of the ammunition columns.

5. Reports to me personally will be directed to the head of the main body.

(Signed) V. KIRCHBACH.

It is perfectly evident that these orders contain all that is requisite for such a march, that the place of everything in the column is clearly laid down, and has evidently been arranged with reference to the country and the prospect of meeting the enemy. No rivers were to be crossed requiring pontoons, therefore they were at the tail of the column, the light bridge equipage being, on the other hand, with the advanced guard. The order in which the advanced guard was to march was left to be detailed by General V. Sandrart, and it appears that it was formed as follows:—

Vanguard, Colonel v. Rex.
1st Squadron, 4th Dragoons.
2nd Squadron, 4th Dragoons.
1st Company, 5th Rifles.
4th Company, 5th Rifles.
1st Battalion, 58th Regiment.
1st Light Battery, 5th Field Artillery Regiment.
Fusilier Battalion, 58th Regiment.
Detachment 2nd Field Pioneer Company.
Main body of Advanced Guard, Colonel V. Bothmer.
Fusilier Battalion, 59th Regiment.
2nd Field Battery, 5th Field Artillery Regiment.
Two Battalions of the 59th Regiment.
Remaining 2 Companies, 5th Rifles.
Remaining 2 Squadrons, 4th Dragoons.
2nd Field Pioneer Company, with intrenching tool columns.
Section of No. 1 Sanitary Detachment.

The order of march of the advanced guard are clearly derived from the requirements of the case. Cavalry and rifles form the extreme point of the vanguard; cavalry and rifles close the march of the advanced guard, and in each case for the same reason, they are more mobile than other troops, can feel out to the front and flank in the one case, and feel out to the flank and rear in the other, thus linking the main

* German mile : half a German mile equal to about 4,000 yards.

body of the corps to its advanced guard. It will be observed that General Sandrart, who commanded the 9th Division, commanded the advanced guard, which was composed of the 17th infantry brigade, strengthened with cavalry, artillery, and engineers. The other brigade of the 9th Division, the 18th, forming the head of the main body, so that in case of an action taking place General Sandrart's command, the 9th Division, would be complete.

It is desirable that the advanced guard should be always composed of a portion of the unit that immediately follows it; thus if it be the advanced guard of a division it should be composed of a portion of the leading brigade, so that if checked, and a skirmish ensues, it may be supported by the remainder of its brigade. Units will thus be complete. It is a mistake, as has often been done, to split a brigade in two, and place one half as advanced, the other as rear guard.

Splitting up the 5th Rifles apparently was with the view of breaking only one battalion; had the 2nd and 3rd companies followed the 1st and 2nd companies, a battalion of the 59th would have had to be broken up; in addition to which the peculiar organization of the rifle battalions, which have more company transport than others (in the Prussian army), allows their being split up with greater impunity.

Advanced guards should be invariably composed of all arms of the service. As a rule the duty of the advanced guard is to take the outposts of the division until the bivouac is regularly formed, and can be relieved, hence it is essential that all arms should be represented.

The Engineers should not be too far from the head of the column or they should march at the tail of the vanguard. A bridge broken down would soon bring the column to a halt, and it is essential that means should be at hand to repair it. It is not advisable to have too great a force of cavalry at the head of such columns; it must be borne in mind that the cavalry divisions should be, as a rule, at least a day's march ahead, and this affords considerable security.

If the mass of the infantry is allowed to follow close upon the cavalry, in case of the latter being driven back it will be ridden down, as it would be unable to get out of the way quickly enough, and the whole be thrown into confusion.

Verdy du Vernois. (Translated by Hildyard.)

It is especially dangerous in a mountainous country to have too many cavalry at the head of the column, for if it be suddenly charged in one of the many defiles that are to be found in such a country, it may be driven back upon the infantry and artillery, and so deprive them of the means of defence.

Clausewitz.

Artillery should be kept together as much as possible on the march, and with the exception of the advanced guard artillery, all the divisional guns should march together between the brigades. They should never be divided by the various regiments, and the tactical rule of having two or more batteries together should be adhered to.

Le Bourg.

In all skirmishes of the advanced guard, after the first moments the artillery should fire slowly and carefully, and husband their ammunition as much as possible, because they are necessarily a long way from their reserves.

In level open countries horse artillery should accompany the advanced guard ; in hilly or close countries, field batteries.

Verdy du
Vernois.
(Translated
by Hildyard.)

Different views exist as to whether the advanced guard artillery should be heavy or light. In any case the artillery of the advanced guard comes into action first, and has to remain there the longest ; and therefore the battery every leader would prefer for the advanced guard is undoubtedly that which carries most ammunition with it, and that the light battery does.

The duties of the troops of an advanced guard are very heavy, as they must send out many flanking parties and patrols, must carefully examine cross roads, and send men to the top of hills to look out for an enemy. The number of men to be sent should be *as few as possible*; the object is to see as much as possible without being seen, and a few selected men will do this work better and have more chance of escaping observation than many men sent together.

Less than two men however should never be sent ; one is pretty sure to return with information. This is especially the case with the cavalry—sending many men riding about up to the tops of hills, galloping down cross roads and along lanes, tends to knock up the horses without doing any good: on the contrary the dust and gleaming of arms draws attention to such movements which otherwise might escape notice. When a dozen men are sent up a hill to look out, they invariably ride one after the other on the top of the hill, well on the sky line, a couple of selected men on selected horses will do the work a great deal better, and the force of the cavalry, viz., its horses, will suffer less. In every troop of cavalry there are men more specially suited for this work than others; these men should be selected and specially taught this work in peace time, and to them the chief part of the scouting should be intrusted. Officers in command of troops and squadrons soon learn the special ideas and ways of their men, and also their method of expressing themselves, which is really very important, as different men rarely report the same facts in the same way.

In a march the strength of the advanced guard should be such as will enable it by manœuvring to hold its ground, and give time for the main body to come up to its assistance, or to deploy into line of battle.

In an advance it is very questionable if there should be a rear-guard beyond one for police purposes. The flank of an army on the march should be well covered by its cavalry, and the escorts of its various trains and convoys should be capable of resisting a few men if any are able to work round the flanks, which is, however, most improbable. Hence it appears advisable to have no rear-guard on the advance, but to divide the force only into advance guard and main body. A strong body of police, with a provost, should close the line of march to arrest stragglers, check marauding, and keep order amongst those camp followers who are the curse of every army, but who are often useful, and generally most difficult to get rid of.

The nature of war renders a reserve indispensable to every leader in action up to the very moment when he must employ it. Whatever joins directly in the fighting is, even in the most favourable case, only in a very limited manner in the hands of the commander, and generally is entirely out of his control ; yet a leader has a decisive influence only so far as he keeps powerful masses of troops at his disposal, or as he understands how to form them for this purpose according to the various movements of an action. Battle therefore must not be given without a reserve, but why the separation of a reserve should be necessary on the march is difficult to imagine ; indeed it is not necessary, and a fighting reserve even, need only be formed just before the commencement of the action. Verdy du Vernois. (Translated by Hildyard.)

Military nomenclature has gone too far here ; let us only consider what the nature of a reserve comprises. All troops so far as they have not yet come into action are reserves for the leader. Hitherto it has been settled in the general proportion ; one quarter of the whole force advanced guard ; one half main body ; one quarter reserve, only varying in a decimal degree. When an action begins it cannot be foreseen whether the advance guard alone will suffice to carry it through, or whether the whole force, to the last man, must be brought to bear.

The advanced guard commences the action, and the whole of the remainder of the troops are its reserves, from which as many are drawn as necessary.

Why then another partition ? Again, is a long interval necessary between these masses of troops ? It certainly is not advantageous for action when a portion arrives half an hour later than it is required. This however is the case, if, for example, a corps on the march separates a reserve, and lets it follow a mile in the rear of the main body. On the march there must be intervals, lest checks in front should be imparted at once to the whole, but by no means so considerable as 1,000 to 2,500 paces ; even less intervals than those laid down would suffice for the various bodies of troops. Besides, it must be considered that these intervals are there in order to be lost under circumstances, and that when this takes place they can only be properly made up in course of time.

Thus the separation of a reserve on the march appears utterly useless ; everything useless is for us dangerous, and danger undoubtedly lies in the usual division mentioned.

When an army is in retreat the rear-guard becomes the most important part, the most dangerous and trying.

Where troops move to the front, the duties of the rear guard are confined to preventing the soldiers disbanding, in sending on stragglers and arresting marauders. Consequently in general the Provost-Marshal intrusted with the police of the army, the mounted police and provosts, march with the rear-guard. But when the army retreats the *rôle* of the rear-guard is far more important. Its duty is to stop the enemy at every point favourable for that purpose, to procure time to the artillery baggage parcs, convoys of sick and wounded to march off. It has to cut the roads, burn, destroy or blow up the bridges ; it has to contain the enemy flushed with success, and to push him back with coolness, to maintain a good appearance so as to prevent the enemy discovering that demoralisation, which almost always takes place during a long retreat. To fulfil this task the best troops and those that have suffered least must be chosen. With the rear-guard the engineers march, intrusted with rendering by their labour the retreat secure, precisely as at the head of ' the column they render its advance easy and pave the way for its success. The rear-guard has nothing but the most requisite baggage, in order that when it has provided time for the army to retire, it may again if possible rejoin it by a forced march. But this is rarely possible, as rear-guards Fallot, Lagrange.

necessarily get loaded with stragglers, badly horsed carriages, and in fact everything the army leaves behind.

The duty of the rear-guard is not to fight, it is to detain the enemy, to compel him to deploy his force, and bring up large bodies of men. In selecting positions for this purpose care must be taken that they can only be turned by a distant flank movement, and consequently cavalry scouts must be kept well out on the flanks of a rear-guard, perhaps a day's march distant; these men should watch for and report any such movement on the part of the enemy. Villages through which an enemy must march should be well barricaded, the roads cut, and a quantity of combustibles, straw, &c., collected, to set fire to when the rear-guard leaves; this retards the enemy considerably.

Bugeaud.

Rear-guards often partially take the offensive; this is sometimes indispensable, to disengage the tail of the column if much pressed, but such an offensive taken by a small body of men should not be pushed too far, for if the rear-guard pursued the enemy too far, while the main body followed its march, too great an interval would be left between the two.

Generally this kind of offensive should be avoided, it leads to small results, and always some of the best men are killed. The troops should if possible be withdrawn by alternate *échelons*. The commander of the rear-guard has two grand objects to fulfil. To fall back and lose as few men as possible, to retard as little as possible the main body, and to stop the enemy as much as possible, Any offensive movement to be really effective must come from the commander of the main body, and in such cases a larger body than the rear-guard should be employed.

Horse artillery is better suited for a rear-guard than field batteries, moving faster and being able to take up positions to cover the retreat more rapidly.

Although a serious offensive movement is undoubtedly dangerous, yet a sudden advance for a short time often checks a pursuing enemy, but such attacks should be for a special object.

Napier.

As the retreating troops approached the river, the ground became more open; and the left wing, hardest pressed, and having the shortest distance, arrived while the bridge was quite crowded with artillery and cavalry, and the right wing was still distant. Major McLeod, of the 43rd, perceiving the danger, then rallied four companies of his regiment on a hill covering the line of passage; he was joined by some of the riflemen, and at the same time the Brigade-Major Rowan posted two companies on another hill to the left, flanking the road.

These posts were maintained to cover the filing of the right wing over the bridge, yet the French gathered in great numbers, made a serious rush, and forced the companies back before the bridge could be cleared, and while a part of the 52nd was still at a considerable distance from it.

The crisis was imminent, but McLeod, a young man endowed with a natural genius for war, turned his horse round, called the troops to follow, and waving his cap, rode with a shout towards the enemy. The suddenness of the thing, and the animated action of the man, produced the effect he designed: a mob of soldiers rushed after him, cheering and charging as if a whole army had been at their backs; the enemy's skirmishers, astonished at this unexpected movement, stopped short, and before they could recover from their surprise the 52nd had passed the river. McLeod followed at a run, and gained the other side without disaster.

Here the troops, retiring by alternate wings, had to get across a bridge; the rear wing covering was hard pressed, it took the offensive, and gained time for the others to file over. The handling of rear-guards is a most difficult and delicate operation, and requires great tactical skill and knowledge, the power of judging distance and time quickly, and penetrating the enemy's intention; in short, in what is known as *coup d'œil.* Marshal Ney was remarkable for the power he possessed in this way, and the retreat of Massena from Portugal, especially the action at Redinha, are excellent examples of this. There is this great difference between a rear and an advanced guard, the former fights in order that it may fall back, the latter fights to hold its ground until supported and this distinction should be borne in mind.

A rear-guard commander should look for and expect no assistance, he must detain the enemy and draw off his force; to send assistance to a rear-guard would be really to delay the retreat, or to do exactly what the enemy is seeking to do. When Bazaine was retiring his army on the 14th of August from the right bank of the Moselle, his object was to withdraw from both flanks, and gradually reduce the circle, covering the rear-guard under the guns of the detached forts Quelien and Des Bottes. When the Prussians attacked the IIIrd Corps at Borny, and the troops which had crossed the Moselle were brought back again, the French leader was really playing the game of his enemies, and disregarding the protection which the fortress of Metz *à cheval* on the river gave him of withdrawing the IIIrd Corps, his rear-guard, when and how he pleased.

Every commander of a body of troops, large or small, should see his command march before him each day. By this means all sorts of irregularities can be stopped. This especially is requisite in long marches, and should be observed by captains of companies, as well as those of higher rank; as troops file into their bivouacs after a march is an excellent opportunity for seeing the state of both men and horses, whether the march has told on them, the columns straggled out unnecessarily, men in their proper places, the order of march preserved, &c.

Another point well worthy of attention is the repose of the men. Men cannot work without rest, and it should be a constant object of leaders to procure this rest; all kinds of noise and confusion should be strictly forbidden, and constant care should be taken that troops are not turned out too early. As an example, suppose an army-order is issued, to march at 4 A.M., as the Prussian orders of the 3rd August, 1870, were; this necessitated a parade of the 5th Corps at 3.45 A.M. When did the divisions parade? when the brigades? when the battalions? Mounted troops whose horses have to be fed and watered before the march, suffer especially in this way. Horses drink badly in the early morning, and it will be always better (if by any possible arrangement it can be managed) to water at a halt.

N

Few who have watched these things but will acknowledge, that to march off at four, the artillery and cavalry trumpets will usually sound two hours sooner.

The execution of orders must never be kept waiting. If the Divisional-General, Brigade-General, or Colonel is not in his proper place at the proper moment, the next senior officer must take command and march off. On the other hand, it is an undoubted fact that if the Commander of an army orders the troops to march at 4 A.M., the Cavalry or Infantry Generals say 3·30 A.M., then subordinate Generals say 3 A.M., the Brigadiers say 2·30 A.M., the Colonels 2 A.M., and so on down to companies; it is exactly the same case for a review or field day. If great care is not taken the troops will thus be under arms three hours sooner than has been ordered.

The Supply of Troops with Provisions on the Line of March.

The supply of troops with provisions hardly comes within the scope of this book, but it is desirable that a few words should be said on it. Some knowledge of the difficulties to be contended with, may reduce the ranks of both the grumblers who never get rations at all, and the fortunate persons who never want for them. Both are probably in error. But some knowledge of how troops must be fed in the field may enable officers to work into the hands of those whose function it is to supply provisions, thus reducing friction and tending to produce cordial co-operation, by which the persons who have to be fed will undoubtedly benefit.

If an attempt is made to realise what was happening when the Crown Prince's army advanced in accordance with the orders given at Page 169, it will be found that long columns of men and horses were spread along the different roads, and that the trains of each corps were parked in the rear, that is to say, the supplies of each corps were parked in rear. When each column halted for the night at the places indicated in the orders, the head of the column did not halt there with all the tail spread out along the road it had marched on, but each corps drew its tail up after it, and more or less formed a line of battle. Thus the roads were cleared, and it then became possible for the trains to advance with food. But it is manifest that if the soldier, having to march 12 to 15 miles, and starting at 4 A.M., and probably not getting settled into his bivouac until 3 or 4 o'clock in the afternoon, had to wait for his food until the train arrived, he would be simply starved. Therefore, it follows that if troops are to be fed in the field, they must carry rations with them, and the rations consumed during the day must be replaced by the train during the night, so that the men shall move off the following day with the same number of rations as previously. *Soldiers, if they are not to starve, must carry rations.* No one who has considered this subject will question the truth of these words; and it is essentially requisite that this *absolute necessity* should be impressed on and clearly understood by the men. A ration of fresh meat and bread put into a canvas haversack and carried under the arm in the sun for 10 hours is not an inviting dinner, and the soldier too often throws it away, refusing to eat it, which would be of little moment if doing so did not render him useless as a fighting element; therefore it becomes absolutely requisite that some means by which the ration may be carried, so as not to be disgusting when required, should be adopted, and that commanding officers should carefully watch that these rations are properly used, and not all eaten at once. It is well known that a soldier in peace time eats a quantity of potatoes, varying with the nationality of the regiment, in addition to his regular bread and meat rations. In the field potatoes, and such bulky food, must to a great extent be viewed as luxuries to be procured more by the skill and sharpness of the men and officers on the line of march than by the efforts of the commissariat. But the want of the large *quantity* of food eaten in peace is for some time not compensated by the larger amount of meat the soldier gets in the field, and although the nutriment he receives may perhaps be greater, yet there is for some time a craving for quantity.* Hence officers must watch to see that the rations intended for two days are not consumed in one.

The best food to carry is undoubtedly bacon, sausage, biscuit, and coffee, it suffers less from carriage than any other, and consequently bacon and biscuit, joined to rice, which can be easily carried, swells much in the cooking, and is a capital substitute for potatoes, must be looked on as the main provision to be carried by the soldier.

But of whatever the ration is composed, some separate and special place, which can be easily cleaned out, should be provided to contain it. The best place for the meat is undoubtedly the mess-tin, and it would be a great improvement if some special place for biscuit, rice, &c., were provided.

One of the Prussian Army Corps, previously referred to, drawn up on parade ready to march off, if inspected, would have been found to have at least eight days rations with it.

These would be divided as follows :—

One day's common ration for immediate consumption, that is to say, to be eaten on the 4th August; three days' reserve rations, consisting of biscuit, coffee, bacon, rice and salt,— special places or bags for the two latter being provided for the purpose in the packs. The five provision columns, viz., two for each Infantry Division, and one for the Corps Artillery and Cavalry, carrying four days' more ; the meat being driven. The order to advance and leave the trains behind was perfectly feasible ; the army could exist for four days without seeing its train if requisite.

But the moment the trains get the order to advance, they move up at night when the roads are clear, and fill up the

* The average weight of a great number of soldiers' dinners is 1 lb. 6¼ oz. cooked, of this the average weight of meat is 5 oz.; it is apparent that the meat ration may be doubled, and although the soldier will then take a much greater amount of nutriment into his system, yet from long custom he may feel his stomach empty.

N 2

rations consumed by the troops, halting again when the troops advance.

How are the trains themselves filled up? As far as possible magazines told off previously in the same order as the corps provision columns, are formed; these magazines are the reserves of which the trains themselves are the expense magazines; and hired transport carriages to the number of nearly 600 per corps are used to haul up the provisions from the magazines to the trains, and fill them up, as they filled the soldiers. It is manifest that there must be some limit to this operation; assuming that the train can move $1\frac{1}{2}$ infantry marches, the limit would be six days, when the magazines must, if the army is advancing, be moved to the front. This would probably be done by pushing up by railway from the great magazines of the country large supplies of food to fresh advanced magazines which would then fill up the train, and this process would be repeated. This supposes nothing to be bought in the country or obtained by requisitions, but all brought from magazines. Practically the commissariat arranges for relieving the strain on the magazines as much as possible by purchasing or requisitioning flour, which is converted into bread by the bakery column, and by the purchase or requisitioning of cattle, which are driven with the train as they advance; of course every purchase lightens the strain on the magazines and train, and helps the advance in a corresponding degree.

Food captured from an enemy has a similar effect, and the rapid advance of the German armies after the battle of Spicheren was not a little due to the vast stores of provisions belonging to the French army captured in Forbach, St. Avold, and other small open towns of Lorraine. A great deal of the comfort and efficiency of a division or corps thus depends on the activity of its commissariat. If the commissariat officer depends entirely on the train, there is every chance of it breaking down exactly at the moment it is most wanted, namely, when the soldier has eaten up all he carries. But an active commissariat will seek to husband what the men carry as much as possible, by the use of what can be procured on the spot; consequently the Prussian system of having the "*eiserne*" ration composed of bacon and biscuit which will keep, is undoubtedly a correct one; the longer its use is staved off the better; the moment it is encroached on it should be filled up again.

It is impossible to read the many personal accounts of campaigns without being struck by the fact that a great deal depends on the qualities of the individual commissary.

One French corps at Metz was well fed to the end of the blockade, because, prior to the blockade, its Intendance had husbanded their resources and used what they could buy from day to day; consequently its reserve stores were not encroached on when the blockade began.

Too much regularity, punctuality, and care cannot be used

in everything regarding distribution of rations; it is in these points, and in carefully watching the soldier that he does not waste his rations, that the regimental officers can do much to lighten the work, and facilitate the duties of the supply department.

In distributing rations it is always best to do so alternately from the right and left as the troops stand on parade. But a corps whose turn is first cannot, if it is not present, and has lost its turn, stop the distribution of rations to another when it has begun.

In the field, the hours of distribution and the number of days' rations to De Gerlache. be distributed must vary constantly, owing to the state of the disposable resources, and the nature of the military operations, or the difficulty and unexpected delays which may impede the regularity of the distribution.

All these variations should be announced in daily orders by the Chief of the Staff after consultation with the Intendant.

Whatever is done must be always governed by the resolve that nothing shall delay or interfere with the military movements, and by the desire to spare the soldiers as much as possible many or unexpected fatigue parties.

Hay and straw can rarely or ever be carried with troops, oats may, but the rations of the two former must generally, at least when on the line of march, be sought in the country.

If war is being made in summer, the horses can eat grass, this, and an extra ration of corn will keep them in good health.

The Prussians have an "*eiserne*" rations of oats similar to the rations for the men, this ration consists of one day's oats for each cavalry horse, carried by the horse, and three days' oats for each horse of the artillery, train, staff, administrative, and regimental wagons; this is carried in the wagons.

War cannot be made without food for men and horses, hence Generals Grimoard. seek to seize posts that will give them the possession of a country abounding in resources, and deny it to their enemy.

No sooner has a division taken up its position than the sous-intendant De Gerlache. should, either himself or by deputy, examine all the farms, stores, and supplies of all kinds, the mills and ovens which may exist in the place or its neighbourhood. He should at once prepare the establishments suitable for making use of the supplies he finds, whether they belong to the enemy, to the country, or private persons, being careful, however, to authorise his acts by proper requisitions, and to leave to the local authorities a sufficiency of food for the inhabitants.

It is impossible to insist too much on order and rule in everything that concerns the subsistence of troops. Let us imagine a division where things are wisely done and strict discipline maintained.

The General remains at the head of his division until everything has been put to rights, its position fixed, the cantonments arranged, the supply of food by requisitions on the villages, and the division of the villages to the force, completed, the guards mounted, fatigues detailed, the camp formed, bivouacs arranged, and kitchens made. The detachments are then sent out in an orderly way, they return in the same manner, bringing what is required. No soldier is absent when the roll is called, and the camp is properly provided.

Let us imagine on the other hand another division, where these details are neglected. It arrives on its ground, halts, the moment it does so the leaders abandon the men, the men scatter, the camp is deserted. One seeks wood, another water, some food, straw, forage; the houses of the people are forced open, provisions wasted, cellars broken into, granaries emptied, the authority of officers despised, their bivouacs entered under pretext of seeking what is requisite, and the furniture of the inhabitants taken from their houses to the camp.

In this pillage (for things must be called by their proper names), the soldiers on duty get nothing. A portion of the others think they would be more comfortable under roofs than in the open air, and they remain there, and the general can hardly get hold of them when he wants them.

However, if this division has fallen on a village well provided, perhaps few men will be lost, despite their disorder, but if the village is not well provided, and a few of the most greedy have seized and wasted what would have been sufficient for all, the last comers wander into the neighbouring villages; they spread over the whole country, live in the houses, and when their corps marches, lose it, and become marauders for the rest of the campaign. Such a division will infallibly lose 2,000 out of 8,000 men in a fortnight, without seeing the enemy. All have seen these things, in that famous campaign where, after having been for years masters of all countries, we were compelled to fight *pro aris et focis.*

War cannot be maintained without requisitions on the people, and it is hopeless to attempt to do otherwise, the power that requisitioning gives a general of moving rapidly is so great, and consequently the force of the army using a system of requisitions is so enormously increased, that the army that does not adopt it will be infallibly beaten by that which does; hence in self defence, all armies must adopt this system, and like any other necessary evil, the truest humanity is not to leave it to chance, but to lay down clear and definite rules for making and enforcing requisitions, rules which shall be such as may protect the inhabitants from pillage and ill-usage, but will at the same time give security to the army. Evils which are unavoidable, like war, and the consequent march of armies in the midst of peaceful inhabitants, may be best mitigated by reducing to system, and enforcing with a strong hand, a strict code of rules. By so doing the misery consequent on the march of hostile armies may be greatly mitigated.

Clausewitz.

Regular requisitions are undoubtedly the simplest and best method of feeding an army, and are the only system that can serve as the basis of modern war. War based on a system of requisitions, and living amongst the inhabitants, possesses such a superiority over that which is based on the exclusive use of magazines, that the latter is really a completely different weapon. No State can dare to meet the former system with the latter, and if by possibility there exists anywhere a Minister for War so narrow-minded, so ignorant, as to despise the universal experience of all wars, and attempt at the beginning of a campaign to use the old method, very soon the general, by force of circumstances, will find himself compelled to have recourse to requisitions, and the system will begin again. If also the expense of the other system be considered, it will be found that the amount of the armament and the extent of the force must be diminished, since no State has money for such arrangements, which would be unprofitable unless both sides agreed to fight in the same way. Such ideas are Utopian.

Fallot and Legrange.

Troops should never be allowed to take firewood as they please, but the proper place to cut it, and the quantity to be cut, should be carefully determined, otherwise the men will cut fruit trees and hedge-rows, and commit irreparable damage without any compensating advantage. Such vexations exasperate the inhabitants, and make them hostile to the soldiers of any army.

Similarly, when green forage is being cut the horses should not be allowed to trample the fields down, but the bundles cut and tied should be carried out to the horses, who should wait halted on a road.

It has been said that troops can rarely march more than four or five days without a halt; when a halt takes place every effort should be used to make it a day of rest, that is to say, that the men should be well fed, and the food carefully cooked; if possible, on such days the men should have an extra ration.

He who imposes on the soldier great privations required for some object of importance, both from sympathy and policy, should not lose sight of the compensation which altered circumstances enable him to give. — *Clausewitz.*

Soldiers in quarters are regularly fed, the hours for meals never alter, the food is excellent, well-cooked, and abundant, it comes to the soldier's mouth without trouble or thought on his part, if he is dissatisfied he complains, and his wrong, if there be one, is immediately redressed. He wants neither salt, pepper, mustard, nor any such luxuries, to say nothing of bread or potatoes. During autumn manœuvres he is fed with pretty nearly the same regularity. He may occasionally have to eat his biscuit and salt pork, but that is not always an unpleasant change; he does not slaughter his own cattle or bake his own bread. This is not a duty connected with the regiment, it is done by some one else, and the soldier and the officer are so accustomed to this regular method of proceeding, so accustomed to see food make its appearance, that both one and the other regard it as coming in the natural course of events. Consequently the necessity of husbanding it carefully, making it go as far as possible, and preserving even stray crusts, is not realised until stern want makes itself felt. It is said that necessity teaches; but far too often, when necessity reads her lesson, those she reads it to are too exhausted, too weary, to learn; that lassitude, which long exhaustion produces, has come on them, and the lesson is forgotten because the mind cannot grasp it. Such lessons, to be profitable, should be taught and learned in peace.

The improvidence of the British soldier in these respects is proverbial, and it can only be checked by the constant, close, watchful care of company officers. And this care must be given if officers would bring their companies, that is the weapon they fight with, the machine they work, into action as efficient bodies. The following extracts from a lecture by General v. Kirchbach, furnished by General Walker, are well worthy of attention :—

General v. Kirchbach commanded the 10th Prussian Division in 1866. He says: The first concentration of the Division, to the number of 13,500 men and 1,500 horses, took place on the 26th June; that night the troops bivouacked; this day they were supplied partly from a provision convoy, halted at Ober Schwedeldorf, and partly by contractors who had followed them from Posen; the straw, 1,600 cwt., and 65 cords of wood, were obtained in the neighbourhood by the Divisional intendance. — *Extract of Lecture, furnished by General Walker.*

The whole staff of the Divisional intendance (except one official left in charge at Schwedeldorf), crossed the frontier the next day, and were left in Nachod to make requisitions while the troops were engaged with the enemy.

Each man carried one day's bread and one day's biscuit, and three day's small stores and coffee, supposed to be renewed each day by the provision convoys, which carried four days' supplies.

Four days' meat was driven with the Division, and 280 country carts carried three days' supply of oats and straw for the corps (the 5th), further supplies being regularly furnished from the magazines in rear. General v. Kirchbach remarks, "One would have thought that these measures would have ensured a regular supply," but this was by no means the case, circumstances willed it otherwise. During the first half of the campaign the troops were entirely dependent on the local resources of the country and on requisitions, which, from the absence of the ordinary authorities, and the impossibility of obtaining any reliable information, were often carried out by compulsion. In Nachod, which had not been deserted by the local functionaries, the supplies of the Division were obtained without much difficulty, 200 cwt. of oats, 50 cwt. of hay, 30 cwt. of rice, 5 cwt. of coffee, 7 cwt. of salt, as well as a considerable supply of bread and salt.

But no transport could be found to carry these supplies to the bivouacs, all the transport being appropriated for the wounded. The troops had therefore to fetch their own rations, which, after a 15 miles' march, and eight hours' incessant fighting, was very inadequately carried out. On the 28th, requisitions were made on Skalitz, after the action fought that day, which furnished little, and the troops were compelled to content themselves with a portion of the provisions carried with them. The 29th, Skalitz was entirely cleared out, and the little obtained the previous day, and the remainder of the carried rations, were all the troops had to stop their gnawing hunger. The following night considerable supplies were found in Chalkowitz, and taken possession of by the commissariat and a strong escort; these consisted of a herd of bullocks, 200 sheep, and a good store of beer. On the 30th June and 1st July we had plenty of meat, beer, and spirits, but bread and other stores were entirely wanting.

This arose partly from the fact that the men, *accustomed to punctual delivery of their rations, had thrown away a great portion of that which they carried during the actions of the 27th and 28th, and moreover had wasted what they received from the requisitions.*

This want would not have been so apparent if the provision columns had punctually followed the troops to the camp at Gradlitz. But marching during the night 29-30 June, a false alarm had caused them to turn back, and they had retreated as far as the Prussian frontier, and when they did arrive on the night 1-2 July, a great part of the provisions were spoilt. Also on their retreat, 40 carts were seized by other corps and appropriated by them during nearly all the rest of the campaign. On the morning of the 3rd July, the Quartermaster Serjeants received the regular rations. The intendant and his staff endeavoured to follow the march of the corps, but encountered so many delays that they only reached the bivouac at Rossnitz on the morning of the 4th, by which time all the villages near had been cleared of anything that the inhabitants had left. While the provision columns of the corps, entangled with those of others, and delayed by the confusion always existing in the rear of a great battle-field, only reached the bivouac on the morning of the 5th to find that a great part of the corps had marched off.

That is to say, from the 27th June to the 5th July, or for eight days, the troops had only one distribution of rations, the rations being spoiled in one case, and too late in the other; during all those eight days, the men had to live on what they carried and could find. This extract shows perhaps more clearly than any elaborate statement can do, how much necessity there is for constant care and watchfulness on the part of the officers that the men do not waste and throw away their food.

185

The war of 1866 was the first Prussian war of any extent for many years, and the men, accustomed to the plenty of barracks, did not realise the necessity of economy and care; during the next war, 1870–1, the troops suffered far less from want of provisions.

THE ORGANIZATION OF THE COMMUNICATIONS OF AN ARMY, INCLUDING RAILWAYS.*

Our language is not rich in military terms, and the expression, *the organization of the communications of an army,* is a clumsy one to express what the Germans call "*etappen,*"—a word which they have taken from the French *étape*. There is no English term which expresses what is meant, and a term has therefore been used which was adopted during the Peninsular, our greatest war, for nearly the same thing. By the words, "the organization of the communications of an army," is meant, therefore, not the maintenance or repair of roads, railways, canals, or telegraphs, so much as the organization which enables an army to obtain the greatest benefit from those means of communication. *(margin: Meaning of "Organization of Line of Communications.")*

When an army advances into a hostile country, it has to be supplied with food, ammunition, and other stores; it has to receive reinforcements in men and horses from the rear; and it has to send back sick or wounded men and horses from the front. If an army of moderate size, say 50,000 men, simply marches 100 miles, without firing one shot, or seeing an enemy, the number of sick that have to be got rid of is very great. Experience has shown that, in a good climate, with abundant food, easy marches, and fair weather, the waste from ordinary causes in a ten days' march of such a force would be between 2,000 and 2,500 men, while the number of galled, foot-sore, or worn-out horses would also be very large. A few wet days or a sharp engagement would raise the number of both very considerably. An inefficient man or horse at the front is a positive disadvantage; he can do no work; and he consumes food which is difficult to get, and often occupies the time of a sound man by requiring to be looked after; consequently, if an army is to be kept efficient in front, there must be a stream of men and horses passing along the lines of communication from the base of operations in the rear to supply the waste in front, and a succession of depôts where sick men and horses may be tended, cured, and again sent to the front.

Further, an army must be fed, and the magnitude of the operation is what many people rarely consider. The action of

* This account of the Organization of the Communications of an Army, including Railways, was contained in a lecture delivered by the late Col. Home at the Royal United Service Institution, and is to be found in No. LXXXII, Vol. XIX, of its Proceedings. It is entered here with the kind permission of the Council of the Institution.

an army in the field, its marches and its battles, the lists of killed or wounded, are what chiefly strike the eye of the looker on; when a man is killed or wounded, or even when he is taken prisoner, his loss is chronicled; but the man is just as much lost if he dies or is invalided from want of food or medical aid. We read of so many killed, wounded, and prisoners, and of so many guns and standards captured; but who notices the losses from privations and hardships? Yet the losses from the latter causes far outweigh those from the former. We read much of the fight at Magenta and the battle of Solferino. Volumes have been written in which you will find accounts of both in the greatest detail; but we rarely see an account of the suffering endured by the French Army from the 9th to the 17th June, 1859; during the first few days the troops were ordered to live on the peasants, and latterly, although in a friendly country, the order was repeated, with the words added, "even to complete exhaustion"—words never used except in the direst extremity.

We read much of the battles round Metz: of the gallant conduct of the soldiers of two great nations; of the skill displayed by the Generals on this side, of the mistakes made by those on that. We read long lists of killed and wounded, but we hear little of the many human lives lost by fever, cold, hunger and want, round the beautiful city of Lorraine.

Few realise the fact that an army requires as much food as a very large city. Each day a large city receives its daily supply of food, there is no stint nor stay for those who can purchase; long custom and gradual improvements have opened up easy means of communication between the consumer and the producer. It is different with an army. An army is a city flung down suddenly in the country, each day moving, each day requiring fresh alterations in the arrangements by which food is conveyed from the producer to the consumer. Yet this portion of the art of war—one of the most important, if not *the most important*—receives but scant notice. "War is the art of being the strongest at any given place," and that portion of the art of war that keeps the greatest number of bayonets in the ranks is surely not to be despised.

It is often asked, why this difficulty about food? The number of mouths in a country is but slightly increased when two armies meet; the total number of mouths in the two countries at war is really diminished. Why then this difficulty? The answer lies here. Suppose there are 10,000 bakeries in England, an addition of ten mouths to be fed by each would make but a slight difference, if distributed. But suppose the additional 100,000 mouths all concentrated in one place, and requiring to be fed all at once, the circumstances are altered.

Three ways by which armies can be fed.

There are really but three ways by which, or by modifications of which, armies can be fed in the field:—

1st. The soldiers may obtain food by being billeted on the inhabitants, or by living from hand to mouth as they march.

2nd. The whole of the provisions may be carted after the army.

3rd. The army may be fed from magazines.

Let us consider these three methods. In the first case, the army would soon cease to be a military body; the men would quickly become a mob of marauders, and cease to be an army. In a thinly-peopled country, moreover, the dispersion of the men in search of food would be so great that little or no progress to the front could be made, and the moment a halt took place, the troops having exhausted the district where they were, would simply starve, precisely as a bullock tethered by a string will eat up everything in its circle and, if not moved, die from starvation, even in the midst of a rich meadow. This was the system generally adopted by the great Napoleon; it is one which we do not read much about in ordinary military histories, and into which we only get an insight by reading personal narratives of the wars at the beginning of this century. And it must be confessed that the genius of Napoleon as a strategist and tactician appears all the more marvellous when the system under which he made war is considered. The marches made by the French Army Corps to blockade Ulm were made in this manner, and French writers say the men suffered severely for many days. Pillage showed itself in that, the finest army Napoleon ever commanded. This must be the invariable result of there being no magazines. A victorious army may march on a broad front in a rich country in such a way, but the moment it concentrates to fight, or halt, it is plunged into the greatest difficulties.

After the capture of Berlin, in 1808, when the French undertook the winter campaign in Poland, their sufferings were very great; whole corps disappeared, broken up into bands of marauders seeking food in the scattered farms of that inhospitable country.

The serious check received by the French Army at Eylau was caused by the demoralisation consequent on this system. The resources of a country cannot be utilised by an army marching through it; they are wasted and lost.

We now turn to the second method, that by which an army is fed by provisions carried with it on wagons; this is possible for a very small force, but for a force of any magnitude it is impossible.

The Comte de Paris has furnished a remarkable calculation on this subject. He says, one road will suffice for only a limited number of carriages; if several roads are available, the number of wagons must be limited, otherwise the army cannot move.

A six-horse wagon will carry 2,000 lbs.; and the supply for each man per day, medical stores, ammunition, and food included, may be placed at 4 lbs. per man.

Such a wagon will supply 500 men for one day; but if the army is a day's march from its base, it will only supply 250 men, for it must go back empty to re-fill at the base. If it is two days from its base, 4 wagons for 500 men are requisite, or 8 per 1,000, or 800 wagons for 100,000 men. But if the army of 100,000 men includes, as it would do, 16,000 cavalry and artillery horses, 200 wagons would be requisite to carry a day's forage, or 800 if the army was two days' march from its base; or 1,600 wagons, horsed with 9,600 horses, but these wagons would be three days away from the base and one day there, consequently they would require 360 more wagons, horsed by 2,460 animals, to feed them; these would require 92 additional wagons, and so on, until we arrive at a total of 2,000 wagons, horsed by 12,000 animals, as being absolutely requisite to feed an army of 100,000 men two days from its base of operations. If the army advances one day further, or three days' march from its base, it would require 3,760 wagons, horsed by 22,000 animals, a column 38 miles long, if the intervals could be kept; but which would extend over 48 miles or the whole four marches; and even this number of wagons does not give a true picture, for there must be a fresh set of wagons to carry the food from, the divisional depôts to the regiments. To move ten days from the base operations, on the basis furnished by the Comte de Paris, would require 10,975 wagons, horsed by 65,850 horses. This is a number which it would be practically impossible to deal with, covering no less than 108 miles, if the distances be kept, but which would really be more than the whole length of the ten days' march.

The third method, or that of magazines, is consequently the only sure, safe, and possible means of making war, provided it be judiciously combined with a system of requisitions.

Along the roads, railways, or canals forming the line of communication of an army, there must be two distinct streams always flowing, viz., that which supplies the army with fresh or convalescent men and horses, as well as food and warlike stores of all kinds (this stream flows from the base to the army), and that flowing in the opposite direction, which carries back sick and wounded men, horses, and prisoners, either to depôts on the line of communication, or to the base itself, and also the empty wagons returning for fresh supplies.

It is manifest that there must be some organization which shall keep order and discipline amongst the heterogeneous masses which compose these two streams, which shall form depôts in proper places; see to the supply of the sick and wounded; push on what is urgently wanted; economise and utilise the resources of the country, whether friendly or hostile; direct those resources to proper places; maintain and repair the telegraphs, roads, railways, and bridges; garrison important points; protect and patrol the communications; check disorders; look after the dispatch of letters; and lastly, be such that, with but a short delay, can direct the whole of the vast traffic into another channel, should the movements of the Army necessitate this being done.

This organization, which the Germans term *etappen*, and which has been paraphrased as the "organization of the line of communications of an army," is that portion of the military art where study and forethought come most into play. It is that portion of the science of war where the bright scintillations of genius, the sudden inspirations of the heaven-born leader, can do little or nothing. But it is on that account the more important; as careful, accurate, painstaking, study, and forethought applied to it, will go far to remove many of the indeterminate causes which mar the most brilliant schemes.

In war there can be nothing absolutely fixed, nothing rigorously systematic. But while this is true, it is equally true that the military machine is composed of many different parts that cannot be made to work for one end unless they all fit into a well-arranged scheme. If all the details of such an organization be not clearly sketched out, well understood and thought over by everyone, no amount of inspiration or feverish excitement will make things go straight when the machine is tried.

Such an organization can only be tried in actual war, it cannot be exercised in peace; but if the principles of such an organization be clearly laid down, and the functions of each person well understood by all concerned, the organization itself will quickly get into working order when wanted.

While, then, rigidity of form is inadmissible, yet it is desirable to have a standard or model, to reach which every exertion should be made, even although such a standard may never be reached. It is very desirable in this matter, as in everything else, to establish some definite and clear principles of organization; details, however important, quickly arrange themselves if the framework or sketch be based on sound principles.

The first great principle which modern experience has pointed out, is the division of the whole subject of supply into two great branches. *Division of supply into two great branches.*

1st. That which works in rear of the army.
2nd. That which accompanies the army

These two great branches should be perfectly distinct, their functions are different, and the class of men and conveyances to be used is in each case different.

The function of the first is to look after and forward stores massed in large depôts, and to push them up, as far as possible, after the army. Referring to the illustration of the bakeries in England, it is the duty of the organization in rear, to seek out, as it were, the food which each soldier would have eaten if he had remained at home, or in garrison, and to send it after him.

The function of the second is to bring up the food from the

advanced magazines to the divisional depôts, at every opportunity, more especially during halts, and at the same time to seek to utilise the resources of the country by requisitions in the immediate neighbourhood of the marching troops.

It is manifest that the service in rear may be of a semi-civil character, the transport may be by rail, hired vehicles, or canals, while the service in the front must be military, and must be performed by bodies having a military organization. As an army advances into a hostile country, the requisitions in the immediate neighbourhood of the line of march will have, to a certain extent, exhausted the country; one object, then, of the semi-civil organization following in rear, will be to extend the area of requisitions, and to tap fresh supplies. In every case the furthest advanced point of the department working in rear should be as near as possible to the army in front, should follow it, and keep, if possible, within one or two marches of it, relieving the guards and detachments left in rear, completing any work that may have been done by the advance, strengthening bridges, repairing roads, laying telegraphs, and bringing up supplies. The transport working in front must, to prevent confusion, be under perfect military control, and must be able to bring up the supplies from the rear, that is to say, from the head or advanced portion of the rear-organization to the Divisional depôts.

The food or supplies, however, have to be carried from those Divisional depôts to the regiments themselves, and a fresh organization is requisite for this, which, being responsible for the supply of the units within the Division, that is to say, the battalions, batteries, and regiments, must be a part or portion of these battalions, batteries, or regiments themselves.

Division of transport into three portions. Thus we are led to a division of transport into three portions and attention is drawn to this division, for in it lies the key of success in this branch of the art of war.

1st. General transport, embracing railway, canal, and road transport, working along the line of communication from the base to the most advanced magazine.

2nd. Departmental transport, which shall convey the supplies from the advanced magazine to the Divisional depôts.

3rd. Regimental transport, which shall bring the supplies from the Divisional depôt to the battalions, batteries, or regiments.

Accuracy of detail and economy of power are only to be found in an intelligent division of labour. By such a division of the transport, the smallest portion is that which, having to be always close to the troops on all roads, and even in the fields, must be highly organized and well horsed. The Departmental transport, which need not move so rapidly, and generally moves at night, and always on roads, may carry heavier loads, or, what is the same thing, may use fewer horses,—while the transport working on the line of communication may, if it is not railway transport, be wagons hauled by relays of horses pressed from the inhabitants, and working a stage close to their own homes, thus avoiding the necessity of sending men and horses to the front, and further, relieving the magazines of the task of feeding horses and men so employed. The first description, General transport, must be under the Commandant of the line of communications, and under him alone; the second description, or Departmental transport, must be under the heads of departments—artillery, engineer, and commissariat; and the third, or Regimental transport, must be under the officers commanding regiments. When it is stated that the transport is to be under these different directions, it is not meant that the horses detached for any one service are invariably to be so employed, but that these are to be their normal or general duties; it being always distinctly understood that any horse or any man in an army is liable for any duty the General commanding may chose to order. It would appear almost needless to say this, but it used to be an axiom in the French army that the "intendant" was responsible for the supply of food, the commanding officer of artillery for that of ammunition, and the commanding engineer for entrenching tools, each having its own train, while the general was responsible for handling the troops in action. This led to its natural results, the heads of each branch of the service rarely helped one another, and the general, shorn of half his attributes, lost his power. In an army-corps, Division, brigade, or regiment, the commanding officer is alone, and can alone be responsible, for not only handling, but also for supplying the wants of his men. He may, and doubtless must, have persons under him responsible to him for carrying out certain duties, but their responsibility is to him, and to no one else.

Many of the arrangements adopted in foreign armies, and which are too often supposed to be modern discoveries, will be found to have existed under different names and altered circumstances, in the Peninsular War. Wellington began with no organization, but originated as he went along, and his organization, adopted from experience, was in principle almost identical with what now holds in the German army. It is well worthy of study as given by Gurwood. *Wellington's organization of his line of communications.*

These were—1st. The regimental mule equipment (pack animals, to follow the troops through the difficult country they had to traverse in Spain). 2nd. The departmental transport, represented by the artillery train, the engineer train, and the commissariat train. The two first chiefly, though not altogether, composed of the corps of artillery drivers, and the latter composed chiefly of the Royal wagon train, while the general transport was represented by vast numbers of hired carriages and animals, comprising the ordnance and commissariat transport, and by boats on the Tagus and Douro, worked by seamen; the whole of the latter being under the general direction of the officer in charge of the communications. Allowing for the altered circumstances, and the absence of railways and telegraphs, the system used in the Peninsular by Wellington was very similar to that now adopted in Europe, with, however, one·important difference, which will be hereafter explained.

Viewing then the question generally, we arrive at this point, that if an army is to be kept up to its fighting strength in front, the communications must be worked by an organization separate and distinct from that in front. It is by no means meant that this organization should be distinct from and independent of the general commanding the army, far from it; the organization working on the line of communications should occupy the position, as regards the army, that an army-corps does, that is to say, the officer in command of the communication should hold to the general commanding, the position that an army-corps leader does. This is most distinctly laid down in foreign armies. If an army-corps is working by itself it is really composed not of two, but of three Divisions—one taking charge of the line of communication, and not being classed or counted as troops of the fighting line; similarly, if several army-corps forming an army are working together, there is another on the line of communication not counted or classed with the fighting troops.

Now this is the point where the modern foreign organization differs from that of Wellington, a difference undoubtedly caused by the small force at Wellington's disposal.

He was obliged to endeavour to look after his communications by means of detachments and convalescents—the results were constant abuses. We read continually in the pages of Napier of the cavalry regiments being dangerously weakened by detachments acting on the lines of communication really as military police. We read of constant abuses, arising from convalescents being detained in rear, and the fighting battalions in front being thereby weakened. Now, in modern armies, the force told off for the communications is complete—it has its own battalions, its own commissariat, artillery and engineer staffs, which hold to the heads of those departments with the army the relations that similar officers do in Divisions to the senior officers of those departments. Thus the troops in front are never weakened by detachments, and a Division of 10,000 men on paper is really as nearly as possible of that strength on parade. The advantages of this as regards discipline are enormous—units such as regiments or battalions are not broken up to find garrison for this post or that important railway junction.

Organization of German line of communications.

There is nothing more remarkable in examining from time to time the strength of the Prussian army in France than to see how closely the real strength of each corps corresponded with the regulation strength.

The advantages of doing away with detachments is too well known to require to be dwelt on here.

Indeed, if an army were to advance into a hostile country

without such organization, it would soon reach the end of its tether, the fighting men in front would be gradually disseminated along the whole line of communication, and nothing would be left in front with which to meet the enemy.

In every army there are and must be a very large number of semi-military bodies, that is to say, bodies possessing a certain amount of military organization, and yet whose function is not to fight, but to work for those who do. These bodies are invaluable; but in front, their presence is absolutely hurtful; in rear, their duties are all important. Amongst these bodies are the bakers, the butchers, the great mass of the telegraph corps, the railway corps, and a large proportion of the medical department. Further, the protection and guard of the various posts in rear may be given to troops inferior in marching power to those in front, and consequently we are again brought by another set of reasons to the fact that a separate and special organization is required for the line of communications.

Nothing more clearly demonstrates the value and importance of a careful preparation of these details than the Franco-German war. Prussia conquered France, not so much from valour on the field of battle, as by the most painstaking care in every detail.

As the Prussian army advanced, it drew Prussian civil institutions after it; and the French statement, that France was invaded not by the Prussian army but by the whole Prussian nation, was literally true. As a general statement, it may be said that the collection of supplies at the base of operations is really the work not of the military leaders so much as of the civil administration of the State.

Acting on this idea, Coblentz, Mayence, and Mannheim were the bases, or great depôts of the German armies at first; stores were accumulated at these places chiefly by the civil government, organized bodies in charge of the communications worked from those points to the army; gradually, as the army advanced, these semi-military bodies followed, and were in their turn followed by a civil organization. First, a Governor of Alsace was appointed, next a Governor of Lorraine; and each functionary exercising the civil government of the State, allowed the semi-military bodies in charge of the communications to be pushed to the front, and finally the grand depôts, originally on the Rhine, were pushed to the Moselle; the force in front, thoroughly military, gradually shading off along its line of communication to the civil governors of the various provinces in the heart of Germany, where each corps had its home and peace station. The young unmarried men were in front, fighting and exposed, the older and married men in rear, each in proportion to his age and his power, doing his country's work.

To place highly-trained military bodies to guard communica-

o

tions, to see after the police duty, to prepare relays of horses, or convoys of stores is manifestly a waste of power. Looking to the two recent campaigns of 1866 and of 1870, it appears that in this organization the Prussians showed their superiority more than in anything else, the whole power of the State being devoted to one object. The Military Estimates in peace maintained the fighting men, and but a very feeble nucleus of these semi-military bodies; their peculiar institution of universal service enabling them to put their hands on as many men as they required at a moment's notice.

Thus when war broke out, every man in the country found his place in the vast machine by which the fighting men in front were kept supplied. The French army had no such organization; and was so frittered away in detachments, and there was so much confusion, pillage, and waste in rear of their army, that, taught by experience, the new French military laws provide that men, who from their stature, or from some slight physical infirmity, are not placed in the ranks, are enrolled for these auxiliary branches of the army. In war, the more complex the military machine becomes, the more important becomes the moral power of armies; and it may be observed that armies only get more complex, because society itself gets more complex: because discoveries and inventions introduced into civil life are adopted into armies; because, in short, men are better educated, and the general standard of knowledge is everywhere higher; consequently, moral force, as a lever that sways bodies of men of the size of modern armies, is more important now than when Napoleon said it was three times as important as physical force. Nothing tends to preserve moral force in armies so much as well ordered communications. It is not merely that regular supplies of food are brought up, that the men are regularly fed—although that goes for something--but the sick and wounded are got out of sight rapidly. Men's minds are not allowed to dwell on horrors, and above all, the reinforcements coming up from the rear, seeing regularity, order, and strict discipline in the rear of the army, are impressed with the sense of the power of the whole machine at work, and spread a healthy tone through the ranks they join.

It has often been said, and with great truth, that German military institutions have not been tried by defeat, that a concatenation of peculiar events has helped Germany in her great successes. This most undoubtedly is true; but if we examine her military institutions, we shall find that her leaders take precisely this view, and they have striven to produce a system that shall be available in the day of defeat as well as in that of victory; and nowhere is this anxious care more evident than in the organization of communications.

The service working in rear must therefore have a special and separate organization. In Germany (France and Austria have followed German arrangements to a great extent) there is an officer who commands the whole line of communications; his place is with the General commanding, or one march in rear of him, and under his orders he has six distinct branches working:

1st. The route service.
2nd. The railway service.
3rd. The field intendance, or commissariat.
4th. The field medical depôt.
5th. The route telegraph.
6th. The field post office.

Each of these departments has its own head, and each is of a civil, or quasi-civil character. Each has its purely military branch in front.

The telegraph department is a good example of the way in which the civil shades off into the military.

It is divided into three distinct branches, all under one head.

1st. The State or home telegraphs.

2nd. The route telegraphs along the line of communication, usually a light, overhead wire.

3rd. The field telegraph detachments which communicate with the Division and army corps. The latter being under the Generals commanding, the Director of military telegraphs deals with them through the Generals.

As the army advances, the route telegraphs are rapidly laid, and the first, or State telegraph department, follows and completes the work, connecting it with the general telegraph-network of the kingdom, the Director-General of State Telegraphs having as his assistant, or deputy, the Director of Military Telegraphs.

Thus there is no attempt to spread the field telegraph detachments out along the line of communications; being well horsed, and an entirely military body, their functions are to make a line each day to unite the Divisions, a line that must be rolled up and re-made the next day. The route telegraphs are more permanent but less military in their character, the great object being to push the State telegraph as rapidly as possible in rear. Thus, by a proper division of labour, the actual number of soldier-telegraphists is but small, and the money spent by the State on soldiers is thus kept as much as possible to pay for the actual fighting men, those who work in rear, being, on account of their prospective service in this way, relieved of a certain portion of the service they otherwise would have to do in the ranks. Men so employed do not require periodical training as soldiers, they do not require more than a distinctive dress, and a habit of respect for superiors. It is not intended to attempt to describe these six divisions or branches of the communications of an army, but the second, or that of field railways, cannot be dismissed without a few words on this very important special branch of the subject.

Changes in war caused by use of railways.

The use of railways has introduced great changes into war, and it is believed that these changes may be summarized somewhat as follows:—

Viewed strategically, they have given an enormous power in concentrating masses of men and horses from the distant portions of a country on certain points; such concentrations, in short, as those effected by the Germans in 1870, on Coblentz, Mayence, and Mannheim. Viewed tactically, their use is restricted. Armies may be massed by these means at a secure distance from an enemy in a short time; but the moment that the distance between two contending armies becomes such that a powerful force must be ready to form in line of battle to meet an opposing army, the railway becomes for the purpose of moving troops of little value; but for the purpose of supplying troops, and removing sick and wounded, its value is at all times very great. Although universal compulsory service is more than sixty years old, we may fairly doubt the possibility of keeping the vast armies in the field that are thus placed in it, if railways did not exist. Suppose there had been no railways during the recent Franco-German war, it is exceedingly doubtful if Germany could have kept 400,000 or 500,000 men in the field. No amount of wagon transport would have fed them in France; and it such a force had attempted to advance, feeding on the country, it must have spread over so wide a front to seek subsistence, and its power to concentrate would have been diminished to such an extent that its numerical value would have been greatly reduced.[*]

Railways must, therefore, be viewed in two distinct lights:—

1st. As means for concentrating armies from distant points, and for placing them on the theatre of war.

2nd. As means for supplying those armies while operating on the theatre of war.

This division is really that between railways actually in the zone of military operations and outside it.

In the former case the military element predominates; in the latter, the civil.

It is manifest that there must be a line of demarcation between these two. This the Germans term the transfer station. Take, for instance, the advance march of the Germans from the Rhine towards the Sarre. The Rhine was for some time the

---

[*] The invasion of Russia by Napoleon is a case in point. Many writers have carefully examined this great episode, and all agree that no organization of carts or wagons could have fed so great a force so far from its base, but that a single line of railway would have done so with ease.

dividing line, Mayence, Mannheim, and Coblentz being the transfer stations. East of these points the civil element prevailed; west, the military element was all powerful. The object being, as the army advanced, to push these transfer stations after it as quickly as possible, they were moved first to the Moselle, and subsequently to the Meuse, in each case the civil railways of the State extending their field of operations further to the west, and allowing the military organization to follow the army. The reason of this distinction is, that an army in the field depends for its supply on the productions of the country in rear of it, and it becomes essential not to dislocate the means of production, and to interfere with the trade and commerce of the country as little as possible. At the same time it is requisite that for a certain space in rear of the army it should have complete control over the railways; hence, a station must be selected where the separation takes place. The French made no such separation; and the consequence was that all kinds of stores, men, and horses were sent from all France to the army when actually in motion, there being no halting place out of the immediate zone of action, where the mass of supplies so sent could be arranged and forwarded as required; consequently the railways immediately in rear of the army were blocked and useless, and the wagons containing the things that really were wanted, never could be got at. No more extraordinary description exists than that of the blocks of railway carriages in rear of the French Army at Le Mans, or in the town of Metz.

At the latter place nearly 7,000 carriages were blocked together in a solid mass; none of the people on the spot knew what the wagons contained—ammunition, food, clothes, arms, intrenching tools, pontoons, and hospital arrangements being mixed up in a confused mass—the power of the railway as a carrying agent being destroyed by its carriages being used as moving magazines. Had a transfer station been used, much of this confusion would have been prevented.

There is always a tendency to follow the lead of those who have been successful, and consequently since the successes of Prussia, there is a great tendency to Prussianize military matters. There is danger in this. There can be no doubt that, broadly speaking, the principles of war must be the same in every country, precisely as the principles which govern the administration of justice, the principles of music, painting, sculpture, &c., amongst civilized nations are identical. But each nation works out those principles in a different way; and any one who is a judge, will a tell a French picture from a German, French music from German. So it must be with war—the principles which each nation has to deal with are identical. But in working those principles out, the peculiar idiosyncrasy of the nation must come into play. The outline of the picture in each case will be the same, but the colouring and detail will vary.

Although it is not urged that we should adopt German customs in this country, it is well to see what German customs are, and how the Germans have worked out the problem of utilizing their railways. When paying a visit to a German officer who filled an important position in a large fortress, the author saw a table which looked like a kind of Bradshaw, and on asking what it was, was told it was the annual mobilization table. "See here," the officer said, "if we will have war, and to-morrow is the first day, I know that at four o'clock a train containing so-and-so will arrive, at half-past five another, and so on, for the nine days during which the operation of mobilization takes place." And he added that each year this table was altered, and every officer of certain grades had a copy of it. This table is really a very simple affair. An army is composed of men, horses, and stores; those men, horses, and stores must in peace time be in certain known places. In war time they must be concentrated in other known places. Consequently it becomes a matter of simple calculation to determine where each of the scattered bodies or units can be best embarked in the railway wagons, and the time it will take to reach its point of destination. The table of mobilization is merely the result of a careful study of the subject. In Germany, a section of the Head Quarter Staff, aided by the Government Inspectors of Railways, prepares these tables and prepares a Bradshaw, which in war takes the place, while the army is concentrating, of the ordinary Bradshaw; certain of the ordinary trains ceasing to be civil and becoming military, and additional trains being added. On the completion of the mobilization, the railway section simply directs what trains are to run as military trains, and all the rest work as usual.

Further, as every unit has its fixed head-quarters, so each army corps has its head-quarters. And it is one of the functions of the railway section of the General Staff, aided by the Railway Inspectors, to select for each corps what is termed a "route depôt station"; to this station everything belonging to the corps is sent, whether going to it, or coming from it.

These route depôt stations have each a commandant. They are selected after careful consideration, and if plenty of store and platform accommodation does not exist, during peace it is made ; at this station the commandant is supreme.

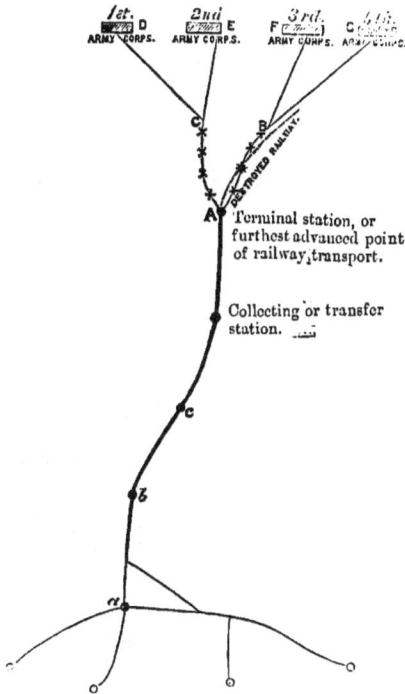

Terminal station, or furthest advanced point of railway transport.

Collecting or transfer station.

Route depôt station of 1st Army Corps.	Route depôt station of 2nd Army Corps.	Route depôt station of 3rd Army Corps.	Route depôt station of 4th Army Corps.

a, b, c, important points which should be the head-quarters of the railway working commission.

A, B, C, road transport by wagon to the route termini B and C, C D, C E, B F, B G, the lines on which the departmental transport works feeding the Army Corps from the route termini B and C.

Further, in peace time a committee for each line, consisting of the traffic manager and a military officer, is appointed. The duties of this committee are the following :—In case a country is plunged into war, there can be only a limited number of possible contingencies. These contingencies are determined carefully. The route-depôt station, and the places to which the troops and stores are to be moved, are also determined. The line committee determine where halts have to be made, where men and horses are to be fed and watered, and on single lines the passing places for trains. These points are all clearly laid down and every one knows them. The commandant at the depôt station simply loads the men, horses, and stores he receives from the district of the corps; the line committee take charge of them and deliver them at the transfer station. It is manifest that the whole of these arrangements require nothing more than a little care and forethought, and a mixture of railway knowledge and military knowledge on the part of those who make them. There is no science required at all.

Imaginary example of organization of railway communications in England.

Let us suppose for a moment that Scotland was a foreign country, with whom we were as likely to fight as we once were. And suppose we had 30,000 men stationed in Hampshire and Dorsetshire, 30,000 in the Midland counties, and 30,000 in Kent. The first step towards a mobilization of these forces for a Scottish war would be the selection of points of concentration for each body of troops; the determination of a route; depôt station; a detail of how the men, horses, and stores should get to that station; and the selection of a line of railway over which each corps was to move; the appointment of a line committee, consisting of military officers and the traffic managers of each line affected; and the determination of certain fixed trains to be used for through-traffic, and also certain places where men and horses might be fed, either breakfast, dinner, or tea, say six hours after starting. These conditions are clear and definite, and require only a little time to arrange. But where are these trains carrying all these men and stores to go to?—where will you disembark your loads? Here we come to one of the most difficult problems to determine, and one on the correct determination of which much depends. Are the Scotch likely to be more advanced in their preparation for war than we are? What is the political state of the country? What is the character of the leader? Is the war popular? Have they many railways to concentrate their troops with? All these questions enter into the determination of this point. It is manifest that if the point of disembarkation is chosen too far to the front, the troops and stores coming up in a long column by rail are liable to be greatly inconvenienced, perhaps not by the actual attack so much as by the threatened attack of the enemy.

If the point is too much to the rear, the full value of the railways will not be obtained, consequently the determination of this point is one of the greatest importance. Let us suppose York is the station selected, then that station becomes the transfer station or collecting station.

Behind that, all transport is worked as described under the regulations prepared carefully beforehand, as much as possible peace-traffic is maintained, and after the first concentration of troops take place certain military trains only are run. The points of departure and the point of arrival once fixed, the concentrations of troops become a simple matter.

Beyond York, no civil traffic of any kind would be allowed; and a military railway director, with very extended powers, would be appointed to work all the railway traffic north of York, acting, however, always under the orders of the officer in chief command of the communications. But let us carry our arrangements a little further, the Collecting Station, York, becomes then at once a great store.

The troops as they arrive are pushed through it at once, some by rail, some by road, towards definite points, where each of the three corps coming from Kent, Hampshire, and the Midland counties would be formed. The station at York would be placed under a commandant, who would issue orders somewhat similar to the following :—

"No trains containing military stores are to pass York."

"Trains with troops and ammunition may, unless specially ordered, pass."

"No train will go to the front that is not full."

"All provision trains will be unloaded, except in special cases, when definite instructions will be given."

"All trains coming from the army will run past York, and not stop there."

Meantime, let us suppose that the Commissary-General of the army in front finds, or thinks he will find difficulties in feeding the troops, on account of some flank movement that is going to be made against the Scotch army. He notifies the commandant of the line of communications of the quantity of provisions he is likely to require suddenly. These are loaded up, formed into trains, and pushed into sidings a few miles north of York, with a small guard which encamps beside them; a telegram from the front brings them on at once.

Similarly an action is expected, and hospital trains are formed, placed in sidings, with nurses, medical comforts, and a guard; a telegram brings them to the front at once, and the sick or wounded are carried far past York to the south.

North of York the traffic would be entirely military, and worked under a military railway director, who would have under him a proper staff for that purpose, and who would arrange for all the traffic being worked in a regular way. But how far can such traffic be worked? How close to the army can the railway transport be brought up to the front? The answer to these questions depends on many things :—

1st. The line; is it destroyed, or likely to be destroyed?

2nd. The nature of the stations available as terminal stations.

3rd. The prospects of a collision with the enemy.

4th. The nature of the roads and the horse-transport of the army corps.

5th. The situation of the army as regards the railway, and the front it was occupying.

But let us suppose a station selected, we will say Darlington, the enemy's army being somewhere in the neighbourhood of Newcastle. Beyond Darlington, railway transport would, except in special cases, cease, and each army corps would have to send its departmental transport to Darlington for supplies. Darlington, the route-terminus, would be the point where the organization of the line of communications would cease; it would be the great point where distribution would commence.

Let us suppose, however, a little further, that the railway has been destroyed north of Darlington, and that the enemy, the Scotch, retreat; the army advances, and the distance from the route-terminus to the corps becomes too great for the departmental transport to work. The officer in command of the communications foreseeing this, and knowing the direction the army is marching in, fixes a fresh route-terminus and establishes a line of horse transport from the railway terminus, Darlington, to the points he has selected; to these points the departmental transport now send for supplies, the transport of those supplies to the route-terminus resting with the officer in charge of the communications, while a strong body of workmen would be put on the railway to repair it, and relay the rails, when the railway terminus would be again advanced, and so on. Att he Collecting Station, York, supplies would be sought, not only in the south, but in the whole region round York, and each commissariat officer of the army corps would seek by requisitions purchased, or other means, to relieve the strain on the communication as much as possible.

Such are the principles on which the Germans work railways, and undoubtedly, so far as we can judge by the application of cause and effect, they are correct. Details have not here been entered into, nor descriptions of how the complicated arrangements requisite for the organization of lines may be best divided between the departments of the army. If the principles are sound, the details will quickly settle themselves. But this we may feel sure of, that though good men may make bad systems work, yet all systems should provide for being worked by mediocre or indifferent men, and many details of the German regulations do not appear to be so framed. But the general principles which prevail the whole are logical, clear, and definite, and this account of them will be concluded by quoting the opening words of their new regulations on this subject.

" The regular working of railways is of the first importance, "not only for warlike operations, but also as most materially "affecting national interests. The greatest care should be taken

"that they are regularly worked; on the lines in rear of trans-
"fer-stations, the ordinary traffic will not be interfered with for
"military purposes, except when absolutely requisite. As a rule,
"the ordinary public trains will run, extra ones being added for
"military purposes. The carrying powers of a railway are best
"developed by constant steady traffic at regular intervals."

"Any interference with the regularity of the railway is fatal."

CHAPTER VI.

The Attack and Defence of Woods and Villages.

If the reports of newspaper correspondents during the recent
war (often incorrect as to large questions, but also very often
singularly accurate as to minor details coming under their own
personal observation) are examined, we find that woods played
a very prominent part in producing victories on the one side,
in accounting for defeats on the other. Somehow a wood
generally helped, or was turned to some useful purpose by the
Germans, and as often it injured their opponents. The more
careful records of the war that have since appeared, although
couched in more general terms, confirm the reports of the
newspaper writers.

The woods on the flanks of the French position at
Spicheren, the woods on the slope of the ravines at Mars-la-
Tour and Gravelotte, are examples familiar to every military
student. The question at once arises, why did the woods help
the Germans? Why were they not equally utilized by the
French.

The answer to this may be found by looking at our New
Zealand fighting; on open ground the Maories could not have
stood up to a body of British troops even of inferior numbers
for five minutes, but in the bush they were at least a match
for them. Most certainly in this case efficient arms had little to
do with success, indeed, long-range weapons in a wood lose
much of their power. What enabled the Maories to check
regular troops in a wood was, by long habits, customs, and
ideas they were accustomed to the wood, and nature had given
them individual self-reliance, while the British soldier had been
trained to lean not on himself as an individual, so much as on
the discipline and concerted action of the body of which he
formed a unit.

It was the same cause that produced a similar result in the

Franco-German war. One of the results of the Prussian method of instruction pursued for many years had been to develop the individual moral force of the soldiers, and to accustom them to fight in small bodies, at the same time accustoming many subordinate officers to the responsibility of command,

The tendency of French instruction ever since the Crimean war had been to control and check what is termed "French *élan*," and to induce officers and soldiers to lean on and seek confidence from the concerted action of large bodies. In a wood such bodies cannot exist, and the direction of events must, to great extent, pass out of the heads of superior into those of subordinate officers. Consequently, self-confidence and habits of individual action within certain limits are, for such fighting, invaluable, both amongst officers and men. Wood fighting is incompatible with the action of masses of disciplined troops. It comes more to be a trial of skill between small bodies or individuals than the concerted action of disciplined men, and the difficulty of seeing what is going on, the personal qualities of the leader produce a smaller result than in open ground.

It cannot be too often repeated that the training of the soldier, if the full advantage of modern arms is to be obtained, must be of a far higher character than it has ever before been, not only must he be able to move and act with others, so that if requisite the full force of a large body in perfect order, acting under one will, may be brought to bear on one point, but he must have confidence in his own individual action. To be able to attain these necessary qualifications, not only must the man originally have an elementary education, without which he cannot grasp what he has subsequently to learn,* but he must be carefully trained to use his own powers of mind and body. Here lies the main difference produced by giving to the soldier improved weapons; to use them properly the man himself must be improved. And to the care bestowed by the Prussians in this individual training and in developing the powers of the man himself is chiefly to be ascribed the power they always seemed to possess of utilizing woods, while the French seemed perfectly unable to do so.

Here more than anywhere else success will be found to spring, from a clear appreciation and recognition of the foregoing facts by regimental officers; without this recognition it is vain to expect constant careful instruction to be given to men in peace by subordinate officers. On such instruction tactics really rest, and the responsibility that officers have thus to bear is far heavier than many will perhaps be ready to admit.

---

* The system of rifle instruction is precisely a case in point; perhaps not one man in five understands the theory that is taught to him, but the one man who does understand, generally can read and write, and the four others, though they may not understand, are improved by *trying to understand.*

It is tactics which win battles, and through battles exercise a preponderat **Pelet.** ing influence on the fate of states.

It is all the more requisite that these points should be brought prominently to notice, because some people, dazzled by Prussian success, and knowing that Prussian infantry are trained for 2½ to 3 years only, are somewhat inclined to run away with the idea that any kind of training does for an infantry soldier. A very cursory examination of Prussian military institutions will show that this is not so.

1st. It is often forgotten that the military raw material of countries where education and military service have been compulsory and universal for two generations must be superior to that of countries where such is not the case, and consequently that the same amount of military teaching goes further in one case than in the other.

2nd. The length of service in Prussia being so short and being compulsory, enables a far greater amount to be demanded and obtained from the recruit, than could under other circumstances be the case. Stoffel says, speaking of the Prussian Army, "The recruits work like niggers."

These causes account for the small time that suffices to train a Prussian infantry soldier both as a fraction of a large mass, and also as an individual.

The method of dealing with woods, villages, &c., may be best examined by referring to first principles. To troops acting on the defensive it is of importance to see without being seen, and to be so placed as to be able to use their weapons with freedom.

Troops acting on the offensive must seek to overwhelm their enemies with fire, and by advancing in individual order, seek to draw off the fire from the main bodies in rear.

Now it is apparent that if both parties are in a wood, neither party will benefit, the shelter afforded by the trees being common to both sides. Consequently, if a wood is to be used for defensive purposes, the *defenders must hold the outskirts of the wood* in that portion nearest the enemy, and must seek to prevent the attackers penetrating into it; if they once gain the wood, unless further arrangements are made for internal defence, the cover afforded by the trees become common to both sides, what is meant may be illustrated by the rules for "loopholing walls." Loop-holes to fire through should be about 4 feet 3 inches from the ground, but if they are that height from the bottom of the wall *on both sides*, two parties can use them, both the attackers and defenders, hence, on the side next the enemy they should be too high or too low for him to use.

Long range weapons lose much of their value in a wood, consequently the object of the defenders should be as long as possible to deny the edge of the wood to the attackers, and keep them under fire. Once the latter get into the wood the fighting is on even terms physically, morally it is all in favour of the attackers who have gained the woods. Woods, as a rule, check, impede, and render the movements of cavalry and artillery difficult and dangerous, they further disorder infantry; but they at all times afford a useful position and protection for the latter arm.

Jomini. No one who has ever seen a battle but will acknowledge the incontestible importance of a wood situated on the flank of a line to be attacked or defended.

Upon the offensive zone of a field of battle, woods, if of great extent, are injurious to the army taking the offensive, breaking up its formation and producing crowding and disorder. Woods of small size, however, aid the offensive considerably, helping to mask bodies of troops, and concealing the positions of reserves. They are more especially of value if they are of such a nature as will admit of cavalry being concealed behind them, which can be brought out at an opportune moment to act on the flanks of an attack.

Woods properly held on the defensive zone are of great value, enabling the front of the army holding them to be extended. A wood of very great extent cannot be so treated, because its perimeter, which must be held, becomes too extensive, and the force acting on the defensive would become too much disseminated. In such cases the position taken up should be in rear of the wood, and sufficiently near to crush the heads of the hostile columns as they attempt to debouch.

Clauzewitz. But impracticable forests, that is to say, those which can only be traversed by certain roads, offer to a defence advantages similar to mountains, viz., they enable the defenders to fight a battle in a favourable position.

An army may, behind these forests, and in a position more or less concentrated, await the enemy as he debouches from the defile to attack him with advantage.

Such a forest has more analogy as regards its effect with mountains than with a river, for it offers long and difficult defiles.

The battle of Hohenlinden affords an example of this. Moreau met the Austrian columns as they debouched from the forest of Ebersburg, and sent Richepanse to attack their flank through the woods from Ebersburg. The Austrians, unable to see in the wood what was going on on their flank, were broken in two, and the moment Moreau saw the wavering in his front produced by the attack on their rear, he assailed and drove them back.

The difficulty of defending a wood of any extent is that the troops are apt to lose in a short time all tactical connection, and escape out of the control of their officers. The difficulty in attacking a wood is that the attackers are in entire ignorance of what the wood contains, how the defenders are disposed, and that the defenders are sheltered from fire, and can shoot down the attackers with all the more ease, because they themselves suffer but little.

If the attack is difficult, the defence is not less so, both may be considered Fisch. the most difficult problems of modern tactics.

It is only by bearing clearly in mind the object in view that any definite ideas can be worked out. To defend a wood by troops, effort should be made to increase the power of the breech-loader on the defensive by opposing obstacles to the enemy and covering the defenders from fire, rendering them as secure as possible, and thus enabling them to pour in a well-directed fire on the attackers. These are the principles of all defences, but in addition, in a wood it is requisite to take special precautions that the troops actually firing, and on the outskirts of the wood, know where their supports are, and that effective measures be taken to communicate between the skirmishing line, the supports, and the main body.

Before putting a wood in a state of defence, it should be carefully examined, and the following points should be chiefly kept in view during the examination :—

    (*a.*) The size of the wood, its length and breadth.

    (*b.*) The nature of the wood, whether open or thick.

    (*c.*) The nature of the edge of the wood. whether marked or indefinite, whether belts of underwood and straggling trees intervene between the main wood and the open ground; whether there are any outlying clumps, or belts of trees, their size, and at what distance from the main wood.

    (*d.*) Whether there are many roads or paths in the wood, whether there are houses, clearings, or open spaces in the wood itself. Whether there are streams or wet places in the wood, and whether the ground is broken or smooth.

    (*e.*) The nature of the position in rear of, and on the flanks of the wood.

Woods in civilized countries are usually cut up by roads, sometimes these are main roads, sometimes mere tracks used to haul timber out; in a wood it is very easy for troops to lose themselves, and it is very advisable that marks should be made on the trees to denote the direction in which different places are to be found. The principal roads may be marked by a staff officer with an axe and a paint pot; but it is requisite that each battalion commander should also mark the way from the skirmishers to the supports, and from the supports to the main body. A simple blow made on the trees with an axe will do this, and a few men should be left to pass orders back; and it is desirable that the skirmishers should know that the supports are close behind them, for, of course in a wood they cannot be seen.

In putting a wood in a state of defence the first thing to be attended to are the salients, and any small detached clumps of trees within 500 or 600 yards, should be either cut down or occupied, such small clumps are peculiarly dangerous as, affording a *point d'appui* for an attack. Plate XX gives a general idea of the defence of a wood. Trees round the salient portions should be cut so as to form a rough abattis. A little thought is requisite in felling these trees, some trees will be better if felled with their heads out, some better if felled parallel to the front; some trees aid the defence and should be left standing. By far the best way to solve all such problems is for the officer so employed to ask himself, "If I were attacking this position, what would do me most harm"? Generally, large trees should not be touched, they afford cover for two or three men, and take time and experienced woodmen to cut.

It is far better to begin operations upon all the salients at once, and make them thoroughly strong than to attempt surrounding the whole wood with a belt of abattis. Cutting down trees is by no means an easy task to men who are unaccustomed to use an axe, with unskilled men perhaps a cross-cut saw will work faster. Although trees afford good shelter from the front, it is desirable not to neglect making shallow rifle pits, which will protect the men on the flanks, while the trees afford cover in front. All cover should, as far as possible, be removed from the front of the position occupied for 600 to 700 yards. This is a very difficult operation, and one, although most desirable, that can rarely be performed. When a wood has an undefined edge, with brushwood, undergrowth, and tongues of trees running into the open ground, it becomes a very difficult question to decide how much shall be defended, how much given up to the enemy.

From 100 to 200 yards of abattis will usually be ample in each place, and the space between, which may be 400 to 500 yards, will afford openings through which an offensive attack may be made.

In all cases every nerve should be strained to prevent the enemy getting into the wood, as he will see the abattis in front of the salients, and as such salients are usually on spurs, it is likely that he may seek to turn them and penetrate by the flanks; to check this, each flank of the abattis should have a return behind it, prolonged into the wood, and should not terminate abruptly; if the enemy then penetrates he will be taken in flank as he tries to advance, and the flank of the defenders of the salients will be covered.

Great care should be taken in using artillery in a wood, if the wood is in front of a line of battle, and can be flanked from the main line, few guns should be put into it; if it forms a portion of the main line, and guns must be placed in the wood, they should never be placed on the roads leading out of the wood where they offer marks to an enemy, but at slight distances to the right or left of the roads in places specially

PLATE XX.

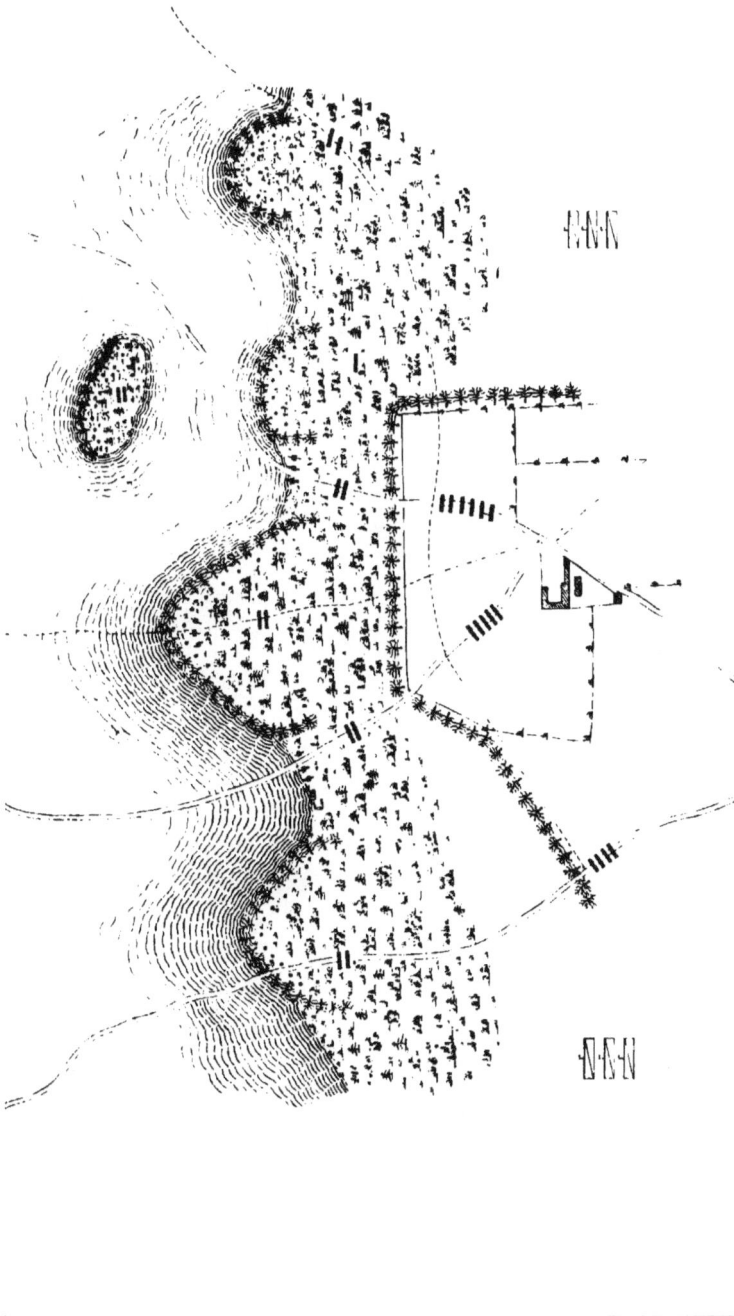

A Wood placed in a state of Defence.

prepared; they should be placed at considerable distances apart, as the splinters from trees do much damage; and, if possible, each gun should have two or more places from which it can fire, previously prepared for, sufficiently near to allow it being moved by hand from place to place.

Troops are really safer in a wood than in a village or in houses, the masonry knocked about by artillery fire is more dangerous than the splinters from trees, which often stop splinters of shells; and above all the retreat is far more secure.

Roads should never be blocked in the wood or at its entrance; unless for special reasons, it is better to break them up at a farm-yard, a village, or some place 700 or 800 yards to the front, and form a small post there to cover the barricade. It is always desirable to prepare for disaster, although never desirable to parade that preparation. Consequently, although the edge of the wood is the place where the great struggle should take place, a second line should be provided somewhere within the wood; this may be at a clearing or barren spot, which often exists in a wood, or behind a watercourse or river; in every case it is desirable to make some line of abattis *parallel* to the line of retreat; such an abattis held firmly, acts as a flank attack on the enemy, and may prevent him extending, when once he has penetrated the wood.

In many woods there is a spot where all the roads converge, at such points there is often a farm, a house, or a small village,* such a position should be put in a state of defence, and a strong reserve put there, which should embrace a few cavalry.

Sometimes in a wood, when the edge has been lost, a skilful use of a reserve will turn the attackers out. When troops have found their way in there will always be some eager spirits who will push on, and others who won't like to hold back; the main body may be disconnected, the second line not yet up, and consequently the hold on the wood but a weak one. The front on which the attackers have entered will in all probability be a narrow one, and a rapid advance, especially on their flanks, will often restore the fight. True, everywhere, in a wood especially, reserves properly held in hand and brought up steadily, will usually turn the day. And this does not refer alone to either an army-corps reserve or a Divisional reserve, but to brigade, battalion, and even company reserves.

In a wood the supports may be weaker than in the case of an attacking force, because the skirmishing or firing line will suffer less, and the true function of the support being to fill up the gaps in the skirmishers' line, it will not be so much needed; hence, the skirmishing line may be longer or occupy more ground, and as there is less likelihood of the skirmishers being taken in flank, than there is if the ground be open, the supports

* At Talavera the rear was supported by a large house in the wood, well placed in case of defeat to cover a retreat leading from Talavera to Arzobispo and Lopeza.—*Napier.*

P

may be distributed in smaller bodies along the rear, while at the same time they may be brought much nearer to the front; this is all the more requisite, as, to support effectually, the officer commanding the supports must be in front to watch the effect of the fire, and on a long line in a wood he cannot see what is going on, consequently the supports must be sufficiently near at hand for the subordinate officers to act on their own responsibility. All the commander of the supports can do is to try and find the most dangerous place, that where the enemy seems most disposed to direct the attack, and post himself there. The commander of the main body cannot watch the fight from the rear, but must do so from the front, and he has therefore to remain in front and send back orders to the main body, which consequently must not be too far off.

Cavalry should be posted on the flanks and in rear of the wood, if an opportunity offers, and they can circle out suddenly, they may produce a great effect. If a small body of cavalry can be concealed in the wood itself and pushed rapidly out, from the fact of cavalry not being expected, it may effect much, but this must be determined by the nature of the wood. If the wood be in front of a position, arrangements should be made to bring a heavy fire to bear on it, and a line of retreat for the defenders should be pointed out to the commanding officer, so that fire may be opened the moment the wood is abandoned, without interfering with the retiring troops. Whenever troops who have once attacked get into cover after heavy loss, there is some difficulty in inducing them to come out again, more especially if met by heavy fire on the other side when they try it.

War of 1866: Prussian Staff. (Translated by Hozier.) The 15th Infantry Brigade now received orders to pass through the wood of Sadowa. This wood forms almost a regular square, and measures about 1,000 paces each way. In the immediate neighbourhood of the road it contains a good deal of high timber, oak, beech, and fir, but the other part of it consists principally of very dense undergrowth. Only trifling detachments of the enemy were found in it, which fell back at all points, but in pursuing them through the thickets the Prussian companies could not retain their close order, and when they reached the skirts of the wood on the other side were received with a perfect hailstorm of shells. It was utterly impossible to advance, and General Bose gave orders to desist from any attempt of the kind, but to hold the skirts of the wood under all circumstances.

The attack of a wood is one of the most difficult and dangerous operations in war.

Von Mulken. The attack of a wood strongly held is only justifiable when the object in view can be attained in no other way.

One of the great difficulties is to know how the wood is held, where the guns and infantry are, and which are the weak points. The reconnaissance of wood prior to its attack should embrace not only the ground in front and on the flanks, but information as to the inside of the wood should be sought from country people, and from maps. The position of the defenders can be best found out by some false attacks, which may induce the enemy to show his position.

It is better to make two or three distinct though simultaneous attacks on a wood than to trust to one; the reason of this is, that the defenders, from the difficulty of intercommunication offered by the trees, have their supports and reserves less under control than would be the case in open ground, a fact which the soldier very soon realises; and the demand for supports sent back from the front, if not promptly responded to, tends to demoralise men who cannot be properly supervised by their officers. The attackers in the open have the benefit not only of intercommunication, but of being completely under the supervision of their officers. Consequently several attacks, if made at the same moment, will produce emulation amongst the men, while at the same time it will have the effect of disconcerting the defenders.

It is desirable to bear in mind that the attack of troops armed with a breech-loader, and holding an open position, is a dangerous and difficult operation, and can be undertaken with a reasonable hope of success only under the circumstances pointed out at page 89.

But when troops armed with a breech-loader are covered by trees, shelter trenches, walls, &c., the attack becomes far more dangerous, because the effective fire of the troops acting on the offensive is seriously interfered with, the defender's fire becomes at the same time all the more accurate and deadly because they suffer but little from the attackers' bullets; consequently the attack on troops occupying a wood or village, or an intrenchment, requires a longer preparation and a greater quantity of artillery fire than if the defenders had no cover. But although it is better to make several attacks, these attacks should not be separate and disconnected, but should work together, one or more being directed on the flanks, while one or more assail the front. The exact nature of the attack can only be determined by the nature of the ground and the amount of cover in front of the wood.

In the attack on a wood, as in all other attacks, as many guns as possible should be got into position, and should be divided into as many divisions as there are attacks; if possible, these guns should be so placed as to fire on all the points selected for forcing an entrance. It is not likely that there will be many guns in the wood, and hence the artillery may push up to some 1,400 or 1,500 yards; a very rapid fire should be begun on the wood, those guns that can support all the attacks firing for a short time in support of each in succession, the actual attack being made by the infantry as previously described. Under fire of the artillery an attempt should be made to penetrate into the wood, through the breach effected by the fires; once the edge of the wood is gained no great advance should be made until a sufficiently strong body of men is in hand, and then

P 2

a careful steady advance should be made with the flanks well supported, as, if the enemy have not been demoralised by the artillery, they will seek to attack and drive out the intruders by operating on their flanks.

De Looze

At the attack of the wood of Skalitz, 28th June, 1866, the Prussians made two attacks. Löewenfeld on the right, with eight half-battalions of the 37th and 58th, Witzleben on the left, with four half-battalions of the 38th supported by six battalions of grenadiers under Voigts Rhetz. The half-battalions at the head of each column were formed in company columns, covered by the skirmishing section, the remainder in a line of columns of half-battalions; the attack was prepared by one 12-pounder and two 4-pounder batteries.

There is one special danger in all wood fighting,—viz., the risk of the general line of attack or defence getting dislocated. Constant attention must be given by officers to this point, and the men should be urged to keep a connection with those on their right and left; should the line get dislocated, the enemy, finding no fire coming from one place, will push in, and by thus dividing it and acting on the flank, compel the retreat, perhaps the flight, of the whole line.

The most remarkable instance of wood fighting that has occured of recent years was undoubtedly that at the wood of Maslowed at Königgrätz. The Austrians made little or no effort to hold the edge of the wood, but fell back and allowed the Prussians to get into the interior and take possession of a great part of the outskirts on their (the Austrian) side, but not of the whole, "because of the great extent of the wood, and the fierce "struggle raging in parts of interior." The Prussians got the whole of a division into the wood, and although they were repeatedly driven back, their line divided and cut in two by large Austrian forces, yet they never could be driven out. This was due to the very skilful way in which the Prussian officers made flank attacks on the Austrians with small bodies of men.

Campaign of 1866: official account. (Translated by Hozier and Wright.)

The companies had all become mingled together as the fight swayed backwards and forwards in the dense wood. No unity of guidance was possible on ground where hills and woods shut out all view of the surrounding country, and all that the commanders of the different detachments could do was to lead their men by their own personal example. In all parts the officers rallied round them whatever men were in their neighbourhood, no matter to what regiment they belonged.

During some of these sanguinary struggles an Austrian battalion lost its way, as troops are very likely to do, and wandering out of the wood on the Prussian side, was charged by and surrendered to a Prussian Hussar regiment, placed behind the wood.

VILLAGES.

Villages have at all times played a very important point in battles. The history of war is full of the accounts of sanguinary struggles for the possession of villages. The villages of Aspern and Essling, with the trench connecting them, saved Napoleon from destruction in 1809. The neglect of the villages in front of Leipzic, undoubtedly helped to bring about the great defeat he sustained there.

In more recent wars the struggles round the villages of Solferino, Wöerth, Vionville, may be quoted.

It is fairly open to question, however, if one of the effects of rifled artillery has not been to reduce the value of villages, houses, and such posts, for the following reasons: increased range and accuracy have enabled artillery to render such places untenable at a greater distance than formerly. A small village put in a state of defence, with houses loopholed, will have its walls so shaken and knocked about by artillery fire that the defenders cannot remain in the house; each shot that comes in bringing down a large number of splinters, and the shells* setting thatch, wooden buildings, hay, &c., so quickly on fire that the villages becomes untenable, this is all the more felt because the defenders of the village are at that state of the fight quiescent, and the mere fact of remaining under a heavy fire of shells, without being able to do anything to reply, tends to demoralise troops rapidly.

Troops when defending a village were usually placed in the houses which were loopholed, some central house, usually the church, being chosen as a reduit to the whole village. Holding a village in this way when modern artillery can be brought against it is simply impossible, and other arrangements must be made.

The whole village, or such portion of it as may be deemed advantageous, must be used as the reduit or redoubt, and must be loopholed and put in defence precisely as ever it was. The streets being barricaded, traverses, &c., made exactly as laid down in books on this subject. But while this is done, arrangements must be made for placing the first or shooting line outside the village. A village is usually surrounded more or less with enclosures, such as hedges, walls, and fences; when these can be taken advantage of, they should be used, and an enceinte formed round the villages by their use combined with that of shelter trenches; in the selection of fences for this purpose, and in the construction of shelter trenches, care should be taken to place them sufficiently far from the houses of the village to prevent the troops lining them being struck by splinters. A distance of 40 yards will suffice for this. But is also desirable that when the defences forming the outer line are carried, the defenders should be able to fire into it from the houses, consequently it will be better to place the outer line at 150 to 200 yards from the houses, if such an arrangement does not give too great an extension to the front; if such be found to be the case, the distance between the outer and inner lines may be reduced one half. The form which the outer line takes must always be an irregular one. If possible, a closed redoubt, even of the weakest

---

* The Prussians have special incendiary shells with each battery for this purpose.

profile, should be placed at the angles. Artillery may be placed in these redoubts, but it is much better in most cases not to do so, but to put the guns under epaulments in rear of the village in such places as will enable them to flank it and cross fire in front. In the defence of villages and woods mitrailleuses will be of great advantage, their lightness enabling them to be readily moved by hand from place to place, and the very efficacious fire they give over a limited area renders them suitable for such purposes. It has always been laid down as a rule that obstacles which detain an enemy under fire are of importance. But obstacles for such a purpose are very apt to give an attacker shelter where he may establish himself, and should be very carefully considered before being used. The most dangerous and difficult ground for troops to advance over is undoubtedly a gentle slope completely seen and perfectly open, and in placing a village in state of defence, the more open the ground is in front and to the flanks the better.

Obstacles may be viewed as opposing the enemy's advance, hampering the defenders if they take the offensive, and furnishing cover to the attackers. The position of obstacles must therefore be carefully considered; perhaps the most efficacious kind of obstacle is a wire entanglement, as it affords no shelter, and is not affected by artillery fire. But a wire entanglement completely forbids the action of cavalry; a few men armed with breech-loaders, and surrounded by wire, would be perfectly safe from a cavalry attack.

Villages may be held for various purposes, and the amount of work to be done to them of course varies with the purposes for which they are held.

Brialmont.

An army may entrench a village. 1st, to shelter a detached post; 2nd, to shelter an advanced post; 3rd, to support a line of battle, either in front or on the flank.

Villages in hollows should never be held, but if on elevated ground, surrounded by woods, and near a river or stream, they may become good posts.

Villages are also of great value when used to support the front of an army deploying into line of battle.

In examining a village prior to putting it in a state of defence, the following points should be chiefly considered:—

> (a.) The nature of the ground round the village, the amount of cover offered to an attack, the nature of the fences, and whether suitable for defensive purposes or not.
>
> (b.) The line selected to form the outer enceinte should be carefully examined, and such walls, hedges or fences as may be available for forming a portion of the line, should be selected, and the places where shelter-trenches or earth-works are required should be marked.
>
> (c.) The houses forming the inner enceinte should be selected, those with timber outbuildings being

avoided if the woodwork cannot be pulled down. The roads leading through the village should be examined, and the places for barricades selected and fresh openings and passages made where requisite.

It is essential that these points should be quickly determined on. There are two errors which officers are apt to fall into under such circumstances: one acting hastily and undertaking too much work for the time and means at their disposal, the other thinking too long of what they are going to do. The outer line should be begun first, and so soon as it is in a fair way of being completed in time, men may be set to work on the other portions.

If the village is held as a detached post it should be carefully surrounded, and everything done to make it as secure as possible, for the troops placed in it have, in such a case, nothing but their own exertion to depend on. When held as an advanced post, the village gets support from the general line of battle, and should be made as strong as possible on three sides, but on the side nearest the defender's position should be open, having a line of shelter-trench, about 250 yards in rear of it, with epaulments for artillery, so that the enemy, when the village is captured, will not be able to use it as a *point d'appui* for further operations. Such a line of shelter-trench in rear of the village will effectually prevent the attacker's flank attack (which he is sure to make) from getting into the rear of the village, and will further cover the retreat of the troops engaged in its defence. Any defensive work may be carried by surprise, or by some accident, such as thick weather, which enables the attackers to come close up; but the moment it is captured is always the very best time for driving out the intruders, before they have time to get into order; hence the garrison of all works, great or small, should have a reserve ready to act rapidly. In defending a village the places where supports are to be placed should be carefully selected, they will be safer when placed in small bodies clear of the village, and immediately behind the troops they are to support. When time is available it will be judicious to cover them by shelter trenches. Although the houses composing the village should be loopholed, troops should not be put into them until the last moment, the men to occupy the different places should be carefully told off, and when the attack gets sufficiently near, they should be taken into the village in small numbers, and carefully posted in the houses by officers. For this purpose a rough sketch of the village should be prepared, and the position of the different bodies intended to hold it should be noted (*vide* Plate XXII, which shows the defence of Le Bourget by the Prussians). At this stage of the attack the assailant's artillery will probably have moderated its fire, being partially masked by its own infantry, and hence the men who should previously have been as much as possible kept under shelter, will come up fresh and in good heart.

So soon as the main body of the troops engaged in the defence of the village are taken into the village, their place in the rear should be supplied by troops from the second line, who should line the shelter trench in rear of the village, and throw forward a strong line of skirmishers between the trench and the village. Feeding the fight in this manner invariably helps the defenders, who are much less likely to be demoralised, when they know fresh troops have come up to support them from the rear. It obtains thus for the defence a part of the advantage which the offensive always possesses, namely, the moral effect of a forward movement, and preserves the same *general* distribution of troops, both for attack and defence.

Important as villages are, too much value must not be assigned to them. And here, as everywhere, a recurrence to first principles is of importance. Fortification is the art of enabling a small body of men to resist a large force. If the fortification or village requires more men to defend it than would be assigned to a similar front of open ground, it really does more harm then good. Shutting up too many men in a village is a great error. The object of holding a village is two-fold. 1st. To deny the cover it offers to the enemy. 2nd. To make a certain point secure, and thus liberate men, who otherwise would be employed at that point as defenders, for offensive action. This latter is the true principle on which all field fortification should be carried out.

If too many men are placed in a village, and the general line of battle is forced, the men garrisoning the village can do little or nothing to restore the battle, and if the second line and reserve fail to drive the enemy back it is likely that the defenders of the village will be captured. Blenheim affords an example of this. The French General Tallard placed a very large force of infantry in the village, situated in a loop of the Danube; when Marlborough forced the French line, the infantry in Blenheim were completely cut off, and had to surrender.

Decker. The defence of villages should not take too many troops which might be useful on the line of battle, and although a position supported by villages is good, it must be given up if their defence requires too many men. It must be always remembered that the defence of villages when men are behind intrenchments acts unfavourably on the morale of the soldiers from the very security they appear to give. All the troops so employed weaken the general line of battle, and the combats which follow are always bloody.

Field fortification can never be a panacea for weakness. And it never ought to be viewed otherwise than in its tactical relation to the general action of the troops fighting. By judiciously using it, it becomes an important and valuable auxiliary. The true key to all such questions is to be found by keeping steadily in view that *the passive defence of any position by an army is an absurdity.*

When an inferior force finds itself in presence of a superior and compelled to fight, it is in danger of having its flank turned by the extension the larger army can afford to make. To obviate

PLATE XXI.

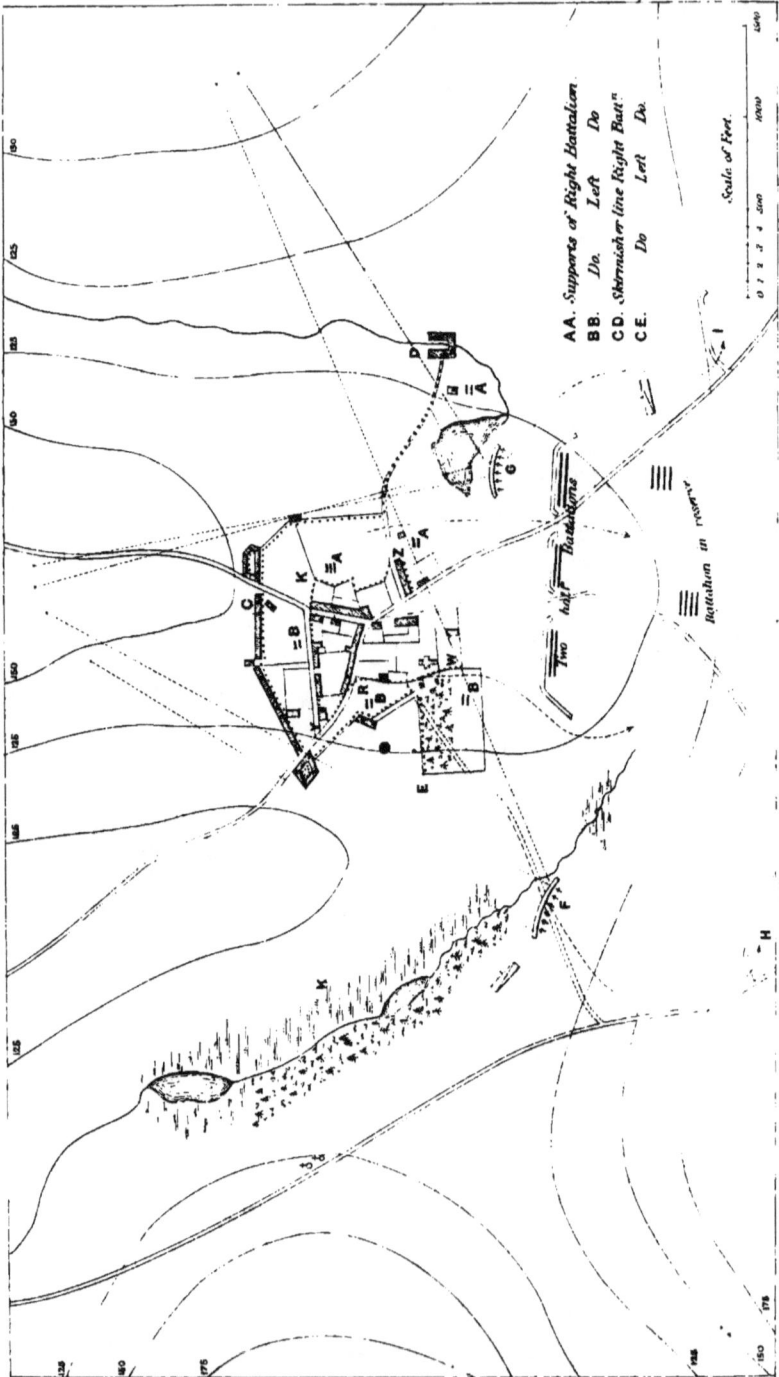

AA. *Supports of Right Battalion.*
BB. *Do. Left Do.*
CD. *Skirmish-line Right Batt^n.*
CE. *Do Left Do.*

Scale of Feet.

Village 800 yards in front of a line of Battle entrenched & defended by three Battalions, two Squadrons and two Batteries.

this danger the army acting on the defensive may, by a judicious use of villages and field works, seek to extend their line, and concentrate the mass of this force on one place where it can strike an offensive blow ; the chief use of fortifications should be to assist this by so strengthening a portion of the line of battle that it may be held by a reduced number of men.

The rules for making shelter trenches, loopholing houses, and putting villages in a state of defence, are given in many of the books on this subject, and need not therefore be repeated. But it is desirable to give an example of a village entrenched as has been just described.

Plate XXI shows a village situated from 600 to 800 yards in front of a general line of battle ; it is supposed to be defended by three battalions, two batteries, two squadrons, and a detachment of engineers. About seven hours is supposed to be the time available for putting it in a state of defence.

The object of holding it is twofold :—

1st. To deny it to the enemy, who, making use of it, the stream, wood, and ponds, could shortly establish a firm foothold within effective musketry range of the defenders' position.

2nd. To delay the attack, to compel the enemy to deploy and extend his forces at a spot 800 yards further off than he otherwise would do, thereby causing him labour and loss of time. Further, to compel him to attack the troops posted in the village, and suffer the consequent loss, before he can unite his attack against the main position. The front covered and protected by the village, extends from the lower pond on the left to the Mill D on the right, a space of about 2,000 yards, guarded by—

3 Battalions	....	....	....	2,400
2 Batteries	....	....	...	260
2 Squadrons	....	....	....	200
Detachment Engineers		....	....	50
		Total	....	2,910

A force which could not pretend to hold such a front, without the aid of field fortification. The outer enceinte has been selected so that in front it is composed almost entirely of shelter trenches, with two closed redoubts of weak profile at the angles, close to and covering the barricades across the roads ; on the flanks, walls are available, which have been used as the line of defences, being of such a height that they can be fired over.

The fence along the road, leading to the Mill D on the right flank, is also put in a state of defence, as is the boundary wall of the Wood E. The wood and the mill thus support the flanks of the village. The little stream, ponds, and marsh K on the left protect that flank, the wood being held by half a company of infantry.

An epaulment to cover a battery, is placed behind the pond near the mill on the right, a similar epaulment covers the other battery on the left.

A shelter trench with two large openings in it, through which the roads pass, is placed 250 yards in rear of the village which is open.

An inner enceinte is formed by loopholing the houses and joining the walls W, Y, K, L.

One battalion is placed in reserve in half-battalion columns under cover of the slope. A squadron is placed near one half-battalion, the other squadron near the left battery, with a couple of men pushed out to watch the road parallel to the wood.

Two half-battalions are sent to line the outer enceinte, which they divided between them. Each half-battalion extending two companies along the front it has to cover, and retaining two companies in support.

The other wings of these battalions are placed in the shelter trench.

The supports AA and BB are kept clear of the houses as much as possible. When the attacker advances to within about 600 yards, the support must be freely used to supply losses, and the two half-battalions, behind the shelter trench, should advance and occupy the inner enceinte, the reserve battalion taking their place behind the shelter trenches. This advance will give confidence to the defenders, who see their own people coming on in support of them. The batteries will, from their positions, flank the village.

If the outer enceinte be carried, the troops defending it should be instructed to fall back towards R and Z; the defenders of the inner enceinte will then be free to use their rifles from the houses, which the attacking artillery dare not now fire at, as they will be afraid of injuring their own men, and the defenders not having been previously in the village, will not have suffered from the demoralizing effect of the cross-fire of the attacking artillery. The cavalry on the flanks will, during the enemy's advance, watch for an opportunity to charge him unexpectedly.

When the enemy get possession of the outer enceinte, the battery on the right should retire to the epaulment, I, prepared for it in rear of the shelter trench, and fire on the assailants when it can see them.

The battery on the left will subsequently retire to H.

Should the attackers succeed in carrying the inner enceinte, the defenders should fall back along selected lines, as shown by the dotted arrows; the battalion in reserve covering their retreat with its fire, and the two batteries firing into the village to check the attackers.

The first two battalions should then reform under cover of the slope. If the village is to be re-captured, the reserve battalion, supported by troops from the second line, should at once undertake the work.

PLATE XXII.

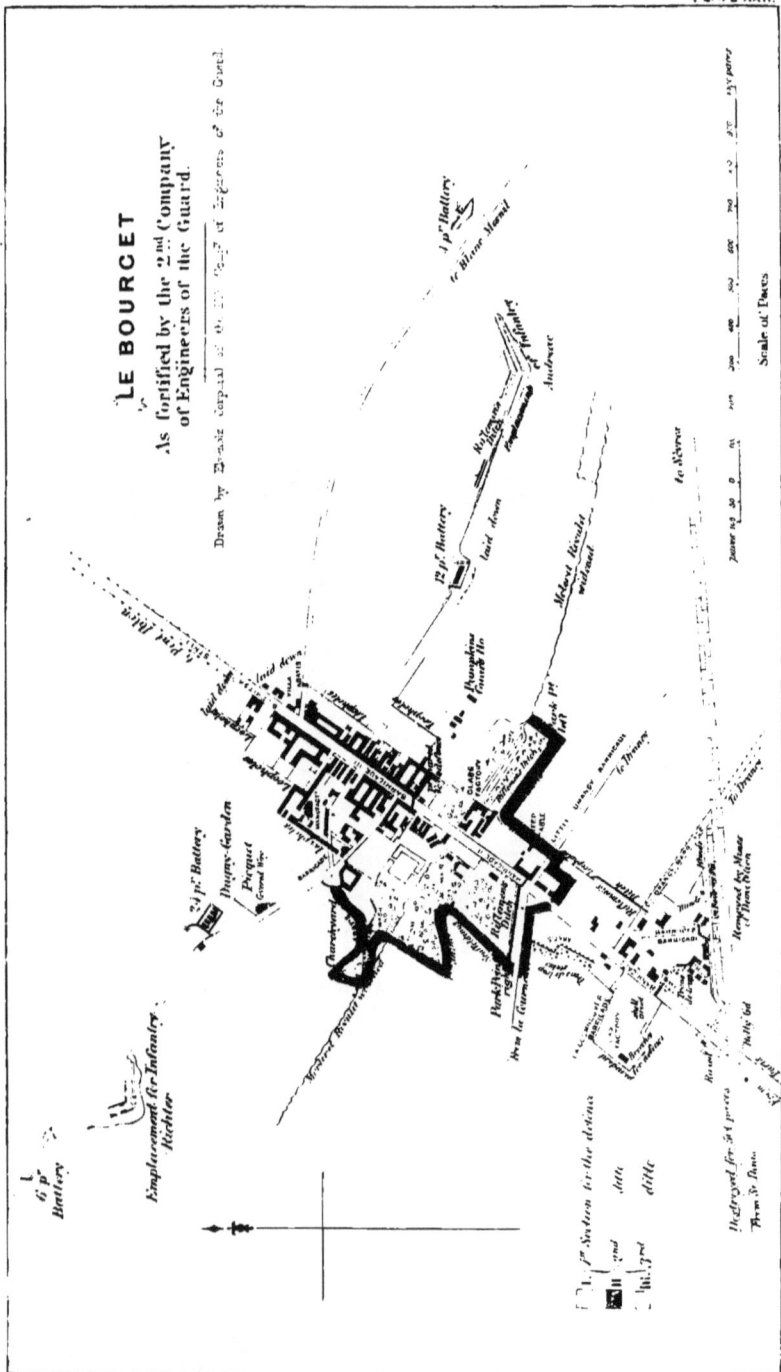

LE BOURCET

As fortified by the 2nd Company
of Engineers of the Guard.

Drawn by Erani Copial

Scale of Paces

By adopting such an arrangement the defence may obtain *some* of the moral advantages of the attack, and the demoralization consequent on leaving infantry in loopholed houses, exposed to a heavy artillery fire, and unable to reply, may be reduced.

As soon as possible after the front is clear of the retreating infantry, the counter attack should be made before the enemy have been able to close the rear of the village which has been purposely left open.

The attack of a village is a difficult and generally a costly operation, and should be attempted only when the object justifies the loss. Many of the hardest fought actions have been those where the attack and defence of villages formed a prominent feature. At Ligny 20 Prussian battalions struggled for the whole day against 32 French battalions, and much of the loss both sides suffered was round the village of Ligny itself.

Attacks on villages cost so many, usually the best men, but I make a rule to avoid them as much as possible.— *Frederick.*

Burning the village will often turn the defenders out, but some thought is requisite before doing so.

To burn a village is the surest way of dislodging the enemy, but if the attackers must pass through the village, doing so stops their advance, and aids the enemy retaking the offensive. *Rocquancourt.*

Generally speaking, the attack should be undertaken somewhat as described at page 95, as heavy a fire of artillery as possible being concentrated on the village, and a considerable time allowed for the artillery to take effect before the infantry are pushed forward.

The attacking troops should be accompanied by small parties of engineers with tools, and a strong body of engineers should be held in hand, ready to push up the moment the outer enceinte is carried, to assist in turning the defenders of the houses out, and strengthening the village against a counter attack of the defender's reserves.

The attack on Le Bourget, at Paris, is a good example of the attack on villages.

Le Bourget is a village of some length, the gardens of which are surrounded by long straight walls 6 feet in height, intersecting each other at right angles. These were prepared for defence by loopholing and heaping up earth, and the entrance to the village was barricaded.

The attack was undertaken from three sides, viz., from Blanc-Mesnil, Dugny, and along the road between them. The two flanking columns sent to the front clouds of skirmishers, which gained ground at the double, and then threw themselves down. The supports and reserves followed these, spread out in extended order, and also at the double. As these latter threw themselves down to rest, the skirmishers again ran forward, and at the same time bore off towards the flanks. When they arrived within range, they again threw themselves down, and opened fire upon the enemy. The gaps which occurred from drawing off towards the flanks were filled up by extending subdivisions. In like manner the flanks were prolonged by single companies advancing one after the other, but always in extended order, so that the concentric attack *The attack of the Prussian Infantry. Duke of Wurtemberg. (Translated by Robinson.)*

which had moreover—as the enemy was approached—become denser in character, kept always assuming a more enclosing form. Each of the extended bodies of troops took advantage of whatever cover offered, in order to rally behind it and collect together. Thus in front of the north-east flank a row of dung-heaps had been left upon the field, which afforded a rallying place for an entire company, which opened from behind these a destructive fire upon troops who came forward to attack. On the other flank the bed of the brook Le Moleret afforded a slight protection and was at once turned to account by a few formed companies, in order to cover an onset against a counter attack delivered from Drancy.

The mechanism of the attack consisted principally *in the rapid change from open to close order directly the most trifling cover admitted of the rallying of a subdivision or company. On the other hand, every advance over open ground took place in widely extended skirmishing lines, which moved on like ants.*

The right wing was left behind ; the centre had not sufficiently extended itself, and had renounced old forms too little, and its losses were enormous ; but the attacking left wing, under Lieutenant-Colonel Graf Waldersee, pressing forward in long thin lines, succeeded in making good an attack of skirmishers up to the garden walls, in silencing the fire from them, and in breaking into the long village, both from its flanks and rear. Its defenders now gave way, General Budritzky was able to enter from the front, and the right flank column to reach the rear entrance without very severe loss.

The recent Franco-German War offers many examples of villages, woods, and posts being defended, and advantageously made use of by the Germans, especially in the blockades of Paris and Metz ; in every case the principles on which these posts were held were identical,—viz., the exterior of the wood or village was held strongly by a thick line of skirmishers, and an interior trench, or defence of some kind, was invariably provided. Thus, if the first line of defence was carried, the second helped the reserve in retaking the first ; in every case such posts were used not as the defence itself, but as adjuncts to the defence, and as means of holding certain important points while the troops acted on the offensive.

The following description of some of the posts is abridged chiefly from the Memoir on the defence of Paris by Viollet Le Duc, from which plates XXIV and XXIII have been copied.

The road to Versailles, the German head-quarters during the siege of Paris, passed across the neck of the peninsula formed by the Seine, having the village of St. Cloud on its eastern, and that of Bougival on its western side, the distance between being about 5,500 yards. The French fort Valerien prevented the Prussians advancing on Paris in this direction, and the Prussians were desirous to check any forward advance of the French towards Versailles. Some high wooded ground runs across this peninsula, gently falling towards Valerien, and steep towards Bougival, St. Cloud, and Villeneuve. (*Vide* Plate XXIV.) The French advanced posts were pushed out as far as house marked A. The Prussian advanced posts as far as the Buzanval Park, B and C. The Prussian line then extended from these places through Garches and Villeneuve. The French redoubt of Montretont. which had been abandoned, was occasionally used as an advanced post by the Prussians,

PLATE XXIV.

THE HEIGHTS OF ST CUCUFA AND CELLE ST CLOUD.

2771

PLATE XXIII

POST ON THE HEIGHTS OF RAINCY

Gardens, Woods and isolated houses some with enclosure walls

Scale of Mètres

Interior Area of the Plateau d. . .

Portion of Bondizel and Gournay Railway

Dir.n of St Denis

Dir.n of Montmartre

Dir.n of Fort Up . . .

Direction of the Railway of Strasbourg

but not always, and from its position appears to have been of little value to either side.

The Haras, an open eminence, formed the central work of the whole, and was the place where the reserves were posted. At one corner of it, D, a hole was broken, and covered with an epaulement, a long barricade, between the Haras and La Bergerie, was formed to take in flank any troops who, having carried the edge of the wood in the Bouzanval Park, should attempt to advance on the Haras, some guns were placed behind epaulements at F, for the same purpose. Small block-houses were placed at the corner of the Haras to give flank defence, and also as places where guards might be placed at all times. A small interior entrenchment, 1, was made in the Haras itself, to prevent its being carried by a rush. Three redoubts. XXX, were constructed to sweep the flat top of the hill. They were formed with a blockhouse in the interior and surrounded with an abattis. At Y Y two epaulements were made to cover the guns sweeping the road leading to Bougival, The outer wall of the Bouzanval Park was loopholed, as was also an interior wall, M N. Celle Saint Cloud was loopholed and barricaded. When the French attacked this position on the 19th January, they carried the first defence, the Bouzanval Park, but were stopped by the wall M N., past which they could not get. They endeavoured to turn it by an attack at the point O and the point R on its right and left. But neither attack succeeded, and both attack suffered greatly from the fire of the guns on the top of the hill.

It will be observed that the flanks of this position are open, and this fact allowed the Prussians to take the offensive from Bougival and the wood in front of it, threatening the right flank of the French troops engaged at R and in the wood about the wall M N.

The plan of these defences is well worthy of careful study; it will be seen that the first or advanced line being carried, there is a second line to support it, and that the position occupied is admirably adapted to the ground, advantage has been taken of the hedges, walls, and existing fences. Troops have not been so much placed in houses as used to defend long lines with skirmishers, thus checking the enemy, and offering a wide front of fire to his advance.

The trace of these works is dictated by an advanced knowledge of forti- **Viollet le Duc.** fication : the hand of an able officer of engineers is seen everywhere. The precautions dictated by prudence are still more numerous. Retreat is pointed out and provided for. In examining these works nothing is so evident as the constant forethought of the Prussian staff to husband their troops and never to compromise them for a trifling result.

Plate XXIII shows the system pursued on the heights of Rainey. The contour of the hill is carefully followed: the edge of the wood held and covered by abattis, and in all cases an inner line taken up to meet the enemy if he succeeds in carrying the first line. Such posts as those shown on Plates XXIV and XXIII are of course the work of time, but they are reproduced here to show the principles on which points of similar importance should be held. And it is manifest that the construction of all such defences must be subservient to a large development of fire, a provision for taking the offensive, and above all, such arrangements as shall enable the skirmishing line to be fed and supported from the rear, thus infusing into the defence the principles of the attack.

In preparing defences of this nature it is essential that the line of retreat of the troops be marked out, so that when the men fall back they may not interfere with the fire of those in rear of them : and it is further essential that distinct notices be clearly put up detailing the names of the various districts into which the defences are divided, and pointing out the nearest road to those districts. No amount of zeal, courage, devotion, or knowledge compensates for the neglect of such details.

Plate XXII. gives a sketch of Le Bourget at Paris as prepared for defence by the Prussians after its capture (described at page 219). This drawing is worthy of study, more especially the care taken to give each part of the defence a reserve in rear, and also the care taken to point out the exact position each detachment should occupy.

APPENDICES.

Page.

APPENDIX I.

Proposed alterations in the Tactical Formation of Infantry in Italy 224

APPENDIX II.

The Instructions of Major-General Crawford for Marches, as issued to the Light Division in the Peninsular War 235

APPENDIX III.

War Establishments of Infantry, Cavalry, Artillery, and Engineers 257

APPENDIX IV.

Table of Losses in various Great Battles.... 263

APPENDIX I.

PROPOSED ALTERATIONS IN THE TACTICAL FORMATIONS OF INFANTRY IN ITALY.

THE Italian infantry formations were laid down in 1869. The result of the war of 1870 has been to turn the attention of the Italian military authorities to tactical formations, and a committee was appointed to inquire into the whole subject; this committee has very recently concluded its labours, and nearly the whole of its recommendations have been introduced into the Italian army since the 1st May last. The report of this committee contains much useful matter: the following is a brief *précis* of the proposed Italian infantry tactics.

An Italian battalion is formed of four companies, each company of four subdivisions (so long as the company is not less than 128 men), each subdivision of two sections, each section of two squads. With a battalion at its full strength, each squad would be about 10 men. The company would be 160 men $= 10 \times 2 \times 2 \times 4$. With four companies, cadres, &c., the battalion would consequently be about 1,000 men, the squad being the first or elementary unit. The squad, working by itself, is commanded by a corporal, who leads it in front of the centre.

When two squads are put together to make a section the corporal's place is on the flanks of their respective squads, their section being commanded by a serjeant. When the two sections are put together to make a subdivision, the subdivision leader is on the right, the sectional commanders becoming serrefiles, but the corporals retain their position on the flanks of their squads at all times. There is no pivot flank, and both the sections in subdivision and the subdivisions in company may be inverted, whether standing in line or column.

Whether halted or on the march, the squads, sections, and subdivisions, at the word of command from their respective commanders, can open out to one, two, or three paces interval.

When not under fire, and indeed on all occasions when a battalion quarter-distance column would usually be formed, the Italian battalion moves in what may be termed a line of contiguous company columns; that is to say, each company is formed in column of subdivisions, with an interval of four paces between the companies, which interval is always preserved. (*Vide* Plate XXV.) It is evident that such a formation has some advantages as regards pliability and power of moving over rough ground. The new regulations fix 50 paces, in place of 20 paces as the interval between battalions in brigade. This peculiar battalion column is that formation best adapted to an object the Italians keep in view—working by the wing instead of the line, or, in other words, pushing the flank or wing of the company to the front, the object being to prevent mixing up companies. (*Vide* page 88.)

The following is an extract:—

" Henceforward we must admit as an indisputable fact that no body of men can remain in close order under the efficacious fire of an enemy's infantry without being exposed to great losses.

"The extended order, which allows an advance to be made with comparatively moderate losses, has, at the present moment, become of so much importance that it must be looked on no longer as a means for preparing for the fighting in close order, but as the normal and only means of fighting both on the offensive and defensive.

"Without seeking to develop the principles upon which large masses of troops are divided into two or more lines, principles which have not varied on account of the introduction of modern arms, all that is requisite here is to point out that for the troops of the first line who come under an effective infantry fire it is requisite that there should be some normal formation.

"Such a normal formation should not be stereotyped, but it ought to lay down such a distribution of the force with reference to the space occupied or disposable, as may allow the greatest possible development of extended fighting, and yet be sufficiently elastic to adapt itself in all cases to the ground and circumstances. The object therefore in view is to find the best normal formation for a battalion fighting in the first line when acting in concert with other troops.

"The condition of working beside other battalions, also in first line, limits the front that the battalion can and ought to occupy. For, viewing the way troops are engaged, there should be no great difference between the action of a battalion working by itself and with others. What characterizes fighting at the present day is the general battle resolves itself into a number of partial battles, having for their object the attack or defence of definite points, such as woods, houses, &c., so that really each battalion in first line, in a general action, has usually its definite object pretty much as if it were working by itself.

"As we must never lose sight of the principle that a passive defence can produce no useful result, and that it ought to be combined with, or at least followed by the offensive, it results that the normal order of fighting should be such as is best adapted to the offensive.

"In order that an offensive may be successful it must be handled with energy, and with the greatest amount of force possible. Successive efforts almost always fail. They break down the *morale* of the troops making them, and confirm and improve that of their opponents.

"When troops are acting offensively, generally they are ignorant of the strength of the enemy with whom they are dealing; and it is always better to attack with too strong a force than to expose portions to be beaten in succession.

"Carry these views to their legitimate conclusion. It would seem at the first blush that the whole battalion should be engaged at once; but when it is considered that the front occupied by a battalion in the front line is usually equal to that it would occupy if it were deployed into line, and as it is requisite to fight in extended order, it follows that the battalion must be divided into two portions, one intended to be used at once, the other to be used subsequently; one to prepare, the other to complete the action. What should be the proportion between these two portions? Let us suppose the front of the battalion covered by a chain of skirmishers; granting that each skirmisher, to use freely and effectually his arms, requires a space of one and a-half yards; the battalion having an average strength of 320 files present. On the field of battle one company is needed to cover this front. Is it, how-

Q

ever, requisite to deploy all the company as skirmishers at the beginning of the action ? In the first moments it is not necessary to have a fire of the greatest intensity ; success is not so much the object at first as feeling the enemy, to compel him to show himself, and to get acquainted with the ground and the state of affairs.

" For this object a company seems too large a force; extending all as skirmishers produces useless loss. An error in the direction at this stage is very difficult subsequently to rectify. It will, therefore, be better at this stage to have a moderate fire, and increase it as wanted. The company should then be divided into two equal portions, the one intended to reinforce the other when required ; the first will be termed the chain, the second the reinforcements.

" Half a company will then form the chain, half a company the reinforcements. It should be remembered that the question at first, is only one of quantity, the method of dividing the tactical elements of the battalion will follow further on. What should be the distance between the chain and its reinforcements ? It ought to be such that the reinforcements should be able to support the chain effectually. Placing them too far off will violate the principle that efforts should not be successive, but that the whole force from the beginning should be in action ; if too near they will suffer from the fire directed against the chain. Let us assume the chain 300 to 400 yards from the enemy's skirmishers. The ground behind the chain swept by bullets, even with the lowest trajectory, will not exceed 60 yards; the reinforcements should, therefore, be placed about 100 yards in rear. They will thus be supports near enough to form one body with the chain, sufficiently far off to escape the fire directed against it. As regards fire aimed against them, they may seek to preserve themselves from it, either by taking an extended formation by laying down, or by the folds in the ground. As for unaimed fire, it is hopeless to try and guard against it. Every commandant of a subdivision who sees his men too much exposed to fire of this kind, must, as soon as possible, change his position.

" The second portion of the battalion, intended not to act at first, and of which the strength is not yet given, we will call the main body. In order not to enforce a passive attitude on it when suffering useless loss, the main body should at the beginning of the action be kept as much as possible out of fire. With this object it should be placed at 700 to 800 yards from the enemy's skirmishers. But, as we have supposed 300 to 400 yards between the enemy's skirmishers and the chain, 100 yards between the chain and the reinforcements ; the distance between the reinforcements and the main body will be about 300 yards. This distance alone is sufficient to point out the advisability of interpolating a fresh line between the reinforcements and the main body, to keep up the connection; but there are still other reasons for this interpolation. It has been pointed out that in lieu of successive efforts, the greatest possible number should be engaged at once. It has been pointed out that to proportion this greatest possible number to the disposable front, and at the same time leave the skirmishers room sufficient to use their arms, a company is all that can be employed in the first line. It has been further pointed out that, at the beginning of the action, this company must be divided into two lines—the chain and the reinforcements. It is easy to understand that the reinforcements being intended to move up into the line of fire, it is requisite to have in rear other bodies to support, both morally and materially, the chain, and fill up its gaps; and direct movements to a flank, seeing the impossibility in most cases with modern arms of making a front attack; lastly, to keep up a connection between the advanced troops and the main body. This interpolated line is called the line of supports.

" What should be its force? To fulfil all its functions, it does not seem advisable to make it of less strength than the chain and reinforcements taken together, or one company.

" As regards its distance from the reinforcements and the main body, it has been fixed by what we have previously said. The supports ought to hold an intermediate position between the reinforcements and the main body, or 150 yards, from each.

" At this distance the supports may be sufficiently covered from the enemy's fire to be able to send effectual assistance to troops placed in advance, and also maintain a connection with those in rear. It should be observed once for all that the intervals given are those that would be given on level open ground. In a close country they may be diminished; but in every case they are limited by the necessity of having the lines sufficiently near to mutually support one another, and sufficiently distant that any retrograde movement of the first may not disorganize the second.

" From the preceding it follows that, taking into consideration the front occupied by a battalion, the division of the battalion into two portions, and the sub-division of the first of these portions into three lines, and the functions assigned to each of these lines, that the proper division of the battalion will be as follows:—

$$
\begin{array}{l}
\text{1 company as chain and reinforcements,} \\
\text{1 company as supports,} \\
\text{2 companies as main body;}
\end{array}
$$

in other words: $\frac{1}{8}$ of the battalion .. .. chain,
$\quad\quad\quad\quad\frac{1}{8}$,, ,, ... reinforcements,
$\quad\quad\quad\quad\frac{1}{4}$,, ,, ... supports,
$\quad\quad\quad\quad\frac{1}{2}$,, ,, ... main body:

these proportions being definitely laid down.

" The most convenient means of working the various companies in the different lines will be as follows:—

" It has been said that the strength of one company is required for the chain and reinforcements, and the strength of another company for the supports. Whether it is better to use one entire company for chain and reinforcements, and another entire company for supports, or to cover the front by portions of the two companies? each portion of the chain having behind it reinforcements and supports belonging to the same company; or, in other words, is it better to work the two companies in line or from a flank?

" The formation from a flank seems the preferable for several reasons.

" It has been seen that the average front of a battalion on a war footing is about 300 yards, it will consequently be difficult, not to say impossible, for a single captain to overlook so wide a front, while by dividing it between two captains, they can better perform the duty assigned to them, and at the same time preserve all the requisite freedom of action, limited only by having to work in concert with

Q 2

troops beside them, and conformably with the instructions of the commandant of the battalion.

"Also, as it must be acknowledged, that it is impossible for any body of troops to remain in close order under the effective fire of infantry, it being admitted that the normal method of fighting can only be individual order, it follows that the chain, the reinforcements, and the supports must get mixed up. When the formation is linear, this mingling of different companies is very inconvenient; when formed from a flank, the mingling of men of various sections but of the same company is less objectionable, and easier to put to rights.

" This formation from a flank, in preference to that from a line, must be applied not only to a battalion, but also to the companies as also to the largest tactical bodies, always with the view of aiding the commandants of the fractions in the duties of the action in front, and reducing as much as possible the mingling of the lines.

" It follows from what has gone before that the normal order of fighting of a battalion in first line, acting in conjunction with other battalions, is the following:—

" Two companies should be pushed forward, termed advanced companies, or first line companies, the others being termed companies of the main body. The first are intended to prepare and develop the attack ; the second to clinch it, as will be shown hereafter.

" The two advanced companies, each divided into chain, reinforcements, and supports, will work in one or other of the normal forms established for a company in a following chapter, according to the ground and circumstances* and the object in view. It is further requisite to deal with a last question—the means of obviating as much as possible the results of mingling the three lines. In other words, what should be the disposition of the chain and reinforcements in the same company ? In accordance with the division of the battalion, it follows that each of the leading companies will have one-fourth of its strength in the chain, one-fourth in the reinforce line, and one-half in support; that is to say, there will be one subdivision in the chain, one in the reinforce line, and two in support. As regards the subdivision intended to form the chain and supports, the principle of working from a flank must be applied in preference to that of working in line, so that two sections of two different subdivisions may be extended in the chain at the beginning of the action, and the two other twin sections shall be in rear ready to be extended when required.

" As the force requisite to cover the front has been divided into two portions—chain and reinforce line, if a fixed interval of a yard and a half is given between each skirmisher, the chain will only cover one-half the front of the battalion, the other half being that left to be covered by the reinforce line afterwards. Should, therefore, more space be given between the skirmishers, so that the whole front may be covered ? or, Should they only occupy one-half the front, leaving between them the intervals to be filled up by the reinforcements when extended ? If the chain cover all the front when it is thickened from the reinforce line, either the men from the latter line must be interpolated between the others, or the sections of the chain must be made to close in, and so leave room in the intervals for the reinforcements to extend.

---

* Not translated.

PLATE XXV.

Normal formation for attack of an Italian Brigade of 6 Battalions or 2 Regiments.

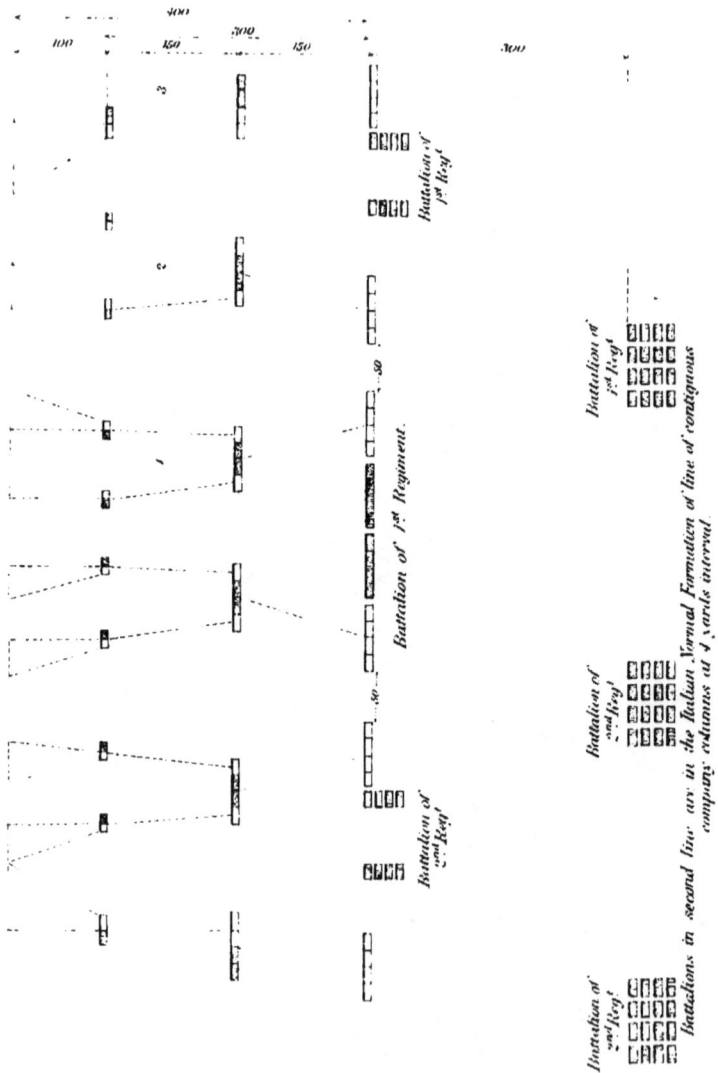

An Italian Battalion on a war footing consists of, independent
of Officers, Non Comissioned Officers and Staff 4 Companies.-
16 Sub Divisions - 32 Sections - 64 Squads - 640 Men, each of
these fractions has a special commander.

" The first method produces a mingling of men together from the first, and thus renders the advantage of forming the subdivisions from a flank illusory. The second would be impracticable under fire, and would produce disorder and considerable loss. It would also be impossible to ask men who had obtained cover to give it up to others. The portions of chain must consequently keep spaces between them, where the reinforcements may be placed. These gaps in the line of fire will not at first cause any inconvenience; they are small, and are covered by the cross fire of the skirmishers on each side.

" It has been clearly shown how the battalion and each of the advanced companies are divided. The front of each battalion is divided and sub-divided so that each body has a limited zone of action, in which it works under the orders of its own leader; each being able within his own sphere, to act on his own initiative, and this must be carried down to even a single man. However limited this last may be, it is not without importance. The great principle of extended order, is not so much a question of loose formation as it is of the substitution of individual and intelligent action, in place of passive, blind, and mechanical obedience, and of the necessity for clear, definite, detailed personal instruction of the soldier, teaching him how to obtain the greatest advantage from his arms and the ground, in order to compensate for the far greater difficulties encountered by the superior leaders. Also the necessity of maintaining very strictly, especially in very small portions, the bonds of tactics and discipline. In action, the section forms the smallest of the elements into which the extended order divides itself, whilst the squad forms the smallest tactical element—two squads acting always under one head. An endeavour should be made to keep the section intact at all times; if this cannot be done for the section, it should be always done for the squad.

" The best method of obviating as much as possible the bad consequences of mingling men, and the dissolving action of modern fighting, is the frequent exercise of soldiers in peace to rapidly reform the subdivision to which they belong, and in case this cannot be done, to put themselves under the orders of the nearest officer or non-commissioned officer, even if they belong to other subdivisions or corps.

" Conversely, it should be required that at all manœuvres the officers or non-commissioned officers should assemble dispersed men as quickly as possible, leading them into action, and placing them under the orders of the nearest superior."

The above extract from the report of the Committee is worthy of study; but before drawing attention to some peculiarities, it will be well to enter a little more into the Italian formations.

Plate XXV gives the formation of an Italian brigade, consisting of six battalions, for attack, showing the smallest tactical element.

In general, the squad when deployed as skirmishers, has its men formed in single rank, the front rank men placing themselves according to the ground, but never more than three paces apart, the rear rank men coming up on their left. But, if requisite, the whole squad, consisting (normally) of 10 men, may be formed in a knot or group under its own leader, either two deep or in a rallying group, or in such a way as shall best sweep the ground with fire.

Skirmishers are ordered to fire only when halted, and never as they advance; men are not to fire when they do not see the enemy. Under fire all movements are made at the double, in a succession of rushes of not more than 60 yards, in order that the men may not be out of breath; when cover is available it is to be used; on open level ground the men throw themselves down.

The two squads of a section are never separated, and always support one another. If both are extended as skirmishers they move in échelon, one supporting and covering the other. If one squad is acting as reinforcement, while the other skirmishes, the reinforce squad may be formed two deep, or with open files, or extended with one or two paces between the files, or extended in single rank with a pace or two between the files, according to the ground and the circumstances of each case.

The subdivision may be extended altogether as skirmishers, or with one section as skirmishers the other in the reinforce line; or, better still, with each section having a squad as skirmishers and a squad in the reinforce line.

As regards the company, its normal formation of attack includes the three lines, chain, reinforcement, and support, which may be formed in three different ways as shown on Plate XXV (1, 2, 3).

(1.) Two subdivisions being in support, two others extended each a section to the right or left, keeping each a section in the reinforce line.

(2.) The two sections extended touching one another, always excepting the regulation interval of four paces: the two squads are then behind the two wings of the chain.

(3.) One subdivision extended, one the reinforce line and two in support, all being in échelon.

It is laid down that it is far better to work so as to suit the ground, than seek to maintain regular and symmetrical formations.

The line of skirmishers has, it will be observed, gaps in it, to be afterwards filled up by the reinforce line. The inversion of the sections in a subdivision, or of the squads in a section, is not considered of any consequence, but the mingling of men of different squads or sections is to be carefully guarded against. One of the chief things recommended is to leave to every person, down to the corporals of squads, complete liberty within certain limits.

In considering the proposals here made, it will be observed that the whole formation of the battalion is based on the squad of 10 men commanded by a corporal. In an Italian battalion there are 116 distinct commands, viz., 64 squads, 32 sections, 16 subdivisions, and 4 companies, or 116 officers and non-commissioned officers. If any of these commanders are killed, the confusion must be great. Suppose a captain killed, a squad leader has to lead the section, a section leader a subdivision, a subdivision leader a company. The division is carried too far. The ultimate unit into which any body of men is divided should be based on the reasons given at page 3. This complicated subdivision is probably caused by the introduction of the large German company into the Italian army, which with a two-deep* formation cannot be commanded by one man, and when the company is extended the difficulty is of course increased.

There must be a limit to subdivision, and there must be some point at which the commander *directly commands* his subordinate officers, who replace him, if he becomes *hors de combat*. The point where

---

* The Germans stand three deep.

division should cease is undoubtedly the company, and for the reason stated.

The opinion expressed by the Italian Committee, that the skirmishers in front of a battalion, 280 to 300 yards, occupy too long a line to be commanded by one man, and the result following on the introduction of the large company into Italy, viz., the cutting up the company into a number of distinct portions in order to get it in hand, are confirmatory of what has been already stated at page 98, of the advantages of the small company; two small companies covering the front of the battalion. It cannot be too often repeated that the large company is in some respects the weak point of the Prussian system, and that a double company formation gives all the advantages (there undoubtedly are some) of the large company without its glaring disadvantages. The advantages of the reinforce line are very questionable, it makes a fresh division without any apparent reason. From the moment that troops are engaged there must, as we have already seen, be a sufficient number of men in the skirmishing line. Acknowledging the truth of the principle " that the offensive should be taken as energetically and with the greater force possible, and that successive efforts usually fail " in theory, it would seem that it is neglected in practice. Suppose the skirmishers meet an enemy with a number of skirmishers double what they bring up. The reinforce line must then come forward, and before it can come up the skirmishers will have suffered much, and the arrival of the reinforcements will not place them in as good a position as if they had been originally in large numbers. The true reason for this reinforce line is apparently to link the supports to the skirmishers, and to avoid splitting the company, the captain's command, into two portions, by too great a distance.

The space left between the sections extended for the reinforce sections to come up would be very difficult to preserve; without the most accurate leading, these spaces would be lost, and then the men must mingle with the others.

Another great objection to such a system is, the captain has his work scattered; he has to lead the skirmishers, order up the reinforce line, and direct the supports, his command being 250 yards deep from front to rear, and about 150 yards wide.

The proposals to work from a flank have been already discussed, the only object in so doing is to prevent mixing the men of various companies together. With large companies this evil is much greater than when they are small, but the evil cannot be avoided, and anyone who looks at the sketch of how it is proposed to work an Italian battalion, will acknowledge that if it advance under heavy fire over rough ground, the men, despite all the complicated arrangements, would get mingled; it is far better to train the men to act when this emergency takes place than to attempt to prevent it. Indeed the Italian instructions provide for this, thereby acknowledging that its prevention is impossible.

The principles laid down are clearly correct, but the method in which those principles are worked out appears questionable.

No formation, however symmetrical, has a chance of success that is not simple, and that will bear that mingling of men that is incident, and must be incident, to every advance over rough ground, especially if the advance is in extended order.

It has been stated in the note to page 88 that this method of skirmishing, from a flank or by sections, meets with much support. The foregoing extract from the report of the Italian Committee puts the case clearly. The following extract from the best and most recent German authority on the subject is worthy of attention :—

Scherff.
(Translated
by Graham.)

"The first or skirmishing line has in the supposed case of a battalion with an assigned object of attack, most undoubtedly a task complete in itself and with one object in view. This task consists in endeavouring to overwhelm with its fire from a front not originally exceeding 300 yards some always smaller portion of the enemy's position which has been pointed out, and thus to shake the defenders before the onslaught of the main body.

"The point which the latter is to force should be first quite clearly made out, the most favorable spot being chosen, after you have approached pretty close to the enemy's position.

"Upon this point the fire will then be concentrated as much as possible, which, with a front of only 300 yards may, with our present arms, proceed from the whole line, even if the selected point chance to be opposite one flank.

"It is evident that all this may be attained most successfully by unity of command, and that on the other hand considerations of space by no means render this unity impossible. The advantages of this unity of command have indeed misled French tacticians into wishing to break up a whole battalion into skirmishers, when the attacking force consists of several battalions. This is carrying it too far, and the arrangement must break down, because no one separate objective can be assigned to such a line. Let us now compare the case of a skirmishing line composed of one company with that of one made up of two halves of different companies (of course we suppose the number of skirmishers in both cases to be equal). In the latter case, we see the line led by two independent commanders of equal powers, in close proximity to one another. This must, of necessity, produce greater difficulties in the way of command than when, as in the former case, the skirmishers are all under one leader. When it comes to advancing by successive fractions, the full value, will not be got out of the two half companies as it will out of the one company accustomed to the signs and signals of its officers. Moreover, the opinions of the two commanders as to the moment at which it is advisable to extend the full number of skirmishers, or as to when it is necessary to ask for further reinforcements from the supports, will agree no better than will their views as to the time when the line should, according to the existing state of affairs, commence the rapid independent fire, which must be continued to the very moment of the final rush.

"As we must understand the effective range for this fire to extend from 200 to nearly 400 paces, it is evident that the line of skirmishers runs the risk of partial checks from the different appreciation of the proper distance from which to commence rapid firing, which may be formed by the two officers, each of whom will only direct his attention to the other, so far as to avoid being left behind by him. Now these partial checks are the worst things that can happen in the preparatory stage.

"Besides, it by no means follows that the two leaders will agree as to the best point for forcing the enemy's line ; hence, there will not be the concentration of fire which is so requisite for the success of the whole enterprise, for we should prefer the less well-chosen point of attack which has been well fired upon, to one better selected but less well fired upon.

"Again ; whilst a skirmishing line composed of one entire company gravitates naturally to its centre, because the one chief will, and must, have influence enough over his lieutenants to control their perhaps conflicting aims, it is not a mere matter of fancy to affirm that two separate companies moving side by side will have a decidedly centrifugal tendency, and (for we must always make allowance for human nature) will be sure to act accordingly in reality, in spite of all theory.

"It will not be a sufficient answer to reply that the battalion commander will be on the spot to remedy all these drawbacks arising from the subdivision of units. It is the business of this officer to conduct the entire attack ; the most important part of his duty is to point out the proper direction for the main body to follow, as on this the success of his battalion will depend. If he undertakes in person the guidance of his advanced companies, those of his main body will be very likely to take a wrong direction, even to get quite out of hand (and this is no idle supposition, but an event of which there have been numerous examples in war). He must, therefore, confine himself to assigning a general direction to the advanced line, whilst he certainly will do well to leave the execution of details to one subordinate rather than to two. Then, again, the other available remedy, namely, that of giving the senior of the two captains in the front line the command of both companies, seems insufficient, on account of the uncertain nature of such an ill-defined office—an office inconsistent with the custom of the service, which, indeed, admits of an officer taking over the command of those of like rank in rear, whilst the chief reconnoitres in front, but is very much opposed to the same being done under the actual pressure of danger and emergency.

"There could be, neither in theory nor in practice, any fair argument to oppose to the formation of the skirmishing line under one sole leader, were it not for the second phase of the question, that of *reinforcements*.

" If you had said to a tactician of the time of Frederick the Great, 'It must come to this : every single foot soldier will shoot whenever he chooses and has the chance ; and the battalion, company, or platoon volley will be a thing of the past'—he would only shrug his shoulders with contempt for such ' an awful state of disorder.'

" Nevertheless, the time has come when the army, without disowning its old traditions, has got on very well in this very state of disorder.

" May not the same thing occur in the matter of mixing up tactical units ? It is an undoubted fact that the practice of doubling in files out of their proper order (a greater innovation when made than any we have now to attempt) has already been adopted as a matter of regulation in the army, has been employed by generals with war experience, and carried out by our recruits twenty, thirty, forty years ago. Cannot our present recruits also do as much ? To this it will be answered that the practice was abolished because impracticable ; and no one will deny that this was at the time a wise measure, because in their then existing state of development, elementary tactics did not require the formation.

" It is no longer possible for skirmishers within effective range of the enemy, and in face of the breech-loader, to take ground to a flank, or to diminish their intervals, without suffering fearful loss, hence nothing is left for a reinforcement coming up from the rear but to double itself up with the skirmishers.

" But if it be once established that we cannot avoid the practice either on a large or on a small scale, it would appear well to accept it frankly.

" As the proverb has it, a danger once recognised ceases to be a danger. Well, then, on the same principle, *regulated* disorder ceases to be *disorder*. In the question now before us we do not then escape this conclusion—we must break up tactical formations either by mixing up the divisions of the same company together or by mixing one company up with another. We maintain that the latter measure is only in appearance worse than the former. If once the original distribution of troops in line of battle is disturbed, it does not much matter, during the heat of action (and we are only treating of that period) by whom the disturbance is occasioned. When such mixing up of men occurs in action, in these moments of danger and of excitement, strained to the highest pitch, personal influence on its own merits will affect the soldier more than the influence of his immediate superior merely as such. He will follow the lead of the brave man, the hero, whether belonging to his own company or not.

" It is in such moments that a superior officer, often entirely unknown to the men about him, will carry them away with him, and that lieutenants have gained their spurs with the aid of men whom they never came across before or since. In such moments, we assert, it does not matter whether the original order is disturbed by men of the same or of another body. But when the fight is over, when it is advisable to restore the original order of things after the momentary disorder, this will be more quickly accomplished if only two units are in question instead of the fractions of one unit, for every soldier knows his own company : thus officers and non-commissioned officers quickly find out the men of their company in the crowd. But many a man may forget to which division (zug) he happens to be attached on the particular day, and the officer who knows the whole company by sight cannot be expected to remember whether John Smith forms part of his division on this occasion.

APPENDIX II.

THE INSTRUCTIONS OF MAJOR-GENERAL CRAWFORD FOR MARCHES, AS ISSUED TO THE LIGHT DIVISION IN THE PENINSULAR WAR.

STANDING ORDERS.

SECTION I.

Preparations for the March.

1. All sounds preparatory to turning out and marching will commence at the quarters of the brigade-major, and be immediately repeated by the orderly bugles attending on the officers commanding regiments.

2. As soon as possible after the first sound, all the buglers are to assemble at the quarters of the commanding officers of regiments, from whence all the other sounds will be repeated.

3. On ordinary occasions, the first horn will sound one hour and a-half before the time of marching, upon which the non-commissioned officers must take care that the squads dress and accoutre, and the baggage, both private and regimental, must be packed and made ready for putting on the horses and mules.

4. In the interval between the first and second horn, the subalterns, in succession, will visit the whole company, in order to see that the non-commissioned officers are doing their duty. The baggage must be loaded on the horses or mules at least 10 minutes before the second horn sounds.

5. The second horn, or rouse, will sound one hour after the first, upon which the companies will turn out on their respective parades.

6. The third horn, or assembly, will sound a quarter of an hour after the second, upon which the captains will march their companies to the regimental parades, and send the baggage to the place appointed by the commanding officer. No officer's servant, or any but the regular bâtman, are to be suffered to be with it after the sounding of the third horn.

7. The fourth horn, or advance, will sound a quarter of an hour after the third, upon which the battalions will march off to the place of the assembly of the brigade.

8. On ordinary marches, when not near the enemy, there will be one subaltern per regiment in charge of the baggage; but when near the enemy, the staff-sergeants who actually march with the baggage, will have charge of that belonging to each regiment, and the assistant provost will have charge of the whole.

9. The quartermaster or, in his absence, the officer who marches in charge of the baggage, will assemble it on the regimental parade at the hour appointed previous to the march, and will conduct it from thence to the place assigned by the assistant quartermaster-general, for the assembly of the baggage of the brigade.

10. If any batman do not come at the proper time to the place of assembly of the regimental baggage, it must be reported by the quartermaster to the commanding officer of the regiment, who will hold officers of companies responsible for it.

11. All guards and inlying picquets will join their companies on the sounding of the second horn.

12. The outlying picquets will receive orders according to circumstances, with respect to the time of their quitting their posts, and whether they are to form the advance or rear-guard of the column, or are to join their respective regiments.

13. It will be considered as a standing order, when not near the enemy, that each regiment will be preceded by two officers for the purpose of taking up quarters; one of whom will march 24 hours before the regiment, and on his arrival will receive the necessary information from the assistant quartermaster-general, or from the quartermaster of the regiment preceding that to which he belongs. The other officer will march the same day as the regiment does, but sufficiently early to arrive at 10 o'clock in the forenoon, when he will have the quarters pointed out by the officer who went on the day before, and who, after having done this, will proceed to the next station.

14. The camp colour men—viz., one man per company, under the command of the quartermaster-serjeants of each regiment, and one officer per brigade—will assemble at the brigade-major's quarters every morning on the sounding of the first horn, viz., one hour and a-half before the hour appointed for the march of the brigade.

15. The officer in charge of these parties will march them in perfect order, and as expeditiously as possible, to the next station, where he will find the officer gone forward with the assistant quartermaster-general, and, after marking out the quarters of each company, he will take care that each party shall remain together until the regiment arrives.

16. The commissary and the cattle, with two butchers per regiment, under charge of the commissary's storekeeper, will, when it is possible, be one march ahead of the brigade. Thus, if the brigade marches on the 15th, the commissariat will be sent forward on the 14th, and either that evening, or early in the morning of the 15th, the meat will be slaughtered, and all the provisions will be in perfect readiness to be delivered over to the quartermasters before they arrive.

17. The quartermasters will march two or three hours before the brigade, or, if possible, the preceding evening. They will ride on as fast as they can, and as soon as they arrive, which will be early in the forenoon, the commissary's storekeeper, butchers, and cattle will proceed to the next station.

18. When the regiments march separately, the quartermaster-serjeants must be sent forward with the cattle and butchers.

19. One of the first duties of officers commanding regiments on arrival in camp or quarters is to cause the communication from the position or quarters of the regiment to all the principal roads by which the brigade may possibly march to be thoroughly examined, and all obstacles removed, in order that each regiment, without the assistance of a guide, and without delay may be able to move in the night, if required, to whatever road in the vicinity of the camp or quarters may be pointed out for the assembly of the division.

20. The number of guides usually required will be six; namely, one mounted guide to attend the commanding officer of the division, one to march at the head of the column, one for the baggage, and three for the sick ; namely, one for each of the divisions as directed in the 6th Article of the Second Section.

21. These guides will be assembled at the appointed hour at the quarters of the assistant quartermaster-general, and by him sent to their stations and delivered over to the proper officers, for which as well as for other purposes, the assistant quartermaster-general will be furnished with such a number of steady orderlies as he may require from the brigade-major or adjutants.

SECTION II.

Of the March

ARTICLE I.

Stations of Officers.

1. All officers are to remain constantly in their stations during the march.

2. The majors are to march in rear of their respective wings ; namely, the first major in rear of the right, and the second major in rear of the left wing; if there is only one major his post is in rear of the regiment.

3. The captains or officers commanding companies are to march in rear of their companies.

4. Commanding officers of battalions, assisted by their adjutants, will move from one part to another as occasion may require their presence for the preservation of order, and particularly for the prevention of unnecessary defiling.

5. In like manner, the majors and commanding officers of companies will quit their habitual stations when their presence is required in any other part of their wings or companies, but will return to them as soon as the purpose for which they quitted them shall be effected.

6. All staff officers, officers of engineers, &c., attached to the division will constantly march at the head of the infantry of the division.

ARTICLE II.

Marching—Silence—Marching at Ease—Halt during the March— Forming up after the March.

1. On all occasions of marching out of camp or quarters, or of moving after a regular halt upon the march, the battalions are to march

off by word of command (and with music, unless particularly ordered to the contrary).

2. The men must be perfectly silent, dress, and keep the step just the same as when manœuvring on a field-day, until the word " March at ease " is given by the commanding officer of the battalion and repeated by the captains.

3. All words of command addressed to men marching at ease must be preceded by the word " Attention," upon which the men will slope their arms, and take up the step, and the most perfect order and silence must be resumed and enforced until the word is given to march at ease.

4. The words " Attention " and " March at ease " coming from the commanding officer of the battalion must be repeated by the officers commanding companies, who, in doing so, must look to the rear, and speak loud enough to be heard distinctly at least by the officer at the head of the company in his rear.

5. When marching at ease the ranks may be opened and the files loosened; but each rank, section, or division must be kept perfectly distinct, and every man must remain exactly in his place.

6. When, at the end of a march, it happens that a line is to be taken up by successive formation, each company may slope arms as soon as formed by word of command from its own officer ; but the companies must not order arms or stand at ease until they are directed to do so by the commanding officer of the battalion, which will not be done until the whole is formed.

7. When either of the majors or officers commanding companies want to pass any notice to the commanding officer of the battalion, or to any other company or section, or to direct the men to keep to the right or left, in order to allow mounted officers to pass through the column, the word must be passed by the officers or serjeants only.

8. Whenever the bugles sound the halt, the head of each battalion is to stand fast, even although it should not be closed up to the preceding one, but the following divisions of each battalion must close up to half or quarter distance, unless the column is entering an alignment or making any other movement preparatory to a formation to a flank.

9. When it is intended that the whole brigade should close up, the head will be halted without sound of bugle, and the word of command " Quarter, half, or wheeling distance " will be passed from front to rear ; and when the rear is closed up, the bugle of the rear battalion will sound the halt as a notice.

10. When the brigade is marching independently of any other, the officer commanding the leading regiment will sound the halt half an hour after it marches off, and afterwards once an hour ; each halt to last at least five minutes. After the men have piled arms, if a longer halt is thought necessary, the commanding officer of the brigade will direct it.

Article III.

Defiling to be Prevented, or Executed by Word of Command.

1. No battalion, company, or section is at any time to defile or diminish its front, or attempt in any way to avoid any bad spot in the road unless the preceding battalion or company has done so.

2. Whenever defiling is necessary, it must be executed with order

and precision, as in manœuvring at a field day, by the proper word of
command, preceded by the word " Attention."

3. When a battalion or company comes to a defile, stream, or bad
place of the road, where it might be more convenient for the men to
defile individually, the officers must be on the alert, and call out to the
men to keep their ranks or sections.

4. Any man who, for the sake of avoiding water or other bad
places, or for any other reason, presumes to step on one side or quit
his proper place in the ranks, must be confined.

5. Whenever a stream, ditch, bank, or other obstacle is to be
crossed, it will be generally found that, instead of defiling or diminish-
ing the front, the very contrary should be done, not only by causing
the files of each section to extend gradually before they arrive at the
ditch or obstacle, but even by forming subdivisions or companies.

6. When a bad place is to be passed, the majors and captains will
go to the head of their respective wings and companies to see it
regularly executed, if ordered. They will remain at the spot till the
whole of their wings or companies have passed, and then will resume
their stations in the rear.

7. It is proved that the defiling of one battalion on the march,
even if done with as much promptitude as is practicable on such
occasions, will cause a delay of 10 minutes, one such obstacle, if not
passed without defiling, would therefore delay the brigade half an
hour, and, in the winter, when obstacles of this kind are frequent and
the days are short, a brigade which is constantly defiling without
cause, will arrive at its quarters in the dark, whereas, if it had performed the march regularly, it would have got in by good time.

8. This order respecting defiling is, therefore, as much calculated
to provide for the personal ease and comfort of the men, as it is essential for the due performance of the movements of an army.

Article IV.

Stragglers.

1. No man is to remain behind, or quit the ranks for any purpose
or on any account whatever without permission from the captain or
officer commanding the company.

2. Officers are never to give permission to any man to quit the
ranks, excepting on account of illness, or for the purpose of easing
themselves, or for some other absolutely necessary purpose.

3. The officers must be particularly attentive to prevent the men
from going out of the ranks for water; when this is required, the
battalion or brigade will be halted.

4. Every man who is obliged to quit the ranks on account of
illness must apply to the commanding officer of the company for permission to remain behind and for a ticket or certificate, which will
be given him if the officer thinks it necessary that he should remain
behind.

5. Those tickets are to be made out in the following form, viz. :—

" The bearer marched off with the regiment, but was unable to
keep up with it.

" (Signed)

" *Commanding Company.*"

6. These tickets must be taken back by the orderly serjeants as soon as the men who fall out rejoin their companies.

7. Officers commanding companies are always to be provided with a sufficient number of tickets, which must be dated on the back before the regiment marches off, and the date scratched out after the march.

8. The captain, or the serjeant walking by his side, must write down the name of every man to whom he gives a ticket or certificate.

9. Men who obtain permission to fall out for a short time to ease themselves, or for any other cause than illness, are not to receive tickets, but they must invariably leave their packs and arms to be carried by the section they belong to until they return.

10. Every man who quits the ranks without leave of the commanding officer of the company without having received a ticket, or having left his arms and pack with his company, as the case may be, must be brought to a court-martial. If ill, he must be tried as soon as recovered; but if not ill, it must be done on the drum-head as soon as the regiment arrives, or as the man comes up, and the punishment inflicted forthwith.

11. The only case in which any man is to escape punishment who falls out under the plea of illness without taking a ticket is that, which can rarely happen, of the illness being so sudden and severe as to deprive him of the power of asking for a ticket.

12. If the orders of No. 10 were not regularly observed and enforced, illness would always be pleaded, and the whole of these regulations for the prevention of straggling would be rendered abortive; and, on the other hand, there can be no cruelty in requiring of the man who is really ill that he should ask his officer for a ticket.

13. No part of the punishment awarded by a court-martial for being absent without leave on the march is to be remitted without permission of the commanding officer of the brigade.

ARTICLE V.

Hurry and Stepping Out to be Prevented.

1. It is of the greatest importance that the men should not on any account be hurried on the march; they are to be instructed that they are never to step out beyond the regular step, still less to run, unless by word of command.

2. When the proper distances of companies or sections cannot be preserved without an alteration in the step, it must always be effected by making the head of each battalion or company step short, instead of allowing the others to step out.

3. After passing an obstacle or ascending a hill, the leading company of each battalion will step short until the last company of the battalion has passed and closed up, although a large interval should be thereby occasioned between it and the preceding battalion.

4. The leading section of each company will also step short until the last section has passed and closed up, even although a large interval should take place between that and the preceding battalion.

5. When the head of a company—suppose No. 4—cannot keep up without overstepping or leaving its own sections at too great a distance, the officer commanding must call out "No. 4 cannot keep up," which

must be repeated aloud by the serjeants on the flanks of the leading sections of the companies in front of No. 4, until it comes up to the commanding officer, who will of course shorten the step at the head of the column, unless he perceives that some obstacle, ascent, or difficult ground in front will give time to No 4 to close up in the meantime. No. 4, if no answer is returned to the notice of its having increased distance, will continue at the regular step.

6. In like manner, if the head of a battalion cannot keep up with the preceding battalion, the commanding officer will forward the notice to the head of the brigade, detaching files at the same time to preserve the communication with the preceding battalion.

7. When obstacles which delay the march are frequent, it may be desirable or necessary in order to avoid loss of time, that each company after passing, should march on at the usual rate without shortening its step, as the following company may overtake it at the next obstacle or ascent; but it can never be necessary, and must never be suffered, that the leading section of a company should march on until the rear section has completely passed and closed up. The intervals between companies may be occasionally increased with advantage and without disorder, but unless each company in itself be kept compact, disorder and disorganization will ensue.

Article VI.
Baggage.

1. Both private and regimental baggage must be packed and got ready for putting on the horses and mules as soon possible after the sounding of the first horn, and the mules must be actually loaded at least 10 minutes before the sounding of the second horn, which denotes the turning out of the companies on their respective parades.

2. No officer's servant, nor any but the regular bâtmen who march with the baggage, are to be suffered to be with it after the sounding of the third horn.

3. The following is the regulation of bâtmen, hospital guards, &c.:—No man of any description is upon any account whatever to be allowed to be out of the ranks for any other purpose.

Distribution.	Officers.	Serjeants.	Corporals.	Privates.

4. The bâtmen for camp-kettle mules will be given by the two adjoining companies, viz., 1 and 2, 3 and 4, 5 and 6, 7 and 8, and 9 and 10 alternately.

R

5. On ordinary marches, there will be one subaltern per regiment with the baggage, who must be provided with tickets to give to any bâtman who is under the absolute necessity of remaining behind.

6. The quartermaster or, in his absence, the officer who marches in charge of the baggage, will assemble it on the regimental parade at the hour appointed previous to the march, and will conduct it from thence to the place assigned by the assistant quartermaster general for the assembly of the baggage of the brigade.

7. If any bâtmen do not come at the proper time to the place of assembly of the regimental baggage, it must be reported by the quartermaster to the commanding officer of the regiment, who will hold officers commanding companies responsible for it.

8. The baggage of the different regiments must not be allowed to intermix with each other; that of each regiment must be kept collected and perfectly distinct—one serjeant at the head of it and one in the rear, and must follow in the same order as the regiments do in column.

9. The baggage and camp-kettle mules of each company must be tied together, and the five bâtmen allotted for the camp-kettle mules will then be employed generally to use their assistance where it may be wanted.

10. The bâtmen must be informed that anyone who quits the regimental baggage without a ticket, either for the purpose of pushing forward, or under pretext of inability to keep up, will be punished by the provost as a straggler, or brought to a drum-head court-martial.

11. If a load happens to fall off, the whole of the baggage of the regiment must stop, and the other bâtmen assist in reloading the mules, and in order not to stop the column the baggage of the regiment must be drawn to the side of the road. The loads can never fall off if proper attention is paid by the officers with respect to the arrangement of baggage, and by the bâtmen to the putting it on; and, therefore, if the baggage of one company occasions frequent delay, it must be reported to the commanding officer of the regiment, who will take care that it be rectified, or that any superfluous baggage shall be left behind.

12. The quartermaster will take care that these orders relating to baggage be fully explained to every individual who marches with it, and will be answerable for its execution, and the provost will punish as stragglers all bâtmen whom he finds separated from the regimental baggage without a ticket.

13. Whenever there is an expectation of meeting the enemy, the baggage will be entrusted solely to weakly men, musicians, &c., and the bâtmen, being effective soldiers, will be put into the ranks.

SECTION III.
ARTICLE I.

Means to be adopted for ascertaining the Number of Men who have Fallen out upon the March, and for Bringing to Punishment those who may have done so without a Ticket.

1. A guard of one subaltern, one non-commissioned officer, and six privates of each regiment, must be left at the entrance of the town or camp as soon as the regiment arrives.

2. The subaltern of this guard may be taken from the inlying

picquets, and sometimes one subaltern per brigade may be sufficient; when this is the case, the brigade-major will notify it; if he does not it must be understood that each regiment furnishes one subaltern.

3. The officer of this guard will be responsible for stopping and detaining every man that comes up afterwards without a ticket or pass certifying that he is sick or a bâtman.

4. A list of the names and companies of the men so detained by this guard must be sent to the commanding officer of each regiment by the officer commanding it.

5. As soon as the battalion is formed, the captains will count the files of their companies, in order to ascertain the number of absentees, and the rolls will then be called in order to ascertain their names.

6. The names of all absent men who are not upon the list of those who received tickets are to be reported to the commanding officer as absent without leave.

7. The number of those who remain behind with tickets must also be reported to the adjutant, for the commanding officer's information, before the regiment is dismissed.

8. The list of men reported absent without leave by their companies must be compared by the adjutants with the list of those detained by the guard mentioned in No. 4, and if the guard report contains names not stated in the company's list, the circumstance must be reported by the adjutant to the brigade-major.

ARTICLE II.

Of the Interior Regimental Arrangements which are to take place on Arriving in Camp or Quarters before the Regiment is Dismissed.

1. On entering the camp or quarters each battalion must form on the same ground which it is to assemble upon in case of alarm, and when formed, the ranks are to be open.

2. If the companies have to form up in succession, each will slope arms and open ranks as soon as formed, by word of command from its own officer; but they must not order arms or stand at ease until directed to do so by the commanding officer of the regiment, which will not be done until the whole battalion is formed.

3. After the reports are collected, as ordered in the preceding Article, the men may be allowed to sit down or walk about behind the ground of formation, which will be marked out by a sentry placed on the right flank of each company; but they must not be allowed to go 10 yards from the spot until the guards and pickets are placed, and all other necessary arrangements are made, unless it rains hard and no enemy is near; in which case the men, except those who do duty, may be dismissed as soon as reports are collected; but no state of weather nor any other circumstance is to prevent the regiment being kept under arms until the reports of absentees are regularly collected.

4. As soon as the regiments are formed and the reports collected, the guards must be placed, and the men or companies warned for in or outlying pickets.

5. In camp the best water and the wood for cooking and hutting will also be pointed out before the men are dismissed, and the necessary directions for opening communications, &c., given.

6. The places for cooking in camp must be pointed out to the orderly serjeants of companies by the captain of the day, and must be

particularly chosen with a view to avoid danger of the grass taking fire, and for the greater facility of superintendence all the companies must cook as near together as possible.

7. It must be explained to the men as a standing order that, when no regular necessaries are made, nor any particular spot pointed out for easing themselves, they are to go to the rear at least 200 yards beyond the sentries of the rear guard. All men disobeying this order must be punished.

8. The captain of the day and the quartermaster under the commanding officers are particularly responsible for the cleanliness of the camp of each regiment; and the field officer of the inlying picket, who is charged with the superintendence of the police and cleanliness of the camp or quarters of the brigade, will give such orders upon the subject as may be necessary to the captain of the day.

9. If the arms are not piled on the ground of formation a stake must be fixed, or some other conspicuous mark must be made on the right and left flanks of the ground on which each company when called out is to form.

10. In towns or villages the alarm post will be fixed, the disposition made for the defence of that portion of the circumference falling within the district of the regiment, and all other necessary directions will be given by officers commanding battalions, and the distribution of billets made by those commanding companies before the men are dismissed.

ARTICLE III.

Of the Exterior Arrangements for the Security of the Camp or Quarters, and Duties of the Field Officer of the Day, on Arrival.

1. On arriving in camp or quarters all the officers of the division and brigade staff, and all the field and staff officers of regiments, will remain mounted and in readiness to assist in placing pickets and in making all the arrangements for the security and internal regulations of the camp or quarters.

2. The field officers of the day for the in and outlying pickets will report themselves to the brigadier, and the adjutants and quartermasters to the brigade-major, as soon as the troops are formed.

3. Whilst the field officer for the outlying picket is taking the necessary precaution to prevent surprise, the field officer of the inlying picket will superintend all the arrangements for the internal defence or police of the camp or cantonments.

4. The field officer of the inlying picket (or if that duty is done by a captain, the field officer next for duty) must as soon as possible make himself acquainted with the position of all the pickets of his brigade, and of the adjoining posts of the brigades on his right and left; as must also the officer commanding the company first for outlying picket, with the position of the company which he is to relieve and its connection with those on its right and left.

5. After visiting the quarter and rear guards and inlying pickets, he will also inspect the guards directed in Article 1 to be placed at the entrance of the camp for the purpose of detaining all men who arrive after their brigade; and he will receive written reports of the number of men so detained, as directed in that Article, and will deliver them to the general himself.

6. The field officer and company of the inlying picket will always be those who are next for the outlying pickets.

ARTICLE IV.

Of the Quarters or Stations of Officers in Camp or Cantonments, and of the Measures to be adopted for Insuring a Ready Communication between all parts of each Company, Battalion, or Brigade, and Prompt Circulation of Orders without Sound of Bugle.

1. When the troops are encamped, the officers' tents must, of course, be pitched in the proper places, and when hutted and lying out without cover, the officers will choose convenient spots as near as possible to the station where the tents would be pitched in a regular encampment.

2. When the brigade is in towns or villages the officers must always occupy a part of one or more of the houses allotted to their respective companies.

3. After every march or change of position or quarters, the house, the tent, or station, of all the officers of each company, is to be pointed out to all the non-commissioned officers present, before, or as soon as the company is dismissed.

4. Officers commanding companies will also take care that at least one non-commissioned officer and two orderly privates may immediately find out the quarters of the commanding officer of the regiment and of the major of their wing.

5. The adjutant and quartermaster and the commanding officer's orderlies, consisting of one private per company and one bugler per battalion, are to have a quarter allotted to them, either in the same house as the commanding officer, or in that immediately adjoining. In camp they are to remain close to the station of the commanding officer.

6. The commanding officer's orderlies must ascertain the quarters of the officers commanding their respective companies before they come to him.

7. In camp, when the battalion is collected, or in quarters after the battalion has been some days in it, so great a number of orderlies in attendance near the quarters of the officer commanding the battalion may, perhaps, not be necessary; but, on first arriving in cantonments or in an extensive or intricate position, it must not be dispensed with.

8. If the field officers are not in the same house with the commanding officer, their quarters should be in as central a situation as may be in the district of their respective wings, and must be made known to at least two or three of the commanding officer's orderlies as soon as the regiment is dismissed.

9. The brigadier-general's orderlies must be sent to his quarters by the adjutant immediately after the arrival of the brigade, having first made themselves acquainted with the quarters of their commanding officer. The commanding officers of regiments must also send some of their orderlies to make themselves acquainted with the brigadier-general's quarters.

10. The field officers of the day will take care that the officers commanding the in and outlying pickets may always know where to find them without the smallest delay, and the officers on duty or in waiting in camp or quarters, as directed in No. 5 of the first article

of the fourth section, will always leave word at the regimental guard, as well as at their own quarters or tent, where they are to be found.

ARTICLE V.

Equal Allotment of Billets.

1. Commanding officers of regiments, in the course of the first day after their arrival in a town, will particularly investigate the manner in which their men have been distributed in the houses of the district allotted to their respective regiments. It is very improbable that the officers employed in the subdivision should in no short a time as is allotted to them previous to their entry have been able to fix the portions to be occupied by the companies with that accuracy which, in a quarter where the troops may remain a considerable time, is necessary, both for the accommodation of the men and in justice to the inhabitants.

2. This allotment, therefore, of equal distribution to companies will be the first object of revision, and after it is completed, officers commanding companies will take the greatest pains to distribute the men in such a manner that no housekeeper may have reason to complain of having more than a due proportion. Commanding officers of companies will also be responsible that the men in each house shall be accommodated with as little inconvenience as possible to the inhabitants.

SECTION IV.

Duties in Camp or Quarters.

ARTICLE I.

Number of Officers on Duty.

1. When circumstances require outlying pickets there will be two field officers of the day per brigade, namely, one for the outlying picket and another for the inlying picket and internal duties of the camp or cantonments of the brigade.

2. When there is not a sufficient number of field officers to do this duty without material inconvenience, the senior captain of one or more regiments of the brigade will take the duty of field officer of the inlying picket, but he will take his tour of outlying pickets.

3. When there are no outlying pickets there will be only one field officer of the day per brigade.

4. The field officer of the day will see that the officers commanding the in and outlying pickets may always know where to find him.

5. The number of officers on duty or in waiting in each battalion (exclusive of those on outlying pickets) will at all times, as long as the brigade remains abroad, and whether in camp or cantonments, consist of one captain and two subalterns of each wing, who must constantly remain in camp or quarters. Lieutenants commanding companies may be ranked as captains for this duty, but the roster must be so regulated that there shall not be less than one effective captain.

6. The officers on duty or in waiting in the lines, as directed in the preceding paragraph, will have charge of the inlying picket by day, when there is one, and will besides do all the orderly and other internal and regimental duties, including the quarter guards.

7. They will always leave word at the quarter or barrack guard, and at their own tent or quarters, where they are to be found.

Article II.

Pickets.

1. The outlying pickets will, in general, consist of one company per battalion, when more are required or less are sufficient, it will be notified in orders.

2. The inlying picket will, by night, in general consist of two companies per battalion.

3. When inlying pickets are required by day they will consist of one-fourth of the non-commissioned officers and privates of each company who are not upon duty, and will be commanded by the officer on duty or in waiting, as mentioned in paragraph No. 5 of the 1st Article of this section.

4. The company's picket will be allowed to leave off duty a sufficient number of men to draw provisions and cook, and the brigade-major will therefore, from time to time, give out in brigade orders the number of rank and file which the companies of the several regiments are to produce under arms on picket.

5. The inlying picket will be inspected, after the evening parade of the brigade, by the field officer of the day, and will remain accoutred and in constant readiness to turn out during the night.

6. If the brigade is under arms before daylight, which will generally be the case in situations which require pickets, the inlying pickets will parade with their regiments; but it will be observed as a constant rule that all pickets are to be under arms before daylight, even if the rest of the troops are not, and, in that case, the inlying pickets of each regiment will place themselves close in front of the centre of their respective regiments.

Article III.

Guards.

1. The quarter guards in camp will consist of 1 subaltern, 1 serjeant, 2 corporals or lance corporals, and 18 privates; the rear guard of 1 serjeant, 2 corporals or lance corporals, and 12 privates.

2. In garrison or cantonments the strength of each regimental guard must be sufficient to give four reliefs; the utmost strength will, of course, depend upon the number of sentries; but it must never be less, when a battalion is assembled, than 1 subaltern, 1 serjeant, 2 corporals or lance corporals, and 18 privates.

3. Exclusive of pickets and quarter and rear guards, there must always, in camp, be a company's guard or watch of one non-commissioned officer and four privates of each company, furnishing one sentry. This watch, except the sentry, may be allowed as much ease in point of dress as if not on duty; in the daytime they must remain within the company's lines, and at night they must remain together in the rear of its centre; the sentry may mount with sidearms, unless when near the enemy.

Article IV.

Orders to Guards.

1. The officer on guard or picket is to write down all orders which he receives, whether these orders come to him verbally or in writing,

and deliver over these orders, in writing, to the officer who relieves him.

2. In order to simplify the duties of the sentries, each individual man is to retain the same post during the whole of the guard or picket; that is to say, each time a man goes on duty as sentry he must have the same post that he had the first time; the most intelligent, trusty, and experienced soldiers being chosen for the most difficult and important posts.

3. The officers will most particularly examine each sentry upon his post respecting the orders that he has received immediately after he is placed there for the first time; and before he is marched off to take the same post a second time, the officer will question him for the purpose of ascertaining whether he recollects his orders.

4. It is the duty of the officers to ascertain that every individual is instructed in what he has to do, and it is to them therefore that the responsibility attaches if any accident or irregularity shall occur in consequence of orders not being accurately given.

ARTICLE V.

Parades and Roll Calls.

1. The time for morning and evening parade will be indicated by the sounds of the bugle, commencing in camp with the regiment that finds the field officer of the day for the inlying pickets, and in garrison, from the main guard.

2. In camp, the field officer of the day of the inlying picket will regulate the times at which the rolls are to be called.

3. At the roll callings, the companies must fall in regularly, and the men must not be permitted to answer louder than is necessary to make themselves heard.

4. The reports of the companies after each roll calling are to be made to the captains of the day, who will be in front of the centre of their respective regiments to receive them; and if any man is absent they will immediately report it to their own commanding officer and to the field officer of the day of the inlying picket.

5. The captain of the day will only report to the field officer of the day half an hour before he is relieved.

ARTICLE VI.

Police and Cleanliness.

1. The field officer of the day of the inlying picket is particularly charged with the police and cleanliness of the camp, and will give such orders as he may think necessary for working parties or otherwise, to the captain of the day of each regiment.

2. The captain of the day, and quartermaster of each regiment, are particularly responsible to the field officer of the day of the inlying picket, as well as to their own commanding officer, for the police and cleanliness of the camp or quarters.

3. Each regimental guard will send frequent patrols after tatoo beating to take up all men found out of quarters.

4. The patrols of each regimental guard will confine themselves to their respective regiments, and if they take up any stragglers of other regiments, they will be sent to the main guard next morning.

5. All applications for patrols from any guard, either from the

provost or from the magistrates, for the purpose of preserving the police of the town are to be complied with.

6. Each regiment will place sentries from its own regimental guard on all the wine-houses within its own district, which must be frequently visited by the captain and subaltern of the day.

7. If any inhabitant should have any just cause of complaint against the conduct of the troops, and it should be impossible to find out the offenders so as to bring them to punishment, some general restraint, by way of punishment, will be laid on the regiment in whose district the offence has been committed. The officers commanding regiments will therefore establish the most vigilant police, each in his own district.

8. Commanding officers of regiments, with the assistance of their field officers and staff, will ascertain the state of all the houses occupied by their regiment, once a week, and if they discover any damage done to them which has not been reported by officers commanding the companies, they will report it to the commanding officer of the brigade, and also, through the assistant quartermaster-general, to the general commanding the division.

9. The most strict orders must be given for the prevention of fire; and the custom, not unusual, of setting fire to huts or straw on leaving a camp must be strictly forbidden.

10. The places for cooking in camp must be pointed out to the orderly serjeants of companies by the captain of the day, which in the summer time must be particularly chosen with a view to avoid danger of the grass taking fire.

11. Towns in which many troops are quartered, and in which there are not proper necessaries and drains, and camps in which troops remain many days, become exceeding filthy, owing to the men easing themselves in improper places. Officers commanding regiments will give due orders to prevent such nuisances.

12. It must be explained to the men that when no regular necessaries are made in camp, nor any particular spot pointed out for easing themselves, they are to go to the rear at least 200 yards beyond the sentries of the rear guard.

13. In towns necessaries must be dug in the yards of the houses, or in the most convenient situations adjoining any large building occupied by the troops. They must be covered over daily, and fresh ones made as often as expedient.

14. Fatigue parties will be frequently employed in removing and covering the filth which, notwithstanding these regulations, may have so accumulated as to render parts of the town or ramparts offensive; and if the quarters of any particular corps be found dirty, some restraint or additional fatigue duties will be imposed on that regiment.

15. When the brigade is stationed in fortified towns, a portion of the ramparts will be allotted to each regiment, which will be considered as its alarm post. The regiment must also be kept responsible for the cleanliness and preservation of the portion of the ramparts allotted to their districts, and the commanding officers will forthwith place the requisite sentries from their regimental guard; the number of which they will report to the brigade-major.

18. The field officer of the day will inspect the ramparts at 1 o'clock daily. The point on which he is to commence and the direction in which he is to make his tour will be settled in orders; and the captain

of the day of each regiment will be in readiness to receive him at the commencement of its portion of the ramparts. The field officer of the day will immediately report to the commanding officer of the division any regiment which has not properly cleansed its district.

17. Those regiments in whose district there is any breach in the ramparts will place a sentry on it, with orders not to allow any person to go up or down the breach.

18. No non-commissioned officer or soldier is to be allowed to go out of the town after retreat nor before daylight.

19. The gates are to be locked at eight o'clock every night. The keys will remain in possession of the officers of the gate guards.

SECTION V.
Issue of Provisions.

1. The quartermaster is to be allowed two assistants, beside the quartermaster serjeant.

2. One quartermaster will superintend the issue of each species of provisions, namely, bread, meat, and wine or spirits.

3. The following will be the distribution for one day of the quartermasters and their assistants :—

Bread.	Meat.	Wine.
Q.M., 1st Regiment.	Q.M., 2nd Regiment.	Q.M., 3rd Regiment.
Q.M., 2nd Regiment.	Q.M., 3rd Regiment.	Q.M., 1st Regiment.
Q.M., 3rd Regiment.	Q.M., 1st Regiment.	Q.M., 2nd Regiment.

4. In order that the fatigue parties may not be kept waiting any longer than is absolutely necessary, the bread and meat will be weighed and counted out for each regiment and company before the parties go for it, for which purpose a subaltern officer of each regiment, and one man per company, will attend at each place of issue; and when the provisions are divided out for the companies the parties will be sent for and marched regularly to the places of issue.

5. One of the subalterns of the day of each regiment will attend the issue of bread, one that of meat, and a third that of wine and wood.

6. When there is not a sufficiency of any articles of provisions to afford a full ration to the whole, care must be taken that each regiment has its due proportion allotted to it before the subdivision for the companies of any one regiment commences.

7. The captain of the day of each regiment will be responsible for the regular performance of all that is directed respecting the reception of provisions. The subaltern of the day will report to him the time and place of issue, and will also inform him when the provisions were received. If there is any irregularity or delay, he will immediately send a report to the commanding officer of his regiment, and to the field officer of the day.

8. After a march, the commanding officer of each regiment will send a report to the brigade-major as soon as the men have received their bread, meat, and wine, in order that the commanding officer of the brigades may be aware of any unusual delay.

9. The commissary and the cattle, with two butchers per regiment, under charge of the commissary's store-keeper, will, when it is possible, be one day's march ahead of the brigade; thus, if the brigade marches on the 15th, the commissariat will be sent forward on the 14th, and either that evening or early on the morning of the 15th, the meat will be slaughtered, and all the provisions will be in perfect readiness to deliver over to the quartermasters before they arrive.

10. The quartermasters will march two or three hours before the brigade, or, if possible, the preceding evening. They will ride on as fast as they can, and as soon as they arrive, which will be early in the forenoon, the commissary's storekeeper, butchers, and cattle will proceed on their march to their next station.

SECTION VI.

Fatigue and Foraging Parties.

ARTICLE I.

Fatigue Parties.

1. All fatigue parties are to be marched regularly to and from the place where the provisions are to be received or this duty to be performed.

2. The men are not to be suffered to carry bread or other articles in their great coats; each man must take a sufficient number of haversacks for bread.

3. The meat must be carried by two men upon sticks, in order that the clothing may not be soiled and made filthy, as is the case when the men carry the meat on their backs.

ARTICLE II.

Foraging Parties.

1. As many irregularities take place under pretence of going for forage, no bàtman is allowed to go singly for forage, except within the chain of posts within the quarter or rear guard of the division, or within such limits of the vicinity of the camp as officers commanding brigades shall point out.

2. When it is necessary to go for forage, regular parties, with a serjeant and corporal of each regiment and that proportion of the camp-kettle mules or horses which officers choose to send, will assemble in the centre of the rear of the regiments under charge of one officer per brigade, who will march them regularly to the forage place, and will be responsible for bringing them all back together, and no officer whatever will be permitted to send beyond the vicinity of the camp otherwise than by the above-mentioned parties.

SECTION VII.

Commissariat.

1. Whenever the division is in settled quarters commanding officers of regiments will investigate in their several districts the best method of supplying their regiments, and the prices which ought to be paid. If, after this investigation, it appears that the mode adopted by the commissary might be improved, they will immediately report it through

the brigade-major to the officer commanding the brigade, suggesting such alterations in the mode of supply as they may think advisable. The major of brigade, after laying them before the brigadier, will transmit them to the assistant quartermaster-general for the information of the officer commanding the division.

2. Commanding officers of regiments will at all times make it a particular part of their duty to ascertain whether the provisions issued are the best that can be procured, whether the prices paid by the commissary are reasonable, and whether the people who furnish the supplies are regularly and fairly paid by the contractor.

3. The commissary will always report the prices of the provisions and forage for the ensuing week, in his weekly report to the assistant quartermaster-general, who will transmit them to the assistant adjutant-general, after they have been sanctioned by the commanding officer of the division. The assistant adjutant-general will then promulgate them in division orders.

4. A ration loaf will be sent with the weekly returns to the commanding officer of the division by each regiment, in order that he may ascertain whether it is equal to that contracted for.

5. The computed weight per measure of corn issued as forage will be notified in division orders at the same time with the prices of the provisions and forage.

6. The commanding officers of artillery and cavalry will state in their weekly report what the corn has weighed per measure on an average during the preceding week.

7. Commanding officers of infantry regiments will also frequently cause the corn issued to them to be weighed, and report the average weight on the back of the weekly states.

8. Whenever any abuse or defect in the provision department is discovered it is to be reported, through the above channel, to the commanding officer of the division without loss of time.

9. If everything goes on regularly and well, it will be notified at the foot of each weekly state, viz.:—"I certify that I have carefully " investigated the mode in which the regiment has been supplied with " provisions and forage during the preceding week, and I believe it to " be the best that circumstances would admit of; the quality as good " as can be procured, the prices reasonable, and the people in this " district regularly paid by the contractor in hard money at the fol- " lowing rates."

10. In fixed quarters the meat will be killed, in cold weather, 24 hours at least before it is used.

11. A weekly muster of the commissariat mules of each brigade, in presence of the brigade-major and assistant quartermaster-general, will take place on the day previous to the weekly returns. The commissary of the brigade will attend this muster.

12. A return made out at this muster, of the state and distribution of these mules, signed by the commissary, and countersigned by the assistant quartermaster-general, or, in his absence, by the majors of brigade, will form a part of the commissary's monthly report.

13. Whenever, in situations of scarcity, provisions of any kind are procurable by any regiment, the quality and quantity, how procured, and to whom receipts were given, must be reported to the commissary.

14. Whenever regiments or individual officers, either from being de-

tached or from any other circumstance, cannot get their rations from the commissary, they must purchase them at the usual prices, taking regular receipts for the same.

15. The commissary will furnish each regiment, and each staff officer; with a form of the receipts which he is to take from the persons from whom he may have occasion to purchase forage or provisions.

16. The account of forage and provisions purchased by regimental officers must be confirmed by the commanding officer and quartermaster, who are to certify what circumstance made it necessary for the officer or officers to purchase them; and that his or their rations were not drawn from the commissariat.

17. The commissary will furnish each regiment and each staff officer with a form of this account or voucher.

SECTION VIII.

Article I.

Inspections and Returns—Weekly Inspection—Nature and Period of Delivery of Reports.

1. The regimental weekly reports are to be delivered by the adjutant to the majors of brigades on the 1st, 8th, 15th, and 25th of each month, before 10 o'clock in the forenoon.

2. The regiments are to parade in marching order on the preceding day: every man fit for duty (excepting only the hospital attendants) must be actually under arms at this parade. All private and regimental mules are also to be paraded, with officers and regimental baggage and camp kettles loaded and ready to march. The reports of the companies are to be strictly examined and compared with their strength under arms, and the weekly reports of the regiments to be grounded upon the actual field state at this inspection.

3. The arms and appointments, and the men's necessaries—particularly shoes, the blankets, canteens, haversacks, billhooks, camp kettles, and intrenching tools, are, on the same day, to be minutely inspected, for the purpose of filling up that part of the report; nothing but a march must be allowed to prevent this inspection. If the weather should be very bad on the day appointed for it, the companies must be inspected in their quarters, but no circumstance will be permitted as an excuse for not delivering the weekly report at the time appointed.

4. Whenever this inspection (which is ordered to take place the day before the weekly reports are given in, viz., on the 7th, 14th 24th, and last day of each month) is prevented by a march or other circumstance, it is to be mentioned at the bottom of the report, and the inspection made the next halting day, and an extra report sent to the brigade-major of appointments, &c., wanting to complete.

5. The officers commanding the artillery and cavalry attached to the division are also to send weekly reports to the assistant adjutant-general on the 1st, 8th, 15th, and 25th of each month.

6. The weekly reports are to be delivered by the majors of brigades to the assistant adjutant-general of the division, and by him to the general commanding, at 11 o'clock precisely on the above-mentioned days.

7. The medical reports are to be delivered to the general, by the staff surgeon of the division, eight times in each month, viz., a weekly

report on the 1st, 8th, 15th, and 25th, in which the admission and discharges are to be reckoned from the preceding weekly report, viz., the
8th from the 1st, in that of the 15th from the 8th, the 25th from the
15th, and the 1st from the 25th.

8. A half-yearly report of admissions and discharges only will be
made on the 4th, 12th, 20th, and 28th of each month, showing the
alterations which have taken place since the preceding weekly report,
viz., the 4th from the 1st, the 12th from the 8th, the 20th from the
15th, and the 28th from the 25th.

9. The regimental medical reports are to be countersigned by the
commanding officer, and delivered personally by the surgeons of regiments to the staff surgeon at the headquarters of the division.

10. The assistant quartermaster-general, on the same days, viz.,
1st, 8th, 15th, and 25th of each month, will make out a general report
—1st, of necessaries, ammunition, and articles of field equipment
wanting to complete; 2nd, of ammunition in store; 3rd, of means of
subsistence. The materials for the first he will collect from the above-
mentioned weekly reports, which will be communicated to him by the
general's aide-de-camp; the second and third from reports which he
will cause to be made to him by the commissary of provisions and
conductor of stores. This report, signed by the assistant quartermaster-general, will be delivered to the general on the following days,
viz., 2nd, 9th, 16th, and 26th, when he will receive instructions respecting the completing and equipment of the regiment.

11. Whenever the brigade is assembled, a morning report will be
given in every day; on halting days at 9; on marching days, if the
brigade moves too early for them to be made out before it marches off,
they will be made out on the march, and collected by the brigade.
major as soon as possible afterwards.

ARTICLE II.

Of Receiving and Dispatching Letters, and of the Payment of Guides.

1. All orders are to be issued by the brigade-major to the adjutant
in person, or when sent in writing, they are to be returned with a
receipt.

2. Officers receiving orders or letters upon service are always to
give a receipt to the bearer, stating the time of delivery.

3. The precise time of dispatching letters upon service is always to
be marked on the outside of them, and also the rate at which they are
to be conveyed.

4. All letters upon service are to be forwarded from intermediate
stations, in the same manner as that in which they arrive; that is to
say, if an officer brings them. they are to be forwarded by an officer, if
a dragoon brings them, they are to be forwarded by a dragoon or
mounted orderly.

5. When officers or dragoons dispatched with orders do not know
the road, they must be accompanied by well-mounted guides.

6. Peasants sent with letters are never to be paid by the person
receiving the letters unless an order to that effect is written on the
cover, but they are to be paid as soon as they bring back a receipt to
the person who dispatches them.

ARTICLE III.

Manner of Keeping Orders, and at what Periods they are to be Read to the Men.

1. All general, division, or brigade orders that are intended to be permanent, or continue in force for any length of time, are to be entered in a book kept by the brigade-major and adjutants for that purpose only; the orders of a temporary nature are to be entered in another book.

2. At the bottom of each permanent order entered in this book the brigade-major will, with his own hand, enter a note by whom and in what manner it was issued.

3. These books must have a methodical index for the sake of reference.

4. Those orders which relate to the conduct of the non-commissioned officers or soldiers, or otherwise concern them, are to be read by the officers.

Manner of Keeping Orders.

Officers commanding companies at three successive parades, and subaltern officers and serjeants will be responsible for their being read to every individual of their respective divisions or squads, who may have been absent when they were read to the company.

5. Those brigade orders relating to the non-commissioned officers and soldiers which are of a permanent nature, besides being read at three successive parades after issuing them as above directed, are also to be read at every weekly inspection during the first month, and afterwards once a month.

APPENDIX III.

WAR ESTABLISHMENTS OF INFANTRY, CAVALRY, ARTILLERY, AND ENGINEERS.

s

INFANTRY.
ESTABLISHMENT in the Field of a Battalion of Infantry.

| Ranks. | Officers, N.-C. Officers and Men. | | | | | Horses. |
	Officers.	Staff Serjeants and Serjeants.	Drummers.	Rank and File.	Total.	
Lieutenant-Colonels	1					2
Majors	2					4
Captains	8					..
Subalterns	16					1*
Adjutant	1	..	..	..	31	1
Paymaster	1					..
Quartermaster	1					1
Medical Officer	1					1
Serjeant-Major	..	1				
Quartermaster-Serjeant	..	1				
Band Serjeant	..	1				
Drum Major	..	1				
Orderly Room Clerk	..	1				
Armourer Serjeant	..	1				
Paymaster Serjeant	..	1	..	..	50	..
Regimental Transport Serjeant	..	1				
Serjeant Cook	..	1				
Color Serjeants	..	8				
Serjeants	..	32				
Pioneer Serjeants	..	1				
Drummers	..	..	16	..	16	..
Corporals	..	..	..	40		
Pioneers and Artificers	..	..	..	13		
Band	..	..	..	20	1,000	
Privates†	..	..	..	903		
Drivers†	..	..	..	24		
Total	**31**	**50**	**15**	**1,000**	**1,097**	**10**

Transport.	Number.	Drivers.	Draught Horses.
Company	8	8	16
Carts { Intrenching Tools	1	1	2
Carts { Small-Arm Ammunition	3	3	6
Wagons, General Service	2	4	8
Spare	..	2	4
Total	14	18	36
Add for Tents, Wagons G. S.	3	6	12
Grand Total	17	24	48

* Transport Officer.
† If Tents are not carried the Privates will be 910, Drivers 18, with 36 Draught Horses.

CAVALRY.

ESTABLISHMENT of a Regiment in the Field.

Officers, N.-C. Officers and Men.	Nos.	Horses.		
		Chargers.	Troop.	Draught.
Lieutenant-Colonel	1	4		
Majors	1	4		
Captains	8	24		
Subalterns	12	36		
Adjutant	1	3		
Paymaster	1	2		
Quartermaster	1	2		
Medical Officer	1	2		
Veterinary Surgeon	1	2		
Total	27	79		
SERJEANTS.				
Serjeant-Major	1			
Quartermaster-Serjeant	1			
Band Serjeant	1			
Paymaster Serjeant	1			
Armourer Serjeant	1			
Saddler Serjeant	1			
Farrier Serjeant	1			
Serjeant Cook	1			
Trumpet Major	1			
Orderly Room Clerk	1			
Transport Serjeant	1			
Troop Serjeants-Major	8			
Serjeants	24			
ARTIFICERS.			480	
Farriers	8			
Saddlers	4			
Shoeing Smiths	8			
Wheelers and Saddle Tree Makers	2			
Total Serjeants and Artificers	65			
Trumpeters	8			
RANK AND FILE.				
Corporals	32			
Bandsmen	15			
Privates*	480			
Drivers* (Transport)	22			4
Total Rank and File	549	79	480	4
Total all Ranks	649	603		

TRANSPORT. (Without Tents.)	Carriages.	Drivers.	Draught Horses.
Wagon, Forge	1	2	4
Wagon, General Service	6	12	24
Total	7	14	28
If Tents are carried, Add— Wagons, General Service	4	8	16
Grand Total	11	22	44

* If Tents are not carried, the Privates will be increased by 8, the Drivers reduced to 14, and the Draught Horses to 28.

ARTILLERY.

ESTABLISHMENT in the Field of a Horse Battery, 16 and 9-pounder Field Battery.

Officers and Men.	R. H. A.	Field.	
		16-pr.	9-pr.
OFFICERS.			
Horse and Field Batteries.			
Major 1			
Captain 1			
Lieutenants 3			
Assistant Surgeon 1			
Veterinary Surgeon 1			
Total Officers	7	7	7
NON-COMMISSIONED OFFICERS AND MEN.			
Serjeant-Major	1	1	1
Quartermaster-Serjeant	1	1	1
Serjeants	6	6	6
Corporals	6	6	6
Bombardiers	6	6	6
Gunners	70	87	72
Drivers	70	73	62
Trumpeters	2	2	2
ARTIFICERS.			
Farriers	1	1	1
Shoeing Smiths	5	4	4
Collar-Makers	2	2	2
Wheelers	2	2	2
Total ...	179	198	172
RIDING HORSES.			
Officers	15	8	8
Staff Serjeants	2	2	2
Non-Commissioned Officers	12	12	12
Farrier	1	1	1
Shoeing Smiths	3	1	1
Trumpeters	2	2	2
Gunners	36	...	...
Spare	6	4	4
Total Riding ...	77	30	30
DRAUGHT.			
Guns	36	48	36
Ammunition Wagons	36	48	36
General Service Wagons and Forge	18	18	18
Spare	12	10	8
Total Horses ...	179	154	128
Guns	6	6	6
CARRIAGES.			
Gun	6	6	6
Ammunition Wagons	6	6	6
General Service Wagons and Forge ...	3	3	3
Total	15	15	15

ARTILLERY.

DETAIL of Divisional and Army Corps Ammunition Reserves, the latter in three Divisions.

Officers and Men	Divisional	Army Corps. One Division.
OFFICERS.		
Major	1	..
Captain	..	2
Lieutenants	2	2
Quartermaster	1	1
Assistant Surgeon	1	1
Veterinary Surgeon	1	1
N.-C. O. and Men.		
Serjeant-Major	1	1
Quartermaster-Serjeant	1	1
Serjeants	6	6
Corporals	6	6
Bombardiers	6	6
Gunners	50	50
Drivers	121	67
Trumpeters	2	2
ARTIFICERS.		
Serjeant Farrier	1	1
Shoeing Smiths	6	6
Collar-Makers	3	3
Wheelers	3	3
Total	212	178

Horses.	Divisional.	Army Corps. One Division.
RIDING.		
Officers	7	7
Staff Serjeants	2	2
N.-C. Officers	9	9
Farriers	1	1
Trumpeters	2	2
Spare	2	2
Total	23	23
DRAUGHT.		
16-pr. Spare Carriages	4	4
8-pr. do.	4	4
S. A. Carts	58	..
Gun Ammunition Wagon, 16-pr.	24	..
do. 9-pr.	18	..
Wagons, General Service	18	116
Forge and Store	6	16
Rocket	20	20
Spare	..	..
Total	263	183

Equipment.	Divisional.	Army Corps. One Division.
Spare Gun Carriage, 16-pr.	1	1
Do. 9-pr.	1	1
Carts, Small-Arm Ammunition	29	29
Ammunition Wagon, 16-pr.	4	4
Do. 9-pr.	3	..
Wagons, General Service	13	..
Forge and Store	1	1
Rocket	1	..
Total Carriages	55	35

ENGINEERS.

War Establishment of a Field Company.

Ranks.	Officers, N.-C. Officers & Men.						Horses.		
	Officers.	N.-C. Officers.	Buglers.	Sappers.	Drivers.	Total.	Riding.	Draught.	Total.
Major	1	..	..	..	..	5	1	..	5
Lieutenants	4	..	..	..	..		4		
Serjeants	..	7	..	..	..		1		
Corporals	..	7	..	..	..	21	1	..	3
2nd Corporals	..	7	..	..	..		1		
Buglers	..	..	2	..	..	2	1	..	1
Carpenters	..	..	..	32	..				
Masons	..	..	..	23	..				
Bricklayers	..	..	..	14	..				
Smiths	..	..	..	14	..				
Wheelers	..	..	..	4	..				
Coopers	..	..	..	2	..				
Painters	..	..	..	6	..	137			
Tailors	..	..	..	4	..				
Collar-makers	..	..	..	4	..				
Clerks	..	..	..	3	..				
Printer	..	..	..	1	..				
Telegraphists	..	..	..	2	..				
Photographist	..	..	..	1	..				
Miners and Quarrymen	..	..	..	22	..				
Pack Equipments	..	..	..	..	4	4	..	4	4
Three Store Wagons	..	..	..	..	6		..	12	
Camp Equipage and Office ditto	..	..	..	..	2		..	4	
Tentage ditto	..	..	..	..	2	22	..	4	28
Forge ditto	..	..	..	..	2		..	4	
Spare Men and Horses	..	..	..	..	4		..	4	
Batmen	..	..	..	..	6				
Total	5	21	2	137	26	191	9	32	41

APPENDIX IV.

TABLE OF LOSSES IN VARIOUS GREAT BATTLES.

Name of Battle.	Year.	Numbers. On each side.	Numbers. Total.	Killed and Wounded. Number.	Killed and Wounded. Proportion to Total Forces.
Malplaquet	1709	... ...	188,000	18,250 Allies.	—
Hohen Friedberg	1745	70,000 P. / 70,000 A.	140,000	5,000 / 9,000	1/10
Prague	1757	64,000 P. / 74,000 A.	138,000	16,000 / 8,000	1/5
Rossbach	1757	22,000 P. / 55,000 A.	77,000	500 / 2,800	1/16
Breslau	1757	25,000 P. / 60,000 A.	85,000	5,000 / 6,280	1/8
Lissa	1757	36,000 P. / 80,000 A.	116,000*	5,000 / 6,574	1/13
Zorndorf	1758	32,000 P. / 50,000 R.	82,000	11,385 / 21,531	1/3 to 1/2
Hoch Kirch	1758	50,000 A. / 30,000 P.	80,000	5,000 / 7,000	1/5
Marengo	1800	28,127 F. / 30,850 A.	58,977†	7,000 / 6,800	1/4
Austerlitz	1805	90,000 F. / 80,000 R. & A.	170,000‡	12,000 / 11,000	1/5
Jena	1806	100,000 F. / 100,000 P.	200,000‖	14,000 / 20,000	1/5
Preussch Eylau ...	1807	85,000 F. / 75,000 R.	160,000	30,000 / 25,000	1/3
Friedland	1807	80,000 F. / 50,000 R.	130,000	10,000 / 17,000	1/5
Talavera	1809	52,000 E. & S / 50,000 F.	102,000	5,928 / 7,260	1/8
Wagram	1809	150,000 F. / 130,000 A.	280,000	24,000	1/12
Salamanca	1812	... ...	90,000	8,000 E. / 22,800 F. §	1/3
Borodino	1812	125,000 F. / 125,000 R.	250,000	80,000	1/3
Leipsic	1813	150,000 F. / 280,000 Allies	430,000	50,000 ¶ / Not known.	—
Vittoria	1813	70,000 E. &c. / 27,000 F.	97,000	10,000	1/10
Waterloo	1815	67,600 E. &c. / 68,900 F.	136,500	14,000 / Not known.	—
Magenta	1859	48,090 F. & S. / 61,640 A.	109,730	4,000 / 5,700	1/12
Solferino	1859	135,234 F. & S. / 163,124 A.	298,358**	14,415 / 13,020	1/11
Königgrätz	1866	230,000 P. / 185,000 A. & S.	415,000	28,000	1/15
Wissemberg	1870	25,000 P. / 8,000 F.	33,000	1,529 / 1,200	1/12
Woerth	1870	90,000 P. / 40,000 F.	130,000	10,530 / 7,501	1/8
Spicheren	1870	41,000 P. / 38,000 F.	79,000	4,866 / 4,078	1/9
Mars-la-Tour	1870	60,000 P. / 140,000 F.	200,000	14,820 / 16,954	1/6
Gravelotte	1870	270,000 P. / 135,000 F.	415,000	20,527 / 15,810	1/11

* 21,000 Austrian prisoners and missing.   † 1,000 French and 3,000 Austrian prisoners.

‡ 19,000 Austrian prisoners.   ‖ 20,000 Prussian prisoners.   § Includes missing.

¶ Includes some prisoners.   ** 2,770 Allies and 9,290 Austrians missing.

The losses in recent battles cannot be taken as more than approximate, the official account of the war not having been published.

The losses in battles before 1870 are given on the authority of a paper in the Royal Engineer Corps Papers by Colonel Cooke, R.E.